Partisans and Partners

Partisans and Partners

The Politics of the Post-Keynesian Society

JOSH PACEWICZ

The University of Chicago Press
Chicago and London

The University of Chicago Press, Chicago 60637
The University of Chicago Press, Ltd., London
© 2016 by The University of Chicago
All rights reserved. Published 2016.
Printed in the United States of America

25 24 23 22 21 20 19 18 17 16 1 2 3 4 5

ISBN-13: 978-0-226-40255-0 (cloth)
ISBN-13: 978-0-226-40269-7 (paper)
ISBN-13: 978-0-226-40272-7 (e-book)
DOI: 10.7208/chicago/9780226402727.001.0001

Library of Congress Cataloging-in-Publication Data

Names: Pacewicz, Josh, author.
Title: Partisans and partners : the politics of the post-Keynesian society / Josh
    Pacewicz.
Description: Chicago ; London : The University of Chicago Press, 2016. |
    Includes bibliographical references and index.
Identifiers: LCCN 2016011296| ISBN 9780226402550 (cloth : alk. paper)
    | ISBN 9780226402697 (pbk. : alk. paper) | ISBN 9780226402727 (e-book)
Subjects: LCSH: Political parties—United States. | United States—Politics and
    government—20th century. | United States—Politics and government—
    21st century. | Keynesian economics.
Classification: LCC JK2265 .P23 201?6 | DDC 324.273—dc23 LC record avail-
    able at http://lccn.loc.gov/2016011296

CONTENTS

PREFACE

Even a casual observer of American politics will have noticed that the two parties are more bitterly divided than ever. Legislatures are paralyzed by do-or-die parliamentary maneuvers, party primaries favor the most ideologically pure candidates, political sound and fury animates TV and the Internet, and hyperpartisan intraparty coalitions like the Tea Party caucus set the tenor of public debate.[1]

But while the two parties have drawn farther apart, most Americans have not—in fact, just the opposite. It is true that that each party's base supporters, those with consistently conservative or liberal views, identify more strongly with their party than comparable voters in the past and are also more likely to vote, volunteer for a political campaign, and even view the opposing party as "a threat to the nation's wellbeing."[2] But these polarized voters represent a small proportion of the public and social scientists argue that they are simply responding to politicians' bitter conflicts, not vice versa.[3] Meanwhile, most Americans continue to hold a mix of liberal and conservative views, remain politically moderate, and are dissatisfied with the political process. In fact, overall rates of party identification have fallen to their lowest levels ever, particularly among younger Americans.[4] Although this second trend may be quieter than the first, it represents an equally fundamental shift in American political culture. Anyone who has talked politics with a range of people knows that the term *apolitical* does not even begin to describe the unaffiliated. Particularly younger Americans are often downright antipolitical, which is to say that they believe that politics itself, not particular parties or candidates, is the problem.

This contrast between ideologically charged party leaders and other Americans' mistrust of party politics is apparent when one compares political attitudes across generations. During the 2008 election, for example,

I conducted interviews in a working-class neighborhood in Iowa, traditionally one of the state's most Democratic neighborhoods. In the 1960s Harold Hughes knocked on the same doors while running for governor. Hughes was a labor organizer who railed against the rich and powerful in campaign speeches and had been court-martialed during World War II for striking an officer. The neighborhood's residents gave him over 95 percent of their vote. Forty-five years later, some of Hughes's traditional Democratic supporters remained. On one occasion, I spoke with Mary, a seventy-year-old resident who often sat on her front porch and disciplined the neighborhood's children.[5] "We've got to get all the moneyed people out of politics," she told me, "get some Democrats in there who will stand up for working people."

What struck me about Mary was not her political conviction per se, but rather how self-evident it appeared to her. People like Mary spoke as if politics were woven into the very fabric of daily life. Their political identification frequently piggybacked on seemingly apolitical local distinctions: they talked of blue-collar or unionized jobs as "Democratic," contrasted charities that service lower-income people with the "Republican" service clubs of the well-to-do, and viewed the affluent hilltop neighborhood once inhabited by their city's business magnates as a "Republican neighborhood." And things were no different among the older residents of this "Republican" hilltop. There I spoke with Donna, who was about the same age as Mary. "The Democrats are for those who don't want to work hard," Donna said, "The Republicans want to help those who are willing to get it for themselves." For Donna, Republicans represented business, education, decorum, and a particular brand of civic-minded noblesse oblige.

While political identity seemed intuitive to Donna and Mary, many younger people found politics confusing and off-putting. One such person was Joni, a twenty-something office worker who lived three houses down from Mary. "Maybe before people said, 'Republicans are the party of rich white men who carry Bibles in their pockets and are this, this, and this,'" Joni said, delineating fixed issue positions in the air with her hands. "But nobody thinks exactly one way anymore. Everything and everybody is just so mixed and with politics you are either in or you are out—it seems so artificial to me. *Who* could say that [politicians] should believe in just one value, vote in this one way? I don't really think that exists anymore. Well," Joni paused for a second, contemplating. "Maybe like *reaaalllllyy* old people [think that]."

The striking thing about people like Joni was that politics seemed to clash with their commonsense understanding of how people solve their public problems. Whereas people like Mary saw public conflict as inevitable and politics as natural, those like Joni saw politics as artificial and inherently flawed. They rejected the logic of sides, rigidly defined identities, and conflict. It seemed obvious to them that politicians would never get anything done so long as they continued to engage in these ways. Many of them joked that politicians lived on "Planet Politics" where herd mentality reigned supreme. "It's like a football game or something," a smartly dressed young professional told me. "You cheer for your side no matter how badly they are sucking." To paraphrase sociologist Nina Eliasoph, people spoke as if politics were a world apart and in opposition to their daily experiences of community life.[6]

Herein lies the puzzle at the center of this book: America's political parties and politicians have parted company with American voters, becoming more divided and partisan as most Americans have grown distrustful of partisan conflict and party politics in general. This apparent contradiction is equally confounding to many political scientists, who model elections like an economic transaction: politicians sell their policy positions to as many people as possible, who buy them with their vote. For example, one popular voting model—the median voter theorem—predicts that when only two political parties are credible, politicians should converge on the preferences of their electoral districts' most ideologically median voter, which suggests that American politicians should follow voters and become *less*, not more, partisan.[7] But in reality the median voter theorem accurately described politicians' behavior for only a brief historical period stretching from the 1940s to the 1980s.[8] Both before this period and especially since the 1990s, most Republican and Democratic politicians have been far more ideologically extreme than their districts' median voter, and many studies, including this one, show that some voters stay home on election day in protest.[9] In every election, ideologically charged campaigners leave many votes on the table—a strong indication that standard models of voting behavior are not especially useful in explaining America's contemporary political culture. In fact, I will argue that the state of America's puzzling political culture has little to do with politicians or voters. Politicians and voters have changed, but only as a byproduct of a more fundamental reorganization of the community institutions in which the political parties are rooted and, therefore, in the grassroots base of America's two-party system.[10]

To illustrate this grassroots shift, I turn to "River City" and "Prairieville," two unremarkable Rust Belt cities, quirky and idiosyncratic in their ways, but nevertheless with an important story to tell us about American politics.[11] I have changed these cities' names to preserve the anonymity of the people I spoke with, whose names I also changed.[12] I originally came to River City and Prairieville to conduct an interview study of their residents' preferences during the 2008 election cycle. But like many social scientists who do qualitative research, I had my research plans upended by an unexpected finding. After interviewing a few community notables to get the lay of the land, it became clear that everyone already had something they desperately wanted to tell me about: "the 1980s" and the "transformation" of both cities' public life that occurred during that decade. From the outset, it seemed evident that this 1980s-era public transformation was somehow intertwined with the peculiarities of contemporary American political culture, particularly its puzzling tendency to be hyperpolitical here, apolitical there. What's more, River City and Prairieville's leaders had many pieces of this story filled in. Before the 1980s, they told me, business leaders clashed with blue-collar leaders over control of the city's public institutions and in the process produced conflicts that mirrored Democratic-Republican divides. Community life and politics were one and the same. After the 1980s, they insisted, leaders could no longer afford to fight lest they lose it all. Gradually, a new type of leader moved to the center of each city's public stage: the *partner*, one who sets divisive issues aside and builds flexible coalitions around doable, provisionally uncontroversial goals. As partners became central, they pushed divisive leaders who clung to the politics of the past to the public margins and before long each city's public sphere became defined by conflict between community-minded partners and partisan activists. By trying to banish politics from public life, partners had created the *partisans*: sign-waving activists who assumed control of the two political parties, nudged primary election campaigns toward the extremes, began to create the substance of media stories about supposedly unbridgeable red- and blue-state divides, and generally promoted the very political polarization that so horrifies partners. In simple terms, River City's and Prairieville's leaders showed me that the binary opposition between community and politics was one reproduced *locally* in their cities' public sphere.[13]

It was later, as I struggled to account for River City's and Prairieville's public transformations, that I realized that their stories were not uniquely their own. This book will show that River City's and Prairieville's public transformation was set in motion by 1970s- and '80s-era federal reforms, which ended the protective regulations that once sheltered the cities' economic institutions and cut off the large, discretionary federal transfers that community leaders had once fought over. In the hypercompetitive environment that followed, community leaders who partnered to market their cities reigned supreme, but not without adopting public personae that proved incompatible with the partisan commitments of their predecessors. The end of America's commitment to Keynesian statecraft reverberated through River City and Prairieville, upended the status system that once characterized their public life, severed traditional ties between community governance and partisan politics, and created the binary community-politics opposition that younger River Citians and Prairievillers increasingly take for granted. Theirs is the story of the post-Keynesian society, and of the tension between political avoidance and political extremism that is inherent to the organization of its political institutions.

Partisans and Partners

This book is about three ongoing trends in American politics. The first is one that academics and popular commentators sometimes identify as a rightward shift among politicians, but which I think is better characterized as politicians' growing preference for market-like solutions to social problems—whether via the private sector directly or public institutions that distribute resources according to competitive and objective criteria.[1] Since the 1970s Republican and Democratic legislators alike have grown wary of interventionist statecraft, punitive regulation, and redistributive policies and more concerned with values like public accountability, choice, and competition. The second trend is partisan polarization, although "conflict extension" is perhaps a more apt description.[2] Since the late 1980s Republicans and Democrats politicians, along with a small proportion of the American public, have taken opposing positions on the full range of partisan issues and fight over every single one.[3] This is a sea change from earlier periods when Republican and Democratic legislators took opposing stances while debating big issues—for instance, the New Deal or civil rights—but overlapped in their positions on less salient issues.[4] The third trend is Americans' disaffiliation from political parties and aversion toward party politics: relative to their pre-1980s predecessors, young Americans especially identify less with political parties and the political process as a whole.[5]

Given that all three phenomena appear ubiquitous, it is tempting to view them as disembodied historical trends that happen nowhere in particular—as simply the nature of the times. But everything happens somewhere. For instance, consider the first trend. Social scientists are still debating the detailed reasons for policymakers' embrace of pro-market policies, but have nevertheless identified particularly important processes that promoted this historical shift: policymakers' inability to understand stagflation and resolve certain kinds of distributional conflicts during the 1970s, the proliferation of conservative think-tanks and business lobby groups, new kinds of linkages between political parties and professional economists, and the diffusion of economic models and styles of reasoning throughout policy circles.[6] My aim in this book is to shed light on the second and third trends: conflict extension among politicians and a small portion of the American public, but political disaffection among most Americans. This goal brings me to Prairieville and River City and a topic that may appear deceptively parochial and unrelated to big trends in American politics: the social world of community leaders, or those who assume leadership positions in local economic, civic, and municipal associations and compete with one another for prominence within their community's public life.

It did not take me long to appreciate that community leaders' social world is situated at a political bottleneck of sorts: they are disproportionately impacted by a myriad of decisions made by faraway policymakers and disproportionately influential within grassroots politics and, more generally, in shaping others' understanding of public life. During corporate merger waves in the 1980s, for instance, it was they who first received phone calls about the acquisition—and frequent liquidation—of their cities' major employers and then toured devastated industrial corridors, wondering what to do next. Like community leaders elsewhere, River City's and Prairieville's leaders had historically assumed control over grassroots Republican and Democratic politics, thereby exerting a quiet, moderating influence on the political system of their day.[7] But by the time I arrived in Prairieville and River City, this was no longer true. Both cities' public spheres were characterized by a conflict between partners who focused on community governance and partisans who engaged in party politics. In this respect, community leaders were the central players within a politically induced transformation of American politics: federal reforms had changed the rules of the game that once characterized community leaders' local world, and they responded in ways that altered the grassroots base of the party system, thereby transforming American politics in turn. In this chapter, my aim is simply to introduce Prairieville and River City and their defining public conflict between partisans and partners, and to begin to separate these places' idiosyncrasies from commonalities between their historical trajectories and those of other American cities. I conclude with a sketch of the book's argument, its connection to other academic literatures, and a summary of the chapters that follow.

River City

River Citians consider the happening harbor district to be their city's symbolic heart, and partners consider it their proudest accomplishment. On a hot July evening, the wrought-iron lanterns light at dusk, drawing a cloud of insects from the river and casting a warm glow on the red-bricked buildings of Main Street. The street buzzes with the voices of young people making their way between sports bars, basement music clubs, and vendors hawking pizza and gyros. From above, more young faces peer down from freshly rehabbed apartments. For many River Citians, this scene represents a new city that has left behind its broken past. "My brother moved out to California for college, and stayed out there," one resident told me, launching into a stylized narrative. "So I took him down to the new Silver Crescent restaurant—the one located where the old brewery used to be. And he said to me, 'Wow, Ellen, this is really great,' and I said, 'Yeah, it is pretty good for River City,' but then he said, 'No, I mean it is just great period.' And that made me stop. I mean, I remember when down here was full of prostitutes and broken-down buildings. And now I can't believe that this is River City."

But River City's partners do not see this contemporary scene, or even the shuttered factories that once stood here, but rather their own entree into public life. Before the 1980s, the blue- and white-collar struggle that defined River City played out here. Workers marched to and from the harbor's factories, lunch buckets in hand, stepping into hole-in-the-wall bars on their way home after work and sometimes on their lunch hours, too. "They used to say that if you stopped for a drink in every bar on Main Street, you'd never make it from one end to the other," a resident of an affluent hilltop neighborhood said with disapproval. From such elegant neighborhoods, the factory owners were daily driven down to work, their hilltop mansions never out of view of the workers below.

"We were an old dirty town," said Kathy Gooding, who some say was the city's first partner. We sat inside a new café, drinking lattes and peering at the place the factories once stood. "[We were] at war with ourselves and frozen in time. We needed to change."

When Kathy was a young woman, River City's captains of industry and union-backed politician struggled for public dominance in the harbor. Here stood the chamber of commerce offices, which served as the social club for business owners, a meeting site for business-friendly civic leaders and local politicians, and Republican Party headquarters. Here, too, the meatpackers' union held rallies for Jones Berry, River City's flannel-wearing, motorcycle-driving mayor.

"The chamber always tried to back the business candidate," Daniel Haas, a 1970s-era chamber president, told me. "But I guess it worked too well, because people thought business candidates were deciding too many important things. Then Jones Berry led a civilian revolt, [he was the] union candidate, the people's candidate, all that stuff. This man was a populist!"

Indeed, Berry's rallies regularly drew thousands and he served many terms as mayor. "That conflict [with business leaders] gave us more confidence in what we were doing," Berry told me. "I wasn't going to change my likes and dislikes [and decided to] defend labor where I could and always listen to the people. If I wanted to ride my motorcycle to city hall, I did that. Because you have to figure that the people elected you to be *their* voice, [they'd] walk up to me on the street and say, 'Just keep doing what you are doing.'"

But then in the early 1980s this local world, and the harbor itself, fell to pieces. Most leaders did not realize it at the time, but their longstanding community struggles had been enabled by federal regulations and transfers, which were gradually rolled back in the 1970s.[8] The manufacturing crisis hit first, soon followed by the twentieth century's largest merger movement—largely a product of financial market deregulation.[9] River City's meatpacking plant was acquired by an outside corporation, then eventually liquidated. Other factories followed suit. The federal dollars that River City's leaders had previously used to reshape the urban environment dried up, too. Democratic and Republican administrations alike had once supported programs like urban renewal, Model Cities, community development block grants, and revenue sharing, which made discretionary transfers to local governments and public commissions.[10] But during the 1980s the federal government virtually discontinued its direct fiscal relationship with cities, as federal transfers fell from 20 to 3 percent of municipal budgets.[11] With federal money gone, River City's factories stood empty, a symbol of traditional leaders' sudden impotence, like broken teeth encircling the mouth of the harbor. A national magazine featured River City's harbor for its cover story on the Rust Belt.

"I was a young mom then," Kathy Gooding continued, looking down at her coffee. "And it was like, 'Oh my god, is this town going to die?' There was not a day when you did not talk to somebody with children leaving for Texas, Arizona, or somewhere. So, you see, our transformation was a conscious choice. [With the] collapse came a new generation. We worked together at every level: a new generation that brought in a new age.

Kathy eventually became assistant city manager and a leading citizen, but in the 1980s she was nobody: a woman in a man's world, a stay-at-home mother and part-time Democratic fundraiser, neither a business owner nor a union leader. Then the president of the city's historical society asked her to fundraise for a harbor museum, which he hoped would grow and anchor future development. And grow it did: from a one-room exhibit to a sprawling $200-million complex that overtook abandoned factories and was later joined by a resort hotel, convention center, casino, and other amenities.

"The museum project was an idea whose time had come," Kathy continued, delving into the details of the museum initiative. "It took partnership and a partnership is like a marriage: it is commitment to the fact that you are not going to break up, because if you do, there is too much at stake. You come in committed to setting differences aside, findings areas where you can work together. [At first] we needed government funding to attract foundation support. So I called our [Democratic] state senator and [got a state funding bill, but we worried that the Republican] governor could veto the bill. Well, my grandfather was a labor organizer and worked all his life at McConnell's Manufacturing, [a factory in the harbor]. I heard that JR McConnell and the governor were friends so I went to a meeting with him and said, 'Mr. McConnell, I'm Elmer's granddaughter and I know he had a lot of respect for you and said you were a man of your word—can you help us do this for River City?' And he just picked up the phone right then, called the governor, and said, 'Jim, some money for the River Museum is going to show up in the budget and don't veto it!' Then he put down the phone and he looked at me and said, 'Kathy, I may be a Republican, but I believe in bringing to River City what River City is due.' That was the beginning, because that had never happened before.

"All throughout, we formed unlikely relationships [like that one]," Kathy added, "public-sector partnerships with the city and county, a variety of other groups. It would be easier to find organizations here that were *not* involved. Then, we competed. We went after every competitive grant—the national foundation for the arts, the EPA, department of the interior and [private foundations,] everything from $25 to half a mil."

Had they thought of it at all, River City's traditional leaders would have funded harbor redevelopment with urban renewal or a different federal program, and probably fought over control of the city commission that apportioned the funds. But by the 1980s discretionary federal funds had dried up. The public funding that remained came in the form of targeted, competitive grants controlled by a multitude of federal, state, and regional agencies as well as private foundations.[12] In this post-Keynesian context, the city's once-fearsome leaders became useless, lumbering anachronisms; to partners, the idea of Jones Berry and Daniel Haas cooperating on a grant was laughable. New leaders like Kathy, JR, and those who followed, outmaneuvered them by agreeing to, in partner lingo, "set divisive issues aside" and focus on contextual, transitory points of consensus. Once leaders agreed to do this, they formed coalitions that represented the museum as different things to different people at different points in time: a Democratic initiative, Republican initiative, historical museum, cultural heritage site, foundation for raising environmental awareness, aesthetic marvel, and many other things besides. Outside funding flowed again, the harbor was reborn, and a new generation of leaders was born with it.

Other River Citians are hazy on these details, but they recognize that something fundamental about their city's public life has changed. One might hear talk of this at the Happy Mug, a coffeehouse that doubles as a bluegrass music venue and a favorite gathering site for the city's self-styled cosmopolitans. "River City used to be just blue-collar all the way," a man at the bar reminisces to a woman who revealed herself as a recent transplant, an employee of a new textbook publisher in the harbor. "The jobs were either in meat-packing or over on the line at Greenfield's [Manufacturing] and everyone and their cousin worked them. [Now we have] new jobs, new people in town, it is just so different." Melissa, a high school teacher who sits at one of the tables, agrees. "This is going to sound terrible, but I think that there was an older generation [that is] no longer as influential and in control," she once told me. "[They are] becoming less active and passing away. [That is why] River City is moving in a positive direction, because the new people want [my] generation to stay. I just get that vibe. I mean culturally [and] in terms of music and art and nonprofits in community it is phenomenal. People are not so set in their ways and are trying to come up with creative ways to make the city better."

Although some details escape them, residents like Melissa know this well: the city's leaders once fought one another and protected their turf. That was perhaps okay for them, but times have changed, leaders now co-operate to find creative solutions, and anything besides cooperation impedes progress. In fact, residents like Melissa instinctually condemn partisanship wherever they see, in community life or party politics.

"We all have to start with a value set, but then we have to work together to get to creative solutions," Melissa told me when I asked her about politics. "Actually, that's why I'm so disenchanted with party politics: I want a good creative problem solver. There are little pockets of that, [but] it is difficult, because [politicians] are beholden to a lot of people. [They] recite just one narrow little point of view. I'm hopeful that [a politician] will emerge with that potential [for] compromise and an ability to find a creative solution. [Maybe] that cultural change [we have seen in River City] will happen nationally."

The post-partisan, creative partner idealized by Melissa may be absent in partisan politics, but those who embrace this ideal are central in community governance. Ben Denison is one such figure. He heads the Development Corporation and, many say, is the most powerful man in River City. The Development Corporation's offices buzz with the shuffle of paper and the ring of telephones, with callers giving and receiving information about everything from a company's need for skilled welders, to plans to refurbish a riverside pedestrian plaza, to out-of-the-box ideas for a summer cultural festival. The Development Corporation takes partnership and fashions it into a sustainable mode of governance. "We act as a kind of broker, bringing different sides so that we can get things done. This is nonpartisan politics at its best," Ben told me, spontaneously contrasting community governance and partisan politics. "[We] form partnerships by finding areas where we can all agree and work together and setting aside the lightning rod issues that divide us. [You] take your blinders off, look at your community through the eyes of the outsider, and if you see a cancer, cut it out. The harbor was just a bunch of garbage and visitors [thought] 'Yuck, what a nasty river town!' Now look at it. People don't say that anymore."

Ben's rise to power was as unexpected as that of the city's other partners. He first arrived in River City in the 1980s, when Jones Berry was still mayor. Like Berry, Ben Denison is a Democrat—although this is something he usually declines to discuss publically—but Ben's similarities to the city's traditional leaders end there. Ben never belonged to a union or owned a business. He is an outsider in a city where traditional leaders once measured length of community engagement in generations. He is not even officially autonomous, working instead as a salaried professional on behalf of the municipal bureaucracies, unions, and businesses that fund the Development Corporation. But in the 1980s the times were changing. One of the few personal effects on Ben's desk is a faded photograph of the "Three Musketeers": Ben Denison, city manager Dirk Vandenberg, and Troy Gooder, the chamber-backed mayor elected after Jones Berry. Each man keeps a photo like it. Like Ben Denison, Vandenberg and Gooder were outsiders removed from the city's traditional leadership class, but their 1980s- and '90s-era partnerships became the stuff of legend and catapulted them to their city's central stage. The city's other partners attribute all the virtues of partnership to them, not least because Ben Denison is a Democrat, Troy Gooder is a Republican, and Dirk Vandenberg is an Independent. The trio's enduring friendship therefore embodies the partners' key virtue: willingness to set divisive issues, especially divisive political issues, aside.

On hot summer nights, partners sometimes meet in the harbor, board an antique riverboat, and paddle around enjoying a dinner cruise as they gaze at the shimmering lights of the new city that their partnerships built. Many traditional leaders who made the transition to partnership are aboard. One is bank president Gus Herman. "[It's] just that new mindset. [Before] it was an adversarial role," he told me. "[Before I knew better, I also] thought I'd get [into a community forum, like] a big bad hero, a business guy [and run things]. See, that was before *I* made that transition, realized that we have to work together in a collaborative way. [Now] I can get on a community board and people know that I am not just looking out for the River City Bank, but I'm looking out for the community at large."

Mayor Ron Bolan is there, too, along with many key union leaders. Once a factory worker, Ron entered politics as Jones Berry's protégé, but then repudiated Berry's oppositional style and embraced partnership. "In the past, boy, [city council meetings] were bad," Ron told me. "They would go until 12 am, and the longer it went, the worse it got: fist pounding, name calling—entertaining, but also embarrassing and not very productive. Partnership has changed the community: everyone has something different to bring to the table, but you have to communicate and figure out what those things are. We're at a tipping point. If we slow that fly-wheel down, the world will pass us by."

However secure things may appear aboard the riverboat, partners know that their coalition, and its grip on power, is tenuous. Somewhere among the city's dark silhouettes, the partisans lurk: those who do not embrace partnerships, cling to politics, and seem always ready to stoke conflicts that would repolarize public life along traditional lines.

Agatha, who has lived in one of the city's working-class neighborhoods for nearly a century, is one such partisan voice. "[Local leadership] just kind of fell apart. They just jump to conclusions—we need this and we need that," she told me. "[Take] the harbor. I was at a wedding down there and oh gosh, we felt like poor mice! We went up into the reception room: a five-piece orchestra, all the kinds of drinks you could want. Now that isn't for poor people. [New leaders must] think they are real society. Not one of them cares about the future of the city. They want to be in the big show. For us, we'd go to church on Sunday, maybe two couples would come home with us and visit, play cards, or play ball or something—that was living!"

Doug, a bank manager, is less concerned than Agatha with the fate of River City's working class but equally critical of community life. He laments the decline of business leaders' singular, unapologetic—and unapologetically Republican—style: the fact that they *represented* their constituents the way that some politicians still do, a sad contrast to partners' marketing gimmicks. "[It used to be that] the guy who owned the butcher shop would get together with the guy who ran the manufacturing plant and said, 'Hey, if we band together and speak with one voice we can be a lot more powerful,'" Doug told me. "And [business leaders] in the past, you could hear a pin drop when they talked, because they told you how they saw it, and the way that it would be. But now [they] get bogged down in these public-private development initiatives, [spend their time] going out and getting grants and then spending them like drunken sailors on holiday to get anything at all in here. [It is to the point where] they want nothing to do with the party. They won't sit through a meeting [or say,] 'I'm a Republican just like you!'"

Partners sometimes dismiss such partisan voices as holdovers from their city's past, but also know that conflicts between community and politics are of their own making. Indeed, many partisan institutions are in the hands of those whom partners ostracize in their community's public life. In the city's working-class North End, for example, the lights are on in the Labor Temple. A rusty sign that hangs above the door reads "Labor Council" creaks slowly in the wind. Inside, Michael Lombarti peers over bifocals and delivers his monthly political report to old men seated in folding chairs. "We got some labor folks on city council," he begins. "And those folks should have labor values at heart. He, Ron Bolan [the mayor], he's a retired union member, he should be an example when he talks. I should be able to see some union values there, but [instead] I see, [council supports] user fees. Because the rich, they don't give a shit. They got their own pools. They don't have to go to the city pool. They don't have to go to the River City library, they can buy the books. Yeah, that makes perfect sense to selfish people! [We] working people, we do things collectively. We can't afford to do this stuff on our own."

Before the 1980s, the Labor Council was the city's most important labor organization, and Michael Lombarti the city's most promising young labor activist. Known among his peers as a "fighter" who does not mince words, Michael was elected "Labor Leader of the Year" soon after becoming president of his local. "A lot of people thought that Michael was going to run this whole show one day, be the head honcho—and he probably could have, too," a labor leader who is aboard the riverboat told me. "[But leaders like] Michael have too much of that old, old, old mentality. They'd rather sit across the table and fight, [not] sit around the table and find a solution that works well for everybody."

After the 1980s, leaders like Michael suddenly found themselves with less to fight over. The factories left or were acquired by outsiders and generous federal transfers fragmented into piecemeal, competitive grants controlled by federal agencies, state governments, and nonprofit foundations. In this new context employers would only come to the city if wooed, and obtaining outside funding required coordination, finesse, and the appearance of unanimous community support that only partners could supply. Michael experimented with partnerships, but ultimately held fast to an oppositional tradition. But for all their bluster, labor leaders like Michael entertain no serious hopes of reasserting community power. Instead, they pour their frustration into one arena that is not dominated by partners: partisan politics. The Labor Temple buzzes with activity at election time, and the Labor Council forms the backbone of the Democratic Party's union drive in the political off-season: they maintain voter rolls, register voters, and wield influence with the city's other Democratic activists and elected politicians.

Across town, the situation is similar at a monthly GOP meeting. Here, those described by Doug as "true-believing" activists meet in the auditorium of a roadside motel—a far cry from the country club accommodations once enjoyed by the party. But the GOP can ill afford better, because the city's business leaders and their once-grandiose donations stay away. Predictably, the GOP has grown more partisan in their absence. On this evening, GOP activists discuss participating in a Pro-Life picket of River City's Planned Parenthood clinic and many decide to join. This will embarrass the city's partners, endanger their plans to woo a subsidiary of a socially progressive computer company, and polarize River City's public sphere into a familiar post-1980s opposition: between consensus-motivated and community-focused partners and nationally directed partisan activists.

Jonathan Speenham, the president of the GOP, was no stranger to this opposition. He served on city council, but lost a race for mayor to Ron Bolan after his Republicanism—and especially his wife's involvement in Christian conservative groups—became an issue. Like the partisans of the Labor Council, Jonathan was sidelined by the city's partners, and like them entertained no hope of a return to community influence. Like Labor Council leaders, too, Jonathan was resigned to his fate, but saw an opportunity to wield influence via the political initiatives that partners avoid. "When it comes to economic development, there are no differences [between Democrats and Republicans]. None! Ben Denison and [the city manager,] they run River City and don't let anyone ever tell you different. We don't get involved with most city issues," Jonathan told me. "Now on social issues, [there is] a core group of Democrats that get deeply involved in those," he added. "Anything related to mental health, health clinics, making River City a 'green city,' the sexual orientation ordinance—that was one we fought for years and the Democratic contingent pushed probably the hardest. We hold the line on issues like those." With leaders like Jonathan in charge, the city's Republican Party has refocused on such partisan hot-button issues, thus coproducing a community-politics rift within the city's public life.

Prairieville

If River City's story sounds familiar, it is because it is not uniquely its own. Its story is not even about cities per se, but rather about community leaders, their struggles, and the ecology of federal regulations and policies in which they operate. River City's leaders are uninterested in such matters; they are pragmatic and focused on the game of public prominence that they play with one another. But this book's central claim is that community leaders' game unfolds in an arena structured by broader economic-political forces. However parochial leaders' struggles seem, they are part of a story that has played out across the United States.[13]

Consider the parallels between River City and Prairieville, a city with a different look, smell, and feel. To get there, one drives west from River City. Creeks and valleys, towns with little hamburger stands, and patches of trees give way to endless cornfields dotted by infrequent farms. Contemporary country music and religious sermons overtake classic rock on the radio, sunsets glow in orange and violet streaks of striking intensity, and the wind howls unchecked, bringing violent weather. One has left the Midwest and entered big sky country.

But look past superficial differences to common threads in Prairieville's story. Here, too, Keynesian-era bureaucracies protected local firms from corporate buyouts and operated a "banker government" of sorts, which made large, discretionary transfers to nonprofits and political bodies, thereby politically constructing an economic, civic, and political sphere that appeared to be under locals' control.[14] In this context, labor and business leaders battled over locally controlled resources, organizing public life into an opposition between business-owning Republican patricians and Democratic union and working-class activists. Only some details differ: whereas River

City's union leaders typically bested their city's patricians, Prairieville's old families were cohesive and maintained a tight grip on power, thus shaping the city according to their vision. Prairieville's old families monopolized local philanthropy via the United Way and funded only their own civic ventures, monopolized control of urban renewal boards and rebuilt downtown according to their own plans, and always elected a chamber-backed mayor.[15] Their opponents managed to elect only one long-serving councilman: Hal Swift, who supporters remember as "a little guy with a big mouth on him, who was not afraid to get up there and tell it like he saw it." Although the relative strength of the sides was different, actors on both sides in both cities traded on an ability to gain control over local and locally controlled federal resources and therefore built networks that penetrated deep into daily life and allowed them mobilize the public in support, thus dividing the public along white- and blue-collar lines.

But as in River City, 1980s-era reforms ended such traditional conflicts by reshuffling Prairieville's leadership class. "Around here it was run for a long time by the old leaders, the old money, the country clubbers—they had this very negative attitude," a real estate agent in his sixties told me. "They did not want change, they did not give a damn about city, and they ran everything in the dark and behind closed doors. [Now] the old money realizes that they have to grow to survive. In the 1970s it was, 'Let's pretend it is the 1950s and keep all the other industries out.' But a lot of them went under in the '80s, and a lot of the ones that were left sat around scratching their heads and wondering why their kids did not want to come back after college. The [new leaders] had to drag what was left of the old-timers into a more progressive direction, drag them kicking and screaming."

After financial deregulation, corporate raiders gradually acquired many of Prairieville's firms, thinning the ranks of the old families. "Thirty years ago, there were probably fifty names you could call on [if you were chairing something]. Now when I am asked to chair something, I don't know who to call on," Charles Browning, the heir of a venerable Prairieville family, told me. "There is not that commitment to the community. [People] get sold out and Boom! There goes the employment base, the corporate headquarters, there goes the family charitable giving [and] community involvement." Suddenly, there were fewer leaders like Charles and—as Keynesian-era transfers were replaced by targeted and competitive grants—those who remained had fewer locally rooted resources to fight over. The city's nonprofit sector shriveled and the built environment crumbled as traditional leaders stood helpless, puzzled by a new world they no longer understood. To achieve their public goals, remaining leaders had to address a new prob-

lem: marketing their city to outsiders. As in River City, self-identified partners stepped in.

When talk turns to partnership, Prairieville's leaders think first of Dani
Dover, the chamber's dynamic new director. One self-identified partner
described her to me as "the first person I go to, to bounce ideas off of,
get support—and there are a lot of people who have her at the top of the
Rolodex—she is a sounding board, a catalyst, a consensus builder." As her
city's central "catalyst" or "consensus builder," Dani Dover is Prairieville's
equivalent of River City's Ben Denison. The two differ superficially. Dani is
a registered Republican whereas Ben is a registered Democrat, Dani got her
start in business whereas Ben was a politician, Dani is a woman whereas
Ben is a man. But there are similarities between them too: both are not
natives of their respective cities, both rose during the turbulent 1980s and
'90s, and both understand themselves as merely channeling the consensus
of the community. Like Ben, too, Dani has a disdain for the rigid, oppositional style of her traditional predecessors.

"We [at the chamber] are more inclusive than we used to be," Dani told
me. "If you asked people about the chamber maybe twenty years ago, they
would have told you it was a good old boys club, and to a large extent it
was. They were very closed off. They did not plant flowers, you know?"
she added chuckling, then pantomimed a curmudgeonly, doddering chamber leader from yesteryear. "'What does building auditoriums have to do
with economic development?!?'" she demanded in mock confusion and
laughed. "Well, that has changed. We try to keep vitality in the community all the time—that excitement. So what you see is a lot more partnerships so that more voices in the community are represented. And we at the
chamber act as a kind of broker," she continued, channeling Ben Denison.
"People will call me all the time with ideas and some of them go on the
back burner, but sometimes we say, 'Hey, that is exactly what we are looking for, let's put the people together.' So you have this constant Rolodex
of people with different interests and you bring them together. And when
people come together things happen."

And indeed, Dani maintains many nontraditional relationships with
other community leaders. She regularly lunches with Abe Skipper, Prairieville's famous—and infamous—former Democratic state senator. Abe,
a worker's compensation attorney, is the inheritor of a long tradition of
Democratic and union activism: a protégé of an attorney who, some say,
nearly traded blows with Prairieville's old families and who union leaders still refer to as "a lion of labor" in hushed tones. To the horror of traditional business leaders, Dani considers Abe Skipper a friendly acquain-

tance. "[Abe Skipper and I] may not agree on everything, but we agree to disagree. We have to keep those lines of communication open, so that we can build partnerships on areas where we do agree," Dani explained. This arrangement is equally acceptable to Abe Skipper. "The chamber is not as political as they used to be—although I still never turn my back on them," he confirmed. "Dani is more the consensus type of person. The old chamber guys thought that fucking labor was synonymous with the chamber agenda. We were bitter, bitter enemies, jeez it was open warfare. Dani has done a much better job of bringing people around the table. She's not [always] going to agree with me and I'm not going to agree with her, but where we can work together we'll work together."

As in River City, leaders' willingness to set divisive issues aside is critical to place-marketing initiatives, because this creates a social space—a "big round table" in partner-speak—that allows leaders like Dani to pull together leaders who will represent the city differently to different consequential outsiders. Abe Skipper would not be right for a partnership to attract a nonunionized employer to Prairieville, but he would be perfect if Dani was applying for grants to open a clinic for former meatpackers now afflicted with carpal tunnel syndrome—provided, of course, that everyone agrees to keep traditional conflicts "off the table." Therein lies the key issue: a partner's utility is predicated on avoidance of a divisive reputation, and partnership is therefore incompatible with traditional leaders' patterns of community engagement, especially their engagement in partisan politics.

For this reason, Prairieville's partners avoid partisan politics, and their avoidance of it fuels a community-politics conflict similar to that which defines River City's public sphere. Nobody appreciates this fact more than Mark Sturley, the president of Prairieville's GOP, on whose shoulders falls the difficult task of negotiating the divide between partners and politics. Before the 1980s, Prairieville's GOP held its meeting at the chamber or country club and counted Charles Browning's father, grandfather, and other Prairieville patricians as key members. But then, business leaders found their public allegiance to the GOP disruptive of their attempts to create partnerships and abandoned the party, leaving party activists hostile toward the "country club Republicans" who only occasionally venture to party headquarters to shake hands with a suitable candidate. With a foot in both worlds, Mark tries to keep the peace.

"That is such a huge division—the country club Republicans tend to be more moderate whereas the activists tend to be more evangelical and right-wing," Mark explained. "[So now] the people who give the money stop and say, 'You have to put up the people that I like,' [and] are holding the money back. The activists, they do the work of the party [and] think they can control the agenda and impose their will. [I mean] now it is like if [a community notable] steps forward to run for something it is like, 'Thank God, we have a candidate.' [Often, somebody unknown runs and] we don't even stop to think anymore if it is someone out there with an axe to grind or someone with a chance to win. So I guess that makes me more of a moderate. Some would say I'm not a true activist."

Just weeks after my interview with Mark, Prairieville's true activists deposed him as party chair, and the division between Prairieville's community governance and partisan politics was complete. At stake in this local transformation is the base of America's party system. Partisan politics was once rooted in community institutions like the chamber of commerce or Labor Council, and leaders of these organizations were party leaders who disciplined activists, focusing their attention of the struggles that occupied them in community life. Since the 1980s, politics became disembedded from community governance: it was in the hands of holdout traditional leaders and a new generation of partisan activists who championed a smorgasbord of political causes and were polarized by their exclusion from, and occasional conflict with, key community leaders. Whereas community and political conflicts were once one and the same, politics now appeared as a world divorced from and opposed to community governance.

Although most of these details were lost on them, Prairievillers—like River Citians—understood enough to situate themselves within this community-politics struggle. Will, a professional in his twenties, sided with community and, seeing few signs of partnership in partisan politics, saw the latter as irrevocably flawed. "I think [Prairieville] is better now," he said. "I don't know if I can put my finger on what is causing that, but maybe it is that the city or the council or whatever, being like, 'Hey, we need to be open, not so into ourselves,' but rather looking towards the outside world [and] starting to think about places where they can work together to get stuff done: the track along the river, bringing in musical acts, things that are good for the city as a whole." Because Will saw it as evident that public life should resemble that of his community, partisan politics seemed inherently problematic. "[In politics] if anything gets brought up it is immediately shot down. It is hard for me to get out and vote. I do, but it's just like—ehh—I don't know what it is really doing," he continued. "[You get] all this talk about viewpoints as either left or right. I just hate to think that way. So many things are good for the country as a whole, but politicians get pulled one way or another. [They need] to stop being so stupid and sit down together to figure things out."

To Linda, it seemed evident that community, not politics, was the problem. In her forties, she was a mother of two and an accountant in one of Prairieville's now non–locally owned meatpacking plants. "Job-wise, I think it has gotten worse," she said. "People have a hard time finding a job that pays more than $8 an hour. I just feel that it is totally unfair [and] I think taxes are outrageous. Here we are trying to make ends meet, but getting it in the butt. This system is so screwed. [And] leaders [in Prairieville] could do a lot. They could do something about these taxes; make it so those of us working our butts off can keep a family home. And jobs. I think the leaders could push INS a lot harder to go into those packing houses, force everybody to do background checks. But Prairieville does not care. All they care about is looking like they are up and running, always bragging about the newest thing."

Having given up on community, Linda looked to politics as a panacea, hoping for a grassroots populist mobilization—an early call for a Tea Party–like movement, which Linda would identify after the movement emerged in 2008. "[Politicians should be] people like us, trying to work hard and get ahead," she told me. "Bring a soldier in, someone who has actually been there, talk to them, because then they might think things different. I prefer the outsider, because you don't have to be a billionaire to have a lot of sense. [They'd] go with their gut feelings. If you get somebody in there knowing what they are doing, they will keep doing the things that aren't working. I want somebody who will just step right in and work hard for those of us who are working hard, but still struggling." In a world controlled by partners, Linda turns to partisans for answers.

Partners, Partisans, and the Politics of the Post-Keynesian Society

The great paradox of politics is that most citizens lack formal political knowledge and yet hold strong political opinions, particularly before elections. In the 1920s Americans' political ignorance so shocked the first public opinion researchers that they fretted over whether it made the nation susceptible to the totalitarianism then spreading across the globe.[16] But scholars quickly accepted the public's ignorance of political issues and turned to measuring it. In the 1960s political scientist Philip Converse concluded that roughly 4 percent of voters could formulate what he considered an informed political opinion—one motivated by a coherent ideology of statecraft and rooted in a good grasp of the facts.[17] Another 10 percent approached this ideal, but faltered in the consistency of their ideological framework or political knowledge. The remaining 85 percent justified their political opinions with reasons that Converse considered uninformed. A plurality expressed allegiance to party or a politically salient category like working class, business class, blacks, Catholics, or immigrants. Others responded less systematically still, justifying their preferences with reference to the "nature of the times," a candidate's appearance, or the media micro-scandal of the moment. By most accounts, Americans' formal political knowledge has not improved since Converse's day, which raises a key methodological question: if people do not know much about politics, how should one conceptualize and study changes in their preferences for candidates, parties, and policies?[18]

Social scientists' initial efforts to study political preferences took American's ignorance of politics as a starting point. One such effort was the 1948 Elmira Study, so named after the New York town where it took place. The study was conducted by a team of sociologists from Columbia University, who approached it as a qualitative case study. The team went for depth—interviewing each respondent four times—over representativity or breadth and conducted a team ethnography of sorts.[19] They observed the activities of parties and candidates, followed the media, sought out places where people naturally talked politics, and generally tried to understand the election's significance for people within their local context.

The Elmira study's conclusions were simple: people implicitly understand the stakes of political contests, but do not typically reason about them in the language of political issues and formal ideologies. Rather, people are social animals and reason about the world socially, exhibiting a natural tendency to think about abstract economic and political processes through the framework of intimately familiar interpersonal relationships.[20] Today, anthropologists refer to this human tendency as indexical reasoning.[21] Certain features of objects, activities, and people come to stand for—or "index"—social groupings, which then index other objects, activities, and people in turn, conjugating into elaborate frameworks that divide the world into categories: the male versus the female realm, high-brow versus low-brow culture, adult versus a nonadult lifestyles, and so on. Similarly, the Elmira researchers found that as an election approached, politics increasingly piggy-backed on—or indexed—salient social divisions, especially the division between the city's blue- and white-collar residents. Blue-collar workers talked about politics at the shop, their grievances against management became Democratic grievances, their working-class lifestyle became a Democratic lifestyle, and so on until they identified as Democrats without necessarily articulating this affinity in terms of policy preferences. As memories of the election faded, political talk dwindled and people became politically disinterested again.

Elmira researchers' findings were consistent with what we know about mid-twentieth-century American politics—and, for that matter, what I learned about River City's and Prairieville's past. The period between the 1940s and 1970s was anomalous in two respects. First, political parties were less divided than today; some Republicans legislators, for example, consistently voted to the left of some Democrats and vice versa.[22] Voters, too, were partisan but relatively moderate. Pre-election surveys suggest that Americans identified as Democrats and Republicans at rates that topped 80 percent, but were relatively unfervent in their beliefs and characterized by low interissue consistency.[23] That is, a committed Democrat was relatively more likely than Democrats today to hold non-Democratic views on issues like foreign affairs, taxation, abortion, or gun control—a preference distribution that one would expect if partisanship was established primarily through social influence.

But then in the 1970s American politics began to change in three ways: the parties diverged ideologically, a small subset of voters grew more ideologically committed to their parties, too, but most people's partisan commitments loosened. Currently, there is no Republican member of Congress who consistently votes to the left of any Democrat, the gap between the two parties' policy positions is the largest since the systematic study of such issues began, and politicians increasingly engage in "conflict extension"— they take extreme positions on their party's entire platform rather than picking and choosing their battles.[24] Analyses suggest that Republican politicians have grown somewhat more likely to hold extreme positions on the full slate or partisan issues than Democrats, but the trend is pronounced among politicians from both parties.[25] This state of affairs is reflected in trends like the emergence of the Tea Party, talk of a red and blue America, politicians who threaten government shutdown, and the common and correct belief that American politicians are more polarized than ever. Like politicians, some voters have become more consistent and rigid in their beliefs.[26] That is, those with consistently conservative or liberal views are more likely to identify strongly as Republicans and Democrats and hold negative feelings about the opposing party.. Overall, however, most people have not grown more consistent in their political views and—what's more—are less likely to identify with parties.[27] Within this aggregate trend lies an even starker intergenerational trend away from partisanship. In the 1960s those in their twenties were similar to their seniors and roughly 70 percent identified as Democrats and Republicans, whereas most millennials identify with no party today.[28] Politicians and the extreme ends of the electorate have grown more partisan, but everyone else has become less partisan or even apolitical. Why?

One way to develop hypotheses about Americans' changing political preferences would be to examine an Elmira-like study today, but this is difficult to do because such studies have fallen out of fashion in the social sciences. The reasons are complex. By the 1960s the boundaries of social scientific disciplines hardened, the study of political opinions fell squarely into political scientists' wheelhouse and became dominated by survey researchers, and the sociological Elmira study became a disciplinary orphan. The study was also theory- or hypothesis-generating by nature and encountered legitimate scholarly criticism: primarily, the statistical generalizability of findings and the difficulty of replication.[29] But to me the Elmira study also had one undeniable benefit over survey research: it produced results consistent with what most people understand as explanation.[30] Contemporary explanations of voting behavior often take the form of demographic change. For example, some argue that party allegiance declined because incomes and education rose.[31] But such accounts just raise more questions: why do high-education and -income people abandon parties? What social phenomena do these variables really measure? By contrast, the Elmira researchers' explanations were rooted in concrete social processes: who people talked politics with, the categories they used to make sense of themselves and others, and the ways they tried to understand political events outside of their immediate experience.[32] In contemporary social scientific parlance, the Elmira researchers were really studying the public sphere, thus grounding their analysis in processes that scholars not interested in abstract accounts of voting behavior and nonacademics, too, find meaningful: the ways that people understand and discuss their public problems.

My goal in this book is to replicate an Elmira-like study in order to explain changes in America's political system since the late 1970s—both the polarization of party politics and changes in the way that regular people think about politics. This may seem like a tall order for a book based on River City and Prairieville, two small cities in one region of the country, but my intention is not to argue that the phenomena I observed therein occur elsewhere. I need not argue this because other scholars already have. That is, I proceed by examining processes that have been documented by others but are typically examined in isolation, look to River City and Prairieville to generate ideas about how and why these processes are interrelated, and triangulate my observations against other researchers' accounts of related historical trends.[33] It is therefore likely that nothing in the following pages will come as a complete surprise to all readers, but given the breadth of scholarship that I draw from everyone should be surprised by something and, I hope, also the book's unique central argument.

Specifically, my argument draws from five academic literatures: studies of US federalism since the 1970s, urban development coalitions, civil society and the public sphere, the grassroots organization of political parties, and studies of how voters establish political preferences.

The book engages first with studies of American federalism by focusing on changes in three policy domains: policies regulating firm ownership patterns, social welfare spending, and urban development. It is generally well known that American politicians from both parties have focused more of their rhetoric on market-like solutions to social ills since the 1980s, but students of American federalism argue that, contrary to popular belief, this shift has not reduced federal spending and involvement in most policy domains.[34] Rather, federal bureaucracies shifted toward a competitive, market-like model of statecraft by promoting private sector competition, outsourcing funding and responsibility for federal programs to states, and delivering transfers and services through targeted, competitive programs.[35] More simply, the federal government has become more business-like, and federal programs generally redistribute less and promote a "race to the top" more than their Keynesian counterparts. I find these arguments consistent with my observations of River City and Prairieville, but whereas scholars interested in federalism focus on the national-level policy, I focus on the effects of policies on grassroots democracy.

This focus brings me into conversation with studies of urban development and grassroots civil society, two literatures that ostensibly focus on similar issues but seldom communicate. Urban scholars and critical geographers note that urban leaders have become entrepreneurial in their efforts to attract outside resources since the 1980s and attribute this to their need to assume federal government functions, a process they refer to as a "rescaling of the state."[36] However, contemporary scholarship focuses largely on urban leaders' formal place-marketing strategies and says little about how political-economic pressures have changed leaders' public culture. Missing are contemporary complements to studies like John Mollenkopf's—a perspective I draw on heavily for historical comparison—who showed how Keynesian-era policies structured community conflicts and, thereby, urban leaders' understanding of politics.[37] Conversely, studies of American grassroots democracy say much about contemporary civic culture, arguing that it has become elite-orchestrated and unamenable to meaningful debate.[38] Nina Eliasoph, for example, argues that grassroots activists see community engagement as incompatible with politics, an argument that aligns with my observations of River City and Prairieville. However, most scholars of grassroots democracy have not advanced a systematic explanation of these changes, in part due to their narrow focus on civic culture and relative disinterest in the things that interest urbanists: how grassroots leaders leverage the necessary resources to bring their plans to fruition.[39] Much of the book bridges these literatures by showing how post-1980s federal policies shaped community leaders' place-marketing coalitions, and how participation in these coalitions shaped how leaders relate to one another and think about public problems.

To this end, the majority of the book focuses on River City's and Prairieville's public sphere: a genre of activity that is recognized by locals as legitimate for adjudicating between competing interests, coordinating collective action, or otherwise initiating action on the community's behalf. Simply put, I am interested in people's ability to speak authoritatively on behalf of others, which has long been a preoccupation of democratic theory. However, I depart from classical conceptions of the public sphere in two ways that are common among contemporary scholars and a third way that is fairly unique to this study. First, I identify the public sphere with norms among a community of speakers and not a place or even face-to-face communication.[40] There is no town square where River Citians and Prairievillers debate, but they share common understandings of how one should address public matters and even of how one should think about them in private. Second, the public sphere is not defined by rational arguments about the common good as some political theorists argue it should be, although people nonetheless make frequent claims about universal values like justice and equality via metaphor, myth, group solidarity, or even slander and mockery of public figures.[41] Third, people participate in public life to establish themselves as worthy of public esteem or authority, not merely to make claims on behalf of others or otherwise do something other than aggrandize themselves in the public eye—unlike many democratic theorists, I see no inherent tension between people's public ideals and private interests. Central to my argument is the understanding that people's efforts to wield public authority are intertwined with their efforts to play the local game—to jockey for public esteem with those whom they regard as peers.[42] My focus in the book is largely on the tight-knit circle of grassroots leaders who simultaneously compete for local prominence and are disproportionately active in community life, thereby shaping the public imagination of their city's other residents. To signal this, I employ a series of metaphors that emphasize my interest is public visibility: the public limelight, the public eye, the city's central stage, and—most centrally—leaders' public game.

In this vein, the motivating insight of the book is that the grassroots public sphere is politically constructed: leaders' public game unfolds within an arena that is structured by a broader framework of federal policies. Federal policies alter the types of public bureaucracies, corporations, and associations that exist in the city and therefore the supply of potential grassroots leaders who typically come from the leadership ranks of such community institutions.[43] Systems of public finance also change how grassroots leaders understand problems and try to solve them. I think it important to emphasize that in focusing on the political construction of the public sphere, I do not mean to imply that federal policies alone are a necessary and sufficient cause for any actually existing public sphere. Naturally, any community's public talk has a long history and is impacted by factors that must by necessity remain exogenous to any study, but it is equally true that public policies have systematic consequences and that, in their absence, any actually existing public sphere would be different. Moreover, in pointing to public policies' influence of grassroots leaders I do not mean to suggest that these leaders are rationally calculating and simply respond to federal incentives. Rather, federal policies generate an opportunity structure that allows leaders who engage publically in particular ways to leverage resources and spearhead projects that catapult them to public prominence.[44] Like most opportunity structure arguments, mine assumes that people act on opportunities for various reasons or, indeed, do not act on them but find their position changed by virtue of the changing context. To extend the book's central metaphor of the public game, federal policies merely determine what moves are likely to "work" rather than shaping leaders motivation for playing the game in the first place.[45] In the 1980s, for example, a few leaders embraced partnership to achieve short-term goals, others to stay in the public limelight, while many key leaders did not become partners, could no longer marshal the necessary resources to wield public influence, and slowly receded from their city's central stage.

Finally, I connect my analysis of the public sphere to studies of American parties and voters. Since the publication of John Aldrich's contemporary classic *Why Parties?*, social scientists have taken a renewed interest in party politics and argue that the polarization of American political discourse is driven by the polarization of partisan activists and politicians, not the general public.[46] Moreover, political scientists argue that this polarization began at the grassroots level after activists took over parties and began exercising influence over primaries.[47] This view is consistent with my observations, but I argue that political scientists lack sound explanations of this grassroots shift. Specifically, I will show that the key change is not the entrance of issue activists into the parties, as political scientists assume, but rather the exit of community leaders and the disappearance of their traditional disciplining role from party politics. I then engage with scholars of political preferences who argue that most people use heuristics, or mental shortcuts, to make sense of the political system. A few studies have shown that such heuristics are sometimes borrowed from salient community cleavages, but none have advanced this insight to explain changing political preferences in terms of changing community cleavages.[48] I do precisely this by showing how the organization of River City and Prairieville's public sphere informs the political reasoning of their residents.

This book synthesizes these five research traditions into an argument that can be summarized as follows: neoliberal reforms transformed the arena in which community leaders play their game, facilitated politics-averse partners' rise to the public fore, and left party politics in the hands of ideologically extreme activists—thus polarizing American politics and some voters, but leaving most distrustful of partisan politics. Along these lines, this book is an effort to map Keynesianism and neoliberalism as multitiered political systems: as sets of policy logics and policies, which coincide with a particular kind of status competition—or game—among community leaders, a particular set of relations between community and partisan institutions, and ultimately a particular commonsense mindset with which community leaders and others view public problems. The structure of the book mirrors this argument and is divided into two parts: Keynesianism and neoliberalism—although my discussion of the latter is divided into two chapter groupings. As shorthand, I refer to these periods colloquially as pre- and post-1980s federalism, but this distinction merely reflects locals' folk understanding of their political context and is not intended analytically—even by the narrowest possible definition, the neoliberal reforms that are central to my argument actually occurred between the mid-1970s and late 1980s. For analytical purposes, I use the terms *Keynesianism* and *neoliberalism*.

Because *Keynesianism* and *neoliberalism* are loaded terms that are used differently across the social sciences, I need make several quick caveats about them. At the national scale, I see Keynesiasm and neoliberalism as defined by the prevailing ideologies of the policymakers who initiated each period's characteristic reforms. Some social scientists use these terms instead to indicate more diffuse political trends. Neoliberalism especially sometimes denotes—roughly—anything bad that happened since the 1970s. For this reason, some social scientists frown on the usage of terms like *Keynesianism* and *neoliberalism* on the grounds that they take the place of precise explanation, but my intention in using these terms is precisely opposite: to focus analytical attention on particular policy shifts and invite precise accounts of their diffuse consequences. To this end, I equate Keynesianism with a period when federal policymakers adopted an outlook that historian Daniel Rodgers has described as "institutional realism": they viewed society as rife with coercive relationships, inefficiencies, and inequalities and had faith in state-directed and bureaucratic solutions to social problems.[49] This orientation led policymakers to engage in economic management and create generous social service and urban development programs, which gave urban leaders wide discretion over program implementation. I equate neoliberalism with a period when policymakers understand society as composed of freely acting individuals, a view that promotes faith in a generalized market and its ability to solve social problems, thus making many state-directed solutions appear coercive.[50] This outlook leads policymakers to reign in public sector spending, but also to create new public bureaucracies that apportion federal funding in a competitive, accountable, and market-like manner and to engage in "downscaling"—simultaneous program cuts and the devolution of responsibility over program implementation to states, nonprofit foundations, and other intermediaries, which typically also apportion funding competitively to municipalities.[51] In pointing to policymakers' ideal-typical pre- and post-1980s tendencies, I do not mean to imply that politicians' outlooks led them to pursue coherent and internally consistent policies, that these policies were championed by politicians from just one party, or that the history of Keynesian and neoliberal policies is neatly periodized—in fact, just the opposite was true.[52] However, it is a historical fact that Republicans and Democrats alike changed their prevailing approach to statecraft in definite ways during the 1970s and to a degree that warrants comparison of pre- and post-1980s federalism as distinct periods. Indeed, the book will show that policymakers' political change of heart reverberated through America's federal system during the 1980s, transforming the organization of grassroots public life and the political reasoning of community leaders and others.[53]

My juxtaposition of River City and Prairieville is motivated by an effort to identify the consequences of federal reforms for these cities' public spheres, the organization of grassroots parties, and the political reasoning of locals, not a standard comparative logic. The findings that I present in the book are primarily ethnographic, but I build my argument by triangulating different observations, data sources, and academic literatures as is commonly done in historical-comparative analyses.[54] River City and Prairieville are idiosyncratic cases that differ from one another in many respects, and I juxtapose them to show that—despite their differences—federal policies reshuffled the public sphere of each in similar ways and with similar consequences.[55] I then draw on scholarship about American federalism, civil society, urban governance, and grassroots parties to show that the causal trajectory that I identify in River City and Prairieville is uniquely consistent with these various literatures. Strictly speaking then, *Partisans and Partners* works simultaneously by juxtaposing academic accounts, and a careful reading of the text and endnotes should convince the reader that a broadly similar public transformation to that which I describe in River City and Prairieville occurred elsewhere and is the most plausible cause of various changes in American politics even absent my ethnographic descriptions.[56] Of course, I arrived at my central argument only by doing ethnographic research, which also adds further plausibility to my argument by showing how processes on the ground lead federal policies, the organization of public life, and the way that community leaders and others think about public problems to intermingle in similar ways across time.

Part I of the book shows that Keynesian-era policies led community leaders to embrace party politics and explores the consequences. Chapter 1 focuses on the old families, local business owners who were once central in Prairievillie's public life. Keynesian policies protected these leaders' businesses from outside acquisitions and allowed them to dominate community institutions by maintaining and mobilizing networks of supporters without cooperating with the union and populist leaders who frequently opposed them. Chapter 2 focuses on working-class leaders who played a similarly dominant role in River City's public life despite, and sometimes because of, their conflicts with business leaders. These two chapters show that Keynesian-era policies structured business and labor leaders' public game in similar ways. Leaders from both sides traded on an ability to mobilize their supporters during conflicts over locally rooted resources and were united by a common understanding of public engagement as the skillful representation of these supporters. Chapter 3 focuses on *politics embedded in community governance*—the consequences of community leaders' pre-1980s political engagement. Traditional leaders' public dispositions led them to see party politics as just another way to represent their constituencies, thus creating a form of grassroots partisan organization that I identify as the *community leadership party*. Community leaders took leadership positions in parties, disciplined partisan activists, and focused them on the social and economic issues that defined community conflicts, thus blending community and politics in the minds of others and allowing them to use community life as a heuristic for making sense of politics. Because policymakers and the media saw traditional leaders as their community's political representatives, community leadership parties displaced partisan conflict by orienting politics toward community affairs and away from the hot-button issues that often occupy contemporary activists.

Part II begins with chapter 4, which shows how neoliberal reforms changed the arena in which community leaders play their public game. These reforms facilitated outside acquisition of locally owned firms, eliminated traditional leaders' access to discretionary federal funding, and created opportunities for those willing to form broad-based partnerships. Chapter 5 shows how neoliberal reforms facilitated the ascendancy of business leaders in Prairieville who identify as partners and repudiate GOP ties. Chapter 6 shows how labor leaders in River City who identify as partners sidelined the city's traditional, and politically engaged, union leaders. Together, chapters 5 and 6 show that both cities' public life became defined by conflict between politics-averse partners and nationally directed partisan activists, between community and politics.

Part III continues my analysis of neoliberalism but shifts focus from community governance to *politics disembedded from community governance*—the consequences of partners' political avoidance, which consists of grassroots party institutions that operate independently of those controlled by community leaders.[57] In chapter 7 I focus on activist-dominated parties, showing how they operate as an echo chamber that further magnifies activists' commitment to the extreme positions that they encounter in the mass media. Activists' desire to respect one another's political commitments leads them to adopt one another's extreme views, refrain from policing use of the party label, and circle the wagons in the face of community ridicule directed at their peers. Because activists dominate grassroots partisan politics and are disproportionately influential in primary elections, they shape political candidates, media organizations, and other consequential outsiders' understanding of social problems, thus polarizing American politics.

Chapter 8 examines how River City's and Prairieville's public life informs the political reasoning of their residents, showing how those who employ partnership as a heuristic are generally confused by party politics and vacillate between political disaffection and political extremism. Chapter 9, which focuses on the 2008 and 2012 elections, reinforces this point by analyzing the failure of any candidate to form a coalition that capitalized on people's widespread discontent with party politics. Although partners initially saw Barack Obama as a postpartisan politician, they were ultimately disappointed and supported Obama only tepidly or not at all. I argue that Obama's campaigns shed light on fundamental contradictions within the political system of the United States, contradictions that are further illustrated by the emergence of hyperpartisan movements like the Tea Party. Finally, the conclusion recaps the book, discusses caveats and the scope conditions of my argument, and considers normative implications for American democracy. The post-1980s public sphere is characterized by a feature that I identify as *structural deceit*, or a tendency to systematically communicate misleading information about people to faraway policymakers, and vice versa. Policymakers, who interface disproportionately with partisan activists, are left with the impression that Americans care deeply about hot-button political issues. Meanwhile, people view their community's governing institutions as a pragmatic alternative to federal politics and are left with the false impression that one can entirely avoid political tradeoffs and focus instead on the kinds of win-win compromises that generate windfalls of outside resources. This two-way structural deceit is responsible for many of the puzzling features of contemporary American politics, notably politicians' parting of company with voters.

PART ONE

Keynesianism

ONE

The Old Families

When older Prairievillers talk of their city's public life, the old families who once dominated it are seldom far from their minds. One such resident I spoke to was Shannon, who moved to Prairieville when her husband Frank, an engineer, took a job in one of the city's homegrown industries. They bought a house in Sheppfield, a tree-lined neighborhood at the city's northern edge that was inhabited by many old families. As was customary then, Frank's new employer counseled him to first drive his family into town from the north to avoid the stench of a meatpacking plant—owned by one of Frank's new neighbors—that skirted environmental regulations and stunk up the city's working-class South End in summer. Shannon never quite found her place among her new neighbors.

"This town has a lot of history, and it is a hard town if you move here," Shannon said. She sat on a dumpy couch with a home-knit blanket laid across her lap. "'Old money,' they call it—my daughter used to always laugh and say that there is 'old money' and 'new money' in Prairieville and that we were 'new money.' Prairieville does not welcome newcomers; it's a gossipy little town. It is just full of these old families that have been here forever and got a million kids everywhere. Like here in this neighborhood we got some, a Browning that lives maybe six or seven houses down from us, and another past that—the Bloor family."

"But you know," Shannon continued, leaning in to share a delicious piece of gossip, "their kids aren't all that successful now either. They may have the backing, but the ones that don't take up the family business, [many] don't make it. Like we had one family two houses down. They were into [warehousing] and had been around the city a long time—so financially they were doing great. But he was a gambler and not a great husband and not a good daddy to the little kids. Eventually, he sold the business and the wife divorced him and moved down to Florida, and I heard those little kids did not make anything of themselves at all."

Such pieces of seemingly apolitical gossip, common among transplants like Shannon and more generally those who identified with the new, cosmopolitan, and partner-dominated city that they hoped Prairieville was becoming, were one way in which Prairievillers discussed changes in their city's public sphere. At the center of such narratives was a particular kind of public actor: a member of the city's business-owning families, or simply old families. Sometimes, people told stories focused exclusively on the old families and sometimes ones about their public struggles with union leaders—the latter type was especially common in working-class neighborhoods. In these stories, members of the old families appeared frequently as villains: they were clannish, conservative, jealously guarded their interests, opposed unions, and kept Prairieville frozen in time. "These old-timers—the city fathers—these old families with their names everywhere and in everything, they did not want change," a former factory worker told me. "General Mills, or maybe General Foods, some big company wanted to move in here, but whatever it was, the old-timers did not want the union. They said, 'No thank you, we like it just the way it is!'"

But sometimes, people remembered the old families fondly, too: as generous and giving, dependable, and—above all—committed to Prairieville. "I don't see Prairieville's prospects as too rosy," one of Prairieville's former Labor Council presidents told me, looking kindly now on his old enemies. "We've got five-, six-dollar-an-hour jobs hanging out our ass, and they can dress that up all they want but hell, even the businesses aren't here, their corporate offices, the majority of that money goes back there," he added, pointing into the air toward imaginary corporate headquarters. "[We're missing businesses] like Glover's Manufacturing, Prairie Tools. The people who started those businesses were part of the community. [Now] you have [these corporate subsidiaries] with no ties. What do they give a shit about Prairieville, Iowa? They have no commitment. We're giving away the goddamn farm to get them here, but there is nothing to keep them from making a drastic decision that affects the entire community."

After hearing many such stories, I came to realize that they were about the particular role that the old families played within Prairieville's public life, not about wealth or business owners per se. In fact, many of members of the old families still resided in Prairieville and were still wealthy; a few even continued to run the business associated with the family name. But older Prairievillers insisted that only a handful of them were really like the old families had been; most had "made the transition" along with other leaders during the 1980s. To older residents, the old families signified a particular form of control that this group once exercised over the city's economy, voluntary associations, municipal decision-making bodies, and Republican politics.

In contrast to today, the past influence of the old families is undeniable. It appears everywhere in the historical record and is even written into the city itself. If one walks down Prairieville's Main Street, for example, the brown and red brick buildings that once housed the economic engines of the city are still marked with their names: Berkin's Department Store, Klueger and Son's Brick and Tile, the Peelmer Building, Browning Construction, the Wheeler Building. Stopping mid-walk in Prairieville's public library, one sees the same names in the picture-filled encyclopedias that document Prairieville's past. Regardless of the time period, the leading citizens' family names and sometimes even first names are the same. In one photo from the 1970s, one sees Charles Springer, Charles W. Browning, and Gilbert F. Jones Jr. posing at a groundbreaking ceremony for a new manufacturer or greeting a visiting Republican dignitary. Another from the early 1950s, features Nick Springer, Charles R. Browning, and Gilbert F. Jones leading the city's Fourth of July parade or beaming proudly while receiving the newspaper's first citizen award. Even further back, the same names appear among the original operators of Prairieville's stockyards. Leaving the library and continuing along Main, one reaches a circular plaza that marks the city's symbolic center. It is dominated by the Willis fountain, a gift from the prominent meatpacking family. Built of imported Italian terracotta that tastefully complements the reddish coloring of the district's surviving warehouses, the fountain's style is classical, but the theme is unapologetically local: a bull on each pillar sprays water from its mouth into the fountain's center, and the fountain itself is inset with plaques showing images of work in the old stockyards. An inscription reads, "A gift to Prairieville and its people, who have brought us so much good fortune." Symbolically and actually then, the old families are central to historic Prairieville and—appropriately—announce themselves in the language of gift and reciprocal obligation: you gave to us so we give back to you.

In this chapter, I explain why the old families emerged as a cohesive actor in Prairieville's public sphere, one that locals perceived as opposed to—or even the polar opposite of—union leaders and their allies. This conflict was important to the public imagination of Prairievillers, because it structured how they thought about politics. Indeed, many older residents still use the division between the old families and union leaders as a heuristic for making sense of national politics, much like the subjects of social scientists' first election studies in 1940s Elmira, New York, who understood politics as a blue-collar/white-collar conflict.[1] My central argument is that there is nothing natural about older residents' tendency to equate politics with a conflict between working-class and business-class sides, or even with sides at all. People saw politics this way—and some older residents still do—because the public actors of their day happened to organize their activities this way. The puzzle in this chapter, then, is how the old families got to be a "side" in the first place. My answer is twofold and focuses, first, on the way that members of the old families organized their public activities and, second, on the broader system of Keynesian-era regulations that supported, and even encouraged, the old families' mode of public engagement.

The cohesive, factional relations that bound Prairieville's old families resulted from the particular way that individuals strove for public prominence or, more simply, the game for public esteem they played with one another. Within this traditional game, members of the old families rose to prominence by giving or—more exactly—by creating a social system akin to one that social theorist Marcel Mauss identified as a total system of gift and counterobligation.[2] Prairieville's old families monopolized economic, civic, and political resources, and doled these out to one another and their supporters, who effectively became their clients.[3] The old families thereby created networks of generosity and reciprocal obligation that penetrated deeply into Prairieville's economic, civic, and political life and, in the minds of Prairieville's residents, blurred the boundary between community governance and national politics. The Janus-faced logic of gift, which Mauss argues puts the receiver under obligation to the giver, is key to residents' divergent perceptions of the old families. To some, the old families were committed and understood that they had to give in order to get Prairievilliers' public esteem. To others, they were cliquish, controlling, and conservative. In fact, they were both at once.

Crucially, however, the old families' game was politically constructed: supported and even encouraged by pre-1980s federalism in two ways. First, Keynesian-era financial regulations created an economic sector of medium-sized locally owned firms that were sheltered from corporate acquisitions and therefore allowed the old families to exist. Moreover, Keynesian-era social service and urban development policies transferred large, discretionary chunks of federal dollars to local bodies, thus allowing and encouraging grassroots leaders to factionalize and compete over these resources. I begin the chapter with a history of Prairieville, which describes the formation of the city's old families and their working-class opponents. This history is followed by sections that focus on the old families' economic, civic, and political activities, and show how pre-1980s federalism reinforced the old families' efforts to exercise collective control over these sectors of community life. Chapter 2 then complements this chapter by showing how Keynesian-era policies promoted a similar organization of public life in River City, albeit with labor leaders gaining the upper hand in the latter case.

A History of Prairieville's Public Life before 1980

In the 1870s Prairieville was a frontier outpost of a few thousand inhabitants, but the railroad changed it overnight into a contender for America's pre-eminent heartland city. Boosters hoped that Prairieville's stockyards would eclipse those in Chicago, turning Prairieville into a key node in America's growing market for meat: livestock would be shipped to Prairieville from the west, slaughtered, and shipped east. Speculators descended, and the city council annexed surrounding farmland, making plans for a city of several hundred thousand—much bigger than Prairieville ever became. Behind the speculators, architects followed and left behind office buildings in the Prairie School style, complete with half-naked natives, gargoyles, and biblical motifs that long ago earned Prairieville the nickname "Little Chicago." Behind both the speculator and architects came a diverse mix of German, Irish, Polish, and Swedish immigrants who worked the stockyards. As the population quadrupled to nearly 50,000 in the 1880s, new immigrants built shanties near the stockyards that dominated the city's southern half, while the original inhabitants moved north to Sheppfield.

Prairieville's fortunes changed with the invention of the refrigerated railroad car, which allowed cattle to be slaughtered closer to the range. The stockyards declined and the economy diversified into meat processing and other industries, but not without leaving an indelible mark on the city. To locals, Sheppfield remains associated with the city's original unhyphenated American inhabitants, while southern neighborhoods bear names like Swedish Village and Polack Hill. Some older working-class residents still recall hearing parents argue in German or Swedish and many nonaffluent Prairievillers are bound by a general sense that they are white-ethnics and therefore rougher and hardier than the city's old families—a pan-ethnic identity that locals celebrate with tales of Prairieville's frontier days, when every weekend brought drunken brawls that spilled onto the streets from downtown's bars.

The 1950s brought another decade of boom to the city with the construction of America's interstate highway system. Prairieville fell on an interstate route, which was extended and expanded during several mammoth projects during the 1960s, thus turning the city into a processing, manufacturing, and commercial hub for its agricultural periphery. The city's packinghouses consolidated into three massive operations, each employing over a thousand workers apiece while locally owned plants manufacturing ice cream, denim products, chemicals and fertilizers, baked goods, consumer tools, and appliances grew into major operations that employed hundreds. Construction of the interstate highway system also cast a long shadow over Prairieville's business community, as homegrown construction firms swelled with federal contracts. Even after the interstate was complete, some of Prairieville's businesses remained focused on building and construction ventures and branched out into related sectors like transportation, warehousing, and wholesale retail.

It is important that Prairieville's period of industrial consolidation occurred during a period when Democratic and Republican leaders alike embraced Keynesian public policy. Popular commentators and academics alike often associate Keynesianism with countercyclical government spending, but I use the term to capture policymakers' prevailing understanding of society, which motivated such policy prescriptions. Historian Daniel Rodgers describes Keynesian-era policymakers' approach to statecraft as "institutional realism": they saw society as rife with power imbalances, dysfunctional norms, and out-of-date traditions, and understood markets as unusually imperfect institutions embedded within this messy social reality.[4] Unlike post-1970s politicians, most Keynesian-era policymakers did not equate the economy with "the market"—a metaphor for society as a whole, which implies a flexible and self-correcting economy—and viewed it instead as a collection of particular markets in need of management and regulation (e.g., labor markets, agricultural commodities markets, mortgage markets).[5] Postwar policymakers' commitment to economic management was reinforced by the era's economic experts. Economic textbooks, for example, addressed macroeconomics before microeconomics, because policy experts assumed that microeconomic price system models would only work if government first established stabilizing conditions.[6] A popular economic and policy teaching tool of the period was the MONIAC computer, a hydraulic system—literally a series of pumps and valves—that simulated the flow of money through the national economy and modeled imperfect allocations of resources that students were invited to correct.[7] In this intellectual climate, mainstream Republicans and Democrats alike accepted tenets of the New Deal like regulation, protections for organized labor, and generous federal programs.[8] For instance, President Eisenhower summarized conventional wisdom in a private correspondence thus: "Should any political party attempt to abolish [the New Deal] you would not hear from that party again in our nation's political history. There is a tiny [GOP] splinter group . . . that believes you can do these things. Among them are a few . . . Texas oil millionaires and an occasional politician or business man from other areas. Their number is negligible and they are stupid."[9]

One key consequence of Keynesian-era policy was a financial system that was more regulated and compartmentalized than the one that emerged after the 1980s. Sociologist Gerald Davis argues that this system arose in the wake of the Great Depression, when policymakers decided that the best way to prevent financial panic was to create multiple financial subsystems that were insulated from one another.[10] The result was three types of financial institutions: investment banks that underwrote issues of corporate stock, commercial banks that lent deposits to firms, and savings and loans that lent deposits to homebuyers. Federal regulations prevented these types of financial institutions from merging, and additional regulations prohibited banks from operating branches in multiple states, thus preventing the emergence of financial conglomerates in any financial subsector (e.g., Citibank or Bank of America in retail banking).[11]

From the point of view of America's largest corporations, the pre-1980s financial system was credit scarce: often, firms could not access the financial capital they needed at favorable rates of interest.[12] America's largest corporations responded by adopting a structure that economic historian Alfred Chandler describes as a multidivisional form: in the absence of external credit, large corporations kept excess profits and used them as an internal pool of credit, which they used to create new divisions as a way to balance their cash flow and insulate themselves from economic shocks.[13] Firms like General Electric are surviving examples of this corporate model. The multidivisional firm was further reinforced by strict federal antimerger policies, which often blocked mergers within the same economic sector. To faraway actors in cities like Prairieville, these realities had one important consequence: corporate acquisitions were rare because—unlike today— corporations viewed them as a way to acquire divisions and balance internal cash flows, not eliminate competitors or repackage and resell a firm for profit.[14]

The federally regulated financial system of the postwar period left the city's firms in the hands of local residents—the old families. Table 1.1 shows that all but one of Prairieville's largest private sector employers (and

Table 1.1 River City's and Prairieville's largest private-sector employers (1975)

	River City			Prairieville		
Company		Employees	Ownership	Company	Employees	Ownership
1. Greenfields Manufacturing		2,500+	Nonlocal	1. Packing house	2,500+	Local
2. Packing house		2,500+	Local	2. Food processor	1,000–2,500	Local
3. Manufacturer		1,000–2,500	Local	3. Construction	1,000–2,500	Local
4. Power company		1,000–2,500	Local	4. Power company	1,000–2,500	Local
5. Manufacturer		500–1,000	Local	5. Manufacturer	1,000–2,500	Local
6. Transport		500–1,000	Local	6. Manufacturer	500–1,000	Nonlocal
7. Wholesaler		250–500	Local	7. Packing house	500–1,000	Local
8. Financial firm		250–500	Local	8. Construction	500–1,000	Local
9. Manufacturer		100–250	Local	9. Manufacturer	500–1,000	Local
10. Manufacturer		100–250	Local	10. Manufacturer	250–500	Local
11. Manufacturer		100–250	Local	11. Manufacturer	250–500	Local
12. Bank		100–250	Local	12. Wholesaler	250–500	Local
13. Bank		100–250	Local	13. Transport	250–500	Local
14. Manufacturer		100–250	Nonlocal	14. Manufacturer	250–500	Local
15. Bank		100–250	Local	15. Bank	100–250	Local

Source: Dun's Million Dollar Directory and local chamber of commerce records. Educational institutions and professional service firms were not systematically included in Dun's business directory and are not included.

all but two of River City's) in 1975 were headquartered in the community and managed by an owner who lived in Prairieville and a local board populated by Prairievillers.[15] These firms' workers were also organized into massive union locals, in part because federal policies were more favorable to unions than today and in part because locally owned firms were easier to organize than the corporate subsidiaries that later replaced them—an issue taken up in the next chapter. Some locals, such as the food workers' union at Miller Baking or the machinists' union at Prairie Tools, represented nearly a thousand workers and employed half a dozen full-time representatives. However, no local union rivaled the meat cutters' union, which represented nearly five thousand workers (roughly 15% of the city's private sector workforce), employed eight full-time officers and representatives, and maintained a sprawling hall that served as the seat of Prairieville's union movement.

In sum, Keynesian-era financial, antimerger, and labor regulations created what most Prairievillers perceived—correctly, in some sense—as a local economy.[16] By this, I do not mean to imply that Prairieville's economy was truly local in some absolute sense; firms bought many inputs—machine tools, fuel, and the like—and sold their products on regional, national, and global markets. Unions, too, were members of federated organizations with a national reach, impacted by regulations established elsewhere, and so on. But crucially, the local pieces of these more complex systems were controlled and contested by community members, who were relatively permanent local fixtures. The economy created a pool of actors—the old families and union leaders—who were bound to local industries and exercised discretion over their profits.

Scholars of urban governance have long argued that those who can mobilize the resources of key community institutions play a leading role in public life.[17] Nowhere is this more true than in Prairieville, where public life consisted of an old family-union struggle. Recall, for example, Charles Browning's report from the introduction: "Thirty years ago, there were probably fifty names you could call on." Charles was the owner of one of Prairieville's largest remaining locally owned businesses—a construction company—and identified with the old families' traditional mode of public engagement. "It used to be my grandpa and his peers, then my father, and now yours truly," he told me. "And we still have the Willis family; probably the Willises and I are the two biggest givers we have left. Heavily involved, good people. But mostly it is gone. With the mergers, [corporate managers feel] like, 'Why should they get so heavily involved around here if they are really just trying to be moving up and leaving in a couple of years?'"

Others recalled the influence of Prairieville's union leaders. "[One day] I'm walking [downtown] and there's a crowd, hundreds and hundreds of people there, lot of 'em were packinghouse workers. They had the whole street blocked off," a labor leader told me. "And they [saw my work clothes and] said, 'C'mon, some politician is going to make a speech.' [The politician] came out on a little balcony and spoke. It was hootin' and hollerin' and agitation. In those days we had Cuttayun's and later Valley Beef, maybe 7,000–12,000 votes for any election, and the [business owners,] they had their people. It was an ongoing battle, the chamber of commerce and the Labor Council, the two of 'em were ongoing, every election. It did not make any difference if it was school board, city council, mid-term, or presidential—we seemed to be always at odds."

Before the 1980s, Prairieville's labor-business clashes were indeed frequent and bitter, particularly at Valley Beef packing plant, the city's largest employer, whose owner was unusually intransigent in the face of union demands for the period. During a 1960s-era Valley Beef strike, someone dynamited a manager's house while several union leaders' houses burned to the ground. "[I lived next to a union leader and one night] they started rolling tires filled with gasoline down [the street toward his house—] trying to burn him out!" a former packinghouse worker told me. "[People who] got involved in it had dynamite thrown through their windows or bottles of gasoline. So I pretty much stayed out of it. I know what those people can do if they are pushed."[18] Eventually, the governor called out the National Guard and transports full of soldiers, their bayonets swaying in the air, rumbled down Prairieville's streets.

The conflict between the city's old families and union leaders extended beyond the economy and into other spheres of Prairieville's public life. Recall that members of the old families saw themselves as "heavily involved" while union leaders argued that "it did not matter what it was," they contested the old families' influence over associational and political life alike. Table 1.2 supports these reports. This table lists the city's most central organizations, or those whose board members were on the boards of many other well-connected organizations.[19] Social scientists use centrality measures to draw generalizations about an organization's relative importance, and Table 1.2 can therefore be interpreted as a list of the organizations in Prairieville that an import leader during the 1970s would likely have considered important.[20] Note the third column: most organizations include members of the old families, or union leaders, but not both types of leaders together. The only types of organizations populated by both business and labor leaders were democratic bodies like the city council or democrat-

Table 1.2   Prairieville's most central associations (1974–1976)

Association	Membership	Democratic or political?	Closeness centrality
1. Central city commission	Both	Yes	5.97
2. City board (community. service)	Both	Yes	5.92
3. United Way	Business	No	5.91
4. Democratic officers	Labor	Yes	5.91
5. Republican donors	Business	Yes	5.88
6. Blood bank	Both	No	5.88
7. City board (human rights)	Both	Yes	5.88
8. Labor council	Labor	No	5.88
9. Bank board	Business	No	5.87
10. Chamber of commerce*	Business	No	5.86
11. Industrial development council	Business	No	5.86
12. Homeless shelter	Business*	No	5.86
13. Bank board	Business	No	5.68
14. City board (plan and zoning)	Both	Yes	5.86
15. City council	Both	Yes	5.84
16. Health planning council	Business	Yes	5.83
17. Hospital board	Business	No	5.83
18. Symphony board	Business	No	5.83
19. Power company board	Business	No	5.83
20. Charity	Business	No	5.83
21. Financial company board	Business	No	5.82
22. Frannie's Table	Labor	Yes	5.82
23. Child charity	Business	No	5.82
24. County supervisors	Both	Yes	5.81
25. Sick child charity	Business	No	5.80
26. Meat packers' union	Labor	No	5.80
27. Labor newspaper board	Labor	No	5.79
28. Child charity	Business	No	5.79
29. City board (art center)	Business	Yes	5.79
30. Republican officers	Business	Yes	5.78

Note: Partisan organizations not listed include Democratic politicians (5.70, no. 60 in centrality), Republican politicians (5.69, no. 64 in centrality), and Democratic donors (5.67, no. 70 in centrality).

*During the 1970s, Prairieville's chamber did not make its board of directors public. I compiled a partial list of directors from other publications. One school board member and Democratic officer was on the homeless shelter board, but no union leaders were.

ically appointed bodies like the city human rights commission, and these were publically central, or populated by leaders who were also involved in other key associations. For instance, Prairieville's most central association during the 1974–76 period was the Central City Commission, a public body charged with debating the wisdom and ultimately overseeing downtown redevelopment, which included representatives from numerous other public commissions (e.g., planning commission, community service commission, human rights commission), the local power company, two local banks, numerous locally owned businesses, the Labor Council, both political parties, and many others besides.[21] The organization of Prairieville's public sphere during the 1970s was mirrored in the speech of Prairieville's older residents, who referred to associations like the chamber, United Way, or symphony board as "business groups" or "business charities," talked about other organizations as "labor" or "blue-collar" groups and charities (e.g., the Labor Council, labor newspaper), and saw it as self-evident that democratic bodies were sites of old family-labor union struggles.

Certainly, Prairieville's pre-1980s economy was a necessary precondition for the labor-business conflicts that defined public life. It created a pool of leaders who were rooted to the city by ties to their firms and understood their interests as place-based. But traditional leaders' control over local industry does not itself account for their conflicts. Indeed, some of Prairieville's remaining business owners and union leaders identify as partners today and see their place-based interests as best maximized by cooperation, not conflict. The key to Prairieville's contentious public past lies in a more careful reconstruction of the relationship between traditional leaders' status competition and Keynesian-era policies, which allowed leaders to rise to prominence through conflict. To this end, I now analyze the factors that once led Prairieville's old families to form rigid, hierarchical factions that spanned economic, civic, and political life.

Old Family Economics

To reconstruct the public orientation of Prairieville's old families, it is easiest to begin with their economic relationships. By this I do not mean to imply that economic relations are somehow primary over other types of social relations; rather, my argument is that the old families' tendency to organize their economic, civic, and political activities similarly reinforced their mode of organization in any one sphere.[22] However, the relationships that Prairieville's patricians formed in the economic sphere were typically interpersonal, whereas their civic and political relationships were often established with an abstract public, which makes reconstructing the logic of the former more straightforward.

I learned much about the old family economics by talking with their members and observing those family-run businesses that remained. Many of Prairieville's patricians still reside in Sheppfield, and a journey to the neighborhood speaks volumes about how the conflicts of the past are inscribed in Prairieville's geography. To get there, one begins in the working-class South End and travels along an avenue that begins as Scarlet Street and changes its name to Royal Highway mid-journey. Scarlet winds through neighborhoods where the houses are constructed of fraying white boards and sit on cinderblocks—a reminder of times before Prairieville's canal system prevented periodic flooding of the South End. During the 1970s, Hal Swift, Prairieville's lone union-backed councilman, represented these neighborhoods and railed against the fact that some of their streets remained unpaved. As one ascends the hills, the houses grow larger and better-kept, and the street's name changes over as one arrives in Sheppfield, a neighborhood shaded by giant oaks, where deer, wild turkeys, and occasional coyote wander in from the wilderness just beyond. To many older Prairievillers, one had just crossed the symbolic divide between regular citizens and patricians, working class and business class, Democrats and Republicans. Unsurprisingly, there is therefore no shortage of lore about Scarlet Avenue's name change. "Scarlet was a madam and she ran a house of prostitution down there," one old working-class resident told me. "Well, the rich folks who live up there, they did not want to live up on a street named after a madam so they had the name changed!"[23]

I interviewed Dale Wilhelm in one of Sheppfield's homes. We sat in Dale's living room, which like that of other old families functioned as a quasi-public space: decorated with antiques and separated from the rest of the house by a set of double doors, beyond which the muted sounds of a TV, the muffled voice of a spouse, or the laughter of grandchildren echoed. In his sixties, Dale had retired from running a small manufacturing plant that supplied machinery to the city's meatpacking plants. He had just returned from playing golf, still wore khaki shorts and a polo shirt, and fiddled with a phone in his lap as we spoke.

"We are so involved in the 'Wal-Mart effect' in this country. It is like sinking sand and we can't get out of it," Dale said, picking up on a familiar theme. "[Our] economic structure is at a standstill because nobody wants to pay anything for anything, so now everything is cheaply made and nothing is of quality. And because of that the division of wealth has gone to where it goes to too few people. CEOs are making millions while their employees just crawl on the ground. But somebody in there is making money—the presidents and the senior executives—a tremendous amount of money, you can be sure of that!"

I was initially surprised to hear such reports from members of the old families. This was 2007, before the Great Recession, Occupy Wall Street, and the popularization of talk about the "1 percent." At the time, talking of inequality with strangers felt edgy and slightly taboo—perhaps akin to discussing the virtues of state socialism today. I therefore initially dismissed reports like Dale's as idiosyncratic, not least because they seemed contradicted by others who described the old families as controlling or egotistical. Indeed, Prairieville's patricians seemed hardly concerned with redistribution when fighting unions tooth and nail. But eventually, I understood that such talk was not about redistribution per se, but an expression of nostalgia for an economic—and noneconomic—system wherein the old families became central by giving. Prairieville's patricians frowned on corporate managers, because the latter no longer participated in this system.

"Prairieville is in a transition between small-town America and big-town America. We are still caught in-between, but the small-town America is disappearing," Dale continued, confirming my hypothesis.[24] "Small-town America thrives on family businesses and the whole community thrives on supporting those businesses and there is not a lot of competitive nature between them. At one time, we had three Fortune 500 companies here in Prairieville that started out as strong, homegrown family businesses—now there are just remnants: [the big businesses] were bought out or consolidated [and] a lot of the smaller businesses had to say goodbye."[25]

"Back then, there was this fundamental bond of trust, and that was most important," Dale continued, spelling out the rules of the old game. "You did not care if you made as much as long as you made enough—enough to feel good, not to worry, feel easy, pay your workers well, and maybe have enough to do a little building, put a new addition onto the house. Now what you have is this corporate society," he added. "These new guys [who run subsidiaries] are different—they are looking to move on and buy a condo in New York and San Francisco, not a house in Prairieville. Even here, a lot of the new people are moving out to Ranch Cliffs," Dale concluded indignantly, referring to the affluent suburb. "They don't even care if they live in Prairieville or not! They just want to pay low taxes."

Economic sociologists have found the types of dynamics described by Dale to be common in stable economic sectors. The key feature of such "embedded economies" is that economic actors enter into multiple types of social relationships beyond economic ones.[26] In such cases, people weigh the need to make immediate profits against the value they place on relationships with one another, and this can have economic benefits in the right context. For instance, owners can use social pressure to police short-term opportunism within their own ranks, thereby obviating the need for costly legal contracts.[27] Pre-1980s community studies of cities like Atlanta (Georgia), Muncie (Indiana), Bridgeport (Connecticut), Rockford

(Illinois), and Minneapolis (Minnesota) found similar sets of relationships to those described by Dale, and my archival research too showed extensive ties between locally owned firms—during the 1970s, for example, virtually every old family business had at least one member of a different old family on its board of directors.[28] The historical record contains evidence of other social relationships besides: back when Prairieville was "small-town," the sons of one old family often worked for a time for other old-family firms, the sons and daughters of Prairieville's patricians intermarried, and so on.[29]

The noneconomic relationships between members of the old families had an effect predicted by Mauss: owners were simultaneously trying to keep their businesses profitable and engaged in a social game wherein they gained status by being "giving" with one another.[30] This is the core of Dale Wilhelm's critique of the "new guys": they care only about personal accumulation, unlike the old families who wanted enough to "feel easy" and then regift the rest to one another and their employees. I witnessed several cases of such largesse while observing remaining old family–owned businesses.

On one occasion, I observed the operation of Weller and Son's Building Supplies, now in the hands of Bill Weller. The night before, a thunderstorm's sixty-mile-per-hour winds wreaked havoc on the city, destroying some huge American flags that Bill sold to other local owners just weeks before. As I waited for Bill, I could see him taking constant phone calls. "Now, Chuck, we can't control the weather!" I heard him protest into the phone and laugh. Finally, Bill waved me into his office with an adolescent grin and explained the situation. "Everybody's calling and hollerin' at me about [the weather]!" he exclaimed, laughing. "But, I mean, we probably will replace [the flags]. We sold [many of the flags to] a lot of the old businesses around here—so they are not only our friends, but we have been doing business with them for over thirty years. We are happy to have their business and they are happy to have ours. So, you know, we are almost glad to help them out."

As economic sociologists would expect, Bill's tendency to view other members of the old families as "friends" led him to replace the flags for free even though he was not contractually obligated to do so. In fact, Bill had sold the flags to other locals without any contract and told me that replacing them for free was a major business expense, especially because his business was then teetering on the edge of profitability. But Bill's willingness to take a loss was not merely an individual act of altruism; it reproduced an economic system described by Dale as "small-town America," and Bill's own place within it.[31] Bill was well aware of the latter fact.

"It has been a gradual decline . . . you know, with the mall-ification of America," Bill said, echoing Dale. "I mean, we used to have meat packing, baking, fertilizer manufacturers, car parts, you name it. A lot of money flowed through all that. It is vastly different working for a family business now. It is a real struggle. Actually we have never had so few employees as we have now." At this point, Bill was giving me a tour of the facility and we entered an expansive warehouse full of long benches scattered with sundry pieces of assembly equipment. "Used to be we had a bunch of people in the back there, building things," he said, motioning to the half-dozen employees. "[But] a lot of my customers have gone away. People who used to buy our products would still love to buy them, but there is no way they can, because there are more fixed costs now and everything is a lot tighter so people need to go low-cost; there is not a lot of disposable income out there for our kind of product. Because, you know, Target, McDonald's, Red Lobster, they won't buy from us, whereas Sam's Hot Dog Stand maybe would have. Everyone is feeling that squeeze so there is not the disposable income."

The economic system described by Bill went hand in hand with pre-1980s federalism. Social relations between Prairieville's business owners predated the Keynesian-era, but federal financial and antimerger policies created a fertile climate for their proliferation—an urban economy dominated by locally owned firms, which had been in the hands of the same families for generations. Studies of America's largest firms also identify the postwar period as one characterized by cohesion between national business elites for similar reasons to those I just identified: in the relative absence of financially fueled mergers and acquisitions, business leaders were able to establish social institutions to coordinate their activities.[32] What's more, relationships between the old families likely carried economic advantages for firms trying to maintain steady uninterrupted profits rather than appealing to financial investors.[33] Consider that the old families were not in direct economic competition; Prairieville's economy consisted of manufacturers producing for different regional and national markets along with secondary support firms like Bill's that specialized in servicing them. In this context, going "high cost" as described by Bill might hurt an owner sometimes, but allowed everyone to coordinate their production smoothly, avoid legal inputs, prevent bankruptcies among key suppliers, and otherwise build up a comparative advantage vis-à-vis manufacturers elsewhere.[34] Naturally, the cohesion of the old families also helped them to coordinate against the two biggest threats to their bottom line: outside corporations and unions. However, my interest here is less in the economic benefits of this system than on how competitive gift-giving between the old families shaped their relations with one another and the community at large.

The old-families system of economic gifts had three important consequences: it bound local business owners together, created a hierarchy among them, and led them to value engagement with community members outside of their own ranks.

First, gifts are by nature indicative of enduring relationships; in both archaic societies and our own, people give gifts to create or maintain long-term ties.[35] Bill Weller's business, for example, had been struggling for years, and he told me that his generosity with the American flags was partially payback for past largesse from others. In giving, Prairieville's patricians both presupposed inter–old family cohesion and actively reproduced it.[36]

The old families' gifts created social hierarchy as well as cohesion. In most social systems, those who give generously rise in social standing vis-à-vis those who receive, putting the latter under an obligation to reciprocate in kind or through shows of deference. For weeks after the American flag incident, for example, other remaining members of the old families I spoke with held up Bill as a paragon of sound business practices. But in cases where owners did not initiate or reciprocate largesse, their status fell. At the extreme, many informants told me that the owner of Valley Beef—historically, the city's largest packing plant—had been "all about the money" and was stingy in his dealings with other local business owners. Members of the old families report having ostracized him due to this stinginess and such reports are consistent with the absence of Valley Beef personnel in historical records of the boards of key business associations like the chamber and Republican Party.

In sum, the gifts of the old families were motivated by a dual logic of gifts observed among archaic and modern societies alike: first, to create cohesive and long-term ties and, second, to elevate oneself vis-à-vis others within this system of relationships. These twin imperatives combined to create a third: Prairieville's patricians reached outside their own circle, attempting to elevate their public esteem with generosity. Herein lies the interesting tension in the old families' public role: they were clannish and controlling, but also displayed a wanton largesse. They distinguished themselves as big fish by being giving or even—as in Charles Browning's report—by being "the biggest givers" in Prairieville. This orientation led members of the old families to engage enthusiastically in civic life.

Old Family Civics

Prairieville's old families approached associational life much like relationships with one another: they used their presence, skills, or money as public gifts for which they expected to receive esteemed community positions in return. Note, however, the subtle but important shift. Whereas in the economic sphere members of the old families gave and received from one another, their civic gifts were often to organizations, initiatives, or even an abstract public. Recall, for example, the Willis fountain. In such cases, the old families theoretically gave to all Prairievillers, but I will show shortly that people understood them as giving to that part of the public that accepted their public standing. Naturally, the degree to which members of the old families actually gave to civic causes varied.

At one extreme was the aforementioned owner of Valley Beef, who brutally repressed the meatpackers' union and was ostracized by Prairieville's other business owners for his stinginess. Unsurprisingly, Valley Beef's owner did not give to civic causes and—more than this—did significant community harm. Until the late 1970s Valley Beef maintained an open-air disposal pit that stunk up the entire southern portion of the city and gave Prairieville two unflattering nicknames: Smelly-ville and Oink-ville. An older resident told me, "I had a cousin that visited me from down south. He said to me, 'Oh you guys have oil in Prairieville.' 'Oil?' I said. 'Yeah, oil,' he says. 'You know that smell!' Well I had to tell him that was just the sewage odors coming from Valley Beef's open sewage pit."

Although my intention is to keep this chapter focused on Prairieville, it is too tempting to forego a comparison with another packinghouse owner who fell on the opposite end of the old families' civic-minded spectrum: Rhomberg Sr., the founder of River City's largest packing plant. In stark contrast to Valley Beef, the River City Packing Company, or simply "the Pack," was upheld by local residents as a symbol of the old families' finest virtues. Rhomberg Sr. began from modest means, but through thrift and ambition grew the packing house into a major establishment that employed thousands and maintained a national distribution chain. Older locals still speak with pride of seeing River City brand hams or bacon selling in distant grocery stores or offered as game show prizes. Rhomberg Sr. was also a joiner, serving on the board of a local bank, the city's newspaper, the local power company, and River City's Republican Party. He gave generously to local charities, notably ones in the working-class neighborhood of his birth, and spearheaded expansion of the city's library. Rhomberg Sr. was even generous toward his employees.[37] In the 1970s, the Pack reportedly paid nearly $20 an hour to its meatpackers, the highest wage paid to blue-collar workers in either city. "He was just a good old regular guy," a former meatcutter told me. "He'd come in every morning and greet all of us, just, 'Hi guys, how's it going?' Once a year for the company picnic he'd rent out a whole train and take us down to Chicago for a ballgame, food, drinks, everything paid for—his attitude was just, 'If you work hard for me I'm going to treat you right.'" Not to be outdone, River Citians heaped many honors on Rhomberg Sr. in life; after his death, the city's council—then dominated by union-backed politicians—voted unanimously to re-name the city's new high school Rhomberg High.

Most members of the old families fell somewhere between these two extremes. But whether they displayed generosity or stinginess, one thing did not vary: by giving to civic causes, they rose in esteem in the eyes of other citizens and established authority over civic life. Exactly like in the economic sphere, the free civic gifts of the old families were not exactly free, because everyone understood them as acts that elevated the public status of givers, endowing them with authority and control over the civic cause in question.

In this way, the old families' civic gifts actually presupposed and called out a public that was differential toward the old families and shared their values.[38] I encountered many older Prairievillers who still spoke as members of this public. "One thing that this city has always had going for it is that there is a group of people here who are extremely giving," a former employee at an old family business told me. "[There is] lots of gifting to public things, [which] has allowed us to get a lot done without falling back on entitlements." But of course, not everyone was deferential to the old families—notably, not labor union leaders and their allies—and the civic gifts of the old families therefore factionalized the public into those who were deferential to the old families and those who were not. Table 1.2 il-lustrates precisely this bifurcation of public life. The city's associations were divided among those populated by business leaders and labor leaders and older residents distinguished between blue-collar and white-collar charities and clubs, even though nonprofits are not legally designated in this way.

In civic life as in economic life then, Prairieville's old families played for status by giving gifts to individuals and organizations that were beholden to and identified with them, thereby building complex networks that touched many and penetrated deeply into daily life. The old families' abil-ity to do this was partially a consequence of their economic position: they owned local businesses and could direct their profits toward their preferred civic organizations and initiatives. Recall, too, that Prairieville's patricians had lived in the city "forever" and had "a million kids everywhere"—that is, extensive social networks composed of affluent people with the time and resources to devote to their pet causes. Members of the old families even expected senior managers from their firms to speak on their behalf in public, and even referred to one another's civically engaged employees as so and so's "man."[39] Recall the report by Gus Herman in the introduction, who was employed by River City Bank in the 1970s: *before* the 1980s, everyone assumed he was only "looking out for the River City Bank" whenever he sat on a municipal commission.

But while the old families' civic influence did grow out of their economic position, it was simultaneously facilitated by Keynesian-era social services policy. As institutional "realists," policymakers saw it as their role to correct various social problems, but they were also operating in a context in which opponents of social spending—although in the minority—effectively used veto points within the American state to block expansion of the federal bureaucracy.[40] The result was a political system that political scientists characterize as the delegated or divided welfare state: rather than creating bureaucracies to address social problems, Keynesian-era policymakers tended to create programs that passed resources onto representatives at lower levels of government.[41] Scholars argue that before the 1980s these federal transfers took the form of "blocky" grants: ones apportioned in large, discretionary chunks to established social service providers, particularly after the War on Poverty era when federal policymakers decided to deliver federal services through nonprofits.[42] Sociologists Joseph Galaskiewicz and Emily Barman argue that this funding regime privileged umbrella agencies like United Way, which funneled local and federal monies alike to other associations—an argument consistent with my observations of Prairieville.[43] After 1969, for example, Title IV-A of the Social Security Act provided no-strings-attached payments to nonprofits that contracted with the state for at least $25,000. This program apportioned funds almost exclusively to established associations like the United Way, which could use the funds more or less as their boards of directors saw fit. In this context, community leaders had little to gain from civic cooperation, but much to gain from conflict if they were capable of winning control over organizations like United Way.

While River City's unions boycotted United Way in 1979 and won representation on the board, Prairieville's cohesive old families resisted such union efforts and maintained complete control. Because of this, Prairieville's unions lacked an associational presence and struggled for decades to fund initiatives like an area food bank.[44] Chapter 4 will show that it was not until the introduction of competitive social service funding in the 1980s that area business leaders, who risked losing funding entirely by not reaching out in a spirit of partnership, allowed Prairieville's union leaders on the United Way board and funded their food bank.

Old Family Politics

As it was in civic life, so it was in politics. The city's old families maintained a network of obligation that dominated local politics. "Back in the early 1970s they had a [public commission] of citizens who got together for a couple months, talking about where the town should go," a professional who had moved to Prairieville in the 1960s told me.[45] "The consensus—at least in the group that I was in—was that they did not want the town to grow. They wanted it to stay exactly the way it was. The powers that be had their henchmen and their cronies, and they wanted to protect downtown and keep new people out. [They] were trying to keep progress out!"

Prairieville's old families controlled politics through the chamber of commerce, which endorsed candidates in local, state, and national elections. The chamber then funded these candidates' campaigns, helped them to mobilize volunteers, and publicized them through its newsletter and via influence on business civic groups. Prairieville's old families were not shy about asking for favors in return. For instance, I examined the correspondences of several 1970s-era chamber-backed councilmen and found them littered with hastily handwritten messages from some of Prairieville's patricians, some of which were simply sticky notes attached to newspaper clippings the latter had deemed offensive. "As a good businessman, I am sure that you will oppose this," read one note attached to an article describing proposed alternation to Prairieville's downtown redevelopment. Chamber-backed city councilmen then made appointments to Prairieville's municipal boards and commissions, and leaders active during the period were virtually unanimous in viewing such appointees as beholden to the chamber. "The chamber ran city council, [which] ran the city. You needed their support to be elected. I don't know how they get their people out, but they did," a union leader who sat on one commission told me, summarizing the 1970s. "With the chamber guys, [our] viewpoints, they were totally different. It was adversarial. It's hard for me to understand their side, it was hard for them to understand my side. With any other board you [sat] on, if there [was] an issue that [was] near and dear to you, [then] chances are the chamber people [came] down different on it."

Indeed, the belief among several career politicians I spoke with was that

Prairieville's pre-1980s chamber only endorsed candidates who fit the rigid profile of the city's business community: a native of Prairieville preferably born to a business-owning family, someone who worked in business or the liberal professions, someone who was anti-union, and somebody who was a staunch Republican. One moderate Democratic politician, who has since received chamber endorsements, summarized the situation like this: "[Their attitude was,] 'By gorsch, here is the conservative, pro-business view and if you disagree you are a socialist radical goofball.'"[46] Despite chamber dominance of the council, labor leaders consistently elected one of their own to city council: Hal Swift (no. 15 in table 1.2, above), who appointed a few union-friendly members to each city board and commission.[47] This influence is reflected in table 1.2, which shows that most of Prairieville's democratically elected or appointed boards had some union-backed members during the 1970s. Unlike River City union-backed politicians, Prairieville's union candidates never managed to wield control over the agenda, but they prevented the old families from monopolizing political power.[48]

The key point is that Prairieville's old families maintained political power by playing a familiar public game: they endorsed chamber-candidates, put their economic and civic resources behind them, and—when they won—had them in their debt. Key to this game is the notion of reciprocal obligation: the old families gave, but also traded on others' willingness to give back—if not in kind, then in deference. The old families' political position was thereby enhanced by their ability to turn economic or civic obligation into political favor, or indeed vice versa. Pre-1980s federalism further promoted this social system via urban policy.[49]

Sociologist John Mollenkopf argued that Keynesian-era urban policies fueled community conflicts, which created an infrastructure for the period's two party system. In the 1930s, Democratic strategists set out to create a permanent Democratic majority by becoming the nation's urban party, a strategy that the GOP initially contested, but then also adopted. Thereafter, politicians from both parties supported generous urban programs and agreed that the federal government should ensure the fiscal health of cities.[50] The parties disagreed only about how federal funds should be allocated: Democrats favored programs targeting needy people and places (e.g., Model Cities), particularly those in declining northeastern cities, while Republicans favored programs targeted at southern, western, and suburban cities as well as programs, like revenue sharing, with few strings attached.[51] In both cases, federal bureaucracies functioned as a "banker government": lacking the capacity to administer programs themselves, bureaucrats delegated authority over broad policy initiatives to local

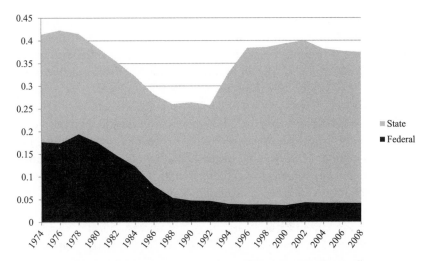

Figure 1.1. Federal and state transfers as a proportion of municipal budgets (1974–2008). *Source:* The Lincoln Land Institute's Fiscally Standardized Cities (FiSC) Database. This database includes only American's 110 largest cities, and state transfers to smaller cities like River City and Prairieville are likely lower.

actors, thereby enhancing their autonomy with federal dollars. Figure 1.1 illustrates that Mollenkopf's account nicely captures the key features of Keynesian-era fiscal federalism: federal transfers as a proportion of municipal budgets were high under Democrats and Republican administrations until the 1980s, when they dropped for reasons that will be discussed in chapter 4.[52] Unlike federal transfers today, Keynesian-era programs were relatively uncompetitive and discretionary. Urban Renewal, for example, was a bundle of programs that expanded until the mid-1970s and provided cities with matching funds for construction projects. And indeed, the Central City Commission—Prairieville's most central association—was initially founded by local leaders precisely to decide how to spend urban renewal monies. Urban Renewal was subsequently joined by Great Society programs like Model Cities, which provided a package of grants for urban redevelopment. The single-largest uptick in federal urban spending followed with the Nixon administrations' revenue sharing programs, which Nixon himself lauded as the nation's historically most generous.[53] Some of these urban programs were technically competitive, but were not by today's standards; of the 190 cities that applied for Model Cities, for example, 166 eventually received funds.[54]

Here again, Keynesian-era transfers created a community arena with few built-in incentives for cooperation, because those who monopolized local political power also assumed near-unilateral control over federal development dollars. Traditional leaders could use these federal dollars for their own gains or as a gift to their supporters, thereby giving others an incentive to ally with them. Consider, for example, the chamber-backed plan to redevelop Prairieville's historic downtown, which replaced many historic buildings with nondescript parking garages and mirrored office towers. Virtually everyone I spoke with, including members of the old families themselves, criticized the redevelopment. Many citizens protested it at the time, too, but chamber candidates on the council, beholden to the old families, appointed an urban renewal commission that was favorable to the old families' plan over the protests of union-backed city councilors, and the project went ahead as they wished. For better and for worse, Keynesian federal policies enhanced, rather than diminished, local political power.[55]

Crucially, however, the old families were not the only party playing their city's traditional game; they were opposed in all things by the city's union leaders and their allies. It is difficult to overestimate the public importance of this opposition, however feeble, because it turned every resident into a potential client and hence ally. Indeed, the prevailing belief among older Prairievillers was that pre-1980s community leaders were more receptive to outside influence. "They've all got their heads up their butts. They think they know better than the people know," a teacher who grew up in Prairieville's South End told me. "City Council meetings, [it used to be] you always knew where and when they were and citizens could go in and voice their opinion. For my first [council meeting] I was just a teenager. They kept raising the prices on the [city] pool. At the time, my dad had just died and it was just my mom. We couldn't go to the pool every day—you know, like the people that live up by the country club, because the prices were just too high for us. So we petitioned the city council to keep the prices the way they were. [Back then, politicians] were more considerate of what a person's situation was. A short gentleman [probably Hal Swift,] spoke up and thanked us for coming in. It's not like that anymore. [Now] it's whatever they think works. They listen, but they don't really hear."

The key point is that there is nothing natural about older Prairievillers' tendency to see public life as a conflict between a business and labor side, one wherein they may be heard by making the right appeals. This perception reflects a historically contingent outcome that was produced by leaders who engaged with the public in a particular way. The city's old families and union leaders once donated to local charities, a "gift" that then placed these charities in a position of obligation and converted them into "business charities." They backed city council candidates, thus converting them into "chamber" or "union" candidates who simply spoke on behalf of their "side." In this way, Prairieville's leaders factionalized a public sphere by calling out, on the one hand, a public that was sympathetic with the old families' business values and was deferential to them and, on the other, a working-class public that was the opposite. It is unsurprising that the city's older residents identify politically as working-class or business-class, because this is exactly how the city's leaders once engaged them.

In fact, I witnessed cases wherein Prairieville's holdout patricians tried wielding public influence by activating a similar network of subordinates, calling out their side in the old way. I once had lunch with Charles Browning Jr. in a spot popular with Prairieville's leadership class. After greeting me, Charles did his usual tour of the restaurant, introducing me to people and chatting about the latest. "Glenn, is that Glenn?" Charles said and then turned to me, "Here I want you to meet somebody." He motioned me over to a table where Glenn was eating cream of broccoli soup with his mother.

Charles introduced us. "Glenn here used to work at Crossroads Computing and now is an attorney in town, but he and his family have been involved in Prairieville for a long time," Charles said, with a nod of respect to Glenn's mom. Charles then switched topics to today's issue: a referendum that would allow for the direct election of mayor.[56] This was Abe Skipper's initiative, who hoped to elect a mayor to breathe fire into the ailing union movement. Charles was opposed to it and asked Glenn what he thought. "Looks like it is going to go ahead, doesn't it?" Glenn responded dispassionately. "Sure does," Charles agreed, "[But] it is like I told you before—Skipper and his people think they are getting one thing, but they may end up with another. If they are not careful, Skipper could get his worst nightmare." Glenn agreed, but did not pursue the subject. After a bit of small talk, Charles and I made our way to our own table.

Once seated, Charles expounded on the direct election issue. "Abe Skipper. He's the one really pushing it. You know that name? He's kind of like a Hal Swift type: a very strong leader for the union movement, a strong advocate for the south side, for *his* side. [Getting up there] and [demanding] the fair paving of streets. At least you know where he stands. [He] does not think it through all the time, but hey, okay," Charles summarized, demonstrating the same begrudging respect toward working-class leaders expressed by members of Prairieville's fading union movement for the old families. Abe Skipper was Charles's opponent and even an enemy, but only a friendly enemy after all: one who took an opposing position in the very same game.[57]

"If they are not careful, Skipper could get his worst nightmare with these social conservatives: no Planned Parenthood, blah blah blah. It [could be] one of them elected [mayor,]" Charles continued. I nodded, mentally noting that Charles described the issue to me using the same exact words he had used with Glenn. We will return to the antipathy between Prairieville's old families and Christian conservative Republican activists in chapter 5. In short, Charles was right: Abe Skipper's referendum passed, and within a few years Prairieville elected a mayor with strong social conservative tendencies. My interest here, however, is in how Charles's talking point made its way through the network of the city's old families and their remaining dependents.

A few weeks after my lunch with Charles, I asked Bruce Nolan, a former senior manager at Miller Baking Company, about the direct election of mayor issue. Bruce immediately mentioned that he had spoken to Charles Browning, who was against it, and his position was unequivocal: people like Abe Skipper think it will strengthen their hand, but "they could end up with their worst nightmare." Indeed, these were words that I heard a few more times. A few days later, I attended a weekly luncheon of prominent Prairieville attorneys, many of whom do business of have other direct ties to the old families, and Abe Skipper "getting his worst nightmare" came up as topics of conversation around the table.

It is not difficult to see how such talking points would have reverberated through Prairieville's Keynesian-era public sphere, making their way from the old families and outward through the factional networks that connected to them to others through ties of fealty and obligation. The senior managers at old family firms would have spoken to their underlings, the city's business associations would have thundered the message to their volunteers, as would have the council's chamber men along with their appointees on municipal boards and commissions. Little wonder that wherever Prairievillers looked, they saw the influence of the old families. But the networks of the old families are largely gone, their influence faded, and local business leaders no longer loom potently in the imagination of Prairieville's younger residents. Indeed, Charles Browning's prognostication on the mayoral election issue raised a few discontented rumblings, but did not derail the plan. He played the old game within a new arena that will be described in more detail in the second part of the book.

In retrospect, it is easy to see many problems with the old families' exercise of public power: they were cliquish, arrogant even, created a system wherein political resources were distributed unequally, and sometimes used their influence to ram through unpopular measures. Their disastrous use of urban renewal is a case in point. I will discuss such normative implications of my argument at length in the concluding chapter. At present, it is sufficient to say that all forms of power can be used toward problematic ends and that the partners who dominate Prairieville's public sphere today do equally problematic things. My interest is less in what grassroots leaders do with their influence than with how they represent the public. Along these lines, the important thing about the old families is that they saw influence as synonymous with an ability to mobilize others and therefore built networks of gifts and counter obligations that penetrated deeply into daily life. They saw it as self-evident that one had to repay the privilege of public prominence with gifts to those whom they represented. Because of this, they and union leaders co-created a public sphere that drew their cities' residents into opposing camps. Their public world was defined by opposition, and therefore by a meaningful choice between two alternative visions of Prairieville.

TWO

The Lions of Labor

"We had some pretty poor elected leadership here in the early 1980s, I don't want to name any names, but there were some people that really did not have a good sense of how business and the community can work together. It was adversarial," Gus Herman said, obviously referring to Jones Berry, River City's motorcycle-riding, hard-drinking, union-backed mayor. We were talking in Gus's corner office and the blinds were partially open, letting in the morning's fresh, malleable light. Gus's desk was built of engraved hardwood, covered in black leather, and sparsely arranged with a metal letter opener, two pens resting in a marble swivel stand, and a plaque that bore Gus's name and beneath it, "President. River City Bank."

But Gus was no well-born patrician; to him, traditional labor leaders like Jones Berry symbolized a broken public past once co-created by River City's old families. Gus himself had rubbed shoulders with his city's old families while working his way up at the bank and even played bit parts in their machinations. But then, sometime in the early 1990s, he stopped trying to be—in his words—a "big, bad business hero," made the transition to partnership, and stepped fully into the public limelight. At the time of my fieldwork, he was best known as president of River City's school board, and appeared frequently in the newspaper at groundbreakings, community meetings, and other local events.

"The new generation [of leaders] really understands that we are all in the same boat, they understand that collaborative approach," Gus continued, contrasting River City's present to its past. "They have that ability to have vision and bring people around—to convince [them] that this is the right direction to go. To get input: 'Gee, I think you are off a little bit, [but] let's try it this way and if it does not work out we will try it your way.' That type of collaborative relationship building—building partnerships. Not to pat myself on the back, but I that is what I helped [bring] to the school district."

My interest in this chapter is in a type of public actor that appears frequently in River Citians' stories about their city's public past: traditional labor leaders like Jones Berry, foils to their city's old families—or indeed, vice versa. River Citians were similar to Prairievillers in that they associated the past with old family–labor leader conflicts, albeit with one difference: whereas residents equated old Prairieville with old family dominance, locals remembered old River City as a union town. All major employers were unionized, blue-collar charities saw to local needs, union-backed mayors thundered in the council chambers, and Democrats held all elected offices. Older locals told me that in those days a union card "meant something" and that "Republicans were not welcome at city hall, except to pay their taxes." These stories were not only about union leaders' decreased clout and visibility. In the mid-2000s, union leaders were still represented among River City's key leaders, but most had "made the transition" and, like Gus, identified as partners. River Citians associated their city's public transformation more specifically with the disappearance or taming of combative leaders like Jones Berry, whose decision to bury the sword—or not—they found intensely interesting.

As I was leaving his office, for example, Gus stopped me in front of a window overlooking a squat, boxcar-like building in an otherwise abandoned lot: the Teamsters' headquarters, and the office of Darrell Bandy, the union local's president and one of the city's key partners. Earlier in our conversation Gus told me that he had put himself through college by working summers at the packinghouse and remembered "what unions once meant for this town." Gus stared pensively. "I see some of the collaborative stuff with Darrell [Bandy]," he said finally. "They realize that [the world has changed and] is more global, but for a lot of [the traditional labor leaders] there is more pressure on them. [Like] you got somebody talking to them from Detroit or whatever saying, 'We need you to do this or we need you to do that, don't back down!' So some of that old atmosphere is still around, but it is not like it was."

Such descriptions of traditional labor leaders, common among partners like Gus, emphasized negative qualities that mirror nothing so much as those that people attributed to the old families. Partners insisted that traditional labor leaders were bound by ties of obligation to one another and therefore insular, incapable of compromise and change, partisan, and combative. But River Citians also told stories that identified traditional labor leaders with positive qualities, ones also similar to those others attributed to the old families: unlike today's leaders, traditional leaders were committed to their city and gave generously to their people. "Used to be a lot better jobs around here, jobs you could take pride in—good union jobs," Gary Pleumer, a resident of River City's working-class North End told me. "But anymore the unions are getting weak because people don't want to join them, because they think they ain't doing nothing. But see, it's the unions that got people the big bucks and stuff. [And now, city leaders] don't care about nobody. Denison, the guy who runs the [Development Corporation is], going to banquets all the time; if you're going to be a big shot like that you should at least earn it—[or] the city manager. They are always right and don't need to listen to nobody. As soon as they start talking I have to get up and leave the room—I can't stand it."

What is at issue in such reports is a fundamental shift in the way that community leaders engage one another and River City's residents. Here as in the last chapter, my central claim is that River Citians understand their city's public past as a conflict between working- and business-class sides because union and business leaders once organized their activities in this way. Stated differently, River City's labor leaders engaged in a strategy that labor historians identify as "social movement unionism," or an across-the-board commitment to working-class issues in community affairs and politics.[1] On any issue—whether a workplace dispute, civic or charitable initiative, local or national election—River City's labor leaders took an opposing position to their cities' old families.[2] By the time of my fieldwork, few publically visible signs of these past efforts remained—no names written into downtown buildings or monuments akin to the Willis fountain constructed by Prairieville's old families. But union leaders' works were nevertheless written in the public common sense of older residents I spoke with, who took it as self-evident that, on any issue, somebody would advocate for the working-class side. My aim here as in the last chapter is to explain how traditional labor leaders got to be a "side" in the first place and why they entered into conflicts with River City's patricians. As in the last chapter, too, my analysis consists of a two-part argument about traditional labor leaders' game for public prominence: I first reconstruct this game's internal logic, then discuss how it was politically constructed—or supported and even encouraged—by Keynesian-era federal policies.

Like the old families, traditional labor leaders believed that one had to give in order to get. They rose to prominence by bringing benefits to their supporters and their city's working-class public. They therefore engaged in economic, civic, and political life by maximizing their control over resources that they then gifted to their supporters. This mode of public engagement brought labor leaders into conflict with local patricians, who were effectively playing the same public game: trying to monopolize the same resources and using them as a pool of gifts for *their* supporters. Within these conflicts, both sides traded on an ability to mobilize their supporters, and therefore equated public leadership with an ability to fight effectively on their side's behalf. Due to the Janus-faced nature of gifts, people interpret traditional leaders' activities differently. To supporters, traditional labor leaders seemed committed and generous. To opponents, they seemed insular, controlling, and combative. Like the old families, traditional labor leaders were both at once, and it is because people tended to identify with one set of actors over the other that they understood the public sphere of their day as structured by labor-business conflict.

Traditional labor leaders' public game was supported by Keynesian-era policy in two ways. Regulations enhanced labor leaders' clout via relatively labor-friendly policies and by protecting locally owned industries, which— as compared to the corporate subsidiaries that replaced them in the 1980s—were less professional and effective in their opposition to unionization drives. Moreover, pre-1980s social service and development funding gave grassroots leaders discretion over federal dollars, thus creating incentives for conflict, not cooperation. I begin with a history of River City, then explore traditional labor leaders' economic, civic, and political activities—and their relationship to Keynesian-era policies—in more detail. The latter investigation focuses partially on River City's Labor Council leaders, holdout adherents of their predecessors' traditional style at the time of my fieldwork. That is, I reconstruct the inner logic of River City's traditional game by examining Labor Council leaders' activities, triangulating their reports against archival sources, and especially by juxtaposing their public orientations to those of another labor organization—United Labor, whose leaders identified as partners and which became publically prominent in the 1980s. In chapter 3 I then show how River City and Prairieville's contested public sphere intersected with pre-1980s party politics to structure the political subjectivities of both cities' residents.

A History of River City's Public Life before 1980

River City was first settled by Scottish and English immigrants in the early 1800s. Its eastward location vis-à-vis Prairieville and strategic position along a bend in a major waterway made it a boom town long before Prairieville. As steamship traffic along the river intensified, River City became an important port, particularly during the Civil War when lead mines and lumber mills in nearby bluffs became strategically important to the Union's armies. At the Civil War's conclusion, River City was a vibrant frontier outpost and—of cities west of the Mississippi—second in population only to San Francisco.

From these extractive roots, the city's economy diversified into manufacturing. Firms specializing in steamboat repair began manufacturing steamship components and, later, other mechanical devices—including a turn-of-the-century mechanized wagon that was popular among locals before Detroit became America's undisputed automobile manufacturer. The Scottish and English families who first settled the area ran these factories and dominated the economy—a dominance that some locals claim continues. Indeed, by the 2000s, a handful of firms were still operated by these first families' descendants: McConnell's Manufacturing, Nottingham and Smith's, Matheson Brothers Supply, and so on.

But virtually since the city's beginnings, inhabitants of Scottish and English extraction were numerically overshadowed by waves of Irish Catholic and German Catholic immigrants. These immigrants were encouraged by the region's archdiocese, which hoped to turn River City into a Catholic frontier outpost. Today, the majority of River Citians identify as Catholic, several Catholic convents operate in the area, and many colleges, hospitals, and charities remain affiliated with the Catholic Church.[3]

As in Prairieville, River City's immigration history structured, and still structures, the city's human geography. While original settlers inhabited fine houses on the bluffs overlooking the river, waves of new immigrants created sprawling neighborhoods of rowhouses in the flood plains below. The Irish settled the south end while the Germans moved north, a division still inscribed in River Citians' language of place: the South End remains "Little Dublin" and the North End the "German area," and this distinction is reinforced by the names of streets, churches, and other landmarks. Such white-ethnic divisions remain salient in locals' minds, who tell stories about "when a mixed marriage in River City was one between a Protestant and a Catholic" or of being tormented as schoolchildren by kids of an opposing white-ethnicity.

Irish and German immigrants brought their names, a penchant for revelry, and one other thing to the city: a tradition of trade unionism. In the nineteenth century, River City was a seedbed of activity for the Knights of Labor, who founded the *River City Union Leader*, a newspaper that achieved widespread circulation and still operated at the time of my fieldwork. The paper's early issues are full of news about trade-based unions like the chimney sweepers, egg packers, typesetters, and upholsterers and their picnics, parades, libraries, and—likely to the old families' chagrin—contestation of local politics.[4] But although labor candidates regularly ran for local offices through the twentieth century, city council control remained firmly in the hands of the chamber men—that is, chamber-backed politicians—until the 1960s.

As in Prairieville, the 1950s coincided with expansion of America's internal market and brought with it industrial consolidation, which here too occurred during a unique period of financial regulation. Recall table 1.1, which showed that the resulting firms were mostly locally owned. A meat-packing plant—the "Pack"—became a major national distributor of processed meats, and other locally owned firms followed suit: Brightwood Metals became a major furniture manufacturer, McConnell's became a manufacturer of housing fixtures, and so on. As in Prairieville, the McFadden Act prevented banks from operating multiple local branches, and River City was left with three locally owned banks and three powerful banking families. As in Prairieville, too, an indigenous sector of supply, professional service, and transportation firms that catered to homegrown industries grew.

For all these similarities, River City's economy differed in an important way from Prairieville's: the city's biggest employer was Greenfield Manufacturing, a subsidiary of a nonlocal corporation. Greenfield Corporation, or simply "Green's" in local parlance, pursued a classic postwar investment strategy and diversified into a multidivisional firm that produced lines of construction and agricultural equipment.[5] The firm outgrew its home city's workforce and looked to places like River City for expansion. Greenfield's first made plans to construct an assembly plant in River City's harbor, but River City's old families—who reportedly feared growing union power and rising local wages—opposed the plan, instructing the chamber men on city council to deny Greenfield's rezoning requests.[6] Undeterred, Greenfield's built its plant anyway just outside of city limits, and soon became River City's largest, and largest unionized, employer. At the time of my fieldwork, some business leaders still recalled lingering hostility toward the plant. "There was a feeling of resentment among a lot of the chamber businesses," a 1970s-era chamber president told me. "You'd train [workers] as welders or machinists and then Green's would offer them a higher wage. I heard a lot of resentment through my associations, [because] it was like the family businesses were a training ground [for them]."

In the minds of older River Citians, Green's appears as a symbol of the old families' intransigence and as shorthand explanation for union leaders' historic dominance over business leaders—a folk theory that I think is not far from the truth. "For many years, this city kept industry out," Jennifer, a resident in her forties, told me. "My instinct is that they did nothing to encourage [growth] and wanted to keep everything the same." At this point, Jennifer asked her mother, who was sitting in an armchair and listening in, about the issue. "Green's wanted to come in; they would not let them," her mother said, "because we had McConnell's, Fletchers, and Matheson Brothers, and they were the three big employers [and] they wanted to hold on to what they had and did not want the wages to go up. They just kept 'em out."

There is no mystery about how Green's altered River City's balance of public power: as a nonlocally owned, but generous and unionized employer, the plant provided no resources for the city's old families but plenty for union leaders and members. By the 1970s Greenfield's UAW local represented 5,000 workers, and was rivaled only by the Pack's 3,000 meatcutters and over 1,500 Machinists at Brightwood Metals.[7] These three industries paid wages nearly four times higher than the city's other industries, and this infusion of wealth into working-class pockets transformed the city's geography as residents of the flats looked for better, less flood-prone accommodations.[8] They went first to neighborhoods on hills leading up to the bluffs, but eventually settled in suburbs that sprouted in farmland just past the bluffs, the newly dubbed "West End." Leaders and residents alike slowly reimagined their city's defining conflict between the flats and bluffs as one between downtown—which residents associated with the old families' economic interests—and the West End's young union families.[9] "My husband was a union man; we moved [to the West End] along with a group of our friends [in the 1960s]," the wife of a retired Greenfield's worker told me. "And he went down to Green's every day—they had a bus that picked them up. I don't know what we would have done if not for Green's, because my husband never went to college, but we had a good life."

As union rolls grew, so too did the ranks of official union representatives. The unions that represented Greenfield's and the Pack's workers each maintained a union hall staffed by office workers and a half-dozen full-time representatives and also pitched in to support a common building: the Labor Temple. According to the local union newspaper, River City's unions supported over 160 full-time or part-time representatives during the 1960s and '70s, a number that fell to under 40 after the 1980s.[10] Like the old families, these union representatives were out in the community, taking a leading role in civic and political life.[11]

As in Prairieville, union and business leaders created a bifurcated public sphere. Table 2.1 shows that they populated opposing coordinating bod-

Table 2.1 River City's most central associations (1974–1976)

Association	Membership	Democratic or political?	Closeness centrality
1. Democratic officers	Labor*	Yes	6.81
2. City board (transport)	Both	Yes	6.78
3. River City Bank	Both*	No	6.77
4. National Bank	Business	No	6.76
5. Chamber of commerce	Business	No	6.75
6. United Labor	Labor	No	6.75
7. County mental health board	Both	Yes	6.74
8. Charity	Both	No	6.74
9. City board (civic center)	Both	Yes	6.73
10. Republican donor	Business	Yes	6.73
11. Boys' Club	Business	No	6.71
12. Industrial development council	Business	No	6.71
13. Bicentennial planning commission	Both	No	6.70
14. Senior citizen charity	Both	No	6.70
15. School board	Both	Yes	6.70
16. Country bank	Business	No	6.69
17. City council	Both	Yes	6.69
18. River City Ambassadors	Business	No	6.69
19. Symphony board	Business	No	6.68
20. City board (citizens' advisory)	Both	Yes	6.67
21. Girl Scout council	Both	No	6.66
22. City zoning commission	Both	Yes	6.65
23. Hospital board	Business	No	6.65
24. City board (mental health)	Both	Yes	6.65
25. Democratic donors	Labor	Yes	6.64
26. Labor council	Labor	No	6.64
27. Labor temple build commission	Labor	No	6.64
28. Girls' Club	Business	No	6.64
29. City board (health)	Both	Yes	6.64
30. Salvation Army	Labor	No	6.63

Note: Partisan organizations not listed include Republican officers (6.60, no. 44 in centrality), Republican politicians (6.65, no. 79 in centrality), and Democratic politicians (6.42, no. 85 in centrality). *Indicates one small-business owner who served as Democratic officer and sat on River City Bank board.

ies like the chamber and Labor Council, opposing political parties, and—mostly—different civic associations. As in Prairieville, labor and business leaders participated jointly as representatives on elected public bodies (e.g., city council, county board of supervisors) or as members of commissions appointed by these bodies (e.g., the City Civic Center and Citizen's Advisory Committee; the County Mental Health Board), which were among the city's most central associations. If anything, the two cities differ only in that River City's unions had a greater public presence. Only River City contained civic organizations like United Labor, which labor leaders created—initially—to coordinate unions' civic and political activities. Such efforts paid off, as evidenced by the presence of labor union leaders on many of River City's key charities and civic association (e.g., a civic association charged with planning the city's bicentennial 4th of July celebration, the Girl Scouts council, a senior citizens' charity), the success of its labor-backed politicians, and the Democratic Party's historical winning-streak.[12]

The key point is that River City and Prairieville's pre-1980s public spheres were more similar than different: dominated by business and labor leaders, who maintained separate networks of influence and competed rather than cooperated. During the 2000s, a few traditional leaders still saw public life as this sort of zero-sum game. Traditional Labor Council leaders, for example, described their public activities as building or strengthening the "world of labor," which included any activity that aided a working-class public: union organizing, volunteering for working-class charities, serving on public commissions, running for local office, or Democratic Party work. "We are all workers, everybody in the country is a worker. It just depends what side of the fence you are on—whether it is union or nonunion, but beneath that we are all the same," a Labor Council leader told me. "Organized labor is not just for organized labor and that is not the picture that *they* want to paint. [They say] we are a bunch of thugs, strikes and things like that. [But] people out there that are really struggling, working three or four jobs just to make ends meet. Things are not good for them. Somebody needs to talk about that. [So we support minimum wage laws], workers [compensation] laws, services here in River City—we have done that, we are the ones who drive that bus."

Much like Prairieville's old families, Labor Council leaders saw public leadership as synonymous with bringing benefits to their side of the public. Theirs was a public game of gift and reciprocal obligation: they saw their esteemed public position as a gift from a working-class public and sought to repay them with service and by representing their interests in public life. But, as previously mentioned, Labor Council leaders' was not the only—or even main—game in town. Roughly ten years before my fieldwork, the Labor Council was eclipsed in public importance by the United Labor Committee, another umbrella organization dominated by labor leaders who identified as partners and frequently collaborated with business leaders on various place-marketing initiatives—a fact that befuddled Labor Council leaders:[13] "Labor people that are involved with [United Labor] want to stay friendly with business. Why they do that, I can't answer," a Labor Council leader told me. "The Development Corporation, that is strictly a business group. It is like joining the chamber of commerce [or] a Democrat getting on the central committee of the Republican Party. You have two different agendas and business is not going to discuss issues friendly to labor. Why would labor people want to be involved?"

In the book's second half, I will say more about United Labor leaders and their rise to public prominence. I introduce them here only to underscore that there is nothing natural or inevitable about the traditional organization of River City's public sphere. Rather, traditional leaders' public activities unfolded within a politically constructed arena that encouraged particular modes of engagement—namely, oppositional faction-building. This is not to say that traditional leaders' public subjectivities were simply a product of Keynesian-era policy; clearly, they and their patrician opponents wove together diverse historical traditions—most of which preceded Keynesianism—into their public personae, just as many of their traditions persisted in hobbled form at the time of my fieldwork. Nevertheless, the differences between pre- and post-1980s public life are stark. My interest here is in the historical conditions that once anchored Labor Council leaders' traditional understanding of public engagement, transforming it into the actually existing public sphere of their day—not, as at the time of my fieldwork, an increasingly utopian vision that other leaders derided as passé.

I have argued that Keynesian-era financial sector regulations and tax policies were a key precondition for traditional conflicts, because they sheltered a "local economy" of old family–owned firms from corporate acquisitions. Keynesian-era policies sheltered unions, too, albeit through a wider array of mechanisms. Popular accounts of labor unions' decline portray the trend as the inevitable outcome of deindustrialization, the movement of industry to the de-unionized south, the decline of blue-collar employments vis-à-vis white-collar ones, and the rising proportion of women and minorities in the workforce.[14] Such arguments are problematic in that they assume that unions are an unchanging organizational form that cannot adapt, for example, to organize the south or incorporate minorities and women.[15] Even so, scholars estimate that demographic and economic changes are only part of the story; anywhere from 20 to 60 percent of union decline can be attributed to changing demographics of workers and the changing nature of work, particularly in manufacturing.[16] The remainder of union decline is due to the legal environment in which unions operate and to changing strategies employed by unions and employers—factors influenced directly and indirectly by federal policies.

First, Keynesian-era labor laws and their enforcement were relatively labor-friendly. Sociologist Holly McCammon argues that unions' legal ability to strike—their most potent leverage over employers—has eroded since the mid-twentieth century, particularly during the 1980s.[17] Unions also began confronting employers that were professional and mercenary in their opposition. Many contemporary corporations employ anti-union tactics like mandatory information sessions, one-on-one meetings with specially trained managers, and legal contestation of unionization votes. Studies show that managers who employ the full slate of such tactics cut the probability of a successful unionization drive in half.[18] Today's corporations routinely do, because 87 percent hire professional anti-union consultants when faced with unionization drives—a practice virtually unknown in the 1970s. By contrast, unionization drives are more likely to succeed when strikers receive support from their community's voluntary associations, especially if the latter pressure employers outside the workplace.[19]

In this light, Keynesian-era financial regulations both protected the old families and indirectly facilitated unionization by presenting union organizers with an easy target: the very same old families. River City and Prairieville's businesses were owned by locals who cared about their reputation and were subject to community pressure. A few owners maintained good relations with unions. The owner of River City's "Pack," for example, cultivated a reputation for generosity via extravagant extras like company-wide outings to Chicago baseball games, high wages, and friendly relations with union leaders.[20] At the other extreme, other owners detested unions and fought them tooth and nail. Unlike the corporate subsidiaries that overtook the local economy in the 1980s, however, local owners lacked the necessary reserve capital to survive long strikes and, when they did hold out, distrusted outsiders like consultants and employed amateurish tactics. Recall, for example, the shenanigans surrounding Prairieville's Valley Beef strike for which Valley Beef's owner paid stiff fines. Most business owners were somewhere in between: by no means friendly with union leadership and ready to contest their civic and political influence, but nevertheless resigned to their basic right to exist.[21] Finally, a few corporate subsidiaries like Greenfield's existed before the 1980s, but were managed differently in a prefinancialized era. Pre-1980s Greenfield's managers sought to manage the corporation's cash flows through steady profits, not signal dynamism to investors by maximizing short-term profits like many firms—including Green's—do today.[22] Green's paramount interest was avoiding work stoppages, and management did not actively oppose unionization. So it was that River City became a union town.

In these ways, pre-1980s federal policies created the necessary preconditions for River City's defining public conflicts: a pool of labor and business leaders, representatives of capital and labor, who were rooted in the city by their connection to local industry. But as in Prairieville, the mere existence of local owners and union leaders did not guarantee conflict. After all, River City retained some local owners and union leaders at the time of my fieldwork, but most had stopped fighting publically. To explain why most once did, I reconstruct the logic of traditional labor leaders' public game and its connection to Keynesian-era policy.

Traditional Union Economics

I learned much about River Citians' relationship with unions while conducting interviews in the city's North End, a neighborhood that locals regard as synonymous with the city's flats. A trip into the neighborhood says much about the way that River City's traditional conflicts were once encoded in space. To older River Citians, the North End remains symbolically working-class, blue-collar, union, or Democratic and—always—diametrically opposed to hilltop neighborhoods once inhabited by River City's old families. "[Growing up] I never went [into the flats] if I had any way to get out of it," the daughter of a bluff-dwelling family once told me. "There is still just a little bit of that left in me—a bit of snot, you know? When we were looking at houses, my husband [who] is not from here said to me, 'But there are some really nice houses down there!' and I said, 'I don't care. I'm not living below the bluff!'"

To get to the North End, one heads north from Gus Herman's downtown office in the River City Bank. Downtown buildings slowly morph into rowhouses, long rectangles that resemble shipping containers stacked atop one another. Their tiny, treeless yards are forever cluttered with plastic children's toys and political signs. "Proud to Be Union," appears in perhaps one yard out of six and stays up year-round, and at election time these are joined by Democratic signs for offices local, state, and national. Upon entering the North End, one begins to smell the river and the rowhouses sometimes break to reveal oddly placed single-family dwellings, enormous Catholic churches with their stained-glass portal windows, and countless bars with neon signs advertising darts, cheap beer, and—here and there—a laminated part-time employment notice. In addition to the North End's characteristic sights, the neighborhood has its characteristic sounds: the earth-shaking clang and rumble of boxcars passing on nearby rails, church bells that ring hourly, a motorcycle revving in the distance, and the whine of saws and other tools emanating from a home improvement project. To older River Citians, this is how a working-class Democratic neighborhood looks, sounds, and smells.

The Labor Temple, Labor Council leaders' base of operations, was located on one of the North End's side streets and might have been mistaken for a family home if not for the forest of political signs that crowded its entrance and a perpetually creaky sign that read, "River City Area Temple of Labor." Most union leaders long ago decamped for the West End, but the Temple remained as ever in the heart of the flats. Inside, Labor Council leaders' diminished capacities were readily apparent. On a typical meeting night, the hall was filled with folding chairs, perhaps sixty in all, facing a lectern and pair of flags: one for the United States and another for the AFL-CIO. Only a handful of leaders typically came: Steve Raney, a representative of a public-sector union and the Labor Council's official president, Warren Daniels, a representative of the Machinists, Michael Lombarti, a communications workers' representative and the groups' unofficial leader, and perhaps three or four others. All the attendees were men in their fifties and sixties.

Labor Council leaders saw the logic of gift and counterobligation as central to their economic role, and many River Citians I spoke with, denizens of the North End in particular, expressed a similar understanding. A leader begins as a normal worker in the plant or on the job site, but then—through election by his or her peers—becomes an official union representative and works only part-time or not at all with salary paid for by others' dues.[23] In the minds of many North Enders, union leaders transitioned from regular people to local elite upon their election, a status that members imagined allowed union leaders to embark on a life of exciting backroom dealings and limitless potential for graft, particularly through complicity with the employer. Moreover, union members I spoke with insisted that their leaders' transition to local elite-hood, whether real or imagined, was financed by their own wages: a gift that allows leaders a new, better life. They therefore expected their leaders to reciprocate by bringing tangible returns: higher wages and benefits. The strength of these implicit norms became evident when union leaders were unable to negotiate a satisfactory contract. Accusations of unreciprocated gifts surfaced immediately and were quickly followed by charges of secret payoffs.

One afternoon, for example, I was interviewing North Enders and met one who had worked at a small corporate subsidiary that liquidated its River City operation. "I worked at [the plant] thirteen years before they pulled out," he told me. "There were just a handful [of us] when it finally closed its doors. I guess that's what we get for our $38 a week of dues, thank you very much," he added. "We were talking about going out on strike and our union rep, he comes in and says, 'Guys, you gotta accept this contract, this is the best they are gonna offer you.' I don't know if he swayed the vote or whatever, but the contract passed. Anyway, so he's riding around on a new Harley, and one of the guys gets smart and says, 'Yup, we know where you got that, you just settled the contract, so the company bought you a new Harley!' He was just like 'whhaaat?!?' He got mad big time. The guy was just joking with him, but then you think, well, maybe they did. You don't know."

The pressure to reciprocate gifts was central to traditional union leaders' understanding of economic representation, and it is easy to see how this imperative was facilitated by River City's pre-1980s economy. Some business owners were not opposed to unions. Others opposed them but were ill-equipped for long strikes, unsophisticated in their union-busting measures, and operating in a legal environment that was friendlier to unions. Perhaps most important, the old families were tied to the city by their own networks, and there was virtually no chance that unionization or strikes would drive them from the city.[24] In effect, labor and business leaders were competing over the same pool of economic resources—firms' excess profits—which they both needed to repay their supporters' and others' past largesse. In this context, traditional labor leaders could visibly go to bat for their members. They bargained long and hard and called strikes if necessary, which sometimes went for months and devolved into intimidation and property crimes. Even if strikes failed to yield tangible benefits, they served a performative function, resolving tensions within a union leader's role by demonstrating solidarity with members. In this light, River City's contemporary economy creates disincentives for labor leaders' traditional economic game, because many firms are nonlocally owned and footloose. For example, the laid-off worker in the preceding paragraph was a machinist represented by Warren, a traditional leader who was nevertheless powerless to prevent his employer from leaving the city or even to confront the firm publically for fear of speeding its exit.

Here, the division between Labor Council and United Labor leaders is instructive, because members of the two organizations represent different kinds of employers.[25] If River City's pre-1980s economy did indeed promote labor leaders' traditional economic activities, then one would expect the leaders of unions based in firms with local ties—which were characteristic of this pre-1980s economy—to still identify with pre-1980s union traditions. Indeed, Labor Council leaders represented locals based in three types of employers, each locally rooted for different reasons: those based in locally owned firms, public sector employers, or amalgamated unions consisting of units based in different firms.[26] United Labor leaders represented locals based in nonlocally owned firms or transport and construction trade locals, which have historically maintained friendly relations with businesses.[27]

As one might further expect, Labor Council and United Labor leaders understood the task of representing their members differently. Labor Council leaders saw representation in the traditional way: bargaining hard, going on strike, and—especially—avoidance of any gifts from management or even friendly relations with them. For Labor Council leaders, "fighter" and "lion of labor" were terms of praise and "in bed with management" the worst insult. Labor Council leaders saw United Labor leaders as doing the latter and often accused them of failing to represent their members. "[United Labor leaders just want to] bring the businesses in here [so] they go fishing to Canada for a week [with management]," an indignant Labor Council leader told me. "But it is unethical. They ain't doing that because they like you. That's business to them—they're investing money to get you do something. It is sad to say, but a lot of 'em are more whoring for jobs than [working for] the labor movement. You can take that a ways, but you can't sell your goddamn soul for a job, [and] I happen to be pretty blunt about it: 'What the hell is the difference between you and a prostitute? [Have] some integrity! You may get a few jobs out of it, but is it representing our community [and your members] in the long term?' But they say, 'Hey, I am representing my members, you stay the hell out of it!'"

By contrast, United Labor leaders saw collaboration with employers as synonymous with representation and argued that risk of capital flight had changed the rules of the game. For example, I once spoke with Doug Whitter, the president of Greenfield's local, a United Labor leader, and key partner. "My father was a [leader in my union] and there was no going to lunch [with management]. They were lucky to share a pot of coffee. I can hear [him] spinning over in his grave saying, 'You had lunch with them?!?' Or if [I had] walked dressed like this, [my members] would have said, 'have you gone sour?!?'" Doug added, motioning to his khakis. "But I can [do that now] or go out and do community work [with management]. People have accepted that we need to work together, but you have to work on it all the time, because it could always slide back the other way. The easiest way to win a union election is to throw out some crazy statement [like] 'Enough with this in bed with business stuff, let's take them on!' Then people say, 'That man is a fighter!' and we'd be right back in the fight. [But most members] understand that we have to get on board with a lot of the positive changes [and] work together."

Traditional Union Civics

Traditional labor leaders also saw volunteering for working-class charities as working in the world of labor and therefore consistent with their public personae. "That is part of what we are about here, it is part of our job," a Labor Council leader told me. "Our job as labor leaders is not just to live in a vacuum where we just deal with our members. Our members have similar kinds of problems as anybody else in the community does and they want to see things here get better for regular working people. . . . It is important for labor to be involved with [working-class associations] because it touches a lot of people."

Indeed, table 2.1 shows that pre-1980s union leaders were heavily involved in various labor groups, which constituted a sector that was distinct from business groups and charities. Labor Council leaders continue such engagement at the time of my fieldwork. Each member of the Labor Council volunteered for two to four charities that focused their efforts on working-class recipients: the food bank, Salvation Army, a program that focused on disadvantaged youth, and others. They devoted fifteen hours a week to such activities on average.[28] In addition, Labor Council leaders volunteered collectively by ringing bells for the Salvation Army every Christmas and by serving a free weekly breakfast to North Enders.

Labor Council leaders' volunteering activities were consistent with the logic of gift and reciprocal obligation. First, giving of either time or resources to working-class charities provided traditional labor leaders another way of repaying the blue-collar community for their own elevated status. Moreover, charitable giving did not merely reciprocate past gifts, but also demonstrated largesse, which elevated labor leaders' social status in turn and gave them the authority to lead. In effect, Labor Council leaders' civic engagement proceeded according to the same logic as representation of their members, except for the fact that the public being represented was broader: not simply workers in their own unions, but—their own words—all "blue-collar families," "Joe and Mary average citizens," or simply their "side." In this way, Labor Council leaders' volunteering was a move within River City's traditional public game that called out an oppositional working-class public that labor leaders could mobilize in turn.

Unsurprisingly, Labor Council and United Labor leaders understood appropriate civic engagement differently. United Labor leaders participated in many civic partnerships with business leaders, which involved donations to underprivileged groups, but were simultaneously intended to showcase harmonious labor-business relations. I will show later that partners value such events, because they consider them a win-win: each side gets something that they want while presenting the city favorably to outsiders. But these partnerships incensed Labor Council leaders, partially because they involved collaboration with business leaders and partially because they generated donations that Labor Leaders considered inadequate to make a difference for their recipients' well-being. "[United Labor leaders,] they'll go out with these so-called charities, [but they're just] business groups," a Labor Council leader told me. "They will play golf with them to raise money for scholarships [and] say, 'We raised money for scholarships, twelve scholarships at $1,000 apiece.' You give out one thousand lousy dollars and then make kids come up and kiss your ring?!? That probably won't even buy textbooks for one year. That's a business charity—it's an excuse for them to play golf and show off!"

In civic life as in economic life, then, Labor Council leaders gave gifts to the city's working-class residents, but also called them out as an oppositional public that polarized their city's public sphere. Labor leaders' ability to play this traditional game was partially a function of their economic position: once, they controlled significant union dues and the loyalty of their members and could direct these toward civic causes. At the same time, unions' traditional civic activities were reinforced by Keynesian-era policies. As described in chapter 1, pre-1980s federal social service agencies relied on large, discretionary block grants to established associations, which thereby became locally rooted conduits of civic monies. In this context, traditional leaders had little incentive to cooperate; if they could capture the United Way's board, for example, they could use its resources to pay back their side of the public.

River City's labor unions had more resources than their Prairieville counterparts and mobilized their retainers and allies to do just that. Labor leaders first founded an association to capture United Way: United Labor, ironically the same organization that was later co-opted by labor leaders who partner. To pressure United Way, labor leaders purchased rally equipment—blow horns, materials for signs, a flatbed truck, and the like—and engaged in a series of pickets and campaigns to convince workers to withhold their annual United Way contributions. These campaigns succeeded in 1979. Labor leaders won United Way representation and were able to fund associations like a food bank, which Prairieville's unions could not support.

What's more, labor leaders' mobilization to dominate United Way led them to accumulate associational resources that they turned to new campaigns. "We were all different unions: construction trades, building trades, teamsters, UAW, meatpackers union," Pete Diller, the United Labor's first president, now retired, told me as we sat at his kitchen table looking at photos. "It was time that we organized and got together to be one voice— a consolidated voice. [After United Labor was formed,] we did things for other unions that were pretty public to show that we were serious. We had a different way of doing it back then. We did whatever we were powerful enough to do. Used to be whoever was most powerful would get what they want. [With United Labor] we had the numbers so we were pretty powerful and did a lot."

"So what kinds of things did you do?" I asked. "Oh, a lot of union drives and things," Pete said. "[A car dealership] in town that was trying to organize and having a lot of trouble. We got a parade permit and [had] a flatbed truck and went and made some speeches in front of the dealership as a show of support—later we had a little parade in front of [the owner's home]. And we endorsed legislation . . . [like] we heard of a law they passed up in Michigan about per-unit pricing. We thought that labels in the grocery store should be individually marked [per quantity of product so that it would be easier to comparison shop].We had [demonstrations] right at city hall." Pete showed me a photograph of his son, aged perhaps ten, holding a sign that read, "Help my Mommy See the Price."

"I guess it was more of a theatrical move—to show our power a little bit," Pete concluded. Whether mobilizations like the one described by Pete succeeded or not, they were significant because they allowed labor leaders to distinguish themselves within River City's traditional game and factionalized the city's public sphere into two coherent sides.

Traditional Union Politics

In politics, too, labor leaders' activities once factionalized public life along a labor-business axis. Their first big success was the election of Wally Porter in the 1960s, a Greenfield's union leader and the first of River City's many union-backed mayors. Wally's election coincided with a federally funded redevelopment of River City's downtown.

"At the time, the chamber had a committee along with some 'concerned citizens groups' to renew downtown," Wally told me about his election. "[In those days, the] Chamber [was pro] downtown . . . because a lot of them thought that this was a million-dollar-an-acre property and they wanted to preserve that investment. They wanted to keep it all downtown [because at the time the big locally owned manufacturers] were downtown

and also some [locally owned] department stores that were very successful. [Some other cities] around here were getting shopping malls and a lot
of people were [going there] to shop. So there was an idea that River City
should get a shopping mall, but the chamber men on the council always
voted it down."

"I went down to this committee and was pretty dissatisfied with what
I saw. So I just declared my candidacy and two other [union] people from
the River City Pack had the same philosophy I had [and declared their candidacy for City Council]," Wally continued. "The Labor Council backed me
pretty hard . . . and all three of us [union candidates] ended up getting
elected. So then we decided that we would simply run the city because we
were in the majority. On the very night [I became mayor] I ordered a rezoning [of the urban renewal district toward the] west end and by February
they were ready to go to construction—we got it fast."

"Was it pretty typical in those days for labor people to be pro-growth
westward?" I asked Wally.

"Yeah, their homes were all out there," Wally replied without hesitation,
"specifically the younger River City Pack, Designer Steel and Green's workers, which were the highest-paid industries in River City. And they wanted
the community to come out their way. They were the young families and
they were going to be the future of River City."

Wally's election shows, first, the extent to which labor leaders' economic, civic, and political activities blended and reinforced one another.
With the postwar expansion of unionized employers like the Pack or the
successful unionization of others like Green's, union leaders acquired organizational capacity, which they used to play for additional civic and political influence. To this end, leaders like Wally approached the public in the
spirit of gift and reciprocal obligation; they saw themselves as supported by
a working-class base and tried to help working-class River Citians in turn
(e.g., by advocating for the West End over downtown). Of course, such activities also institutionalized River City's working-class public as a political
actor; it is in part *because* Wally won the election that the West End's young
union families became a recognized political force that could claim to be
"the future of River City."

But Wally's election also speaks volumes about pre-1980s federalism.
Urban renewal was a Keynesian-era program par excellence, because under
its auspices federal bureaucracies functioned as a "banker government":
they established broad program priorities but allocated discretionary federal grants to democratically appointed local commissions. Because of this,
Wally was able to redevelop downtown without entering into coalitions

with the business leaders he had just bested in the election. As in the non-profit sector, federal policy aligned control of the city with institutions that operate at the urban scale and thereby created a local political system that tolerated, and even encouraged, factional conflict by allowing leaders to exercise near-unilateral control over federal resources. To foreshadow the book's second half, contrast this with the neoliberal environment that Kathy Gooding, the River Museum fundraiser, encountered in the book's opening vignette. To get the museum, Kathy was forced to enter into coalitions with countless other leaders to represent the project favorably to dozens of federal, state, local, and nonprofit agencies. By contrast, pre-1980s federalism allowed Wally to initiate downtown redevelopment with a stroke of his pen.

The tradition of union-backed mayors that began with Wally continued, with some interruption by chamber-backed candidates, until the 1980s. Residents of River City today associate this tradition most with Jones Berry, who served as mayor for over a decade and colorfully embodied River Citians' working-class style. The local joke went that Berry, a motorcycle enthusiast who passed his time in the scummy roadhouses of the city's flats, so frightened chamber leaders that they put sandbags around their country club.

It should go without saying that such public oppositions—between labor and business, workers and owners, unions and the chamber, gritty debauchery and high-society propriety, white ethnicity and nativism, the roadhouse and the country club, the flats and the bluffs, and countless such distinctions communicated via a myriad of public pronouncements, tales, jokes and innuendos—indexed nothing so much as the national conflict between Democrats and Republicans. Indeed, Labor Council leaders saw it as self-evident that local struggles and national politics were one and the same. "We look out for people that are going to support working-family issues," a Labor Council leader told me when I asked him about city council endorsements. "Like increasing sales tax—that is not something that is going to help working people. The problem with a lot of 'em on the city council, the ones that the *other side* . . ."

"Wait," I interjected, "what do you mean by the 'other side'?" I asked, seeking clarification because city council elections in Iowa are nonpartisan.

"I hate driving a wedge down there and saying it is Republican and Democratic, but [that is] the bottom line," he replied. "The Republican Party is not going to do anything to benefit working people. That's just not what they are about—that's not their agenda. And that is the Democratic agenda—to help working people and to lift us up instead of pushing us down. It does not take long with [City Council] for that to jump out at you. There is no party at City Council, but everyone knows what is going on."

There is nothing natural about a grassroots public sphere wherein people establish such identifications with the Republican haves and the Democratic have-nots, or even one wherein people identify with sides at all. Here as in the last chapter, my point has been that this public sphere was rooted in local structures consisting of grassroots leaders who maintained networks of largesse and obligation that penetrated deeply into local life, which were supported in turn by the federal policies that promoted this form of public engagement. Indeed, River City's and Prairieville's traditional leaders occasionally tried to call out an oppositional public in the traditional way in the 2000s, but the local and federal context worked against them.

On one occasion, for example, I attended a Labor Council candidates' night forum. Such events once drew all local, state, and national candidates endorsed by the Labor Council, but on this occasion only one had come: Denise Coolidge, a school-board member. Although endorsed by the Labor Council, Denise went against the group's strong protests in siding against cafeteria workers in contract negotiations.[29] "We were some of your earliest supporters, and we put a lot of resources into that election, so it burns when you turned on us," Steve told her after discussion turned to re-endorsement. Everyone sat up tensely.

But after Denise left the room, the mood shifted. "Well, Denise is probably going to get re-elected—I'd even definitely say she will get re-elected—so if we don't endorse her we will lose the only real voice we have on the school board," Steve said. I nodded as I wrote in my notebook. Denise was very popular with other civic leaders and had been getting great press in the local newspaper for her ability to set divisive issues aside and work to improve local school facilities. "I'll call her up later and let us know our decision," Steve said.

There are parallels here to the political practices of the old families, like Charles Browning's attempt to sway opinion on Prairieville's direct-election of mayor referendum. Like Prairieville's old families, Labor Council leaders exerted control over public life through meetings like this one: they backed Denise, and therefore expected her to be their voice. In years past, scores of important key politicians would have come and labor leaders assembled in the Labor Temple, perhaps fifty leaders in all, would have taken the message back and presented it to their locals at the next meeting, a meeting likely held in one of the dank bars of the city's North End within earshot of other residents. These same leaders would have carried the message to the working-class associations that depended on their largesse, where those who ran these organizations might pass on a political endorsement to working-class residents along with housing assistance, a free meal, or a safe place for the children to play. In the council chambers too, labor-backed politicians would have thundered about the upcoming election, making local newspaper headlines. But in the absence of such networks of gift and reciprocal obligation within River City's economic, civic, and political life, Labor Council leaders and others are powerless to factionalize the public along these traditional lines. They are just a handful of old men in a room, playing the old game in a new arena that is no longer amenable to it.

"[Look at] school board: we got some business people on there and then we got Denise, and she wants to do good," Michael told me after the meeting. "School board [is] a hard job: no money and it takes you away from your family—plus, I'll be frank with you, a lot of people feel intimidated. Because boy, these [business] people are smart, they can write, talk good, whatever. A lot of people, if [Gus Herman] president of the River City bank calls you up at home and says that River City needs this, well they just collapse [and] working people get hosed. So as they kill us, this is what happens. [We can't represent] average Joe and Mary citizen [and they] are the ones that need to be represented."

THREE

Politics Embedded in Community Governance: The Community Leadership Party

Frannie Steele was Prairieville's foremost Democratic activist, the political powerbroker of her day. She died several years before I began my fieldwork, but her husband, Daniel, still functioned as the Democratic Party's unofficial photographer, and I stopped by their house often to look at black-and-white photographs and talk about the old days. The Steeles' house was situated on an unassuming tree-lined street, where the cars rolled by slowly, observant of playing children. Much like the neighborhood on the outside, the house's interior suggested a disappearing Midwest: wall-to-wall carpeting, plush-cushioned, American-made couches, and cherry wood tables with lace tablecloths.

On one visit, I resumed my habitual interest in the house's nooks and crannies, and was struck again by the seamless integration of the personal and political therein. Many objects of memory, like family photos and service medals, appeared often in the homes of older Prairievillers; the Steeles' house was no different. But integrated with these, without commentary or pretension, were mementos suggesting a life less ordinary: pictures of Frannie in the midst of a raucous picket line, posing with the governor, or with Daniel at the Democratic National Convention. Before I had time to look in detail, Daniel returned with two mugs of coffee, a box of photographs, and a videotape that he had finally found of Joe Biden's eulogy of Frannie—my reason for the visit. Before looking at the video, we sat at the dining room table to look through the photographs.

"There it is, that's Ms. Frannie talking," Daniel said upon finding one photo, calling his wife by her pet-name as usual. He turned the photo right side up so that I could see it, and as he did so I caught sight of the crooked scar that wound around his wrist like a centipede—an injury left by the printing press in Daniel's basement, which once produced many of the materials distributed by Prairieville's Democratic Party. In the grainy photo, I made out a speaker on the podium before a sea of denim-clad workers. "Here now, we had a rally when the meat-packers were out on strike—up in the park; we had probably 5,000 union members out there," Daniel said, narrating the event. "I was just out taking pictures, not paying attention, and I had to turn around and say, 'Who the hell is that woman speaking?!?' But that was Ms. Frannie! That was the only time I heard her speak publically." Other Democratic old-timers had also told me about Frannie's shyness and preference for the back room.

"So then she get up there and—would you believe it—out of her mouth come some of the most beautiful phrases of labor talk you ever heard in your life," Daniel continued. "She knew it all, all the issues. I guess she probably knew more about politics than just about anybody. Then, when she got done—and it was only a short speech—the place come down. Hollerin' and clappin' and screamin'. She stopped the whole damn thing. The next speaker come out and he says, 'What's there left to say? She said it all!'" Daniel paused, uncharacteristically somber. "So then [I always kind of thought] that I never really knew my wife, [because, right then,] I could not believe my eyes. That was not my wife. That was that inner person. It just come out of her."

Frannie may not have spoken frequently in public, but her inner person nevertheless imprinted itself on the Prairieville, and even the American, political system of her day. In hindsight, her story seems unlikely. She was born during the Depression in the Valley, Texas's perpetually impoverished border region. There she met Daniel while he was in the army and married him. The two could not make a life on Daniel's earnings, so they uprooted after hearing that a railroad company near Prairieville was hiring unionized brakemen. To avoid paying for motels, they drove all night through the starry skies of the Great Plains.

Before long, Frannie had found her place. In a decade, she went from Democratic volunteer to president of the county organization. Soon after, she began holding weekly meetings in her home. Here, union leaders, labor lawyers with working-class clientele, and politicians met at Frannie's dining room table to establish a common agenda and before long "Frannie's Table" became local shorthand for Prairieville's Democratic establishment. Daniel had pictures of the whole thing.

"There's O'Malley, look, settin' right there where you are settin', the chief of police. And look here, Stewart Warner, he's now state senator," Daniel turned the photographs around toward me as he thumbed through them. Judging by the broad collars and facial hair worn by the grinning men at the table, these pictures were from the 1970s. "And Abe Skipper, this was back when he had more hair. And look there's Culver senior [a long-serving Iowa governor], the new Culver is his boy, he's running for governor now," Daniel continued, referring to the candidate who would win the governorship that election cycle.

As was often the case when I looked at photographs with Daniel, my mind drifted to political conversations with Prairieville's younger residents. "With [a lot of politicians] I just feel like they are not someone I can respect," a recent college graduate in Prairieville told me. "It is like they have lived their whole pampered existence in some kind of bubble. For once, I just wish somebody who has lived a real life would run." More than one young person compared politicians to extraterrestrials from "Planet Politics." By contrast, party leaders of Daniel's generation never made such distinction between politics and daily life.

For example, Daniel's next photograph was of Al Gore. "That was when he ran for president the first time, he and Ms. Frannie got along so well," Daniel said matter-of-factly and moved on. And indeed, Al Gore was sitting in my seat, looking baby-faced and examining the same porcelain donkey that still adorned the table. Other Democratic Party luminaries soon emerged in the photographs: Bradley, Hart, Gephardt, Dukakis, Bill Clinton. And then the coup-de-grace: a VHS tape of Joe Biden's Senate-floor eulogy of Frannie. We went into the living room to watch it. Senator Biden said Frannie was a "great American," who embodied the "promise of politics": willingness to "work hard in the service of others and of all people."

Frannie's unlikely journey—from the Valley, to Prairieville powerbroker, to a eulogy by a future vice president on the floor of the United States Senate—says much about the American political system of her day. Her story would certainly have been impossible in the Prairieville that I encountered in my fieldwork. By this, I mean first to make a relatively mundane point: Frannie would not have fit in with contemporary Democratic activists. She was formally uneducated, not prone to political pontification, and a Southern Baptist with ambivalent feelings about issues like abortion to boot. More important, the structural position that Frannie once inhabited—one that straddled key community institutions and simultaneously served as the grassroots base of one of the two parties—no longer existed in River City or Prairieville on either the Democratic or Republican side. In this respect, Frannie's story is less about her than the changing integration of American grassroots democracy and party politics.

In this chapter, I continue to analyze River City's and Prairieville's pre-

1980s public sphere, but shift focus from community leaders' game for public esteem to community leaders' importance for party politics. In the second part of the book, I will argue that community leaders' withdrawal from party politics created a set of arrangements that I characterize as *politics disembedded from community governance*: grassroots parties that are in the hands of ideologically motivated activists, who are not community leaders and have extended and hardened partisan conflicts. This chapter sets up this argument by examining a period just before the 1980s when politics was still embedded in community—a time when institutions like Frannie's Table stitched together the activities of community leaders with party politics and led most people to see the latter as a simple, unproblematic extension of the former.

Central to my argument in this chapter is a form of grassroots political organization that I characterize as the *community leadership party*. The community leadership party is an ideal type, or a model of party organization that captures analytically useful similarities between River City's and Prairieville's Democratic and Republican parties, pre-1980s.[1] These parties shared three characteristics. First, community and party leaders overlapped: most party leaders played a leading role in community life *and* most key community leaders were publically affiliated with one of the two parties. Community leadership parties were also hierarchical: community leaders translated their public esteem into intraparty influence and disciplined lower-status activists. Finally, party leaders focused largely on the bread-and-butter economic and social issues that motivated their community initiatives, not the hot-button issues that excite contemporary activists. Because the community leadership party is an ideal type only, River City's and Prairieville's actual parties deviated somewhat from the model. Nevertheless, both cities' pre-1980s Democratic and Republican parties were more similar to one another than to what any of them became after the 1980s, and the community leadership party best encapsulates their overarching commonalities.

I begin the chapter by stepping back and considering River City and Prairieville against the historical backdrop of America's party system. Other scholars of American political parties also note that community leaders like Frannie Steele were once central to grassroots electioneering, then lost ground to ideologically motivated activists after the 1980s, but fail to provide a convincing explanation of this grassroots transition. Returning to my analysis in the two preceding chapters, I argue that community leaders engaged in party politics because they saw it as an extension of their community personae: as something that would elevate their esteem in the eyes of their supporters and peers as surely as an economic payout, a civic initiative benefiting their people, or as advocating for one's side on a municipal commission. I then describe each city's parties and conclude by showing how older River Citians and Prairievillers used the historical overlap between their city's community and partisan institutions as a heuristic for making sense of politics. Many of them still saw politics as an extension of community conflicts and were able to establish moderate but stable partisan preferences by reasoning about political divides in terms of the working- and business-class sides that defined the public sphere of their day—something that their younger counterparts were typically unable to do.

American Party Politics in Historical Perspective

To better appreciate the unique nature of American political parties, it is instructive to consider the different phenomena that the term *political party* references in everyday speech. Political scientist V. O. Key first identified these as the party-in-government, the party-in-the-electorate, and the party-as-organization.[2] The party-in-government refers to all the activities of elected politicians. The party-in-the-electorate refers to voters and everything they do to influence one another. Finally, the party-as-organization refers to the formal and informal institutions that formulate and carry out a party's agenda. Key's critical insight was that people implicitly assume that the three different meanings of party co-imply one another and are substitutable. If Congress passes a series of far-right reforms, we assume that this is because the GOP has a well-established party infrastructure and is supported by a majority of ideologically committed, right-leaning Americans. But in fact Key's three definitions of party are often decoupled, with the current historical moment a case in point. Parties-in-government are more influential and polarized than at any time since the Great Depression: the policy positions of all congressional Democrats are to the left of all Republicans and interparty relations are downright hostile.[3] However, this is not because Americans have become more polarized; most voters are less committed to parties today than during the more moderate partisan climate of the 1960s. Nor is the legislative strength of parties exactly the result of formal party organizations, because American parties have traditionally been—and continue to be—lacking in bureaucratic organization relative to, for instance, their European counterparts. Rather, many political scientists argue that contemporary partisan polarization is the result of a reorganization of parties' informal grassroots base.

The organization of American political parties has historically been based in informal grassroots associations, a state of affairs that largely persists today. After the American Revolution, political leaders were tasked with mobilizing a rural population dispersed along a dangerous frontier and balked.[4] America's first parties, the Jeffersonian Republicans and Federalists, functioned exclusively as parties in government: systems for coercing congressmen to support their party leaders' agenda, which made no effort to mobilize the public.[5] When mass parties did emerge in the nineteenth century, partisan leaders formed them on the cheap by weaving together existing factions, local and state parties, and political machines into loose national networks. The broad contours of this system remained in place until the 1960s when leaders like Frannie Steele first became active.[6] By this, I do not mean to imply that America's political system was static during the nineteenth and early twentieth centuries. For instance, sociologist Elisabeth Clemens argues that Progressive Era grassroots lobbies on behalf of women, labor, and farmers formed new alliances with political elites, thus sidestepping political machines and transforming American politics.[7] Nevertheless, American politics was and largely still is the provenance of grassroots coalitions that align with politicians and other partisan actors who lack the bureaucratic capacity to create a formal party organization.[8]

Figure 3.1, which shows the aggregate historical expenditures of both parties' presidential campaigns, all congressional campaigns, both political parties, and nonparty organizations (including PACs, Super-PACs, and

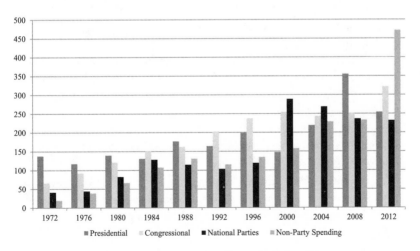

Figure 3.1. Election year political expenditures in millions (1972–2012). Adjusted for inflation to 1972 dollars.

issue advocacy organizations), demonstrates that the bureaucratic incapacity of American political parties was particularly pronounced during the Keynesian era. This period's biggest spenders were campaigns, especially presidential campaigns, which dwarfed spending by political parties. In 1968, for example, the Democratic Party's myriad committees spent just $19.2 million (in comparison to $48.2 million expended by presidential campaigns), a sum that stretched to pay salaries, upkeep on the national office, and the nominating convention, and aid Democrats running for president, Congress, and state and local offices.[9] The GOP fared only slightly better with $41.5 million in expenditures. At this expenditure level, the Democratic National Committee (DNC) and Republican National Committee (RNC) could afford to pay fewer than thirty employees apiece.[10] Indeed, a 1960s-era DNC chairman complained that his party organization only had the power to "hold the convention and establish rules for who could come."[11]

As formal organizations then, political parties were basically nonexistent before the 1980s: a handful of figureheads in a room, who—like their nineteenth-century predecessors—were unable to maintaining a national infrastructure capable of spearheading electioneering activities.[12] Although post-1980s political parties are more effective fundraisers than their traditional counterparts, they too lack the will or capacity to create a national bureaucracy; effectively, party leaders are now just figureheads in a room with an advertising budget. To the extent that voters are mobilized by political parties, therefore, it is by representatives of particular campaigns, not RNC and DNC representatives, which is a particular problem for campaigning politicians. Campaigns are episodic events by definition, but must be organized quickly, in many places at once, and in accordance with a dizzying array of place-specific conditions. For a campaign to succeed, someone must gather supportive signatures, file paperwork that accords with local election laws, maintain up-to-date voter lists, run a phone bank, conduct a get-out-the-vote drive, and book appropriate venues for campaign events. To be effective, campaigns need this solution: a grassroots organization or group with electioneering experience, local know-how, and a willingness to work on the cheap or, ideally, for free.

Community institutions like Frannie's Table were campaigns' Keynesian-era solution to America's lack of formal party organizations. Although studies of mid-twentieth-century informal party organizations are sparse, existing ones describe broadly similar arrangements to those in River City and Prairieville. Journalist Alan Ehrenhalt, for example, conducted a historical survey of dozens of cities, counties, and states and found each place's pre-1980s party politics controlled by a "tight-knit local elite." In Marin County, California, a "good old boys club" of chamber leaders set the Republican agenda. In Sioux Falls, South Dakota, "six old families and a nucleus of chamber types" dominated public life. In Utica, New York, a powerbroker with union ties ran local government and the Democratic Party and was opposed by Republican chamber leaders. In Greenville, North Carolina, community life and Republican politics were orchestrated by directors of the city's banks, major law firms, and textile mills; they were opposed by a weak Democratic coalition of transplants to the city, rural voters, and lower-class residents.[13] Alabama's politics was a contest between the "Conservatives," a coalition of landowners, insurance company owners, and medical industry executives, and "The Alliance," a coalition of black leaders, unions, teacher's associations, and trial attorneys.[14] In each case, party politics was the provenance of community leaders: typically, local business or landowners who identified as Republican and a Democratic coalition of whichever leaders had the organizational capacity to oppose them—oftentimes unions.

Political scientists argue that traditional grassroots organizations like these encouraged pre-1980s politicians to engage in conflict displacement, thus moderating politics.[15] Federal, state, and local politicians needed the goodwill of grassroots party leaders to win elections, but these leaders' super-ordinate concerns were with community life and they often disagreed about the contentious political issues of the day—particularly in different cities and regions of the country. Imagine, for instance, the differences in political opinion that must have existed between Utica's blue-collar leaders and leaders of Alabama's "Alliance." In this context, successful politicians wove together broad coalitions by taking firm stances on one contentious issue at a time—the New Deal in the 1930s or civil rights in the 1960s—but moderate or ambiguous stances on other issues. This incentive for moderation disappeared during the 970s and 1980s as ideologically motivated activists took over traditional grassroots parties. Political scientists argue that this grassroots transformation gave politicians an incentive to engage in conflict extension.[16] Unlike traditional community leaders, post-1980s activists are ideologically committed to their party's entire platform and frequently identify most with hot-button political issues, which gives politicians every reason to take hard stances on contentious issues across the board.[17]

In the second part of the book, I will have more to say about post-1980s partisan activists and discuss why their takeover of grassroots parties—rather than, for instance, Americans' changing political attitudes or changes in campaign finance—is the main cause of America's polarized politics. My interest here is why Keynesian-era community leaders were once central to party politics to begin with. Political scientists and sociologists alike attribute traditional leaders' control over parties to procedures for selecting national convention delegates. Before the 1970s, party insiders like politicians, fundraisers, and powerbrokers controlled delegate selection and thereby their party's agenda.[18] Afterwards, Democratic and Republican parties began selecting delegates via primaries and caucuses, which gave ideologically motivated activists an opportunity to take over.[19] Scholars argue that party-controlled delegate selection procedures increased traditional party leaders' influence for two reasons: it insulated them from social movements and strengthened the hand of urban machine bosses and powerbrokers.

The first argument is made most forcefully by sociologists Doug McAdam and Karina Kloos, who argue that insider-controlled nominations created a wall between postwar parties and social movements.[20] According to this account, changes in delegate selection allowed activist-backed nominees—especially Ronald Reagan—to initiate a "slow release" revolution by outcompeting traditional politicians and encouraging "scores of his protégés to enter GOP politics" at the grassroots. On the Republican side, for instance, constituencies like Christian conservatives, the NRA, and low-tax lobby groups took over local party chapters, thus polarizing local politics, state politics shortly thereafter, and eventually congressional politics by the 1990s.[21] Like McAdam and Kloos, I will argue that social movements have greater influence over activist-led than community leader-led parties and thereby contribute to the post-1980s polarization of American politics.[22] But the explanatory portion of McAdam and Kloos's account is inconsistent with the sequencing of historical trends in American politics. In fact, activists' party takeover of grassroots parties occurred concurrently with or even before Reagan's presidency, which suggests that the latter was not the prime mover of the former. For instance, Alan Ehrenhalt describes how a right-wing coalition dubbed "the crazies" by the local media took control of Colorado's landowner-dominated GOP in the late 1970s, and successfully fielded candidates for local, then state, then federal office—a process of bottom-up party takeover that he also observed among Democrats.[23] And logically, too, it seems unlikely that Reagan—a divorced, relatively unreligious Hollywood actor—somehow catalyzed a coalition between Christian conservatives and other right-wing activists. Even if Reagan nudged this coalition along, it is more plausible that changes at the grassroots—

notably, traditional community leaders' exit from party politics—created an opportunity for Reagan by leaving local GOP chapters unattended. The key question is why traditional leaders abandoned grassroots politics.

Political scientists argue that traditional leaders did so because changes in party nomination procedures restricted their ability to extract patronage from political elites.[24] This account portrays traditional party leaders as patronage-seeking "material activists" and "party bosses" who leveraged their control over national parties into the graft they needed to build local patronage systems.[25] Then 1970s-era reforms cut off traditional party leaders' access to graft, their party organizations crumbled, and ideological activists took over. Although the patronage politics account does address the key issue of community leaders' engagement in grassroots parties, it too suffers from logical and historical inconsistencies. Logically, it is unclear why traditional "material activists" should have been singularly focused on national conventions. Recall that American political parties are organizations in name only, which gives national delegates little power over anything besides selection of presidential candidates; delegates also vote on a party agenda, but lack the capacity to compel others to follow it. Because of this, one would expect materially interested leaders to be equally or more interested in congressional, state, and local politics, wherein nomination procedures did *not* change in the 1970s, and which traditional leaders—had they been primarily interested in graft—could have presumably continued milking.[26] What's more, historians of urban governance identify the decline of urban patronage systems with Progressive Era good governance reforms during the early twentieth century and New Deal urban policy, which establishing federal programs as an alternative to machine-style graft.[27] By the mid-twentieth century, urban machines had largely disappeared outside of a few large, immigrant-receiving cities— notably, Chicago. For this reason, 1960s- and '70s-era elective affinity between grassroots and national party bosses seem unlikely.[28]

And indeed, political scientists' account of machine-like urban governance misrepresents Keynesian-era community leaders, at least Prairieville's and River City's. In some sense, traditional community leaders were indeed materially motivated, because—as I have taken pains to point out— they spoke the language of material benefit and reciprocal obligation. But they were not exactly bosses. Political machines are quasi-bureaucratic systems wherein bosses control their retainers' jobs and other means of livelihood, which makes machine-style graft more akin to a salary than a gift: party bosses simply command their clients' votes much as an employer commands employees in the workplace.[29] But in River City and Prairieville, traditional leaders' material focus revolved instead around an ideology of gift and counter obligation. Traditional leaders acquired the capacity to lead by demonstrating themselves as giving to their side. Their gifts were rarely individual payoffs. More common were collective gifts like a successful unionization drive, donations to an appropriate charity, electioneering in support of the right council member, or an urban development initiative that proved pleasing to one's blue- or white-collar supporters.[30] Most important, community leaders exerted control primarily by virtue of their central position within their city's public game: via an ability to convince and cajole others from a position of public esteem, not by being able to command those whose livelihood they controlled.[31]

On closer examination, too, my account of community leaders' use of the velvet glove better captures trends in American electoral politics than political scientists' focus on party bosses' iron fist. Consider again American presidential nominations: based on political scientists' account, one would expect a clear shift from insider-backed presidential nominees to activist-backed nominees during the 1970s. The actual history is murkier, suggesting instead that traditional leaders' party dominance was characterized by periodic activist-fueled party takeovers followed by regression to a more moderate partisan mean. It is noteworthy, for example, that activist-backed challengers secured party nominations *before* 1970s-era reforms: archconservative Barry Goldwater won the Republican nomination in 1964, when many of the GOPs big-money backers accepted many tenets of the New Deal.[32] But then, the Republican pendulum swung back to moderate party insiders like Richard Nixon and Gerald Ford. Similarly, Democratic Party activists successfully capitalized on new delegate selection rules to nominate peace candidate George McGovern in 1972, but he was later followed by centrist party insiders like Walter Mondale. Indeed, even activist-backed Ronald Reagan was followed by George Herbert Walker Bush, a conflict-displacement politician par excellence. Although Bush served as Reagan's vice president, he purged Reagan staffers as president and refused appointees from the GOP's right wing, talked about homelessness and AIDS, invited gay activists to the White House, appointed a pro-choice doctor to head the Department of Health and Human Services, and broke with his party on issues like gun control and environmental regulation.[33] Even a charitable reading of history suggests that party reforms only created opportunities for social movements to momentarily capture political parties, but afterwards these parties slowly gravitated back to their more moderate base, a process that continued into the 1980s.[34]

To better appreciate the social mechanisms between parties' traditional regression toward a moderate mean, consider one traditional leader-activist pairing: Frannie Steele and Abe Skipper, an activist who eventually became Prairieville's state senator. Like many of his generation, Abe entered politics during the Vietnam War as part of the activist wave that swept George McGovern to a strong showing in Iowa's 1972 caucus. Abe continued to support outsider candidates in 1976, when he backed antiwar Democrat Fred Harris, who was then traveling the country by RV. "In those days, I had all the answers, wanted to save the world," Abe told me, smirking, before describing how he swung his precinct for Harris. "[I caucused near] Hilltop College, where I'm an alum. There weren't that many people at the [caucus], it was almost evenly divided, but not looking good. So we sent Jenny [another activist], who was just beautiful, across the street to the boy's fraternity. She trolls the fraternity houses, grabs like 13 or 14 frat boys, they stay [to caucus] maybe fifteen or twenty minutes—they did not even know who the hell the candidates were, but that's how we won the precinct."

With youthful enthusiasm on his side, Abe Skipper next made plans to unseat one of Prairieville's labor-backed state representatives—a move that Frannie and her allies feared might allow a chamber-backed Republican to snatch the seat. The scheme landed Abe at Frannie's table, where he went willingly at her invitation. "Abe, he come knocking on the door, sat at this table for 2–3 hours, [he was] just a young college kid saying he wanted to run in the primary and, boy, that was a no-no," Daniel Steele recalled. "And the whole time, he just talked and talked—Ms. Frannie did not say a word, and finally he says, 'Ms. Frannie, I'm going to run for office, but I'm not old enough this time—I have to wait until I'm old enough!' And that kind of tickled Ms. Frannie, that he'd spend all that time talking just to say that he was not going to run."

But Prairieville's Democratic establishment was not done with Abe Skipper. Sensing potential in him, Frannie asked Hardy Schmidt to take Abe "under his wing." Hardy was an attorney who represented injured workers and edited Prairieville's labor newspaper. Under his tutelage, Abe secured a job as a unionized meatpacker during the summers, put himself through law school, and became a labor attorney. "[Hardy] was cut from that old labor style and was pretty redneck and all that: not very tolerant of coalitions," Abe Skipper told me. "But boy, did [Hardy] do a lot for labor—everybody in Prairieville who carries a union card owes something to Hardy Schmidt! And man, he could smell shit and schemes coming a mile away that you could not even see. To this day, every time I look at something in city government, I'm reminded of something that Hardy Schmidt said, or did, or taught me. [For many years he] energized the Labor Council and politicized it, so that what you had here was a de facto two-party system, chamber and Labor Council." Eventually, Abe was elected to the statehouse, but by then he was a community notable rather than just an antiwar protester. He was ready to compromise with other Democrats, sacrificing ideology on the altar of collective expediency. For example, he continued to criticize America's military interventions after Vietnam, but unlike some contemporary activists did not refuse to support any candidate who had ever voted for a war.

I found that this stabilizing base of the party was largely missing in Prairieville at the time of my fieldwork: the Frannie Steeles, the Hardy Schmidts, and an entire institutional infrastructure that brought young activists into contact with the community they hoped to represent, teaching them to balance their beliefs against political reality and their constituents' needs. In Iowa especially, presidential candidates and other politicians still make herculean efforts to tap into this infrastructure today.[35] I went to backyard barbeques that featured sitting US senators who flew in on private jets to address a handful of party insiders. One Democratic activist I knew accidentally called a well-known candidate on his personal cellphone while shopping at Walmart, and the candidate was not only undisturbed, but took the opportunity to lobby her for support. Presumably, national party leaders would prefer the alliance of a powerbroker like Frannie Steele to an ideologically committed, but locally insignificant activist. The problem is that institutions like Frannie's Table no longer exist in Prairieville, River City, or other American cities. Those who simultaneously took positions of community leadership and engaged in politics for the love of the game are simply gone.

Given my previous discussion of pre-1980s community leaders, it should be evident why so many once readily participated in party politics. Keynesian-era policies sheltered an indigenous class of local labor and business leaders, whose competition for community esteem was further structured by federal policies that left federal resources under the jurisdiction of local bodies. In this context, community leaders engaged in public life by forming warring coalitions, saw their position of community leadership as synonymous with their ability to mobilize and represent their side, and saw partisan politics as another way to do so.

On sees ample evidence of community leaders' simultaneous engagement in party politics in tables 3.1 and 3.2, which list Prairieville's and River City's most central leaders during the 1970s. I constructed these tables using lists of leaders' associational activities and assessed centrality

Table 3.1. River City's most central leaders (1974–1976)

Leader	Local Democratic bodies	Formal partisan affiliations	Closeness centrality
1. Manufacturing company executive	Civic Center Board and Mental Health Board	Republican donor	57.08
2. Newspaper publisher	Citizens', Transit, Civic Center Board, Health Board	Republican donor	56.34
3. Machinist union leader	Civic Center and Mental Health Board	Democratic officer	54.81
4. Bank executive	School Board	Republican officer	54.24
5. Developer	Mental Health Board		53.80
6. Packinghouse owner	Transit Board	Republican donor	53.58
7. Packinghouse manager	City Council, Mental Health Board	Republican donor	53.36
8. Teamster union leader	Transit Board	Democratic officer, donor	53.25
9. Attorney	Civic Center Board and Mental Health Board		53.04
10. Physician			52.93
11. Small business owner		Democratic officer	52.93
12. Bank owner		Republican donor	52.93
13. Manufacturing company executive	Civic Center Board		52.93
14. Bank executive			51.68
15. Bank executive	Civic Center Board and Health Board	Republican donor	51.48
16. Teacher	School Board	Democratic officer	51.38
17. City planner	Civic Center Board and Health Board		51.27
18. County supervisor	County Supervisors and Mental Health Board	Democratic officer	50.97
19. Community activist	Mental Health Board and Health Board		50.60
20. Manufacturing company owner			50.41
21. Construction company owner			50.29
22. Mayor (dentist)	City Council, Transit Board	Democratic donor	50.29
23. College administrator		Republican officer	50.29
24. Teamster union leader			50.29
25. Judge	Mental Health Board		50.00
26. Advertising executive	Civic Center Board		50.00
27. Manufacturing company owner		Republican donor	50.00
28. Bank executive	School Board, Civic Center Board, and Civil Service Board		49.81
29. Bank executive			49.81
30. Attorney	Transit Board		49.53

Table 3.2. Prairieville's most central leaders (1974–1976)

Leader	Local Democratic bodies	Formal partisan affiliations	Closeness centrality
1. Construction union leader	Central City Commission	Democratic officer, Frannie's Table	27.24
2. Bank executive	Central City Commission	Republican donor	26.56
3. Construction business owner	Central City and Art Museum Commission	Republican donor	26.47
4. Bank president	Central City and Art Museum Commission	Republican donor	26.41
5. Power company executive	Central City Commission	Republican donor	26.24
6. Retail business owner	Central City Commission	Republican donor	26.16
7. Bank president	Central City Commission	Republican donor	26.14
8. Small business owner	Central City Commission	Republican donor	26.07
9. Manufacturing business owner			25.99
10. Bank executive	Central City and Art Museum Commission	Republican donor	25.91
11. Packinghouse union leader	Human Rights and Art Center Commission	Democratic officer	25.91
12. Construction business executive	Central City Commission		25.87
13. Credit union president	Central City Commission	Republican donor, officer	25.87
14. Bank executive	Central City Commission	Republican donor	25.81
15. Hal Swift (packer's union)	City Council, Planning Commission	Democratic officer, Frannie's Table	25.66
16. Unknown	Central City and Human Rights Commission		25.66
17. Wholesale bus president	Central City Commission	Republican donor	25.65
18. Bank executive	Central City Commission	Republican donor, officer	25.65
19. Catholic activist	Central City CC and Human Rights Commission		25.63
20. Democratic politician	City Council, Community Service	Democratic officer, Frannie's Table	25.61
21. Manufacturing bus executive	Central City Commission		22.57
22. Manufacturing business executive	Central City Commission		22.57
23. Car dealership owner	Central City Commission		25.55
24. Bank executive	Central City Commission		25.53
25. Construction bus executive	Central City Commission	Republican officer	25.49
26. Dentist	Central City Commission		25.39
27. Mayor (physician)	City Council, Central City Commission. and Civil Service Commission		25.37

Table 3.2. (*continued*)

Leader	Local Democratic bodies	Formal partisan affiliations	Closeness centrality
28. Food process bus owner	Community Service Commission	Republican donor	25.33
29. Meatpackers' union leader	Community Service Commission		25.29
30. Supervisor (manufacturing executive)	Central City Commission	Republican politician*	25.29

Notes: Frannie's Table = A compatriot of Frannie Steele, who participated in weakly meetings at her home.

I misplaced records of most county supervisors' 1970s-era partisan affiliations, but all ran as partisan candidates. Number 30 was a manager in a locally owned manufacturing plant and therefore probably a Republican.

using a closeness measure, which counts leaders as *central* if their associational engagements make them the fewest steps removed from those of other leaders. In sum, one can read these tables as a rough proxy of leaders who were most visible to their peers or, more simply still, most likely to be considered important by other important leaders.[36] Of particular note in the tables are columns 3 and 4, which list central leaders' engagement in local and party politics. Of River City's thirty most central leaders, twenty were members of at least one city elected body or commission and fifteen publically supported the Democratic or Republican Party—that is, they worked on the party's behalf, or were publically known as generous donors to the local party, not just supported particular candidates or voted.[37]

Of Prairieville's thirty most central leaders, twenty-nine were members of at least one city elected body or commission and nineteen publically supported the Democratic or Republican Party.[38] Here as in the oral histories, community leaders simply were party leaders before the 1980s, and vice versa. I now discuss the particularities of each city's parties before considering these parties' impacts on the political reasoning of older Prairievillers and River Citians.

The Community Leadership Party

Before the 1980s, River City's and Prairieville's Democratic and Republican parties shared three characteristics that I have identified with the community leadership party: community leaders held leadership positions within the party; their community status translated into intraparty standing and allowed them to discipline activists; and they engaged in partisan activities that advanced their community-directed goals. I now illustrate this by discussing all four parties, moving from most to least ideal-typical community leadership party.

The Democrats

River City's pre-1980s Democratic Party was the most ideal-typical community leadership party. In chapter 2 I showed that traditional union leaders viewed Democratic politics as a crucial constituent of the "world of labor" and were still involved in get-out-the-vote drives and other electoral initiatives. Historically, River City's Democratic Party was virtually synonymous with the labor movement. Older informants recalled that the "Labor Temple became Democratic headquarters" at election time, and their recollections are consistent with pre-1980s reports in the local newspaper, which detail phone banks, canvassing, and other electioneering coordinated from the Labor Temple. The Labor Temple was also River City's pre-1980s storehouse of voter lists and the *Labor Leader* newspaper served as a medium of political communication that featured ads for all Democrats running for local, state, or federal office.

Culturally, too, River City's Democratic Party was a blue-collar, union party. This is not to say that all Democratic activists and politicians were union leaders or members. Nevertheless, meaningful participation in any political culture requires people to foreground some aspects of their identities while suppressing others, and River City's Democrats celebrated their connection to working-class lifestyles to the exclusion of other identities.[39] Historically, a handful of doctors, lawyers, and even small-business owners participated in Democratic politics, but they publically touted working-class credentials when running for elected or party office: their Catholicism, their white ethnicity, the hard work of their parents in manual employment, or simply their working-class style. Perhaps the best exemplar is Jones Berry, River City's long-serving mayor. People saw Berry as a union mayor, but he was actually a high school teacher and, therefore, technically a white-collar professional.[40] But Berry's personal style was more blue-collar than that of any union leader, and his rumbling motorcycle, refusal to wear a suit, and tales of benders in the city's flats left little mystery about his local allegiances.

In Prairieville, the division between unions and Democrats was perhaps more pronounced. Most older Prairievillers associated the Meatpackers' Hall with unions, but saw the Steeles' house as the Democratic Party's "home" and Frannie as the party's "mother."[41] "I started out working as a canvasser as a kid and met Frannie," Stewart Warner, Prairieville's state senator at the time of my fieldwork, told me, launching into a common Frannie Steele narrative. "She recognized me, as just a young guy, going door-to-door, working hard, getting a lot of voters signed up—although not raising a lot of money, which was my other job," Stewart continued, laughing. "See, Frannie had a very, very sharp memory and she always recognized people, especially the hard workers. Well anyway, I went to college, but politics always intrigued me and I always wanted to get back in, so then it was right back to Frannie's table. She remembered me from ten years earlier, when I came back asking for her advice and input about [running]. She said, 'You should run,' so I did. Daniel snapped some pictures of me that day while I talked with Frannie and the others upstairs. Then, Daniel ran off some fliers from the basement and I was off. Yeah . . ." Stewart paused, smiling, "that was the way it was in those days. It all happened in that little house."

Culturally, too, Prairieville's party was less of a blue-collar party than River City's, in large part because union-hall behavior did not fly in the Steeles' home. Traditional leaders never described Frannie using honorifics like "lion of labor," which they applied to one another to celebrate tenacity and combativeness. Their recollections of Frannie were similar to Stewart Warner's in that they praised Frannie's intuition, fairness, and especially her memory—indeed, many described her as a sort of repository of knowledge about past gifts given to the party. Frannie's house also did and still does display a modest middle-class décor, and she did not tolerate drinking, shouting, and the kinds of confrontational tactics that sometimes characterized union meetings. Daniel Steele told me that her biggest disagreement with Hardy Schmidt occurred after union leaders deemed a prospective candidate too business-friendly, berated him, and picked up their notebooks and left, leaving the candidate sitting alone with Frannie. "You will never do that again," Frannie hissed into the phone afterwards.

But aside from such wrinkles, Prairieville's pre-1980s Democratic Party was thoroughly union. The era's important labor leaders were all Frannie's Table regulars: both Labor Council presidents during the 1960s and '70s were part of Frannie's inner circle, as was Hal Swift, a former meatpacker and populist councilman who was probably Prairieville's most recognizable labor leader during the 1970s. In fact, Hal and Frannie were so close that she managed his campaigns and assumed his council seat while he recovered from a heart attack. Also central to the party were two labor lawyers, Hardy Schmidt and Harry McDonald Sr., close collaborators of Frannie who also edited the city's labor newspaper.[42] Despite their professional credentials, labor attorneys dealt almost exclusively with working-class clients, were themselves a product of the shop floor or only one generation removed, and identified simply as labor leaders. Abe Skipper is a case in point. His flower-child roots notwithstanding, Abe was related to Marty Skipper, a 1960s-era president of Prairieville's Labor Council, worked himself as a unionized meatpacker, and spent many years as protégé to Hardy Schmidt.

Furthermore, distinctions between Prairieville's unions and Democratic politics disappeared entirely during elections. Union-sponsored events like Prairieville's Labor Picnic were the city's biggest *electoral* initiatives, doubling as candidate forums and opportunities for registering new voters. Union leaders also directed get-out-the-vote drives among union members and other Democrats alike, a practice that required creative bookkeeping because it was illegal.[43] "[In the 1970s they passed a new election law]. It was the damndest things, because nobody really understood it or what to do with it," a union leader told me. "As a labor person, you might go door-to-door [canvassing] and have one labor person on the block [and] 10 Democrats, but [the law said you couldn't mix the lists]. You had to separate them, but keep 'em together. So what we did was drill 3×5 [cards and] ring 'em [so that] we could flip 'em and go door-to-door-to-door. If you clamped [the cards] they stayed together, but if you shook 'em, only one batch would fall out. Every election they would [prepare] those walking decks—30 or 40 hours at a time [to get] them ready."[44]

As in River City, Prairieville's Democratic politicians and activists foregrounded their working-class identities. Among surviving traditional activists, the comment that such-and-such "gave so much to the labor movement" persists as the highest form of compliment. I also found no archival evidence of Democratic mobilizations based around the sort of identity politics that unites many of Prairieville's contemporary activists. This is not to say that traditional leaders were necessarily intolerant of differences in belief, ethnic background, or sexual orientation. Indeed, I found records of pro–civil rights speeches by Prairieville's Democratic leaders in the 1960s, but—crucially—such speeches called out for tolerance on the basis that black Americans were also working people, and therefore Democratic constituents. Unlike contemporary activists, traditional activists did not foreground diversity as a basis for solidarity and emphasized working-class commonalities instead, thereby effectively displacing potential conflicts or issues that did not map onto labor-business divides.

On one occasion, for example, I spoke with Daniel Steele after the funeral of another long-time activist. "We just lost our friend Darrel Westland, and he was always far out, he was different, but he was consistently different—he was always consistent that everybody should get a fair shake in life," Daniel said. "He was a cartoonist; I have some of the cartoons that he drew for handbills—we'd print them off by the thousands. [Anyway] I went to the memorial and all the old-timers were there, more Democrats than I seen in twenty years. They got up and they told stories, about how when nobody else would speak up, there was Darrel standing up and speaking in front of city council. But not one word about religion—not one word! [The next day] I'm telling a guy how I was really moved by the whole thing, and then I says, 'But nobody talked religion there.' [The guy says,] 'Darrel was an atheist, he did not believe.' I could not believe that I knew him for forty years and did not know that. It was amazing. But he was always champion for the little guy, always champion for the underdog, he was always front and center. It was, 'You can't have it for that group, unless the other group gets some of it!'"

The Republicans

The old families, too, assumed leadership over their cities' GOP, with Prairieville's business leaders more vocal in their Republicanism than River City's. The longest-serving president of Prairieville's GOP was a wholesale business owner, descended from one of the city's oldest families, and brother to president of Prairieville's largest bank. Another popular business owner served as a Republican state senator. Prairieville's old families also hand-picked candidates. "Years ago, [I supported] our congressman, Brad Trippley," Charles Browning told me, launching into a narrative I heard often among Prairieville's patricians. "One day Greg Mackey, of Mackey Baking Company, called me up and said we should check this guy out. Trippley [grew] up in Prairieville, went to Yale, became a well-known journalist, and then came back here to run for Congress. Greg Mackey [oversaw] his campaign and I was probably his biggest financial supporter."

Prairieville's business leaders also mobilized their associations toward electioneering activities. Prairieville's chamber endorsed candidates, allowed them to run their campaigns from chamber offices, and served as a site of candidate fundraisers. The Republican-ness of Prairieville's chamber is everywhere evident in materials like the organizations newsletters, which are filled with opinion pieces penned by business leaders that rail against the "entitle-ists," a term applied to union leaders and Democrats alike. Prairieville's other business associations were characterized by a similar assumed-Republican-ness. In 1976, for example, Prairieville's Rotary Club conducted a straw poll and 88 percent of Rotarians reported Republican sympathies, with 6 percent favoring the Democrats and 6 percent reporting no party preference.[45]

It should go without saying that the involvement of Prairieville's business leaders made the pre-1980s GOP radically different from its post-1980s incarnation: an elite, businessman's party that was unapologetically pro-business and anti-union. Indeed, my historical investigation revealed none of the religious-tinged, populist initiatives that energized GOP activists at the time of my study. In the same 1976 Rotary poll, for instance, nearly half of Rotarians supported legalized abortion and most did not see it as an important political issue. Members of the old families also adhered to Mainline Protestant faiths, which they saw as a mark of distinction from the Catholicism and revivalist Christianity embraced by Prairieville's lower classes. The only religious figure in the city's United Republican Club, for example, was an Episcopalian minister descended from one of the city's old families. This is not to say that religious conservatives were nonexistent within the ranks of pre-1980s GOP activists; indeed, many Christian conservatives first became involved in the GOP in the 1970s. However, these activists either did not foreground religious issues or the businessmen who handled pre-1980s party communications saw fit to ignore them. The latter is likely, because I will show in chapter 5 that remaining members of Prairieville's old families were hostile toward Christian conservative activists at the time of my fieldwork, viewing them as embarrassingly low class.

Relative to Prairieville, ties between River City's business community and Republican Party were weaker, and River City's GOP was generally the least ideal-typical community leadership party of the four. Even here, however, the pre-1980s party boasted high-profile business leaders among its ranks. For example, Fred Pommel was chamber president during the 1970s and served as secretary of the GOP. Another member of the old families who was brother to the city's newspaper publisher served as a GOP officer alongside Fred. A popular car dealership owner served as a Republican state senator. Like in Prairieville, too, River City's chamber endorsed Republican candidates for office, helped them to coordinate their campaigns, and supported these candidates in its newsletter and other publications.

But for all these similarities, many older River Citians described their business community's traditional Republican allegiance as tepid. Older GOP activists, for example, complained that members of the city's old families failed to hoist political signs at their workplaces for fear of losing customers. A few business owners confirmed that being "openly" Republican in overwhelmingly Democratic River City—as opposed to privately supporting the GOP—could carry economic costs. For example, Troy Gooder served as River City's mayor in the 1990s and switched his partisan identification from Independent to Republican after leaving office. The next day, he told me that the city newspaper called and asked if he feared that his real estate business would suffer. I never heard a similar complaint in Prairieville and whereas the Republican-ness of Prairieville's business leaders was accepted as gospel by all, I spoke with a few River Citians who thought there might be secret Democrats among their city's business leaders. For instance, some residents suggested that Ned Schrank Sr., the historical owner of the city's largest bank, had Democratic sympathies. And indeed, the assumed Republican-ness of River City's business community was quickly shed during the city's transition to partnership during the 1980s, when the chamber ceased endorsing candidates and elected an openly Democratic businesswoman chamber president.[46]

Nevertheless, the relationship between River City's and Prairieville's business communities and Republican institutions was more similar than it was different: rumors of GOP defection among the businessmen's ranks were particularly delicious in River City, because everyone assumed that all businessmen were Republicans. "Back then, we were all Republicans," a former manager at one of River City's factories told me. "You had the city fathers who were on the chamber: there were the McConnells, the Mathesons, the Fabers. All of them had their own little empire. [They] were afraid that any [nonconformity] would jeopardize [it]. It was quite an experience. It was the man in the gray flannel suit, so to speak. If [the owner] was at the top of the pole, well you allahed to him. If he said jump, you said, 'How high?'" In these ways, the networks of union and business leaders who defined River City's and Prairieville's public life effectively acted as informal party organizations: they organized campaigns, maintained voter rolls, engaged in party-building initiatives, and mobilized voters. Simply put, the opposing factions that defined each city's pre-1980s public sphere were—organizationally speaking—also each city's parties.

What Regular People Think

Herein lies the key to pre-1980s electoral politics: partisan distinctions were intuitively apparent to people, because they were woven into the fabric of their community's daily life. Political scientists have consistently shown that most people know and care little about the substance of public policy, and I have therefore proceeded in the tradition of the Elmira study, which argued that people use local distinctions to make sense of national politics. When Elmirans talked politics, apolitical group identifications—particularly blue- and white-collar identities—became bases for political preferences. It is not difficult to see parallels to pre-1980s River City and Prairieville, where residents also identified with blue- and white-collar sides. My contribution has been only to show that residents' tendency to identify with such sides was neither natural nor self-evident. Rather, this tendency was created, first, by community leaders' game for public prominence, which factionalized community life and, second, by Keynesian-era policies that supported and encouraged leaders' public game. In the words of sociologists Cedric De Leon, Manali Desai, and Cihan Tuğal, political elites—here community leaders engaged in grassroots parties—*articulated* for others which social characteristics were politically salient through their words, deeds, and patterns of associational activity.[47] I now explore the consequences of their pre-1980s activities by turning to Prairievillers and River Citians who I identify as traditional voters: those who, like their counterparts in Elmira, used traditional community cleavages to make sense of politics.[48]

Before discussing traditional voters, I need make a methodological caveat. I see my study as consistent with the Elmira tradition in that my primary interest is in the social contexts that reproduce particular ways of reasoning about politics. I am therefore less interested in how particular voters behave on election day, the current preoccupation of much of voting behavior research in political science, than in broader macro-historical patterns: social contexts that people use as heuristics, or intuitive models for making sense of politics, and why they change. To this end, my aim in this section is to show how people who *did* use pre-1980s public life as a heuristic for making sense of politics reasoned and ultimately why they tended to establish firm but moderate partisan identifications.[49] I do not mean to imply by this that these residents used *only* pre-1980s community cleavages to make sense of politics or that there was a one-to-one correspondence between people's use of community heuristics and their eventual vote decisions. Nevertheless, I do think it reasonable to conclude that as pre-1980s community cleavages disappeared, so too did people's tendency to use them as a heuristic for making sense of politics, and make this argument more formally in chapter 8 and the Methodological Appendix.[50]

A Politics of *Sides*

Reflect for a moment on all of the ways in which pre-1980s public struggles once interpenetrated residents' daily lives. To the eyes of older Prairievillers

and River Citians, a person's form of earning a living, their forbearers' occupations, their white-ethnic lineage, their civic engagement, and even
their neighborhood identified them as a natural ally of union or business
leaders. For traditional voters, these identifiers were simultaneously political. To them, a blue-collar job was Democratic and a white-collar one was
Republican, the food bank was Democratic and the symphony board was
Republican, the "bluffs" Republican and the "flats" Democratic, and so on.
Traditional voters' defining feature was an ability to establish such connections between daily life and national politics and, thereby, stable political
preferences.

One such respondent was Gil, in his seventies and a former middle
manager in one of River City's locally owned firms. We talked first about
local history and 1980s-era plant closings came up. "I felt bad for the people working at the factories because they were losing their jobs," Gil said.
"There were lots of people with just high school going to work at Green's.
And in the first year they were making more money than me, a college
graduate," he added, expressing a resentment I heard often from older
business-oriented River Citians. "A lot of that was that unions were strong.
It was just, 'This is what our members want. We better get it!' And look at
where that got them. So there was a lot of resentment [toward unions] but
it was sad too, because a lot of 'em had houses and mortgages and then
suddenly were without a job."

Later, our conversation turned to national politics. "And it is like [the
situation at Green's] with the Democrats," Gil said, spontaneously making
a community-politics connection. "The Democrats, their constituents are
poor, whereas the Republicans, they do represent the people with a little
more money. But I think the Democrats misrepresent [the poor]. Look at
all these years of the welfare state; it does not seem to have done anybody
any good. We still got a lot of poor people, so I think it is money not being
spent wisely. The Republicans are more middle of the road, for less government and for controlling spending, not trying to change the equation or
even it out, but to smooth the way for people working hard."

Note that Gil seamlessly grafted national political debates onto community narratives about River City's "blue-collar element." Political scientists refer to this type of reasoning as the use of a political heuristic: use
of an intuitively familiar aspect of daily life to make sense of otherwise
unfamiliar national political realities.[51] To Gil, it seemed self-evident that
public life is a contest between two types of actors: those working for themselves, and those like unions who coerce others into giving them a hand-
out. Gil reasoned about politics as a member of the former category, blam-

ing the latter for preventing River City's "progress." Because the Democrats were more union-like and the Republicans more like those working hard for themselves, Gil felt Republican. Of course, Gil's ability to establish this community-politics link required distortion of the facts, especially at the level of national politics: by the 2000s welfare hardly existed as an extensive federal program and many Democrats were as pro-market in their rhetoric as Republicans. Late into the Bush presidency, Republicans also had a disastrous record of controlling spending. But these errors were unimportant, because Gil's way of reasoning about politics was intuitive and local, not policy oriented and national. He first established affinity for an intuitively comprehensible community division, then projected this distinction onto a plausible set of national actors.[52]

Naturally, traditional voters sometimes identified instead with their city's blue-collar, Democratic side. One example was Shirley, a Prairieviller in her seventies. "There are not as many unions now as when I was growing up and that is not good," Shirley told me. "I was in a union twenty years and worked as a steward for ten, and that did us a lot of good. I think it was good for [Prairieville] too, because the unions were for the working person. We've seen the time when we could have got a lot more industry in here," Shirley added, referring to the sad state of Prairieville's economy. "[But] the city would not let it come in. I don't know why that is or who it was exactly. Maybe [they did not let new firms in] because their wages were higher. [So] it helped people that the unions were here and I think the people, they realized this. The unions were looking out for everybody."

"I'm all for unions and probably will be till I die I suppose. I'm a lifelong Democrat, too, because I think the Democrats are more for the working people," Shirley added, hardly missing a beat. "The Democrats are looking out for the working person first. The rich people try to get by without the taxes, but some people just got too much: got their TV, got their this, got their that, they don't need to have somebody looking out for them so that they get more. When we grew up, we played cards, bunch of us would get together, take turns, any holiday that come up the whole family would get together, we celebrated it, all got campers, go down to the lake, spend time down there, all eat together. The Democrats are more for that idea. Seems like you don't see that anymore. Now everybody has one of everything all their own. Isn't that a dirty shame?"

Although Shirley identified with different sides in the struggle, she understood public life similarly to Gil: as a contest between blue-collar union leaders who Shirley sees as "looking out for everybody" and an unknown force—the city or the "powers that be"—that prevented growth for their own selfish reasons. Shirley took this basic opposition deeper into her personal life, contrasting collective family leisure, which is more union-like, with individualized consumption, which is "selfish" and less union-like. She then projected this localized distinction onto national politics and identified with working-class, collectivist Democrats over selfish Republicans. Here again, details of national political policy were unimportant; in fact, Shirley mentioned no policy details when justifying her political preferences in her own words.[53]

Many traditional respondents like Shirley and Gil were able to establish political preferences with virtually no political knowledge.[54] Consider the case of John, a former meatpacker in River City, and Patsy, a homemaker in Prairieville. Both were in their eighties. I spoke with over one hundred voters, and John and Patsy were by far the most politically disinterested and uninformed. For instance, neither could recall that Kerry had been the Democratic nominee just three years after the 2004 election despite Iowa's around-the-clock political advertisements. Nevertheless, both expressed consistent partisan preferences during the three interviews that I conducted with them and both voted in 2008: John Democratic, and Patsy Republican.

"I always been my own way, did what I wanted to do—and I'm not too much into the politics. I vote maybe once a year, vote for president and then think, 'The hell with the rest of them,'" John said. "But if I do vote, I always vote Democrat, because, well let's see . . ." he paused, composing his thoughts. "When the Democrats are in, they had jobs for the people, but when the Republicans got in, they kind of took 'em out. This is the only way I can think of wordin' it: it's like with a union. Like, you better vote for this guy, because if you don't vote for this guy you ain't gonna get what you want. That's the only way I can think of putting it into words for you. That's what I think of a Republican versus a Democrat."

"A friend of mine used to do accounting [for a factory] and there were people there making $20 an hour just to sweep the floor," Patsy told me, working up to justifying her GOP preference. "Half the time they were just sitting there! People used to say it was hard to get a good paying job around here *with* a college degree! I feel like the Republicans want to create jobs and make it easier to for people trying to make it for themselves. The Democrats try to help a bunch of little groups who don't want to work hard and they do that to get their votes."

Traditional voters typically established strong partisan identifications, but also occasionally expressed political ambivalence. One exemplar of this tendency was Dan, a fifty-something River Citian who identified as an

Independent. "I work in a plant nearby here and for ten and a half years I was in the union—so then I was Democratic," Dan told me. "Then I got the management job and over time it has gotten to where I agree with the Republicans over the Democrats a lot of the time. There is a lot of good on both sides. Both parties are trying to do what is the best, [but do] it in different ways. Like they always say, the Republicans are for the rich and business and the Democrats are more for the working man and the wage earner. Well, we need both. You have to try to balance that before deciding which side to give your vote to."

Although Dan did not identify strongly with one side in his community's traditional conflicts, he accepted that community life and politics should be animated by conflict between two sides in principle. Therefore, his Independent position in no way implied a lack faith in the legitimacy of America's political system, as it often did among the partners that I discuss in later chapters. In fact, just the opposite: Dan saw *both* parties are trying to "do what is best." While most traditional voters did not necessarily attribute positive motives to both parties, the belief that America's political system was structured in a reasonable way and functioned more or less as it should was widespread. Like traditional leaders, traditional voters understood political engagement as a zero-sum game animated by norms of gift and reciprocal obligation: to participate in politics is to support one's side by voting, thus putting one's side under obligation to support people like oneself. Recall John's statement, which I quoted above: "[Politics] is like with a union. Like, you better vote for this guy, because if you don't vote for this guy you ain't gonna get what you want. That's the only way I can think of putting it into words for you."

It is easy to find fault with traditional voters like these. American political culture is characterized by the deeply held belief that political preferences should be based in carefully reasoned public policy positions. Relative to this ideal, traditional voters lack political sophistication; indeed, their preferences have little to do with policy at all. River City's and Prairieville's partners often criticized traditional voters along these lines: "they'd vote for a shoe if the shoe had the right party label." I will discuss the normative implications of River City's and Prairieville's public transformation more fully in the book's conclusion, but I think it important to foreshadow these concluding remarks by drawing attention to two features of Keynesian-era politics: voters' tendency to establish consistent preferences and to view community and partisan struggles as parts of a common political conflict.

As I argued in the book's introduction, there is nothing noteworthy about traditional voters' political ignorance or their use of political heuristics. Political scientists have always found that the vast majority of people lack a good grasp of political facts and make political decisions emotionally, due to appeals to group solidarity, and in other ways that depart from philosophers' democratic ideals.[55] Because this basic state of affairs will probably never change, the tradeoff is not between voters educated in the minutia of public policy and those who use heuristics as mental shortcuts to make sense of politics. Rather, the possible tradeoff is one between voters who use different types of heuristics.[56] In this light, traditional voters' method of reasoning about politics promoted meaningful democratic participation *because* it gave them a way to reason about politics in the absence of political information. As a heuristics, pre-1980s community life was a good one, because it gave people a reliable way of connecting what they did know (i.e., affinities for a community side) with what they did not (i.e., public policy debates). Traditional voters' heuristic was an inexact political lens, but nevertheless one that—I think—gave them a better than random chance of supporting candidates that pursued policies favorable to the community side that championed their economic and social interests.

Moreover, and along similar lines, the distinctive feature of the Keynesian-era public sphere was its ability to communicate an underlying reality about policymaking: that politics is often a zero-sum game, which benefits some people more than others. That River City's and Prairieville's public institutions communicated this fact to residents is unsurprising, because Keynesian-era policymakers operated a "banker government" that passed on discretion over broad policy priorities onto local bodies, thus making community leaders—and, by extension, their supporters—co-participants in the federal state.[57] As low-level co-participants in the state, traditional voters overwhelmingly viewed the organization of their political system as legitimate. "Being a teacher, I'm definitely a Democrat, so that's my stand on that," Terry, a forty-something River Citian told me, before expressing a basic faith in the rules of the political game. "And as much as I hate Bush, I do feel like both parties also have a responsibility to the citizens they represent. The Democrats try to represent the middle class, keep an eye out for them. And I've always thought that the Republicans represent money, they represent the upper class. The two parties are very important, because we have to make sure we don't have like a monarchy—just a government that is run solely by one group of people."

But government by one group of people, or rather a politics without sides, is precisely what the partners who came to dominate River City's and Prairieville's public sphere want. To them, public life is synonymous with partnerships, or flexible and shifting coalitions that require participants to set politics aside and focus on win-win initiatives. Partners looked to party politics and recoiled from what looked to them like an old-style factional conflict, which paradoxically left grassroots parties in the hands of issue-activists who pushed America's political system toward the extremes. In the second part of the book, I now turn to 1970s- and '80s-era neoliberal reforms, their connection to the public ascendancy of Prairieville's and River City's partners, and the many consequences of partners' stewardship over public life.

PART TWO

Neoliberalism

FOUR

The Political Construction of Partnership

In the second part of the book, I shift focus to 1980s-era changes in River City's and Prairieville's public sphere, for it was during that decade that the lions of labor and the old families—long the sole players on their cities' central stage—moved to the periphery of public life. Now, a new kind of leader was found at the center of any successful initiative: the partner. The contours of my argument emerged soon after I began research, because River City's and Prairieville's leaders had strong intuitions about the origins and consequences of partnership. They insisted that partnerships were necessary for the place-marketing initiatives that became central to public life during the 1980s and viewed leaders who spearheaded such initiatives—Prairieville's Dani Dover and River City's Ben Denison—as their cities' most important and perfect partners. They further argued that key difference between traditional leaders and partners revolved around styles of public engagement. Traditional leaders participated in public life by giving gifts or receiving them, an act that factionalized the community into opposing networks maintained by largesse and reciprocal obligation. By contrast, the ideal-typical partner neither gives gifts nor receives them; instead, she builds partnerships around win-win initiatives supported by all parties, an act that creates an unfactionalized public space ripe for future partnerships.[1] Partners insisted that the disposition required to create such partnerships clashed with partisan political displays and viewed their city's parties as foreign and ungovernable.

The second part of this book develops these arguments, substantiates them with historical records, and situates them against the backdrop of bigger changes in American federalism and party politics. That is, I show that 1970s- and '80s-era federal reforms transformed community leaders' public world, their political orientation, and ultimately their role in American partisan politics. This chapter focuses on the structural opportunities created by neoliberal reforms: I show how these reforms changed community leaders' ability to leverage outside resources, thereby transforming the arena in which they play their public game and creating an opportunity for partners to rise in public life. Chapters 5 and 6 then delve into the details of Prairieville's and River City's post-1980s public game, detailing how partners actually sidelined their city's traditional leaders and exploring the dispositions that enhance and handicap particular partners' ability to rise in public prominence—particularly partisan political displays, which partners see as incompatible with their public personae. Chapters 7, 8, and 9 then analyze political consequences, which I categorize as *politics disembedded from community governance*. Partners' activities reorganize the city's public sphere into a conflict between community-oriented partners and politically oriented partisans, which breeds confusion among citizens, polarizes activists, and promotes the divisive politics that so horrifies partners.

Central to these arguments is the public persona of partners: the qualities, dispositions, and presentations of self that they view as useful and praiseworthy among those in positions of public leadership. In focusing on what can be summarized as community leaders' public culture, I aim to underscore that community leaders did not simply respond instrumentally to new constraints and opportunities presented by 1970s and '80s-era reforms. Rather, these reforms transformed community leaders' social world, upending existing status hierarchies and changing leaders' sense of public self. By this I do not mean to imply that community leaders' public culture is a coherent belief system imposed from above, which—like a religious doctrine or political manifesto—provides a guide to thought and action. My analysis runs counter to academic criticisms of "neoliberal" urbanism, which portray community leaders as ideologically opposed to federal social programs, union-friendly policies, and putative corporate regulations, in part because I found some partners to be privately supportive of policies ranging from the libertarian to nostalgia for New Deal–style union protections, regulations, and social programs.[2] Their overarching commonality was only an agreement to set politics aside in public. By *public culture*, then, I mean sometimes akin to sociologist Pierre Bourdieu's notion of *habitus*: an embodied practical reason or a commonsense predisposition for certain types of mundane judgments of propriety and utility that allowed partners to seamlessly form relationships and coordinate their activities, and generally gave them a "feel for the game."[3] To put the matter simply, the 1980s changed what it meant to be a community leader.

For River City's and Prairieville's partners, nothing was more interesting than this public transformation. I often had the impression that partners wanted to talk of little else but the 1980s, their own ascent, and the tacit rules and norms that regulated their exercise of public authority, and then at length and with an attention to detail that reminded me of accounts I had read of Nuer herdsmen discussing cattle or Trobriand Islanders discussing the Kula trade: for partners, partnership was a matter of personal identity, a means of achieving other goals, and an end in itself.[4] Partners meticulously dissected the dispositions of their successful peers, often by contrasting partner-like qualities with those of traditional leaders, and thereby evaluating their own behavior and that of others along a continuum between traditional and partner-like poles.

For instance, partners associated flexibility with their own kind and viewed traditional leaders as pathologically rigid, a distinction they sometimes illustrated with age metaphors. Traditional leaders were old, stuck in their ways, and incapable of change, whereas partners saw themselves as youthful, although those who said this were quick to add that youthful action is unrelated to chronological age. Rather, partners laid claim to a particular version of youthful adolescence: not to broodiness and antisocial tendencies, but to a bravado that borders on arrogance, to not knowing one's limits, to a belief—naive perhaps—that anything is possible. For similar reasons, partners identified with entrepreneurs, especially early Silicon Valley entrepreneurs who threw caution to the wind and just went for it.

To the trained eye of a partner, signs of partnership were equally apparent in one's personal biography. Traditional leaders were parochial, whereas partners were cosmopolitan, a quality that they believed gave them the wisdom to see that some differences are unbridgeable and best avoided. In truth, partners were more likely than traditional leaders to have lived outside River City and Prairieville, but even those who had not identified with symbols of worldliness. "I'm sure you understand, you probably speak a foreign language," one lifelong resident of River City told me after an extended tirade about traditional leaders' intransigence. From this assumed worldliness, a number of optional tastes followed: a passion for travel, even if just to Chicago but ideally to a foreign country, an interest in exotic food or drink, a distaste for overstuffed couches, woolly carpets, pastel curtains, and other types of traditional Midwestern décor.

Partners saw worldliness as intertwined with another characteristic that they associated with themselves: education. To them, traditional leaders were a "bunch of hicks in the sticks," even though many key partners— union leaders who partner, for example—lacked formal education. By contrast, many traditional business leaders held elite credentials like degrees from big-name universities. But for partners, education was about one's capacity to transcend local tradition and adopt an outsider's perspective, not credentials. Many a partner expressed a penchant for scholarly or pseudo-scholarly pursuits like ancient history, studying a foreign language, or simply a passion for National Public Radio or public television. This belief in education was sometimes expressed via a second age metaphor: little kids and adults. Traditional leaders, partners believed, were like little kids who are petulant and fought over the smallest provocation, whereas partners saw themselves as capable of taking a measured step back, reflecting, and then seeking consensus.

In personal comportment, partners' appearance was always a bit unconventional, unexpected, or off. They mocked the three-piece suits and country club weekends of the old families. Male partners avoided ties on all but the most formal occasions, while women preferred pantsuits—perhaps decorated by a single, idiosyncratic broach—to the dresses and heavy makeup worn by traditional women leaders. Upon spending more time with a partner, one was sure to notice a pair of sneakers worn with a suit, a joke that was just too sarcastic, an admission for a secret penchant for unrefined pleasures like cheap beer, fast food, online fantasy games, or an embarrassing 1980s band. Such apparent lapses from a partner's ideal presentation of self were part of the performance and signaled that the partner was just a regular person, did not take herself too seriously, and was open to working with anyone on anything.

Partners were doggedly nonpartisan in their self-presentation and viewed traditional leaders as politics-drunk, frothing-at-the-mouth fanatics. Yet they did identify with certain social causes, particularly the civil rights movement and other movements for racial, gender, and sexual orientation inclusion. This orientation meshed with partners' belief that public engagement should consist of inclusive, broad-based coalitions. But partners' actual record on inclusion was mixed. Women were more represented among their ranks than among traditional leaders, and some male partners joked that women's alleged lack of ego and superior interpersonal skills make them more adept at building partnerships. Partners also strove to include historically disadvantaged racial and ethnic leaders in their initiatives. But on the flip side, partners' propensity for avoiding divisive issues had historically made them more reluctant than some traditional leaders to support early calls for racial or sexual orientation equality.

Beyond these characteristics, which partners adopted selectively as a performance of their own capacity for partnership, some leaders attached relatively idiosyncratic significances to partnership. A handful of female partners, for example, likened traditional leaders to star-crossed but uncommitted lovers who are ready to split up at the slightest provocation. By contrast, they argued that partnership is like a marriage: a commitment to building a long-term relationship by setting divisive issues aside. Conversely, virtually all partners shared some beliefs in common. All partners saw traditional leaders as conflict-prone, cliquish, and ineffective; among partners, the term "divisive" was a universal term of derision and universally indexed their city's traditional leadership class. By contrast, all partners equated partnership with inclusion and saw it as necessary in a post-1980s context. Partnership was a "well-oiled machine," or some other functional analogy, that kept their cities from returning to a state of economic and social collapse. But for this to occur, a differently organized public life was necessary, and this belief was reflected in perhaps the most common partnership metaphor of all: the big round table. Traditional leaders sat across the table and fought, but partners sit around the table, set divisive issues aside, and work together to find solutions that would work well for everyone. This effort, partners believed, was their city's sole saving grace.

"[Many] of the old families that were pillars in the community have transitioned out of the area," a popular partner in Prairieville told me. "What is good about it is that we have seen new leaders emerge. Like Dani Dover, I'm sure you've heard that name. [These leaders bring] new ideas: 'Look at all of us. All of us are at the table.' Some in the business community have not made that 'ah ha!' yet, because for a long time there was no big round table; those family businesses made the decisions so it was more sitting around and waiting for initiatives to come down from. [Now] the seats around the table are being populated differently. It is sharing ideas for making the community better."

My aim in this chapter is to specify why qualities like flexibility, youthfulness, entrepreneurialism, cosmopolitanism, a disregard for local tradition, distaste for factional loyalty, nonpartisanship, and technical virtuosity suddenly began to "work" for partners during the 1980s.[5] This question brings me first to the period's neoliberal reforms and an analysis of how they transformed the arena in which community leaders play their public game. Reforms in federal bureaucracies charged with regulating the financial sector and allocating social service and urban funding altered the supply of key economic, civic, and political resources. Before the 1980s these resources fell under the jurisdiction of local commissions, but after the 1980s they were dispersed among various public, private, and nonprofit institutions outside of the city. Community leaders' capacity for public action therefore became dependent on their ability to market initiatives to outsiders, which I show that River City's and Prairieville's leaders began doing within "big tent" development organizations. I conclude by examining several successful initiatives orchestrated within these big tents, showing how community leaders' willingness to adopt an undivisive and flexible presentation of public self allowed them to assemble coalitions that leveraged outside resources by presenting the city as different things to different audiences.

Readers immersed in contemporary urban scholarship should find aspects of my argument familiar, particularly my analysis of the causal connection between changes in American federalism and urban partnerships. For example, urban theorist David Harvey also identifies the 1980s with a reorientation of urban governance toward entrepreneurial partnerships, or "public-private [collaborations] in which traditional local boosterism is integrated with the use of local government powers to try and attract external sources of funding, new direct investment, or new employment opportunities."[6]

My argument is somewhat different because I argue that partnerships allow leaders to successfully market their cities by strategically presenting them as different things to different consequential outsiders, not merely by allowing leaders to blend private- and public-sector resources.[7] But more significantly, I depart from mainstream urban scholarship primarily in my analysis of community leaders' public culture, which urbanists typically treat as nonexistent, a reflection of neoliberal policymakers' priorities, or as a sort of opiate of the masses that reflects community leaders' economic interests.[8] By contrast, I analyze the cultural logic of community leaders' public activities by further extending the anthropological metaphor of game-play: community leaders exert disproportionate influence over public institutions, but are simultaneously constrained by one another's understandings of proper and praiseworthy public action.[9] For example, traditional leaders' public culture of gift and reciprocal obligation constrained rich and poor alike. The owner of Valley Beef was Prairieville's richest man and could have given more generously than most, but he refused to play the generosity game and became a pariah without public influence.[10] Similarly, partnership is central to a public world that is far more complex than a simple reflection of community leaders' economic interests. Traditional leaders did not simply wake up one morning, take a hard look at 1980s-era reforms, and jointly elect to form partnerships so as to protect their assets. Indeed, many of them never embraced partnership and bowed out of public life instead. Rather, 1970s- and '80s-era reforms changed the arena in which leaders jockey for public esteem. This new system of structural constraints and opportunities co-evolved with a new public game defined by nuanced rules of praiseworthy and profane behavior, which led partners to engage one another in particular ways with unintended consequences— notably, their withdrawal from party politics and the subsequent polarization of America's political system.

How Neoliberal Reforms Changed the Rules of Community Leaders' Public Game

Social scientists of various stripes characterize the late 1970s and early 1980s as a turning point in American political economy. Political scientists often identify the period with the beginnings of rising economic inequality in the United States or even a "New Gilded Age"—trends that they alternatively attribute to the post-1972 successes of Republican politicians and a rightward shift among politicians in both parties.[11] For others, the 1970s represents a shift in the way that Republican and Democratic policymakers discuss and address social problems. For instance, historian Daniel Rodgers argues that politicians abandoned "institutional realism" during the 1970s: an understanding of society as thick with "context, social circumstance, institutions, and history," which suggested the need for active tinkering by political leaders.[12] Recall, for instance, that leading economic textbooks during the Keynesian era discussed macroeconomics before microeconomics because policy experts presumed that state intervention provided the stabilizing conditions necessary for the microeconomic price system to work.[13] But after the 1970s, policymakers and experts increasingly viewed society as akin to a self-regulating market and worried that political programs would do more harm than good.[14] Like sociologists and urban geographers, I equate the 1970s and '80s with the beginnings of neoliberalism, a term I also employ as shorthand for common policy logics that supported reforms in three federal policy domains that have a disproportionate impact on community leaders: financial regulation, urban funding, and social service provision.

Before wading into the details of federal policy reforms, I think it instructive to identify neoliberal reforms' common threads, particularly where my discussion diverges from common narratives about the 1980s. Popular commentators and academics alike often present the 1980s as a period when right-wing politicians aggressively slashed social programs and deregulated various economic sectors. The reforms of the period are, according to this narrative, first a creature of the political right and second pro-market and anti-state in orientation—a revamped laissez-faire Liberalism akin to that of the nineteenth century. Observers often lump in contemporaneous trends like militarism or the war on drugs under the neoliberalism rubric, too, such that the term means—roughly—bad things that Reagan, Thatcher, and other right-wingers started in the 1980s. This tendency to equate neoliberalism with radical right-wingers is understandable because politicians on the right were often vocal supporters of deregulation and public sector rollback during the 1980s. Consider Ronald Reagan's famous pronouncement: "Government is not the solution to our problems; government is the problem." But my account departs from this common neoliberal narrative in two respects: I argue that support for neoliberal reforms came from both Democrats and Republicans and that these reforms did not reduce the federal government's fiscal or regulatory power over localities but rather transformed the nature of American federalism.[15] These points are important and worth emphasizing.

First, Keynesianism fell out of fashion and neoliberal ideas gained currency in policy circles on both the left and right during the 1970s, impacting Democratic and Republican politicians alike. Historian Phillip Mirowski traces the intellectual roots of neoliberal reforms to conservative debating societies (notably, the Mont Pelerin Society), policy journals, and think-tanks, which were populated by opponents of the New Deal who were then outside of the political mainstream: economists, historians, and other intellectuals as well as the "Texas oil millionaires" and "the occasional politician or business man" whom Dwight Eisenhower had dismissed as numerically "negligible" and "stupid."[16] Such organizations proliferated during the postwar period and ultimately found a new platform for their ideas with the emergence of broad-based business lobby groups in the 1970s, which advocated for cross-sector business-friendly policies rather than pursuing industry-specific legislation as they had traditionally.[17] During the 1970s policymakers were receptive to these organized challenges to New Deal–style statecraft because the economic malaise of the period contradicted key Keynesian assumptions like the mutual exclusivity of rising inflation and unemployment, thus shaking politicians' faith in their ability to steer the economy. None of the economic experts seemed to know "why [the models] misfired," and policymakers were on the lookout for new ideas.[18] In this context, neoliberal ideas, proposals, and metaphors slipped across political divides, becoming a policy fad among politicians across the political spectrum as well as the experts who advised them.[19] For instance, those who advocated for reforms of financial sector regulations included Republicans, Democratic insiders like Jimmy Carter and Senator Ted Kennedy, and even populist left-wing groups like Ralph

Nader's Consumer Protection Agency, which argued that regulation promoted overly cozy industry-government relations, bureaucratic mistakes, and corruption, and generally favored the wealthy.[20]

But while many 1970s-era reformers made laissez-faire-like calls for rollback of state intervention in the economy, their actual policies did not shrink the federal government or limit its influence. Early opponents of the New Deal were particularly influenced by Friedrich Hayek, who glorified markets as both less coercive than political bureaucracies (and hence morally superior) and as uniquely suited to incorporating information about the full range of human desires (and hence more economically efficient than political bureaucracies).[21] Those influenced by thinkers like Hayek therefore held up market society as a superordinate value, but argued that it could only arise through state intervention—following Hayek, through "planning for competition."[22] When think-tanks and journals influenced by this viewpoint began issuing policy prescriptions, they advocated for elaborate market-like bureaucracies to correct market failures (e.g., markets for pollution credits), legal supports for corporate activities, and various kinds of mechanisms that insulate market-competition from democratic interference (e.g., auditing and accountability devices, new forms of public management, subcontracting schemes, reliance on services from quasi-private organizations like credit-rating agencies).[23] And indeed, 1970s- and '80s-era reforms typically expanded the state. Political scientist Jonah Levy has analyzed myriad reforms of health care, education, and utilities, and shown that even those reforms that proponents championed via laissez-faire rhetoric increased public expenditures.[24]

To put the matter simply, neoliberalism is an ideology of statecraft, not an economic doctrine that seeks to limit the influence of the state.[25] Neoliberal reformers' overriding commonality was a preference for impersonal, market-like systems of resource allocation—whether in the public or private sector—as preferable to planning via public bureaucracies. They viewed this ideological stance as consistent with three types of reforms: some that actually rolled back public sector expenditure, but also those that made systems of federal funding allocation accountable, competitive, and generally market-like, and those that devolved funding and responsibility over federal programs to states and nonprofits (which often spent a portion of these monies and also converted those they did pass on into competitive, narrowly defined grants).[26] But despite their varied nature, neoliberal reforms had one common feature: they replaced Keynesian policies that had once localized control over consequential economic, civic, and political resources, and thereby undermined local leaders' ability to shape their communities without appealing to outsiders. Consider the effects of these reforms on community leaders' ability to leverage economic, civic, and political resources.

Financial Deregulation and Community Leaders' Economic Game

The defining features of America's Keynesian-era financial system were regulation and compartmentalization, which subdivided financial activities like commercial lending, investment banking, and mortgage origination into different institutions and restricted banks' ability to establish branches in different states. From the viewpoint of America's largest corporations, this system was "credit scarce" and firms responded by holding onto their profits and investing them in their own divisions.[27] Relative to contemporary corporations, Keynesian-era ones infrequently purchased other firms, because they lacked the capital and due to the era's more stringent anti-merger policies. River City's and Prairieville's urban economies were the result and consisted largely of locally owned firms and corporate subsidiaries like Greenfield's, which had parent companies that managed conservatively to create an uninterrupted, predictable income stream.[28] From traditional leaders' perspective, their city's economic landscape appeared rooted in place and their economic game consisted of efforts to monopolize local industries' profits and redistribute them to supporters.

But by the 1970s federal financial regulations showed signs of strain. Interest rate controls were insufficient to prevent inflation during the 1970s and periodically kicked in, shutting off the supply of credit to willing borrowers, particularly would-be homebuyers.[29] Such regulatory interventions were doubly burdensome for lower- and middle-income borrowers, because other federal regulations capped the interest that financial institutions could pay on savings accounts at *below* the rate of inflation, meaning that would-be borrowers' savings depreciated as they awaited mortgages. Populist consumers' rights advocates like Ralph Nader and seniors' groups lobbied Congress for deregulation, which responded with bipartisan bills that loosened financial sector subdivisions.[30] Saving and loans, which had previously been restricted to originating and servicing mortgages, could now offer savers higher interest rates and use additional capital thus levied to make speculative investments. Congress also loosened rules surrounding 401(k) accounts, allowing middle-class workers to invest their savings in mutual funds. People's savings flowed into an expanding financial sector, allowing firms to finance their operations by issuing stocks or bonds—provided, of course, that investors were willing to buy them.[31]

Sociologist Neil Fligstein argues that 1980s-era financial sector expansion and deregulation coincided with a new corporate ethos: the shareholder-value conception of the firm.[32] Managers who embraced this ethos ceased trying to self-finance their operations and reorganized their firms to appeal to investors. The chief operating officer, who manages the operations of different divisions, was eclipsed in importance by the chief financial officer, and managers generally pursued aggressive layoffs to signal dynamism to investors.[33] Moreover, managers realized that they could make profits by buying and selling other firms and looked to their traditional suppliers, distributors, and competitors as "bundles of assets" to be acquired and managed directly, resold, or liquidated.[34] The twentieth century's largest corporate merger wave followed. By the mid-1980s firms acquired their suppliers and distributors six times as frequently, and their competitors four times as frequently, as they had during the 1970s.[35]

The corporate mergers of the 1980s were particularly concentrated in America's manufacturing sector, which was struggling after a decade of sclerotic profits. Manufacturers' malaise stemmed partially from 1970s oil shocks and competition from the developing world, but financial deregulation turned these problems into a full-blown crisis. As investors borrowed to take advantage of new financial opportunities, interest rates soared and fluctuated erratically, a particular problem for manufacturers who buy inputs on credit and were unable to make profits in a high interest-rate regime.[36] As a manufacturing crisis swept across the Rust Belt, financially savvy corporate managers saw opportunity in locally owned and under-capitalized firms like those that anchored Prairieville's and River City's economy: these firms held valuable assets, but their cash on hand and ability to resist takeovers was low.[37]

It is for this reason that Prairieville's and River City's history during the 1980s was one of corporate acquisitions and layoffs. Indeed, outside acquisitions only slowed in the late 1990s because by then all but the most stubborn of local owners had sold or lost their firms. In the 1970s all but a handful of Prairieville's and River City's largest employers were owned locally, but table 4.1 shows that by the time my fieldwork began in the mid-2000s, most of old family businesses were gone. Concurrently, corporate subsidiaries like Greenfield's responded to crisis conditions by scaling back operations to maintain cash-on-hand in case of takeover attempts; River City's plant laid off 3,000 workers in 1980s, which—along

Table 4.1. River City Prairieville's largest private-sector employers (2005)

	River City			Prairieville	
Company	Employees	Ownership	Company	Employees	Ownership
1. Greenfields Manu	1,000–2,500	Nonlocal	1. Food processing	2,500+	Nonlocal
2. Call center	500–1,000	Nonlocal	2. Manufacturing	2,500+	Nonlocal
3. Manufacturer	500–1,000	Local	3. Packing house	1,000–2,500	Nonlocal
4. Power company	500–1,000	Nonlocal	4. Power company	1,000–2,500	Nonlocal
5. Manufacturer	500–1,000	Nonlocal	5. Manufacturer	500–1,000	Local
6. Manufacturer	500–1,000	Local	6. Construction	500–1,000	Local
7. Casino	250–500	Nonlocal	7. Manufacturer	250–500	Local
8. Hawkeye Manu	250–500	Nonlocal	8. Warehousing	250–500	Local
9. Wholesaler	250–500	Local	9. Food processing	250–500	Nonlocal
10. Manufacturer	250–500	Nonlocal	10. Casino	250–500	Local
11. Transport	250–500	Nonlocal	11. Construction	250–500	Local
12. Transport	100–250	Nonlocal	12. Call center	250–500	Nonlocal
13. Wholesaler	100–250	Local	13. Construction	250–500	Local
14. Manufacturer	100–250	Local	14. Manufacturer	250–500	Nonlocal
15. Manufacturer	100–250	Nonlocal	15. Manufacturer	100–250	Local

Source: Dun's Million Dollar Directory and local chamber of commerce records. Educational institutions and professional service firms were not systematically included in *Dun's* business directory and are not included.

with bankruptcies and cutbacks of smaller locally owned firms—brought the city's unemployment rate to 25 percent. Most River Citians who were alive in 1982 had a story about it. "I was married at the time with two small children," the ex-wife of a Greenfield's worker told me. "Everyone use to call it 'Black Friday' because one Friday afternoon just before Christmas our husbands did not come home [because they were discussing layoffs at a union meeting]. They had a cutoff date—everyone hired after the date goes, anybody hired before can stay. It was everywhere constantly. My daughter's orthodontist—he was in practice with three others and all three of them left town—things like that everywhere. To tell you the truth, I did not think River City would ever recover."

The merger waves of the 1980s changed community leaders' local game by, first, thinning the ranks of its traditional players. With each corporate buyout, Prairieville and River City lost an old family, as many former owners left town to retire in sunnier locales while others scaled back their public engagement. The layoffs that frequently followed acquisitions also hobbled unions, which could no longer afford to pay full-time representatives; recall that in River City, the number of official union representatives fell from over 150 to under 40 during the 1980s. Moreover, those traditional leaders who remained could no longer take the "localness" of their city's economy for granted. Every time that the union of a corporate subsidiary went on strike, for instance, it risked driving that employer from the city. Increasingly, remaining leaders saw the fate of their city—and indeed, often their own existence as public figures—as synonymous with their ability to attract and retain outside corporations. Their super-ordinate economic problem became marketing the city.

Nonprofit Funding Reform and Community Leaders' Civic Game

In pre-1980s Prairieville and River City, traditional leaders exercised discretion over the lion's share of local and federal social service funding. But in the Rust Belt especially, 1980s economic crises disrupted this system of charity. Corporate buyouts and mergers thinned the ranks of local business owners and well-paid union members alike, thus reducing the supply of local charity.[38] Rampant unemployment also strained existing services, creating cutthroat competition for existing federal grants. "It was worse than we ever imagined it could be," a nonprofit worker in River City remembered. "I used to sit in the office and deal with personal catastrophe after personal catastrophe. People lost their jobs and their homes. People that had been making 20 dollars an hour at Green's were on food stamps. Social workers, young women who ran agencies and were lunch friends, were fighting over grants to keep their projects going."

River City's and Prairieville's leaders struggled for social service funding against the backdrop of ongoing federal reforms, which—unlike other neoliberal reforms—were almost exclusively a product of the political right. The Reagan administration particularly viewed federal bureaucracies' discretion over social service funding as synonymous with top-down authoritarianism and outlined a New Federalism policy to return autonomy to local charities.[39] New Federalism had two planks: downscaling of nonprofit funding to states and the allocation of remaining federal funding via market-like mechanisms.

During the 1980s, federal bureaucracies downscaled both responsibility and funding over social service priorities to states. Congress first phased out discretionary federal programs like Title IV-A of the Social Security Act and slashed social service block grants. But conversely, social service transfers to states nearly doubled during the 1980s.[40] Advocates of downscaling argued that it would increase autonomy and accountability, because state bureaucrats were closer to the people and could make better decisions than their counterparts in DC.[41] In reality, state bureaucrats simply spent federal monies on their own priorities, causing a sharp reduction in funding for many local nonprofits.[42] Moreover, state grants proved qualitatively different from federal grants: whereas the latter were large and broadly defined, state grants tended to be small, narrowly defined, and competitive. Community leaders scrambled for the same federal funding as before, but this money was now delivered to them via intermediaries in small pieces; they now needed to cobble together multiple grants to pursue a significant initiative.

New Federalism had a similar effect on social service funding that remained nominally federal. Such funding had once flowed directly from federal bureaucracies to local nonprofits, which they believed to be capable stewards of the public interest.[43] By contrast, the Reagan administration supported bills that apportion funding to pools that are open to competition from for-profit providers, government agencies, and other nonprofits.[44] This created increased competition for service contracts, increased the importance of outcome metrics, and coincided with the emergence of another competitor for scarce nonprofit funding: middle-men foundations. Sociologist Emily Barman, for example, argues that some United Ways began to act as private foundations that monitor the philanthropic activities of other nonprofits and specialize in convincing federal funders and private individuals that they can more effectively invest their charitable dollars.[45] From community leaders' perspective, obtaining federal funding had once been a relatively straightforward matter of submitting an application to the right local body or federal agency, but afterwards they found themselves scrambling to demonstrate that they could perform tasks—reduce teen pregnancy, provide job training, and the like—more effectively than other nonprofits, private foundations, for-profits, and the state. Gone were the days when community leaders could achieve their civic aims by winning control of local commissions that controlled access to federal resources, as River City's labor leaders had done, for example, after winning representation on the United Way Board. In a post-1980s context, labor and business leaders' game for public prominence unfolded in a new arena wherein they needed to market their initiates to various outsiders in order to leverage civic resources.

Urban Funding Reform and Community Leaders' Political Game

During the 1980s the allocation of urban development funding changed in many similar ways to social service funding. Since the Great Depression, Democratic and Republican politicians alike took it as self-evident that the federal government should have a relationship with cities characterized by generous transfers. Differences between the two parties hinged largely on how this funding should be delivered, with Democrats favoring programs like public housing and urban renewal that targeted needy people and Republicans favoring federal transfers that left local leaders greater discretion. Indeed, I argued in chapter 1 that revenue sharing, the most generous and ideal-typically Keynesian urban policy, was the brainchild of the Nixon administration and passed Congress with GOP support.

The first attempted break with Keynesian-era consensus occurred at the behest of the Carter administration. Carter publically announced his dissatisfaction with "the doctrine of salvation through bricks . . . the idea that we can bulldoze our way out of urban problems," and generally criticized the waste, duplication, and inefficiency of federal urban policy. As an alternative, Carter officials proposed the aptly named New Partnership. Although this policy failed to pass Congress, it is interesting because most of its federally initiated proposals occurred anyway during the 1980s and 1990s, only without federal guidance and support. The New Partnership called for a downscaling of federal development policy to municipalities, or even neighborhoods, where local politicians and bureaucrats would collaborate with private developers to catalyze development deals. The federal government would facilitate these local partnerships through tax incentives and loan guarantees to private businesses, through a National Development Bank that would lend to private developers, and via urban development action grants (UDAG), the primary finance arm of the New Partnership. Unlike Keynesian-era grants, UDAGs were not intended to allow locals to steer development, but rather to "sweeten the deal" for private developers. They would be issued on a competitive basis to cities that had obtained redevelopment pledges from private developers, not primarily based on local need.[46]

But Carter's New Partnership model arrived before its time, and—ironically—Democratic and Republican commentators dismissed it as incoherent.[47] One columnist lampooned it as "10 recommendations supported by 38 strategies . . . or maybe 10 strategies supported by 38 recommendations."[48] Congress voted down most of the New Partnership proposal, passing only one minor increase in mass-transit funding. The task of capitalizing on Carter's neoliberal impulses fell to Reagan.[49]

Like Carter officials, Reagan administration officials entered office with an announced intention of fundamentally altering the relationship between cities and the federal government—the second plank of their New Federalism initiative. But unlike the Democrats, Reagan's appointees did not play around with half-measures. They planned to eliminate fiscal relations between cities and the federal government outright via a two-pronged strategy of federal cutbacks and downscaling. Reagan administration officials began by initiating bills that eliminated federal revenue sharing, slashed community development block grants (CDBG), and rolled back programs like mass transit and public housing, which had been apportioned predominantly to cities. During the 1980s the Department of Housing and Urban Development (HUD) received deeper cuts than any other federal agency and saw its expenditures decline from 8 percent of the federal budget to just 2 percent.[50] Recall figure 1.1, which showed the consequences: federal transfers plummeted from roughly 20 percent of municipal budgets in 1980 to just 3 percent in 1990. Reagan administration simultaneously transferred both responsibility and funding for urban initiatives to states, but figure 1.1 shows that such transfers did not initially compensate for cutbacks in direct federal aid. In simple terms, there were suddenly fewer development dollars flowing to cities.

Subsequent administrations backpedaled from the Reagan administration's anti-urban stance, but initiated urban programs that differed from generous, discretionary Keynesian-era transfers. For example, CDBGs began increasing again in the 1990s, but Republican and Democratic administrations advocated replacing formula-based apportionment with a competitive, means-tested system much like the one used to apportion social service block grants. The Obama administration has continued this argument by proposing that more CDBG funds be apportioned instead through a competitive system that increases accountability.[51] Concurrently, subsequent administrations apportioned other urban monies via state bureaucracies. The latter policy shift is evidenced by figure 1.1, which shows an increase in state transfers to cities since the 1980s. Much as in the case of nonprofit funding, federal money directed through states was partially absorbed by state bureaucrats, and the remainder was converted into smaller, more competitive, and more directed grants.[52] Here again, local leaders quested after the same federal monies as before, but within an arena wherein these monies confronted them as a complex system of competitive grants administered by federal agencies and states rather than well-financed local commissions that they could capture.

Despite the many parallels with nonprofit policy, post-1980s urban development policy differs in one critical respect: unlike nonprofits, municipalities have recourse to debt-financing via the bond market.[53] Although American cities have always issued municipal bonds, their ability to do so was highly regulated after the Great Depression. Then, in the 1980s, many states redefined municipal economic development as a vital community function, which—like public safety or fire prevention—requires no oversight. Subsequently, urban actors grew more speculative in their use of new, exotic municipal bonds like securities backed by tax increment financing (TIF) revenue.[54] Urban leaders' reliance on speculative bonds has driven up municipal debt, which makes investors wary of municipal defaults, and makes urban leaders dependent in turn on the positive evaluations of credit rating agencies.[55] Rating agencies determine a city's creditworthiness partially by evaluating to what extent stakeholders appear willing to "put politics aside" in servicing municipal debt.[56] Here too, then, community leaders found that realizing their goals required cooperation, or at least the appearance of it.

The Big Tent Development Organization: Making the Big Round Table in Practice

In the 1980s Prairieville and River City's leaders competed for public prominence in a new arena wherein they had comparatively little to gain— and much to lose—from the factional struggles. In this context, those who continued to engage one another in the traditional way slowly fell from their city's central stage, whereas partners, who claimed to sit "around the table" and formed new kinds of "big tent" organizations, strode boldly forth. River City's and Prairieville's first big tent organizations formed in the early 1980s to pursue legalized gambling. With the manufacturing crisis in full swing, Iowa passed laws permitting dog racing and later riverboat gambling, which legislators hoped would alleviate rampant unemployment. But in a policy stance that became common during the 1980s, state agencies demanded that cities demonstrate community support prior to receiving licenses. Partners' coalition-building discourse, with its emphasis on setting politics aside, soon appeared in newspaper reports focused on River City's and Prairieville's efforts to showcase community support for gambling. "There was this terrible sense of hopelessness," a 1980s-era chamber-backed councilperson recalled. "[Like] we are an old city, we've come back from other blows but this is too tough—we can't do anything. And then the oddest things happened, which was uncomfortable for me because I'm antigambling. A group of passionate people decided that [gambling] would be salvation of the city. And you know what? It was. It really wasn't the money, although that comes in awfully handy. It was that we came to a consensus and acted on it. People started to think, 'God, we can do this, maybe it isn't even so hard—we can come back if we just work together.'"

River City's leaders acted first, in part because they hoped to use a riverboat casino to reverse blight in the harbor district. They formed the River City Racing Association, a portentous organization that embodied many of the features of subsequent big tents. The organization guaranteed a portion of its seats to elected officials, municipal bureaucrats, labor and business leaders, and the heads of local charities. It also straddled the public-private divide, acting sometimes like an autonomous entity and sometimes like an arm of the city's municipal bureaucracy. Officially, the Racing Association was a fully independent nonprofit, although a plurality of its funding came from the city. The organization also assumed de facto control over a public revenue stream: casino profits. According to state statutes, riverboat casinos must turn over a portion of profits to the city, which is entrusted with funneling this to local philanthropic initiatives, but city council allowed the Racing Association board to disburse casino profits as it saw fit.[57] Prairieville's efforts to attract gambling unfolded similarly: Frannie Steele's group partnered with the chamber-backed council members to found the Prairieville Gaming Association, which included many types of leaders on its board, was mostly funded by Prairieville, and exercised de facto control over casino profits.

These features of River City and Prairieville's gambling boards became the norm for subsequent big tents: inclusion of a wide array of local stake-holders and an ambiguous relationship with municipal government. Lead-ers in both cities founded Development Corporations soon after, which—by the time of my fieldwork—were each city's most central organizations. Many partners also viewed River City's Ben Denison and Prairieville's Dani Dover, who headed these organizations, as their cities' most important leaders: as a central "broker," "consensus-builder," or "catalyst," or one who holds a "master rolodex" of the city.[58] "The chamber did its traditional things: ribbon cuttings, downtown business pageants and represent the interests of business in politics," a founder of Prairieville's Development Corporation told me. "An affiliate of the chamber—the industrial develop-ment council—sometimes did some smokestack chasing, but it was not economic development as we understand it today. It was done against rather than with the community. [We wanted] to get along better with la-bor and the community as a whole. [So our bylaws specify] an equal distri-bution between business, labor, and civic interest. It got to be about trying to find that middle ground."[59]

Ben Denison, the director of River City's Development Corporation, described its founding similarly. "[The Development Corporation was founded] in 1984 when River City was pretty much at rock bottom," he said. "We decided to develop a big tent organization that excluded no one and would incorporate all factions of the community in order to develop consensus. There was a chamber of commerce in River City, but it was felt to be too cloistered, because it did not include organized labor and was more of a club than a community development organization. [We decided] that this big tent should include business leaders, as the chamber already did, but it should also include leadership from organized labor, the educational community, and elected officials regardless of political identification. [We needed] a permanent seat for the mayor—not *a* mayor, if we happen to like him, but rather *the* mayor. It wasn't a matter of having one voice, but rather of having all voices: a big tent that would incorporate everyone and bring people together around problems we could actually solve."

Like the River City's Racing Association, both cities' development cor-porations were independent nonprofits mostly funded by their cities that assumed jurisdiction over public monies: supply-side economic incentives like property tax abatements, TIF revenue, and monies leveraged through municipal bond markets. "Our strongest partnership is with the city," Dani Dover told me. "You always have the feeling that they want it to work and are willing to be flexible and do anything required to get it done. [It's rare] that [we expect] something that does not happen. It almost never happens." Ben Denison was equally explicit. "We kiddingly describe our relationship with the city as, 'We make the promises and city fills them,'" he said. "We have carte blanche from the city to include incentives on proposals to companies, conditional on the approval of city council, but we don't check with them first. TIFs, land grants, applications to the Iowa Values Fund—we make a judgment about what would be appropriate."

Dani Dover and Ben Denison's self-reports suggest that big tents are more formally inclusive than past business organizations and became central to River City and Prairieville's post-1980s public sphere, even becoming virtually synonymous with each city's *big round table*. Tables 4.2 and 4.3 substantiate these claims. Recall that River City's and Prairieville's traditional labor and business sectors engaged in economic, civic, and partisan political institutions that were populated only by members of their own kind. Cross-factional interactions occurred mainly on conflict-ridden municipal bodies and commissions. In partners-speak, traditional leaders "sat across the table and fought." But by the 2000s, community leaders met regularly as members of big tents like development corporations, gaming associations, downtown development groups, labor-management councils, and other cross-factional partnership like Prairieville's intergovernmental transportation alliance and another partnership to increase awareness and services to the city's Hispanic population.[60] During the 1970s such associations were nonexistent but, as tables 4.2 and 4.3 show, of River City and Prairieville's thirty most central 2000s-era associations they comprised, respectively, five and six of thirty.[61] These tables show an analogous change in the city's civic sector, wherein many other key organizations like both cities' United Way, River City's Community Foundation, or Prairieville's food bank are also populated by business and labor leaders.

The structural centrality of partner-dominated associations was accompanied by another trend (I discuss in the next two chapters: the structural marginalization of local and partisan politics. Democratically appointed commissions were once central in River City's and Prairieville's public sphere. In the 1970s, eight to nine of their cities' thirty most central association were democratically appointed, but by the 2000s this number fell to five and three. Branches of the two parties, particularly the Republican

Table 4.2. River City's most central associations (2004–2006)

Association	Membership	Democratic or political?	Closeness centrality
1. Development corporation	Both	No	4.06
2. United Way	Both	No	4.06
3. Racing association	Both	No	4.05
4. Labor management council	Both	No	4.05
5. River Museum	Both	No	4.04
6. Development initiatives	Both	No	4.03
7. Charity	Both	No	4.03
8. Democratic donors	Labor	Yes	4.03
9. Omnibus charity	Both	No	4.02
10. Chamber of commerce	Business	No	4.02
11. College board	Business	No	4.02
12. United Labor	Labor	No	4.02
13. Financial company	Business	No	4.01
14. Community college	Both	No	4.00
15. River City Bank	Business	No	4.00
16. Labor council	Labor	No	4.00
17. College board	Business	No	3.99
18. City board (planning)	Both	Yes	3.99
19. City board (utility)	Both	Yes	3.99
20. Media company	Business	No	3.98
21. Country Bank	Business	No	3.98
22. School board	Both	Yes	3.98
23. Main Street development	Business	No	3.98
24. River City Ambassadors	Business	No	3.98
25. Building trades council	Labor	No	3.98
26. Electricians' union	Labor	No	3.98
27. Democratic politicians	Labor	Yes	3.98
28. Auto workers union	Labor	No	3.98
29. City council	Both	Yes	3.98
30. County supervisors	Both	Yes	3.98

Note: Partisan organizations not listed include Republican donors (3.97, no. 34 in centrality), Labor COPE (3.96, no. 44 in centrality), Democratic officers (3.95, no. 85 in centrality) and Republican politicians (3.85, no. 85 in centrality).

Party, also saw a decline in structural prominence.[62] The public heart of the pre-1980s cities resided in political spaces like the council chambers or party office, where leaders competed for prominence by advocating on their supporters' behalf. By the 2000s, it moved to the nonpartisan big round table.[63] I now show why this mode of engagement allowed partners to leverage outside economic, civic, and political resources, before showing in the chapters that follow how partners capitalized on such structural opportunities to squeeze traditional leaders from public life.

Table 4.3. Prairieville's most central associations (2004–2006)

Association	Membership	Democratic or political?	Closeness centrality
1. United Way	Both	No	4.81
2. Chamber	Business*	No	4.80
3. Development corporation	Both	No	4.79
4. Democratic officers	Both*	Yes	4.77
5. Development initiatives	Business	No	4.77
6. Gambling board	Both	No	4.77
7. Hospital board	Business	No	4.76
8. Symphony board	Business	No	4.76
9. Community college board	Both	No	4.74
10. Hospital board	Business	No	4.74
11. Labor council	Labor	No	4.74
12. Regional transport partnership	Both	No	4.74
13. Foodbank	Both	No	4.74
14. Medical center	Business	No	4.72
15. Art museum board	Business	No	4.72
16. City council	Both	Yes	4.72
17. City enterprise zone commission	Both	Yes	4.72
18. Community foundation	Both	No	4.72
19. Community theater board	Business	No	4.72
20. Teamsters' union	Labor	No	4.71
21. Bank board	Business	No	4.71
22. County supervisors	Both	Yes	4.71
23. Latino awareness partnership	Both	No	4.71
24. Construction company	Business	No	4.71
25. Heritage Foundation	Both	No	4.71
26. Public library foundation	Both	No	4.70
27. Prairieville growth organization	Business	No	4.70
28. Banks board	Business	No	4.70
29. Transit workers union	Labor	No	4.69
30. Youth foundation	Both	No	4.69

Note: Partisan organizations not listed include Republican donors (4.64, no. 49 in centrality), Republican officers (4.63, no. 50 in centrality), Democratic donors (4.63, no. 53 in centrality), Democratic politicians (4.59, no. 66 in centrality), and Republican politicians (4.46, no. 88 in centrality).
* During the 2004–2006 period, the chamber did not disclose its board of directors and I compiled a partial list of directors from public announcements. A few small-business owners were Democratic officers during the 2004–6 period.

How Partnerships Help Leaders Rise within Their City's *Economic* Game

Prairieville's and River City's 2000s-era economy consisted of potentially footloose corporate subsidiaries. In this context, community leaders could distinguish themselves by attracting a new subsidiary to their city. But this was no small feat, because corporations ran multistage searches for new investment sites, which sometimes pitted hundreds of municipalities against one another. Leaders who successfully attracted corporate subsidiaries engaged in two ancillary tasks that required a degree of flexibility unknown to their traditional predecessors: first, they created expansive incentive packages and, second, marketed their city directly to corporate headquarters. The role of partnerships in facilitating these two tasks is evident in two of River City's success stories: attraction of a Sunflower Foods meatpacking plant and a Microprocessor Corp. data-processing facility.

River City's Sunflower bid began after the firm announced that—based on its location and demographics—River City was one of a dozen finalists for a medium-sized plant. River City's leaders considered themselves a natural choice, because "the Pack" had recently shut down, leaving hundreds of experienced meatpackers unemployed. To grease the wheels, Ben Denison's development team began assembling a package of incentives for the company.

But, crucially, many of the incentives that Denison's team proposed were under the control of state bureaucracies, and attaining these was itself an exercise in marketing. Iowa's economic development grants are typical of post-1980s funding in that cities compete for them by showing that they will be put to good use by—among other things—demonstrating broad-based community support for a new employer. To demonstrate community support, partners create boards that include multiple stakeholders: business leaders, labor leaders, public sector officials, women, visible minorities, and so on. Development personnel argue that such boards must unanimously approve a project for state funding to be viable, and, indeed, I will discuss a case in chapter 6 when the state refused to grant incentives due to one negative vote on such a board. But in Sunflower's case, River City's board unanimously supported incentives, and Sunflower received $6 million in dollar job creation grants from Iowa's Department of Economic Development and additional monies to alter infrastructure around its plant site from Iowa's Department of Transportation. River City sweetened the deal with local incentives, which required city council approval. Here again, development personnel argue that corporations take umbrage at anything less than unanimous city council approval. Luckily for those spearheading the Sunflower bid, the council unanimously approved the incentives, offering the corporation land in the city-owned industrial park at a 75 percent discount.[64] Development personnel also pledged to offset the costs of Sunflower's plant with tax increment financing (TIF), a practice that allows cities to capture property tax receipts created by private sector–generated "growth" and allocate them toward development projects rather than school districts, fire departments, and other public services according to normal fiscal formulas. In this case, River City's used $3.5 million in TIF-revenue to pay for Sunflower's capital improvements, essentially earmarking the firm's property taxes for construction of its own facility.

But money was not everything, particularly because Sunflower was considering other cities willing to match, or even exceed, River City's incentives. Like other finalists for Sunflower's plant, River City's development personnel assembled a coalition of local stakeholders and flew to corporate headquarters. This coalition had a clear theme: harmonious labor-management relations. Coalition members included business and labor leaders who partner, president of the city's Labor-Management Council, and Ron Bolan, River City's mayor, who was a former line worker at Greenfield's and a vocal advocate of partnership. "At one meeting, I sat down with a couple of [their] VPs, the city manager and Ben Denison and we just talked about the community," Ron told me. "When [Sunflower] made their big announcement, they talked about that meeting and said that made the decision for them. They saw how progressive River City had become and they liked the fact that we talked about partnership and how we all work together to make projects happen."

But crucially, the type of coalition that lured Sunflower cannot work in all cases, because no two companies are exactly alike. Indeed, development personnel insist that a good marketing coalition involves "unlikely partners," or is "creative" and "unique." Such artistic analogies are apt given the creative license that is inherent to marketing. Urban theorist Michel De Certeau, for example, argues that thre is not a single, real version of complex human constructions like cities; the city exists as something different for each person who experiences it.[65] To give a mundane example, consider that it is possible to take different tours of the same city: "Woody Allen's New York City" tour versus the "*Sex and The City* New York City" tour. Along similar lines, development personnel do not simply present the city to outsiders when forming coalitions, but rather create a single coherent reduction of the city that is fundamentally different from the real thing. When marketing River City to Microprocessor Corp., for instance, development personnel represented the city differently than during efforts to lure Sunflower.

Microprocessor's plan for a data-processing center included the eventual hiring of hundreds of information technology professionals, and was therefore considered a remarkable catch, both by local leaders and state bureaucrats. River City's chances initially appeared slim, but improved markedly after Microprocessor Corp eliminated 70 percent of nearly 400 possible sites based on metrics like median wage levels, cost of living, and local rents. The company then eliminated most remaining sites due to lack of transport infrastructure or workforce characteristics. River City distinguished itself early at this stage, when representatives of the Development Corporation partnered with local colleges to personally hand-deliver 500 resumes to Microprocessor's corporate headquarters. Eventually, Microprocessor had twelve finalists and proceeded to phone interviews and on-site visits.

As soon as River City was announced as a finalist, development personnel flooded Iowa's Economic Development Department with applications, all of which received unanimous approval from a local board. All were approved. Microprocessor received a state economic development grant that provided $9,000 for every future employee and a state income tax credit worth over $2 million. Sunflower also benefited from a new state program that reimbursed firms for training Iowa's workers, ultimately receiving an additional $7 million in grants. Not to be outdone, River City kicked in a TIF "match" for Microprocessor's state grants that was valued at $12 million. Because Microprocessor desired payment instantly, development personnel floated a bond backed by this projected TIF revenue, essentially giving the firm the $12 million upfront, which the company then repaid by paying its normal property taxes. Then there were sundry benefits thrown in, ranging from a city-financed shuttle to ferry employees from a parking garage to Microprocessor's facility to pledges to hire a Development Corporation employee to work full-time on helping Microprocessor with employee recruitment. All of these incentives passed city council unanimously. In the parlance of River City's partners, the city hummed like a "well-oiled machine."

But economic incentives were only part of the story, because here again other finalists for Microprocessor's bid met or exceeded River City's incentives. To distinguish themselves from the pack, River City's development personnel presented the city as an educated and progressive diamond in the rough—effectively, the polar opposite of the blue-collar image they had presented to Sunflower Foods. Key to this self-presentation were six local college and university presidents, all present for Microprocessor's on-site visits. Development personnel also pulled together the heads of cultural and artistic organizations and advocates of various progressive causes like marriage equality and environmental sustainability. River City even lobbied Iowa's state legislature to pass one of the United States' first same-sex domestic partner bills during this period, which community leaders justified on the grounds that it would convince companies that Iowa was not inhabited by a "bunch of hicks in the sticks." Ron Bolan, the city's mayor, was also prominent in this marketing coalition, because he had advocated for a green city initiative as part of his electoral campaign. So it was that River City appeared as two different things to two different companies.

It should go without saying that my description of these marketing efforts does not constitute approval for them. I have argued elsewhere that the use of public monies for private sector incentives, particularly via debt-financing, is fiscally risky and democratically problematic.[66] But the key point here is the form of social organization—partnership—that helped community leaders to attract outside subsidiaries to their city. Whatever the ultimate consequences, those who attracted Sunflower and Microprocessor distinguished themselves in the public eye, rising in esteem in the eyes of their peers and other residents. Indeed, it is not every day that a computer company opens a major facility in the Rust Belt, and those who partnered to bring in Microprocessor were hailed as local heroes. But to successful lure corporate subsidiaries, partners acted in ways that were anathema to their traditional predecessors.

In particular, those who participated in efforts to attract Sunflower and Microprocessor took divisive issues off the table and adopted a flexible, changing presentation of self. The city's mayor, for instance, presented himself as a blue-collar leader in one context, an advocate of environmental sustainability in another. Partners' flexible self-presentation was important because it allowed their city's brokers to assemble effective partnerships, instrumental to attaining corporate incentives. This is partially because partnerships allowed community leaders to blend public and private sector resources, but even more important was development personnel's ability to create coalitions that signaled broad-based community support to state agencies. Indeed, development planners looked with pity on cities whose applications for state grants were marred by excessive democratic contestation. "A lot of your smaller communities, will come with a big delegation and a long laundry-list," one of Ben Denison's lieutenants told me. "[And one representative] will say, 'Don't trust [my town's other representative,] he's a liar!' You've got to have somebody in Des Moines who can say, 'Look, this road is critical for us, for our community development." Community leaders' willingness to engage as partners then allowed development personnel to flexibly market the city to corporate subsidiaries.

The key point is that successful place-marketing required leaders to adopt a fundamentally different mode of public engagement from that of their traditional predecessors. Gone were the days when Jones Berry called the city manager a "chamber stooge" and the world went on as before, hardly noticing. Development personnel cannot work in an atmosphere like that. "Our city council meetings were once like a Jerry Springer show . . . a circus," Ben Denison lamented to a business magazine shortly after the Microprocessor announcement. "[This success shows] that is no longer the case." In a post-1980s neoliberal arena, would-be place-marketers rise in public esteem when they engage in public life like the city's new mayor, who presented himself as a labor leader who partners, a green city advocate, and many other things besides.

How Partnerships Help Leaders Rise within Their City's Post-1980s *Civic* Game

After the 1980s, the success of community leaders' civic initiatives also depended on their ability to set divisions aside and enter into broad-based partnerships. This is illustrated by labor leaders' efforts to create Prairieville's food bank, which they had historically viewed as central to their visions of a blue-collar-friendly city. These plans did not bear fruit until the 1990s when labor leaders partnered with business leaders. Before then, working-class politicians like Hal Swift railed against Prairieville's lack of an emergency food system along with a general lack of social services for lower-income residents, unpaved streets and periodic flooding in the city's working-class neighborhoods, and other inequities. But the city's old families were unmoved. Before the 1980s, they dominated organizations like the United Way and municipal commissions, which controlled access to both local and Keynesian-era federal funding. The only "food bank" that labor leaders could manage was a checkbook held by the Labor Council president, from which he sometimes cut checks to desperate strikers.

Then, in the 1990s, labor leaders stumbled upon partnerships. By then, organizations like the Gambling Board, Labor-Management Council, and Development Corporation had set a precedent for labor-business cooperation. In this spirit, business leaders had even allowed two labor representatives onto the United Way board, although the resources available to this organization were greatly reduced after 1980s-era federal cutbacks and declines in local donations. The two principals in initiating a food-bank partnership were Jerry Winslow, then-president of Prairieville's Labor Council, and Matt Planton, a Democratic state senator from one of Prairieville's working-class districts.

"Matt and I would go to these conventions around the country, [we'd] be driving all night, and we were always brainstorming, [like,] 'I wonder if this would work?!?'" Jerry told me. "Anyhow, [we] convened a meeting [of the United Way's] member agencies, which ran [separate food drives] to fill their pantries for maybe one month [out of the year. We asked them:] 'If you could have food twelve months out of the year, would you do it?' And naturally they said, 'Yes!' Then we went [to managers of restaurants, department stores, and food-processing plants and said,] 'Hey, I know you just throw away lot of food, and I know that you care about the community. Maybe we could get you a little slip that lets you just write [the food] off [on your taxes]. The people in need would appreciate it, too!' A lot of the labor leaders could not make [this] transition," Jerry added after a moment of reflection. "[Before] the mindset was, 'This is what we want, put it on the table. If we don't get it we are going to go out on strike!'"

Matt and Jerry's food-bank initiative worked only in the context of America's changing emergency food system, which reorganized and expanded during the 1980s and '90s.[67] In 1981 Congress passed the Omnibus Budget Reconciliation Act, which scaled back emergency assistance to individuals via programs like SNAP, but—in the face of public outcry—policymakers simultaneously released excess agricultural commodities to the public, most memorably government cheese.[68] From policymakers' perspective, releasing agricultural commodities was a market-friendly alternative to individual relief, because it was inexpensive and incentivized domestic agriculture. But delivering food to recipients was burdensome, and policymakers relied instead on nonprofits. By the 1990s these consolidated into a single organization: Second Harvest (later renamed Feeding America), which distributes all surplus agricultural commodities via a network of regional food banks, which bid on the food using points apportioned to them according to the number of clients served. Supplies of emergency food also rose in the 1990s with passage of the Good Samaritan Act, which protected corporate donors from legal liability and offered them a tax writeoff for donated food. Before the Good Samaritan Act, corporations disposed of 80 percent of their excess food for fear of lawsuit, but afterwards they did so with impunity and—because they donated largely unsellable food—at profit.[69] Matt and Jerry's brainstorming therefore occurred in a world in which emergency food was there for the taking, but community leaders could only do so by setting aside divisive public identities and reconceptualizing the food bank as a community-wide win-win, not an institution that would primarily serve their side. Once they partnered with area business owners, Matt and Jerry pooled the United Way's agencies recipient lists to leverage more emergency food from Second Harvest and drew on local businesses' unused food.[70] Jerry and Matt indexed their commitment to such partnerships by inviting several business leaders onto the food bank's board of directors.

In fact, Jerry and Matt's decision to create a big-tent-like board proved fateful, because local donations were inadequate to fund food storage and distribution, particularly after a sudden wave of corporate acquisitions robbed Prairieville of its Fortune 500 companies in the 1990s—an event discussed in the next chapter. During this crisis, the food bank's board demonstrated board-based community support and allowed the organization to win state, federal, and foundation grants to cover operating costs. Partnership saved the food bank again when Iowa elected a new governor in the 2010s who announced that the public financing of food banks "crowded out" private charity, depriving citizens of the opportunity to support homegrown nonprofits. But after much public outcry, the governor announced that Iowa would defund only those food banks that failed to demonstrate community support via a "local match" of $50,000 in donations. Prairieville's food bank had never raised such a sum, but business leaders pitched in, argued in newspaper editorials that failure to raise the local match would be like "leaving money on the table," and successfully raised the sum, thus allowing the food bank to keep its doors open. In a post-1980s context, Jerry and Matt's partnerships with business leaders won them much esteem in the public's eye and even in the eyes of their traditional predecessors, who had tried but failed to create a food bank for decades. These partnerships then saved the food bank, thus allowing Jerry and Matt to stay in the public limelight.

How Partnership Helped Leaders Rise within
Their City's Post-1980s *Political* Game

As it was in economic and civic life, so it was with urban development projects. No case demonstrates post-1980s incentives for partnership better than River City's historical museum partnership (discussed in this book's introduction). In the 1980s federal funding dried up and the harbor's boarded-up factories stood vacant. Kathy Gooding, a previously marginal Democratic activist, spearheaded the initiative, which she reported required a "transformation" of public culture that "had never happened before." Contrast Kathy Gooding's museum initiative with Wally Porter's effort to do the same thing in the 1960s (discussed in chapter 2). Wally operated within a Keynesian-era arena, wherein municipal commissions had access to federal urban-renewal funding that covered two-thirds of project costs. In this context, Wally could avoid collaborating with business leaders and actually achieved his aims through conflict—specifically, by contesting the chamber's hold over city council and becoming River City's first union-backed mayor. Recall his self-report: "We decided after the election that we would simply run the city because we were in the majority. I ordered a re-zoning . . . and it got done pretty fast—by the summer they were breaking ground."

By contrast, Kathy and her collaborators operated in a post-Keynesian arena without access to large, discretionary grants like urban renewal. Of her initiative's eventual $200-million price tag, only $8 million came from direct federal appropriations. Instead, development occurred on a pretense—a historical museum—that Kathy and her allies thought would appeal to a wide array of federal, state, and nonprofit grant-making agencies. The eventual list of funders included the EPA, Midwest Arts Foundation, Federal Highway Administration, Institute of Museum and Library Services, Iowa Department of Cultural Affairs, Iowa Department of Transportation, Iowa Great Places Foundation, the Leopold Center for Sustainable Agriculture, Iowa Math and Science Educational Partnership, Iowa Space Grant Consortium, National Endowment for the Humanities, National Endowment for the Arts, National Marine Sanctuary Foundation, National Oceanic and Atmospheric Administration, The Prudential Foundation, the Kresge Foundation, the McKnight Foundation, the Hy-vee Foundation, the National Park Service, America's Scenic Byways, Preserve America, Smokestacks and Silos National Heritage Association, Vision Iowa, State Historical Society of Iowa, and NASA.

It is no coincidence that River City's leaders regard the historical museum as synonymous with the emergence for a new generation of partners. To fund the museum, leaders resolved differences behind closed doors, checked egos, and generally set divisive issues aside. This allowed them to signal harmony to outside funders and to strategically form coalitions that presented the museum as an education center, an architectural marvel, a historical heritage site, and on and on. After it was all done, partners' superiority was there for all to see: the harbor was once a symbol of River City's humiliation, but now bulldozers puttered back and forth beneath construction cranes that gleamed golden in the sunlight. One imagines River City's once-proud traditional leaders looking on, like dinosaurs watching an asteroid fall to earth. But it does not follow from this that traditional leaders abandoned their old ways or relinquished control over public institutions to partners. In the next two chapters, I tell the story of how partners pushed divisive traditional leaders and politics more generally from their cities' public spheres.

FIVE

Prairieville's Business Community in Transition

"Christian Nazis!" blared the headline of the *Prairieville Reporter* just after the 2006 mid-term election. This headline was a quote from Mark Sturley, the chair of Prairieville's Republican Party. He had spoken with the press on election night and, in the heat of the moment, blamed his party's loss on "Christian Nazis": activists committed to fringy, far-right causes who, he claimed, had co-opted the GOP. This statement, and Mark's subsequent ousting as head of Prairieville's GOP, became a piece of national news, was quoted in newspapers all over the country, and formed part of the narrative about the GOP's electoral defeat. In retrospect, this event appears like a portent of things to come: the Republican defeat of 2008, the rise of the Tea Party, and a perennial conflict between the activist and moneyed constituencies of the Republican Party evident, for example, in fractious presidential primaries. But this was 2006. At that time, the national media painted the Republican Party as a seamless monolith, incapable to losing elections in the wake of back-to-back victories. Most national commentators expressed surprise that a Republican leader should turn against activists within his own party. However, Mark's statement was no surprise to those familiar with Prairieville's public life.

"I know a lot of [the prominent Republicans in town through my law practice]. They don't want anything to do with the far right," Harry Mc-Donald Jr., a Democratic activist and son of a celebrated member of Frannie's Table, told me, echoing an attitude common among members of the city's gleeful Democratic establishment. "Frankly, I think it embarrasses them, because—you know—they may be Republicans, but they are not out there. So they have stepped away from the party. [They may still] donate to individual [Republican] candidates, but they won't give to the party and they want nothing to do with it."

On the Republican side too, people interpreted the event as symbolic of a growing rift within the GOP. On one afternoon, I spoke with Norma Gentry, vice chair of Prairieville's Republican Party. We sat in a little downtown café as business people wandered in from nearby offices to escape the dusty summer. All around, they leaned on wire-rimmed tables, sipping iced coffee, with their shirt-sleeves rolled up. I knew some of the people in the room and knew that they identified as partners, not as business leaders in the vein of Prairieville's traditional, and traditionally Republican, old families. "I am definitely an activist," Norma said, lowering her voice and leaning in, "but there are a lot of people sitting in this room who are just donors."

"Activists and donors are the two major groups. I don't see a lot of crossover between them," she continued. "The people sitting here in this room, some of them will donate money—sometimes to the party or at least to candidates, maybe show up at an event occasionally, but they will never make phone calls or knock on doors. And activists will say, 'Why should this and that person be invited to such and such an event, they don't do anything?!?' Yeah well, over the years they may have given so many thousands of dollars [so they always get to go]. And that is frustrating, because when you staff an office, you are going to staff it with activists and then maybe sometimes the people that bring in the food, the office furniture, the computers—those are going to be your donors, but that does not happen much anymore. So then activists will say, 'Why should all the tickets [to political events] go to these country club Republicans?!?'"

More than anyone else in Prairieville, Mark Sturley straddled the divide between Prairieville's GOP activists and the city's newly partisan-averse business leaders; in fact, he was the only person I encountered who identified as both a partner and a GOP activist. I initially asked Mark about his place within Prairieville's public sphere using the terminology of GOP activists, whose favored term for the city's closeted-Republican partners was "country club Republican."[1] Because this term was one that nobody applied to themselves, I often began interviews with activists by asking them if they identified as activists or country club Republicans as a kind of icebreaker. To this, Mark Sturley had given a surprising response.

"Well, I'm a little different," Mark said after a long pause. We were having breakfast several weeks before the 2006 midterm elections. "I have been part of the country club and have traditionally given money to the party and to a number of campaigns, but I've also been an activist. Actually, I'm probably one of the more active activists here. But you know, I'm not what some would consider a true conservative either." Mark shifted in his seat, switching tracks for a minute to talk about the activist–country club Republican distinction more generally.

"That is such a huge division. The country club Republicans tend to be more moderate whereas the activists tend to be more evangelical and right-wing.[2] [So now] the people who give the money stop and say, 'You have to put up the people that I like.' More and more they are holding the money back. They think the party is being dragged too far to the right [and] resent *how* [the party] is winning the elections. The activists do the work of the party, but now more and more the country club Republicans, they won't even attend meetings. The activists think they can control the agenda and impose their will [so now] we have the workers, but not the money. [And] we [need] to do a better job finding candidates who are respected in the community. Now it is more like if somebody steps forward and says they want to run for something it is like, 'Thank God we have a candidate!' We don't even stop to think anymore if they are someone out there with an axe to grind or a chance to win or not. [I think that] to become more effective again we have to reach out to the moderates."

Mark's statements nicely summarize the growing gap between the majority of American voters and adherents of the two parties, especially party workers. Generally, 1960s-era voters were committed to one of the two parties, but held moderate views on most issues that did not necessarily align with the positions of their parties. Party workers and politicians were much like everyone else: moderate and heterogeneous in their views.[3] By the 2000s, most Americans expressed dissatisfaction with both parties at unprecedented rates, but those who identified with the two parties were more extreme and consistently partisan than 1960s-era party faithful. Party workers and politicians especially became much more polarized than their district's voters.[4] Social scientists who study everyday public talk encountered a similar gap between daily life and politics in the 1990s. Sociologist Nina Eliasoph, for example, observes that people spontaneously distinguish between "community"-directed and desirable action and "politics," which they view as divisive and try to avoid.[5] Similar attitudes are evident in Mark's statements when he wished that the GOP ran candidates who were "respected in the community" rather than activists with a political "axe to grind." Indeed, Mark's troubles generally signify an increasingly unmanageable conflict between community and politics in Prairieville.

Many social scientists who study American politics assume that the growing community-politics rift is purely the result of change among elected politicians, party activists, and other partisan actors. This is understandable, because research shows that political candidates and party workers have grown more polarized since the 1960s, and this polarization—as well as particular manifestations like Fox News—are something that academics love to complain about in their free time. Conversely, social scientists have traditionally idealized grassroots community life, a tendency that has existed within the civil society literature since foundational theorists like De Tocqueville.[6] Indeed, scholars ranging from Jürgen Habermas to Robert Putnam portray grassroots initiatives as an immediate expression of community will, a fount of true democracy, and a realm unspoiled by the instrumental, calculating spirit that pervades partisan politics. Perhaps it is natural to blame it all on political actors: they have grown more brazen in their politics and left committed, community-minded leaders behind—in fact, this is precisely what many academic books about the polarization of America's political discourse argue.[7]

By this point in the book, it should be clear why such attempts to put all the blame on political actors are facile. I argued in chapter 3 that America's parties have little bureaucratic capacity and derive any organizational coherence from informal community associations. If Keynesian-era politics was relatively more moderate, it was due to the moderating effects of community institutions like Frannie's Table or the chamber, which disciplined activists and shifted their attention away from the hot-button issues that motivate contemporary activists. Consider, too, that American politics has changed in degree over the last several decades, but not in kind. Now, as in the 1960s, politics is a contest between two parties. But community has changed in kind. River City's and Prairieville's public life was once defined by a two-sided conflict that community leaders saw as simultaneously political, whereas contemporary public life consists of a division between community leaders who partner and avoid politics and those who do not partner and are politically engaged. We are not yet at the smoking gun, but all the clues point to community, not politics, as primarily responsible for the rift between the two—although, of course, my overarching argument is that changes in community governance were caused in turn by a transformation of American federalism in the 1970s and '80s.

In the next three chapters, I show how River City's and Prairieville's turn toward partnerships produces the polarization of American politics. The argument culminates in chapter 8, which shows that both cities' parties conform to a new ideal typical form of organization: the activist party, which is divorced, or disembedded, from community governance and characterized by intraorganizational dynamics that polarize activists and lead them to support extreme political candidates. The key difference between the activist party and Keynesian-era community leadership parties is the absence of contemporary community leaders in the former's ranks. This chapter and the next one therefore set up my eventual argument about grassroots parties by analyzing why partners avoid politics. The argument is simple: partners' public personae are incompatible with party politics. By this, I mean first that partners' mode of public engagement—the construction of shifting, flexible coalitions—is practically complicated by public political attachments, which are divisive and—partners believe—prevent people from working together. Moreover, party affiliation is a liability within the game of public prominence that partners play with one another, because it indexes qualities that are incompatible with partners' public ideals. Partners distinguish themselves by being open to working with anyone and hence unfactionalized and undivisive, whereas party ties index factional attachments and divisiveness, and generally make partners appear more like their cities' traditional leaders. In the words of sociologist Erving Goffman, partisanship carries a stigma, one that can spoil a partner's public identity and lead to outright ostracism.[8]

This chapter focuses on business leaders in Prairieville, explains why they embraced partnerships, and shows why they simultaneously abandoned party politics. I begin with a post-1980 history of Prairieville's public life, which contextualizes subsequent discussions and provides additional evidence for my argument about the link between neoliberal reforms and partnership. As in River City, Prairieville's business leaders began the transition to partnership in the 1980s, but then—through a stroke of unexpected luck—emerged as momentary winners during the corporate merger wave of the late 1980s. Prairieville's boom replicated the conditions of the Keynesian era because it gave community leaders the illusion of local control and, predictably, they abandoned their move toward partnership, only to then retreat back as boom turned to bust. I then shift focus to three of Prairieville's key leaders who renounced their party affiliations upon transitioning to partnership. After discussing commonalities in their style of public engagement, I show why these partners' community roles clash with party affiliation. Finally, I conclude with Mark Sturley's ouster from the GOP and use the event to show how the reorganization of Prairieville's public life leads local leaders to understand and frame public conflicts as ones between community and politics.

New City That Wasn't: Prairieville's Financial Boom and Bust

Prairieville's 1980s-era history was initially similar to River City's and that of many American cities: cutbacks during the manufacturing crisis were followed by corporate acquisitions and plant closings that devastated the city's economy. In 1981 Valley Beef—the city's largest employer—was acquired by a holding company, which liquidated some of its Prairieville operations and sold what remained to a food-processing conglomerate. Several smaller homegrown industries like Prairie Tools soon followed. The owner of Valley Beef was universally unpopular and therefore hardly missed, but Prairie Tools was owned by the Altoons, one of the city's oldest and most respected families. After selling the company, Harry Altoon Sr. set a pattern that other former owners soon followed: he retired to Arizona as his extended family scattered, thus eliminating one of the pillars of Prairieville's business class. Corporate acquisitions also coincided with layoffs, and hence fewer union dues with which to support full-time union representatives. For example, Prairieville's meatpackers union began the 1980s with nearly a dozen full-time representatives, but was down to four by 1990.

Initially, then, the 1980s coincided with a moment of crisis for Prairieville's leaders. Traditional leaders had experienced boom-and-bust economic cycles before, but the 1980s thinned their ranks and confronted them with the unfamiliar challenge of retaining and attracting outside investment. It was in this context that leaders first experimented with partnership. For example, Frannie Steele partnered with chamber leaders to start the Prairieville Gaming Association, the city's first big tent. "The first time I ever saw [business and labor leaders] getting together was when Ms. Frannie was getting the riverboat started," Danny Steele told me.

"[There was a guy] Sam Ellis, who was on city council, a staunch Republican. He and Frannie did not see eye to eye on anything [before, but] I think Ms. Frannie knew that to get the boat to work she would need broader input so Sam Ellis [became] her financial advisor. Then Candice Shiller, she was chamber too, got to be on Frannie's board [along with other business representatives], maybe six total." Shortly after, Prairieville's leaders founded the Prairieville Economic Development Corporation as an alternative to Prairieville's chamber, and the Labor Management Council soon followed, with old family luminaries like Charles Browning Sr. as founding members.

But then in the late 1980s, Prairieville's trajectory diverged from River City and most other American cities, as the city played host to several homegrown corporate success stories. Indeed, it is ironic that Prairieville's remaining old families complained about the "global economy" and the heartless economic rationality of the "new men," because their 1980s-era forbearers were nothing if not willing globalizers. For example, the family that owned Miller's Baking Company began acquiring distant food-processing plants, eventually growing to nearly 7,000 employees. Tidal Chemicals, a local fertilizer manufacturer, likewise acquired plants in other cities. Prairieville's power company also changed its name to the Midwest Energy Company and bought up the region's utility companies.[9] Finally, the 1990s coincided with the rise of Crossroads Computing, an early manufacturer of personal computers. The company was founded by Ken Nate, who grew up on a farm at the outskirts of Prairieville and began assembling computers in his garage as a teenager. Within a decade, his assembly plant supplied an exploding national market for computers, which shipped in boxes decorated with the rolling green hills that commemorated the company's bucolic beginnings. By the 1990s Crossroads had cracked the Fortune 500 and employed over 3,000 professional workers in Prairieville.

The merger movement brought Prairieville some setbacks, too. Tidal Chemicals no sooner acquired its regional competitors then it too was acquired by a larger holding company. But the city's successes were more spectacular than its losses. By the early 1990s Valley Beef's parent company relinquished its controlling shares and Tidal Chemicals' new parent company announced plans to relocate its headquarters to Prairieville. In 1995, then, Prairieville was to be the headquarters of three Fortune 500 companies, unusual for a city its size and unheard of in the Rust Belt. Affluent suburbs like Ranch Cliffs exploded and airline connections to the city proliferated. A specialized firm even formed to ship fresh seafood directly from the West Coast to the restaurants that fed Prairieville's young professionals.

Prairieville's finance-fueled boom was especially significant for business leaders, because it counteracted neoliberal trends that robbed them of local control. Corporate mergers had thinned the ranks of the city's old families, but those who remained could draw upon, and redistribute, a huge pool of resources. The "big fish" in Prairieville's business community had always maintained dominance by giving, and windfalls for Prairieville's secondary sector were spectacular indeed. For example, many locally owned construction companies struggled in the 1980s, but rebounded after winning a contracts to build new corporate headquarters for their peers. Similarly, Prairieville's civic sector, once hobbled by New Federalism, was revived as corporate foundations dispersed their embarrassment of riches. Even Prairieville's blight-bitten downtown got a makeover as princely corporate headquarters transformed entire city blocks. Corporate foundations funded public buildings like the city's futuristic library, which replaced warehouses in the old packing district, and towered like a chrysanthemum of mirrored glass over restaurants and bars that swarmed with a young, clean-cut clientele. Business leaders once again walked with heads held high.

Given my central argument in this book, it should come as no surprise that Prairieville's business leaders shied away from partnership during the 1990s: partnerships allow community leaders to market the city to outsiders, but Prairieville's leaders momentarily had no need to look outside. And indeed, Prairieville's big-tent organizations all floundered. The Labor Management Council failed outright. "The reason that fell apart is that management just kind of stopped showing up—you can't have a labor management committee when all that shows up is labor," the Labor Council's president told me, "they always had something else they had to do. But now there's all these business and professional people who are talking with me about getting it started up again."[10] Similarly, high-profile business leaders discontinued their involvement in Prairieville's Economic Development Corporation, instead founding and funding the chamber's development taskforce as a business-dominated alternative. But then the financialized economy of the 1990s struck back, humiliating Prairieville's business community and showing them that their local control had been illusory.

In the late 1990s, Prairieville's homegrown industries fell like dominoes. Midwest Energy was acquired by an even larger energy holding company, Miller Baking Company was purchased by a major distributor of processed foods, and the company that owned Tidal Chemicals was acquired and left Prairieville even before fully relocating its corporate offices. In a final blow, local prodigy Ken Nate relocated Crossroad's headquarters to Silicon Valley, citing his inability to attract talent to Prairieville as the cause. By 2000 Prairieville's Fortune 500 companies were gone, leaving only shuttered headquarters behind. Boom had turned to bust.

For many residents, Prairieville's present was a bitter contrast to the amenity-filled, world-connected city of the 1990s. Many Prairievillers bemoaned their city's lack of airline connections, which declined from a dozen to one inconvenient and expensive connection to Kansas City.[11] The young professionals who swarmed the city's streets also disappeared along with the restaurants and nightlife that catered to their tastes, thus leaving the city's downtown dark and depressing. "[There was] a restaurant here for a long time called the Lavender Pony [and it was] truly phenomenal," Mark Sturley, Prairieville's ousted GOP president told me. "I was going to have them do an open house for me, [but they] said, 'We will do your open house, but that is probably the last event [we're] doing.' Because of the last

100 or 150 [customers they kept track of], 80 percent had moved away. Without [good] jobs, you just don't create the kinds of positions that allow for places like the Lavender Pony."

It was in this atmosphere of shock and disarray that Dani Dover assumed control of the chamber's development taskforce and began a second drive toward partnership. Dani and her fellow partners sometimes focused on rekindling labor-business collaborations, but—perhaps more than their River City counterparts—embraced a "build cultural amenities and the corporate headquarters will come" strategy. Indeed, the city's most celebrated partnerships revolved around amenities like music festivals, art fairs, and farmers' markets. Prairieville's best-attended public event during my field-work, for example, was a lecture by the former mayor of Austin, Texas. "He was great!" the president of the Growth Coalition, one of the groups that sponsored the event, told me. "[It was a] city brainstorming session, because he was responsible for a kind of renaissance down there as far as making it more attractive for young people. We had a room of hundreds of people, just shot ideas at him and he shot ideas back. We have since implemented some of those ideas." Scholars who study economic development are pessimistic about the benefits of amenity-driven economic development, but Prairieville's partners believed in this strategy at the time of my fieldwork, and it was largely through successful quality-of-life partnerships that leaders distinguished themselves within Prairieville's public game.[12] To show the public norms that underlie such partnerships, I turn to three of Dani Dover's frequent collaborators, who embody the public style—and political aversion—of Prairieville's other partners: Daniel Feegan, the planner of a local music festival, the young professionals of Prairieville's Growth Coalition, and Terry Masconi, the city's organic food guru.

Daniel Feegan's Musicade

Next to Dani herself, Daniel Feegan was easily Prairieville's best-known citizen. People associated him with the Friday Night Musicade, a music festival that drew 20,000 concertgoers and nationally recognized acts to Prairieville, and smaller projects like restoration of Prairieville's old Opera Theater. "This man Daniel Feegan, he's a mover and shaker," an older Prairieviller told me, illustrating Daniel's golden reputation. "He and his friends were sitting around one day and in their mind's eye created what is now known as the Friday Night Musicade. Around here, nothing changed for a long time and then we had a little bit of progress and a little bit of progress, [but then] Daniel [came along and started] getting behind things

[and] made it happen. Some people just have that unique ability to bring people together."

One afternoon I interviewed Daniel in the headquarters of the National Pipe and Concrete Company, a small business that been in his family for generation. Daniel leaned back in his swivel chair as we spoke, feet up, showing off a pair of boots and blue jeans. Our conversation was interrupted by frequent phone calls, which consisted mostly of Daniel giving rapid engineering advice—Daniel had graduated from Johns Hopkins with an engineering degree, where he also began promoting student music festivals.

"None of this is fun!" Daniel muttered finally after hanging up the phone and returning to the topic of Prairieville. "One of the things that [made quality of life a focus] was Crossroads Computers," Daniel said. "Because in their heyday they were bringing a lot of people from out of town. And there was a lot of discussion [and] the big point was, 'We are bringing some guy in to work at Crossroads, but his wife has nothing to do.' [We decided that] we needed things like the old Opera Theater, we needed more restaurants, we needed more bars, we needed to redo the downtown corridor." The phone rang again. "Ahhh fuck, I swear to god!" Daniel exclaimed, reaching for it and interrupting our conversation.

While Daniel talked, I reflected on the tension between his public persona and actual biography. Many of Prairieville's residents identified Daniel with a new, youthful generation that drove the city's old families from power, but Daniel himself *was* a member of the old families—or rather descended from one. Daniel did not self-identify this way and—in fairness—seemed nothing like his city's graying patricians. He also openly critiqued their public style. "The chamber used to be terrible, total boys' club," he had once told me. "Very close-minded. Had I called [them] about doing Friday Night Musicade, whether they would have returned my call or even given a shit, I don't even know. Not big consensus builders and very galvanized. [It was] support your guys or sit it out on the sidelines as naysayers." His old family roots notwithstanding, Daniel probably could not have risen so high so fast in pre-1980s Prairieville. The National Pipe and Concrete Company was small and his family therefore lacked the capacity to be as giving, and hence as prominent, as the Altoons, the Millers, or even the Brownings. Prairieville's traditional public game must have seemed even less appealing to Daniel after the 1990s, when corporate acquisitions thinned the ranks of the city's old families, and—to quote another business leader—"there was nobody left to call on." Nevertheless, Daniel rose quickly after throwing his lot in with Dani Dover, but not without engaging in public life in a fundamentally different way from his predecessors.

"God, none of this is fun!" Daniel muttered again as he hung up the phone, interrupting my thought. "Anyway, where were we?" he stretched out easily, his feet right back on his desk, and turned to what made initiatives like the Musicade possible in the first place: Dani Dover. "It is all about personality and it is all about Dani. Dani is the single most important consensus builder in the community," Daniel said. "[She is] incredibly modest, incredibly enthusiastic, and has the ability to look at something as say, 'Yeah, this can happen,' or 'it won't.' And if it can happen, she knows the right people to call—I mean, if she calls me and says, 'Hey, we gotta work on such and such,' it is something I am always excited about.'"

"See, you get these webs," Daniel continued, making social network diagrams in the air with his hands. "Otherwise it is a lot of people just floundering around. Dani is the first person I go to, to bounce ideas off of, get support and there are a lot of people who have her at the top of the rolodex—she is a sounding board, a catalyst, a consensus builder, whatever you want to call it. You need somebody to say, 'Great idea, but you need to work it this way. Let me call so-and-so, figure out how to help you work all these different systems.' And I serve that role, too, for a certain part of the city. People will call me asking what to do, but then of course if it gets big enough, then I will turn around and call her."

Here, Daniel spoke to a central piece of my argument: the connection between place-marketing initiatives like the Musicade and the way that leaders engage publicly, especially the relationships that they form with one another. Prairieville's patricians saw cross-factional collaborations as distasteful if not an outright taboo violation and were therefore neither interested in nor adept at initiatives like the Musciade. To Daniel, then, they seemed out-of-touch naysayers, hamstrung by their own rigid relations who "end up sitting on the sidelines" of Prairieville's post-1980s public game. By contrast, Daniel identified as a partner who sits at Prairieville's big round table. He did not see public life as organized around two rigid sides, but rather as a floundering and undifferentiated mass of leaders, each with unique talents, which is best catalyzed into shifting coalitions from the center by a catalyst like Dani, who holds a master rolodex of sorts that allows her to foresee which coalitions are likely to work. This public organization was useful because it allowed leaders to assemble into changing coalitions that drew on different types of resources and appealed to different audiences. When helping Daniel with the Musicade, for example, Dani catalyzed a coalition that included business leaders with experience getting corporate sponsorship, a local business owner who sponsored the event, Prairieville's Democrat-dominated parks department, and a variety of local artists and musicians.

The key thing to note is that the characteristics that make Daniel useful within Dani's partnerships, and thereby a prominent leader in Prairieville's post-1980s public life, are different—even opposite—from the public attributes celebrated by Prairieville's old families. Traditional leaders believed that you had to give in order to get, and valued loyalty and the gestures of largesse that they saw as inducing factional ties. By contrast, Daniel's utility to Dani had nothing to do with obligation. He was useful because he had experience planning music festivals and was able to get other artistically inclined leaders excited but, more than this, because he was willing to work actively with anyone *without* polarizing participants along traditional fault lines—in effect, because he saw himself as a free-floating individual unrestrained by factional obligations.

And indeed, I found that partners like Daniel were ambivalent about the logic of gift and reciprocal obligation or, more generally, their initiatives' capacity to bring concrete benefits to others. "I'm a big believer in quality of life, but there is always a big disconnect between perception and reality," Daniel mused. "Everybody wants trails and parks, but nobody uses them, they just want to know they are there. It gives people a lot of self-esteem or community-esteem. [Take the] old Opera Theater. People just love it, even though they only go maybe two or three times a year. They love to talk about it—you know, Dylan played there or Willie Nelson played there—they might not even have gone, but when they are talking to their friends from out of town they can say, 'Oh yeah, we've got all this stuff.'" Unlike traditional leaders then, Daniel was not looking to give gifts that brought sections of the public under obligation to partners like himself. His partnerships were successful because they made Prairieville look good to outsiders, and Daniel could do so more effectively precisely when he was *not* hamstrung by the public style and factional obligations of his old family forbearers.

In fact, partners' aversion to factional obligations cut both ways: partners like Daniel did not make across-the-board commitments to Dani Dover's public agenda. True to partners' iconoclastic persona, Daniel held opinions on economic development matters that differed from the prevailing consensus. "There is a [state] fund [that Prairieville draws from] to market the state, and I wonder how much mileage we actually get out of it," Daniel told me, referring to one point of disagreement with Prairieville's other partners: a partnership to create pro-Prairieville advertisements by using local funds to leverage matching state grants. "[They] spend it on radio ads and billboards and I think that is all a fucking waste of money, because that does not get people feeling better. What would get people feeling better is to give $5,000 to any reasonable event that needs help to grow or to start, whether it is a pie fest or a music experience. That gets people talking positive. [With] billboards you call someone, buy some shit, the ads always look cool, but it is stupid and you get nothing from it."

Here, Daniel's report speaks to another quality that partners associate with their own public personae: a willingness to keep divisive issues off the table. Had Daniel made his opposition to "stupid billboards," radio ads, and the like public, he might have endangered this place-marketing effort. During my fieldwork, the same could have been said of any ongoing quality-of-life initiative: at least some partners disagreed with some aspect of what other partners were doing. Traditional leaders faced similar problems of public coordination, but resolved them through hierarchical relationships defined by fealty and obligation. By contrast, partners resolved public-coordination problems by simply agreeing to disagree—they participated in only those partnerships they agreed with and refrained from publically criticizing other ones. This allowed skilled brokers like Dani to maintain the appearance of consensus simply by including the right mix of partners in each partnership.

A similar spirit of agreeing to disagree pervaded partners' interpersonal relationships. Unlike traditional leaders, they neither expected nor celebrated personal loyalty. For example, Dani Dover ran unsuccessfully as a Republican candidate for lieutenant governor, down-ticket from a GOP stalwart. The campaign was noteworthy in that Dani pledged to introduce a pragmatic, nonpartisan, and distinctly partner-like ethos into state politics—a similar pledge to that made by River City's Ben Denison, whose failed congressional campaign is discussed in the next chapter. But most of Prairieville's partners, Daniel included, did not support Dani because of her far-right running mate. "I could not stand the guy she was running with," Daniel told me. "But [we] have learned to set that aside, just say, 'I know that you are this and I am this, but let's just agree to disagree.' I'm very close to Dani, but she knows I did not support her. She probably does not feel great about this, but I said, 'Look, if you were running for governor I'd support you and work on your campaign, but the guy you are running with, I don't care for. Agree to disagree, on to the next thing." It should go without saying that traditional leaders would have seen this event as a major betrayal, probably one serious enough to permanently sour a relationship. But Dani and Daniel were able to move past it because their relationship did not imply total, faction-like obligation. They simply agreed to disagree, kept divisive issues off the table, and awaited the next initiative that they could both support.

The Prairieville Growth Coalition

Like Daniel, the Prairieville Growth Coalition (GC), a young professionals' group, was held up by Prairieville's leaders as a paragon of partnership. It was by observing this group's activities that I came to appreciate an aspect of partners' public game that I noted in passing when discussing Daniel: in addition to avoiding factional ties with one another, partners neither value strong ties to local constituencies nor expect one another to be able draw on the kind of deep community support that traditional leaders considered essential.

Winterfest, an annual event spearheaded by the group to get young people out in winter, provided an apt illustration. The year that I attended, Winterfest coincided with a warm snap, which melted the snow and raised the humidity of the air, shrouding Prairieville in a fog from which pieces of rusted postindustrial landscape periodically appeared like ghosts. The event was held in Prairieville's civic arena, and I arrived to see dozens of youngish people, dressed business-casual, milling around and laughing in big open circles or talking in smaller groups. I made my obligatory greetings and then went to talk to Louise Bedel, the group's president. In the background, attendees lazily planned a city-wide scavenger hunt on giant flip pads. Although this event was much publicized by local media as both fun and an important networking opportunity, the turnout was modest. Louise sat off to the side, eating chili from a Styrofoam bowl as we talked, periodically pushing around saltine goldfish with a plastic spoon.

"I grew up [elsewhere] and always thought, 'Prairieville is a small town, who cares what is going on over there?'" Louise said. "When I moved here, people were like, 'Why would you want to move to Prairieville?!?' If people that are from here don't even want to be here, why would I want to be here? And we as a group, I think, have really flipped that over. We want others to look at us more positively, because right now people don't look at us positively or negatively, they just don't care. And then why would somebody want to bring 200 jobs or whatever to a place they don't care about [or] if people say, 'Ugh . . . we hate it here!'"

In public settings, too, GC leaders presented themselves as a group of youthful professionals who—unlike traditional business leaders—were willing to partner with anyone on anything. "We want young thinking about things," Louise told me, for example. "Young thinking is just saying, 'Let's make a clean break from the past, come up with a good idea, see who is interested to get involved, and then just get it done!'" Like Daniel Feegan, then, GC leaders explicitly repudiated Prairieville's traditional public culture. But unlike him, they commanded no significant resources and were not initially regarded as peers by Prairieville's leaders. The group began in the early 2000s as a Republican political club populated by low-level managers and professionals. By the time of my fieldwork, the group shed its political leanings, but its events—like Winterfest—were sparsely attended. For instance, the GC hosted a monthly cocktail hour that was often attended only by the organization's board of directors. In effect, the GC had neither the capacity to actually mobilize Prairieville's young professionals nor any meaningful connection to them.

But interestingly, Prairieville's other partners were undeterred by the GC's limited reach and regarded the organization's leaders as key players. They gushed, for example, about how GC leaders did not take credit, were willing to partner with anyone, and simply wanted to "get it done!" In previous chapters, I discussed how traditional leaders were puzzled by precisely this: some prominent partners originated from "isolated little groups," were "cut off [and] out there on their own," and did not "represent anyone." But consider the advantages of membership in a "cut off" group in a public game that that revolves around partnerships.

The fact that the Growth Coalition did not truly "represent anyone" enhanced the group's flexibility, and therefore its capacity for participating in multiple partnerships. For instance, the GC distinguished itself via a partnership to create downtown art installations, an idea they got from listening to a lecture by the former mayor of Austin. The sculptures were funded partially by a federal grant and a variety of local sources: a grant from Prairieville's labor-dominated Gambling Board, donations from area businesses, municipal labor donated by the city, and active participation from the city's art community. Had the GC maintained strong ties to any of these other groups' constituencies, other leaders might have seen the downtown initiative as suspect.

But GC leaders spoke on behalf of no one, were seen as neutral, and therefore easily presented the initiative as a win-win. In effect, cut-off groups like the Growth Coalition could distinguish themselves in their city's post-1980s arena for the same reason as development personnel like Dani Dover: they were seen as neutral brokers who bring others to the table.

But in a way partners *did* view the GC as representing young professionals, and herein lies another difference between traditional leaders and partners: the two groups understood representation differently. Traditional leaders understood representation as speaking on behalf of and therefore able to mobilize, but partners understood it as serving as a stand-in for—in the sense, for example, that a painter creates a visual representation of landscape. While the latter kind of representation would have been fairly useless in traditional Prairieville's conflict-ridden public sphere, it is useful in post-1980s marketing schemes because outsiders need not know anything about a group's local significance. And in fact, GC leaders were constantly drawn into partnerships by the city's other leaders, precisely because their inclusion in any coalition broadcast the image of a young, educated, professional city to the outside world.

The Growth Coalition illustrates that partners need not command the loyalties of Prairievillers to become central players in post-1980s public life. Whereas traditional leaders traded on their ability to construct vertical networks that penetrated deeply into daily life, partners inhabit a thin layer of interaction with one another, a sort of reflective looking glass that shows outsiders what they want to see. A partner's resources or ability to mobilize others can occasionally be a useful thing to have at the table, but it is not always essential. Instead, partners' public game revolves around representing the city to outsiders and partners regard rigid, divisive attachments as incompatible with this goal. Indeed, it was GC leaders' renunciation of factional ties that allowed its otherwise insignificant leaders to move quickly onto Prairieville's central stage. In fact, Prairieville's other partners told me that they first took note of GC leaders when they renounced two factional bonds that characterized traditional business leaders—Prairieville's chamber and GOP.

Shortly after the Growth Coalition's founding, Prairieville's chamber offered GC leaders free office space, which they refused. "We decided not to be connected to the chamber [so that] we don't need to go to them, or the city, or anything to execute a plan," Louise told me. "They work with us and we work with them, but it is important to keep that line uncrossed so that they can do their thing and we can do our thing [and] keep our thinking our own."

A former GC president confirmed Louise's perspective. "Now we can back anything without being the puppets or pawns of any other organization," he said. "We are very independently thinking. If we support something that none of these other groups support, we want to be able to write letters to the editor or speak about it without ramifications. And it has worked great. Now we are at a point—and this is what we wanted—that if a project comes up people will come to us directly and say, 'GC group, will you partner with us on it?'"

Similarly, the Growth Coalition repudiated its initial GOP ties. The organization was founded in support of a Republican campaign, but the group's leaders shed this image—and expelled those who wanted to maintain Republican ties—after deciding to engage seriously in Prairieville's public life. "I think that is the trend of the younger generation," Kevin Becker, a former president of the group, told me. "We don't want to be tied to any political party or group, to put arbitrary divisions here and there. We want to be an independently thinking group."

Louise agreed. "With politics, you are either in or you are out," she said. "All the new people who joined said, 'Okay, as long as it is not political. Let's make a clear break from this politics thing.' [We are] more about community, about bringing together ideas for how to make the community better. Politics can draw people away, because it is cut-and-dried, Republican and Democrat, and if you base it on this then you are going to have people shut down. They won't show you their true person, because they need to fit a persona or mold that we have given them. [Then] if we don't agree and end up arguing about it, how am I going to get you to work with me?"

Terry Masconi and the Greening of Economic Development in Prairieville

Although the municipal office of rural development was not traditionally an important one, Terry Masconi made it into a cornerstone of Prairieville's economic development strategy. Like members of Prairieville's Growth Coalition, Terry was noteworthy because he was a relative nobody prior to adopting a partner's persona. It was also by watching him operate that I came to appreciate the hard distinction that partners make between private belief and public action: partners were generally more tolerant of personal—even potentially divisive—idiosyncrasy than traditional leaders, but saw any attempt to establish ties or factional alliances around points of division as absolute anathema to their public personae.[13]

Terry's biography was deeply intertwined with Prairieville's changing fortunes. He moved to Prairieville from California to work at Crossroads Computing in the 1990s, but stayed behind when Crossroads went to California . He worked other jobs, ran unsuccessfully for local office, and finally took his current position. At the time of my fieldwork, Prairieville's partners regarded him as a central, if perhaps odd, player in economic development efforts for his advocacy of locally grown and sustainable food—a prescient focus given the explosive interest in urban agriculture, organic farming, and green architecture since. "The stars aligned for this job," Terry told me as we talked in his city hall corner office. "All my life I have always thought of food as health, food as identity, community identity, and family identity." Terry was fifty-ish and wore a clean, nicely pressed suit paired with a tie that was loosened almost down to his chest. Just weeks earlier, he had cut the wavy gray hair that once fell crazily down to his shoulders—"I've lost my powers like Sampson!" he quipped a couple times as we talked.

Terry's claim to fame was a set of programs designed to encourage organic farming, which—being the first of their kind—garnered him multiple NPR interviews. His stock in the community rose thereafter, and key leaders like Dani Dover often had him at the table when discussing new partnerships. "All my life, I have had problems with the homogenization of everything," Terry declared, explaining his public philosophy. "New York versus Chicago pizza—this is a distinction rooted in localities and differences. You could drive to Colorado to get Coors beer. There was romanticism about having beer from somewhere else, but I think those days are gone. You know that if you go to a certain town you will have a Best Buy, a Target, and all that. [And] our local labor has been sucked out by these large corporate structures, where they are getting that labor at a lower and lower cost," Terry continued without missing a beat, although in my mind he had just jumped from the safe topic of preserving local differences to a divisive antibusiness position. "And then there is this insidious notion that economic growth is going to be, 'We are going to get an ethanol plant here, it will employ forty people, it will require a $100 million investment, the county is going to give a tax abatement, so that they don't pay all the taxes associated with the facility, because we really need those fifty jobs,'" Terry added, ending on a more divisive note still.

It should be evident that Terry's opinions were out of step with those of Prairieville's other partners. Terry's critique of ethanol plants was particularly noteworthy because he made it during the peak of the mid-2000s oil price spike, when most partners were busy imagining a future when ethanol plants remade Iowa's economy. More generally, too, Terry's critique of publically funded incentives cut to the heart of Prairieville's partnership regime, because many—if not most—partners focused on attracting or retaining employers in large part through such incentives. But these were Terry's usual talking-points, ones I heard him make often when mingling with other leaders. At the time, it surprised me that Terry saw no tension between his outsider critiques and his ability to be a reliable partner and, indeed, a critical insider.

"Yeah, at first I'm sure the [business people] thought, 'Oh, that's just some quack down there, that Terry Masconi,'" Terry told me, shedding light on this issue. "And yeah, I'm a liberal myself, and kind of a wild guy— when I go down to a chamber dinner I'm in their face, but it really does not make any difference. Many in the chamber crowd are all now very excited. They've traveled, seen the Whole Foods in Omaha and Minneapolis and Chicago. They've seen organics in California and in Florida. So [they are excited] not just for their own health, but they can see the economic potential. Everyone [in Prairieville] has their own place which they eventually fit into [and] people understand the kinds of things that I am saying. The other people are people with good intentions, we all want to make things better, we just disagree at times about how to get there—the key is finding the areas where we can work together."

A "wild guy" like Terry would certainly not have fit in with the chamber crowd of yesteryear. But in the context of Prairieville's post-1980s public game, Terry's eccentricity was an asset to other partners given the existence of key "brokers" like Dani Dover. In this context, Terry simply agreed to disagree with other partners in most respects, and participate enthusiastically in the partnerships with which he agreed. Unlike traditional leaders, Terry did not need to support other partners across the board to maintain his public standing, only to keep his dissent private and to gush publically about any ongoing partnerships. In the latter respect, Terry was a master of presentation.

"I don't think that anyone is doing a holistic economic development approach here, except for me. I know it is a cliché to say this, but the proof is in the pudding," Terry told me. "[Take] the organic conversion policy: anyone who converts to organic gets a [county tax] rebate. [Or another deal with] the community college [to provide] a certificate in organic farming. It was their initiative and we partnered on it. Now [they've leased] some land from the county [and operate an organic farm]. We made a deal with Whole Foods to buy [that] food [and] we did that through the organic broker [which I set up]. And then with the food grown on the farm, we did a recipe contest for the best salsa and sauce—so now we have a label for organic salsa from Prairie County.

"To me that is real economic development," Terry continued. "We've got to make this place cultural. We have the old Opera Theater, the Musicade—James Taylor just played there—we have an art center. We need to develop quality of life: a community that inspires young people to say, 'I can work here on this farm, or in this kitchen, I can do that here.' Everything apart from that, to me, is just a lot of publicity. We have history here:

delicious local apples, Prairie Valley watermelon. If we can get those names associated with this place, then we could really go somewhere. People will always pay more for quality and value and that is what this economy is looking for: mojo. If you build it, they will come. People will always come if you have your own vision. So that is what we need to work on, our own vision."

Terry's case illustrates some aspects of partners' public game that I discussed with respect to Daniel Feegan and the Growth Coalition. Partners gain public esteem by entering into flexible coalitions around win-win initiatives, and they do not necessarily value those who can speak on behalf and truly mobilize local constituencies—something that traditional leaders considered synonymous with public leadership. For instance, Terry admitted to me that most local farmers distrusted him and were unenthusiastic about organics, but this hardly mattered as Terry's utility within partnerships lay in "representing" a green Prairieville to outsiders, not "representing" farmers (i.e., speaking on their behalf). But more than this, Terry's case illustrated that the consensus upon which Prairieville's place-marketing partnerships depended was actively constructed and, therefore, potentially tenuous. Terry's integration into Prairieville's public life depended on skilled brokers like Dani, who created initiatives that looked like a win-win from a pool of leaders who might appear divided if arranged differently.

Herein lies the key reason for partners' aversion to public divisiveness. At any minute, partners who identified as one useful thing—an advocate of organic farming—could have identified as a different divisive thing: an opponent of ethanol plants, or worse. The well-oiled machine was always at risk of breakdown, particularly if the factions that once defined public life re-emerged. Partisan politics was one point of division that threatened to refactionalize the city, and this is a why partners viewed those with a public party affiliation as suspect.

Country Club Republicans and Activists

In the first part of the book, I showed that traditional leaders saw partisan politics as an extension of community life: they had no qualms about being divisive, fought on behalf of their side in public, represented their constituents on conflict-ridden municipal commissions, and viewed party politics as a simple extension of all this. To them, political engagement was just another way to gain esteem within their city's traditional game. Partners' political orientation was virtually the opposite. They saw sides as restrictive, disempowering, and ineffective, and distinguished themselves by avoiding divisive identities that could inhibit the seamless formation of partnerships. Moreover, partners were more interested in projecting a positive image to outsiders than in bringing benefits to their people or speaking on behalf of a local constituency. For these reasons, partners had ambivalent feeling about both local and party politics.

"[Many things] do not work well with city [commissions], because you have all the bureaucracy and the roadblocks," Daniel Feegan told me, exemplifying a typical partner's orientation toward local politics. Such attitudes were reflected in partner's avoidance of local democratic bodies; recall table 4.3, which shows that city commissions were structurally peripheral within each city's 2000s-era public sphere. Daniel continued: "You need public meetings and freedom of information [for] some things. If you are going to raise water rates or garbage rates or something, you gotta have public meetings, because that affects everybody and people [need] a chance to get up there and bitch. But [public meetings] make it difficult for the city to do things creatively. You can't work out really complex ideas in ten heated minutes. Entities like cities and counties are really hamstrung." For partners, local political bodies were unattractive because they encouraged public discord and inhibited flexibility and creativity

The GC repudiated Republican ties early in its history because its leaders wanted to be "more about community." The group's leaders underwent a similar personal conversion. Louise Bedel described herself to me as "not a very political person: I want to be educated, but I don't see myself as cut-and-dried, one way or another," while Kevin Becker, the GC's former president, reported not caring whether "you are a Democrat or a Republican, as long as you represent me well. [I will] support anyone who makes me feel like they understand." Along similar lines, Terry had been a lifelong Democrat and Daniel voted Democratic in college, but both felt similarly to GC leaders at the time of my fieldwork.

"I have supported [Democratic] Party things at times, but I've kind of decided over the last couple years that I'm [registering] Independent, I switched," Daniel told me. "I don't hold the Democratic Party in a whole lot higher esteem than the GOP. They both have their problems and run shitty candidates. . . . The two-party system sucks anyway and hopefully it will all blow up when people realize that. [Then we will have] no more of this galvanizing bullshit: 'I'm a Democrat and you are a Republican; I'm a conservative and you are a liberal.' You can't—I mean, whatever, whatever, who cares? Unless everyone is working together, you can't get anywhere anyway!"

"Whether you are a conservative or a liberal does not make any difference." Terry told me, mirroring Daniel's sentiment. "You have to go to where the truth is and talk about common sense. Both parties could use more of that. You are always talking abortion, trying to take a position on Iraq, and just really focusing on all these wedge issues. You are forgetting about all the basic issues in American politics: healthy environment, self-reliance, equality of all people before the law—what we are and what the American people can identify with. Right now we have become so fragmented, polarized, pitted [against] each other so that nobody can see clearly. A lot of things could get brought up that aren't. If somebody could tap into that, they could win."

This co-occurrence is striking: three different people, all of whom identified with a political party in the past, repudiated party affiliation upon becoming key players in Prairieville's public life. But what is significant is not each leader's repudiation of politics per se, but rather the similar reasons for it, which illustrates an incompatibility between the logic of post-1980s community engagement and politics. In their own ways, each leader argued that *being* a community leader is incompatible with the qualities associated with political party members. Daniel, for example, perceived party membership as "galvanizing" (people into conflict) and therefore ineffective—note that "galvanizing" is the same term that he applied to Prairieville's traditional patrician class. Terry took the argument further by implying that he might support a party that became community-like (i.e., focused on points of consensus over divisive issues).

Of course, Daniel, Terry, and GC leaders were unusual in that they were close associates of Dani and regarded as exemplary partners; not all of Prairieville's business leaders repudiated politics so completely. Nevertheless, these three cases illustrate a basic contradiction between the logic of partnership and politics. Such contradictions are common in social life. Consider some everyday examples: contradictions between traditional masculinity and involved parenting, between rebellious teenage culture and participation in high school activities, and so on. Implicit in such cases is the notion that social interaction is analogous to playing a role or part and that the performance of some roles (e.g., that of rebellious teen) is incompatible with the performance of others (e.g., organizer of the school's pep rally).[14] Because such contradictions are ubiquitous in social life, we typically take it for granted as natural that certain types of people do not do certain types of things. Along these lines, most partners simply saw it as natural that community leaders should avoid politics. This is not to say that all avoided politics entirely. Cultural contradictions rarely constrain absolutely, because people find ways to negotiate and reconcile contradictions, establish themselves as exceptions to the rule, or simply flout social convention. Some of River City and Prairieville's partners circumvented community taboos against public partisanship by, for example, engaging in politics only before elections, supporting candidates on the grounds that they were consensus builders, or critiquing a party or its candidates as divisive—but actually, few partners did even this and hardly any formed the unquestioned attachments to parties that were normal for traditional leaders. Partisanship was simply an unacceptable liability within their public game.

By the time of my fieldwork, partners were centrally established in Prairieville's public sphere and their aversion toward politics had spread to others. For instance, a few of Prairieville's business leaders had not fully embraced partnership and behaved traditionally in some circumstances and like partners in others. Many of these leaders were the "donors" discussed by GOP activists in this chapter's opening: those who traditionally led the party and still occasionally donated money, but were increasingly discontinuing even financial support. Charles Browning (discussed in chapter 2) was one example. Although his father and grandfather held positions of GOP leadership before him, Charles was unsure. We spoke about this over lunch shortly after Mark Sturley referred to GOP activists as "Christian Nazis."

"This guy Mark Sturley," Charles said, pausing for a moment to reflect. "He called them religious Nazis or something like that, okay? Right-wing fascists. And I thought, 'Yeah, he got that one right!'" Charles chuckled. "Here [The GOP] just lost the House, Senate and governor's race. When you dance for the extreme 15 percent, you are going to lose every time. I would never get involved [with the county GOP] again. I could never hack it. The GOP nationally has repositioned itself to a fault," he continued. "Now they fight for this 15 percent over there or that 15 percent over here. Seventy percent of us in the middle don't know what to do, just throwing up our hands, so disgusted with what is happening. The GOP has moved so far to the right on this social agenda that they have forgotten what is reasonable and they leave me out. I mean, if I went down to the courthouse I'm probably still registered as a Republican, but I've been meaning to get that switched over for a long period of time, register as an Independent. And I need to do that, just to make a statement.

"The [Republican] congressman we have now, he's out there—I would not send him a dime and always vote for whoever is running against him," Charles added, expressing a frustration I heard often among Prairieville's traditional donors. "When I was growing up, [our congressman] was smart, very smart guy, effective [and] from the same generation as my brother. [Our current congressman is] not from here. I don't know him and I don't want to know him. So then this last go-round, Daniel Feegan calls me up, because there was this young guy, running as an Independent [in our district]. Daniel Feegan and I get along great. He was on public radio the other day trying to raise money, so I called in, 500 bucks, you know. His family and our family go back a long ways—Daniel is great, great, great guy. And I went up there, met with this young guy, and just did not think he had a chance. This guy just did not know what he was talking about. But Daniel calls me up again and he says, 'Charles, this is it; we have to support this guy! He's running as an Independent. It is the road of the future.' And I said, 'That's fine, I agree. I would if I thought he could be effective.'"

Charles's public orientation differed in some respects from Prairieville's hard-core partners, because he vacillated between traditional and partner-like statements. Charles was speaking as a traditional leader, for example, when he said that contemporary GOP leaders are not "from Prairieville," and that he did not "know them . . . and does not want to." By contrast, past GOP candidates were from Prairieville, "very, very intelligent" and from the same generation (read: social circle) as Charles's brother. In sum, Charles viewed current GOP politicians as outsiders to Prairieville's traditional business faction who did not merit inclusion. At other times, however, Charles critiqued politicians as a partner: as too "divisive," "extreme," and for leaving too "many people out," particularly people in the middle where Charles discursively positions himself.

These short quotations offer clues to Charles's changing orientations. At the time of my fieldwork, most business leaders engaged as partners. In fact, Charles experimented with partnerships himself: he gave a speech to the Growth Coalition and participated in "Schools Now!" a partnership between business leaders and Democratic lawmakers to improve public schools. As many of Charles's peers embraced partnership, they abandoned the GOP, leaving it in the hands of activists. Increasingly then, Charles's public world was divided between community partnerships that involved many of his peers—patrician-turned-partner Daniel Feegan, for instance— and "wacky" GOP politicos. No wonder he avoided politics.

It is important to note that former Republican donors like Charles were not simply reacting to the county GOP's polarization. They simultaneously drove this polarization by staying away from the party, thereby fomenting the resentment that GOP activists felt toward country club Republicans. "I guess there has been a changing of the guard here [and] I guess I'm new guard," Landry Oliver, the new GOP president told me some months after the furor over Mark Sturley's statement faded. Under Landry's leadership, the GOP reoriented its strategy. "The new guard is more socially and fiscally conservative then our predecessors—maybe not even that much more conservative, but much more energetic," Landry explained.[15] "We need to [focus on] local races [and] engaging people here with the values in our platform. There is more of an emphasis on that in the new generation. Because in [each election] there are people who show up because of conservative values, and then they are always the ones who stay behind and do the work. [And] I know Sturley said we were going to tap into this [local] big business money. So that is basically an appeal to—in his view, which I don't think is a healthy one—is that you have to push out people that are more socially conservative. [Mark] pledged to me that he would not do that when he ran [for country chair], because otherwise I would have run against him. So would have a lot of other people. The social conservatives are the ones that have been doing the work for a long time, so why should they be the ones to be pushed out? No! What we really need is a new way to reach people, get people excited and energized."

Thus speaks politics disembedded from Prairieville's community life. Whereas traditional leaders' political views revolved around bread-and-butter-issues like taxation, unionization, and government regulation, political activists like Landry are unconstrained by community considerations. They are not community leaders and—indeed—are shunned by them and operate instead within a political space divorced from other community institutions. In the next chapter, I analyze a similar disembedding of politics from community life in River City before proceeding to an analysis of activist parties like Landry's in the chapter that follows.

SIX

The Ben Denison Campaign: How Partners Failed to Colonize Politics

When I first began fieldwork in 2006, River City's leadership class was abuzz with the candidacy of Ben Denison, who was running in the Democratic primary for Congress. Partners in particular could talk of little else and packed any venue where he spoke. One afternoon Ben gave a speech at the Rotary Club, a traditionally business-dominated and Republican association. But like so many others, many Rotarians had made the transition to partnership.

As the opening speaker introduced him, Ben sat motionless in his impeccably pressed grey suit, shifting in his seat slightly and pushing up his rimless glasses. He then approached the podium to applause and occasional exclamations from the audience, finally towering above it with an impressive frame that exceeded six feet.

"My name is Ben Denison and I am running for the privilege of serving you in the United States Congress," he began to deafening applause. "But my friends, you know me. Now [I want] to learn a little about you. [So] I have a poll—a nonscientific poll—to do. Would please—everybody who is registered Democrat please raise your hand?"

Tension filled the room as only a few hands went up, waving back and forth like lone blades of grass in a barren field. Ben grinned, seemingly enjoying violating partners' taboo on public discussion of politics. "Oh come on, you chickens!" an audience member finally shouted, eliciting a wave of rumbling, good-natured laughter, including from Ben himself. "Now, everyone who is a registered Republican please raise your hands," Ben continued as a narrow majority of hands went up. Ben then asked about Independents and perhaps a third of those in attendance raised their hands.

"The reason I ask you is this," Ben continued, carefully annunciating his next words. "Is I . . . *don't* . . . *care*," he paused dramatically. "I know what

I am, I'm a Democrat and I know why I'm a Democrat. But frankly, I don't care what your politics are. There's enough going on in this nation, folks, where we have to forget about the left and the right. This race is about right and wrong. You and I both know what this race is really about: it is about you.

"So the last ten years, what a ride!" Ben continued. "You have educated me in those years as director of River City Development. Your community was the butt of jokes when it came to the economy. Today it is a model of how a community can turn itself around and I'm so proud to have been a part of that. [If I win this race] it will be because of folks like you—people who *know* me. Folks who know that we will not agree 100 percent of the time, but who know that I will work my heart out for them."

"This race is not about Washington, DC, and it is not about partisan politics," Ben continued, fixating on his trademark campaign theme. "I am not running for Congress to change *the* world. I'm running for Congress to change *our* world, one life, one family, one job at a time. You know with what I do at the Development Corporation—if I go down to [the city where Green's corporate headquarters is located] and I say, 'My name is Ben Denison and I am director of the River City Development Corporation and I'd like to help you,' they'd go, 'Yeah, right, what's in it for River City?!?'" Ben paused to let the laughter in the room subside. "But if I say to those same folks, 'My name is Ben Denison and I am a congressman and I would like to help—will you allow me?' I think the answer will be 'Yes!' So remember this: nobody understands what is going on here like I understand, nobody can go to bat for you the way that I can go to bat for you, nobody can produce for you what I can produce, and no one" and here Ben paused for dramatic effect "no one loves River City like I love River City."

The speech was followed by enthusiastic applause and a series of "questions" that mostly expressed support for Ben's candidacy—including several from people who claimed never to have voted Democratic. And indeed, Ben's campaign attracted widespread support from Republican business leaders. "I'd consider myself more of a Republican, at least that's how I've always voted," a banker and an early supporter of Ben's told me. "But I guess I'm more on an Independent now, because there are Democrats I like. I like Ben Denison a lot and have contributed pretty heavily to his campaign. I've known him for years—he's a straight shooter [and] he seems to be more pro-business than a lot of Democrats, since his role at the Development Corporation is to work with and attract business to the community. He's a team player and does a better job than most."

Partisan politics, a subject usually avoided by River City's partners, was suddenly all that anybody wanted to talk about, if only to voice enthusiastic support for Ben Denison. In the informal meetings and phone calls between acquaintances and friends that constitute the backstage of River City's public sphere, Ben's candidacy symbolized nothing short of the final leg of the journey that River City began in the 1980s: the moment when the city's partners would finally tame the world of partisan politics—that last stubborn vestige of pre-1980s conflict—with the logic of partnership. Their victory over the city's traditional leadership class would then be complete, a fact not lost on many Democratic activists who mobilized against Ben. This was a morality play with an uncertain ending. Each played their part to the upmost.

But in this case, as in so many others, partisan politics proved to be partners' undoing, a bridge too far. Ben did attract the support of much of River City's leadership class, but Democratic activists were bitterly divided and many campaigned for his rivals. Ben's victory among regular citizens was also far more ambiguous than among other partners and—due in part to his lukewarm reception among the former—he ultimately lost the primary to a PAC-backed candidate from another city. Disappointed, River City's partners settled on a familiar explanation: grassroots community consensus had, once again, lost to divisive partisan politics.

In the last chapter, I discussed why Prairieville's partners generally avoid politics and thereby reproduce a public sphere defined by conflict between community and politics. In this chapter, I make a similar argument about River City, but focus more on exceptions to the rule of partners' partisan avoidance, or—to be more precise—constitutive exceptions to the rule: activities that violate partners' taboo against political participation, but upon closer examination reinforce the binary opposition between community and politics that structures River City's public life.[1] I focus especially on partners' tendency to publicly criticize politics, malign partisan activists, and occasionally run for political office as consensus, antipolitics candidates, dynamics that were at the heart of Ben Denison's campaign.

This chapter serves the secondary function of a sort of insider's critique of River City's partnership regime, and of partnership as a public ideology by extension—one that is unavoidable given the realities of partners' stewardship over public life. Say what you will about traditional leaders, but there was no subterfuge in their public style: they valued open conflict over the distribution of society's resources and the public sphere they oversaw was conflict-ridden. By contrast, partners equated their public style with consensus, but the public sphere that they oversaw was not without conflict. Partners blamed this fact on activists obsessed with hot-button issues or politically motivated traditional leaders, holdovers from another era who refused to exit gracefully from River City's central stage. But the truth was more complicated. For instance, those who opposed Ben Denison's candidacy were former community leaders who had been ostracized by partners and saw the Democratic primary as an opportunity to exact revenge.

In this light, my key argument is that the binary opposition between community and politics is one reproduced *locally* within River City's public sphere. The partisans who thwart partners are not outsiders from Planet Politics or holdovers from another era, but rather partners' own doppelgangers: actors created by partners' peculiar form of domination over community life.

The chapter works up to the doppelganger argument by examining the origins of River City's partners, the inherent tensions in their public role, and the way that conflicts with political actors can resolve these tensions. I begin with a history of River City's transition to partnership. This section provides context for subsequent discussions and further illustrates the link between neoliberal reforms and changes in public life. I focus especially on the mechanisms that reshuffled River City's public sphere, showing how leaders who did not change their traditional style were pushed into irrelevance when they could no longer mobilize the resources they needed to impact public life. I then turn to contemporary partners and discuss tensions that they experience between, on the one hand, their ideological commitment to consensus and, on the other, the reality of public discord, their desire to side with majority over minority opinion, and some partners' need to speak on behalf of particular constituencies rather than River City as a whole. Partners' ability to label conflict as "political," or even to start a political conflict, helps to diffuse these tensions. I conclude with two cases of public conflict that partners decried as evidence of politics gone wrong, but which were actually of their own making: one between community leaders and Republican activists, and the one between Democratic activists and supporters of Ben Denison's primary campaign.

Pathways to Partnership: A History of
River City's Post-1980s Public Life

In River City, the crises of the 1980s struck quickly and totally devastated the city's traditional institutions. The year 1980 was River City's high-water mark: employment levels at Greenfield's, the Pack, and Brightwood Metals were higher than ever before, and River City's population peaked. Then, in the winter of 1981, the order to streamline operations came down from Greenfield's headquarters, a day that locals still refer to as Black Friday.

Things were hardly better in River City's homegrown industries. River City's packinghouse was now in the hands of Rhomberg Sr.'s descendants, who decided to follow the advice of management consultants, streamline operations, and use capital thus levied to acquire their regional competitors. Much to River Citians' dismay, the Pack's owners replaced the River City brand with the distinctly non–local-sounding DKL Foods logo. Then they laid off a thousand workers and slashed the wages of those who remained. "The sons never seemed to be able to run that plant the way the old man could," a former meatpacker recalled. "As soon as they came in they put turnstiles on the doors, and the wages started to come down. We had incentive before, but then they said, 'No, we don't need that.' It [went downhill] after the old man left. When the place shut down, I was not sorry to see it go."

Unlike in Prairieville, homegrown industries like the Pack quickly became the victims rather than the benefactors of corporate mergers. By mid-decade, DKL Foods was acquired by a national brand specializing in processed foods, which slashed the workforce again and shuttered the plant soon after. Many of River City's other local firms were also bought out during this period, thinning the ranks of traditional business and labor leaders alike.[2] The fortunes of labor leaders were perhaps more dramatic that those of local business owners, because defunct union leaders went back onto the job site or shop floor to make ends meet rather than leaving the city. The once-proud meatpackers' union, for example, was unable to support any full-time representatives after the Pack shut down. "I know a guy here in town, old Marty Manx, he was a big guy over on the meatcutters' union," a working-class resident told me. "Back then he was making a ton of money, a big figure around town and now—we went into [a grocery store] and saw [him] working back behind the meat counter! That's all 'cause they broke up the union."

River City's economy seemed beyond repair. When asked about the period, many older residents tell an urban legend about a sign that appeared over downtown and read, "Will the last one to leave River City please turn off the lights?" Some residents claim that a savvy entrepreneur even reproduced the slogan for a t-shirt that River Citians wore en masse. In fact, neither such a sign nor t-shirt ever existed, but the mood of the 1980s must have been somber indeed.[3] Halfway through the decade, unemployment peaked at nearly 25 percent and photographs of River City's broken-down harbor was featured in several news stories as iconic of the newly discovered Rust Belt. It was in this atmosphere of shock and disarray that some of River City's traditional leaders first dabbled with partnerships.

"The wakeup call happened [when employers] weren't just laying off union guys any more. These were real cuts—we were laying off management. too," Fred Pommel, a banker, chamber president, and early advocate of partnership told me. "Then there was the whole thing that the packinghouse is leaving town [so the union needs to give concessions]. They did cut wages, and then they [were bought out and liquidated] anyway. So there was that recognition that it is a bigger world than the city limits, [and] that we have to work together to get the jobs and keep them." Pete Diller, the president of Greenfield's union at the time, mirrored this sentiment. "[Management was] eroding our workforce. It was terrible," he said. "[One time] a guy says [to me], 'Geez, guess who is doing my old job I used to do at Green's making $24 an hour? My wife [at a small shop that contracts with the plant], for $8 an hour.' So when they said, 'You better give us what we want or we are going to move [the plant to Mexico],' I thought, 'It might take 'em a while, but they will to do it.' That's when a lot of us got the message. They could do what they had always threatened to do. Better try to work together with 'em."

Although there is no reason to discount such accounts, strategic adoption was not the primary mechanism that reshuffled River City's public sphere. Indeed, most prominent traditional leaders were unwilling or unable to become partners—I will show shortly that even Fred Pommel was unable to do so.[4] Rather, 1970s- and '80s-era reforms closed off the supply of locally rooted resources that traditional leaders once fought over, creating a structural opportunity for those who engaged in broad-based partnerships. After leaders like Fred and Pete founded big tents like the Development Corporation, others were free to dabble in partnership and many did. However, most traditional leaders found the public culture of big tents distasteful. Those who remained partners tended to be leaders who were peripheral to pre-1980s public life, but they were soon catapulted to prominence as their partnerships began to attract outside resources to a struggling city. The history of the Labor Management Council exemplifies this process.

Fred Pommel was also a founding member of the Labor Management Council. "There was a bad environment between labor and management, because it was—you know—the old way: 'You do what you do, we do what we do, stay out of our way unless you want a fight!' But the '80s changed everything," he said. "It's like my dad used to say: 'In this city there are five manufacturing families and two banking families. Whatever they say goes, thank you very much!' Well, all that was over. Then a couple forward-looking labor guys—Marty Manx and Peter Diller—got together with a couple [bankers and other business leaders] and started having that conversation. Not a lot of people knew about it at first. It wasn't secret exactly, but the [chamber] membership would have been surprised had they known what was going on."

In fact, four labor leaders showed up at the organization's first meeting: Pete Diller, Marty Manx, Michael Lombarti, who was then Labor Council president, and Fred Billingham, a little-known leader who had just been elected business manager of the carpenters' local. In time, Fred became River City's most prominent union leader while Michael Lombarti—then arguably the city's biggest union leader—began a long, contentious exit from River City's central stage.

"When we started, there was a lot of labor people pissed off at us saying, 'Hey, you going to sleep with management?'" Fred Billingham recalled. "See, in the mid '80s, they were going to shut the lights off and everything, and River City had a bad reputation in terms of labor and management. And guess who showed up: Fred Pommel, who was president of the chamber, sayin, 'Hey, we gotta get rid of this black eye we have created here!' So a few of us [on the labor side] got together and said, 'Hey, let's create this thing.'"

"[But] after about ten years, Michael, I don't know, I guess he thought like [some of the other Labor Council leaders]," Fred continued. "They just dropped out and are still dropped out, [because] we were really starting to work together and I think a lot of them think, 'Hey, it's still union fighting management out here all the time'—that old mentality." Fred paused pensively, then continued, striving to account for traditional leaders' refusal to abandon the old way. "I think they'd rather sit across the table and fight. A lot of the older guys tried this, and maybe they thought that this was going to be something different than it was, maybe, 'Oh this is a way really for the unions to get control. Oh boy, we are going to have management trapped under our little finger!' But it wasn't that way. Everybody else here realized that it is a two-way street. [We said,] 'Hey, let's sit around the table and find a solution that works for everybody."

The Labor Management Council was founded to solve an ideal-typical post-1980s problem: to broadcast an image of labor–business harmony and thereby attract outside employers. All of the organization's surviving founders reported agreeing with this strategic goal in principle. But the actual process of marketing to the outside—however strategic it may initially have been—clashed with traditional leaders' public style. Traditional leaders saw themselves as fighters, a presentation of self that allowed them to mobilize support from the gallery of the democratic forums that controlled access to the local and locally controlled federal resources of their day. But organizations like the Labor Management Council had no gallery section and, what's more, control of the organization guaranteed access to no significant local or nonlocal resources. Moreover, the organization could hardly broadcast harmony if its own directors were fighting over control. Leaders like Michael Lombarti did not want to be part of this new world and ultimately dropped out. "[Some labor leaders] will get on these bullshit boards—and I don't mean city council or school board—because those run the city and we have an opportunity to have control of those, but some of these other [development organizations]," Michael told me. "[These leaders] get co-opted and forget that you are on those goddamned boards to take the labor agenda [to the business people]."

It was not only previously peripheral players like Fred Billingham who catapulted past River City's traditional leaders during the 1980s. Many people whom traditional leaders had not considered public peers at all were suddenly making waves: the heads of educational, artistic, and cultural groups and—of course—economic development personnel. Because such figures commanded neither significant resources nor loyalties, they did not participate in the gift exchange that once structured the city's public sphere. But as in Prairieville, River City's cutoff groups participated effectively in post-1980s public life because of their capacity to easily shift their presentation of self in different partnerships.

One such leader was Patricia Collins, the president of River City's community college system. "We touch everybody, so for us to be at the table [means a lot]," Patricia told me, touting a partner-like ability to be all things to all people, then went on underscore how her organization could represent striving working-class residents, adult learners, the ESL community, high tech and manufacturing firms, or downtown property owners, depending on the needs of a partnership. And, indeed, during my fieldwork Patricia was central in a workforce development partnership to attract medical technology, a partnership between social service agencies to expand the mental health center, and a partnership between cultural associations to obtain funding for downtown art exhibits. So it was that she became a central player in River City's public sphere.

As in Prairieville, then, partners who adopted flexible, changing, and multiple presentations of self quickly moved to their city's central stage. The rise of these new leaders put competitive pressure on traditional leaders who embraced partnership in turn. To stay in the limelight, they too now needed to expand the range of identities that they could adopt. By the 1990s traditional leaders turned partners began to mirror leaders like Patricia in their public pronouncements: they presented themselves as community leaders first and foremost; labor or business ties, they insisted, were but one of their many public identities. "In the past we were very adversarial. The chamber was an organization that protected its turf, like, 'If it's business related, you deal with us and only with us,'" a chamber leader told me. "[It was] a narrow point of view, so often we were just sitting on the sidelines. [Instead, we should] find creative solutions to the same old problems that allow us to bring in our different gifts."

Fred Billingham echoed this tone. "United Labor is very community oriented," he said. "We put on the Labor Day parade, we get involved in [a summer music festival], we might hold a fundraiser, we work closely with different charities. We work *with* the community on a lot of projects. The Labor Council would never get behind [most initiatives]. We are the labor group that says, 'Hey, it's going to create jobs, be great for the community, let's do this. We've got to be part of the positive changes around here.'" Traditional leaders were now "more about community" than the business or labor sides that had once structured public life; in local parlance, they had fully made the transition to partnership. Anything that indexed traditional modes of public engagement was now a liability.

Despite idiosyncrasies in their 1980s- and 1990s-era trajectories, then, River City's and Prairieville's central community institutions were taken over by partners for reasons that are consistent with my argument about 1970s- and '80s-era neoliberal reforms. That is, traditional leaders embraced partnerships for their own idiosyncratic reasons or did not embrace them, but—crucially—those who partnered rose to prominence in their city's post-1980s arena while those who did not fell. Along these lines, Prairieville's and River City's public life differed only in that partners hold over public institutions was firmer in River City. Recall that Prairieville's partners retreated briefly from partnership during the 1990s. There, the line between traditional leaders and partners was blurrier, and some leaders like Charles Browning even inhabited a kind of in-between space and acted sometimes in partner-like ways and sometimes in traditional ways. Not so in River City. Even those who had been key in River City's transition to partnership were not guaranteed a seat at the city's big round table as partners periodically ostracized those who seemed too divisive.

For instance, Fred Pommel, the chamber president who worked behind the scenes to start the Labor Management Council, was subsequently encouraged by his peers to withdrawal from public life. "The guys getting involved all said, 'Okay, it can't be the chamber umbrella-ing this and no it can't be [the Labor Council. But] it was funny, because [for me] it was like, 'I'm really for this, but I will have nothing to do with it!'" Fred said, laughing and at peace now with his exit from public life. "I was always suspect because of my pedigree. There was no way any of the labor guys were going to have anything to do with me—I was too divisive. So I was for it, but I could not be a part of it, because I was suspect, too divisive. And you know what? I don't blame them."

Fred's damaging "pedigree" was a perfect fit with River City's traditional game: noted for his business sense and affability, Fred sat on several business charities and worked on the campaigns of two stridently anti-union Republicans. But in the partnership-dominated city, Fred's biography became a liability because union leaders read it as "too divisive." Of course, everyone assumed that business leaders were Republican in private, but Fred's public support for union-busters was something else altogether. Sensing that he was an impediment to cooperation, Fred therefore withdrew from public life. At the time of my fieldwork, partners looked on Fred with respect but did not consider him a key player.

How Community Consensus Creates Partisan Conflict

So it was that River City's traditional leaders either made the transition to partnership or were publically marginalized. To a great extent then, River City's public life was dominated by partners who disagreed about the details of local development strategies or community initiatives, but agreed that everyone should take divisive issues off the table and focus instead on win-win initiatives. Yet the city's public sphere was not free of conflict. This was because in excluding political actors from community life, partners relegated them to a sort of purely political petri dish, one where they were free to polarize one another and focus on campaigns that were more divisive than anything traditional leaders ever supported. Partners themselves exacerbated this community-politics divide, using political conflict for their own advantage. During my fieldwork, I observed partners stoking partisan conflict to resolve three kinds of tensions within their public role: between the ideology of consensus and actually existing discord, between their desire to do the popular thing and avoid offending a vocal minority, and between their desire to support a particular constituency and speak on behalf of the community as a whole.

Contradiction 1: Actual Consensus versus Socially Constructed Consensus

The key tension within the ideology of partnership revolves around partners' understanding of consensus. By consensus, partners do not mean a situation in which everyone agrees with an initiative. For instance, Prairieville's key partners like Daniel Feegan and Terry Masconi disagreed with many other leaders' initiatives, but maintained consensus by agreeing to disagree, keeping their discord private, and participating enthusiastically with others on other initiatives. The consensus valued by partners therefore presupposed a public sphere dominated by partners, because it could be constructed only if others viewed discord as private and accord as public. The problem here is obvious: what to do when others want to publicly disagree? Partners found it useful to tar such opponents with the political brush.

Much of River City's 1990s-era public life hinged on the uneasy tension between partnership and public discord, because one group of traditional leaders—River City's Labor Council—refused to bow out of public life. Throughout the decade, the Labor Council bickered with the United Labor Council, which was by this point populated entirely by labor leaders who partner. The two organizations disagreed especially about who had authority to appoint labor representatives to River City's public commissions. The conflict was finally settled in 1998, when Hawkeye Building Supplies, a corporation headquartered elsewhere, announced plans to build a new manufacturing plant in River City.

Hawkeye's announcement was only River City's most recent piece of good news as several development partnerships had paid off and were finally drawing visitors, not vice, to the harbor. In a speech shortly before the Hawkeye incident, Ben Denison proclaimed that "all the positive changes" ensured that "never again will the lights be turned off." But leaders' ability to attract Hawkeye was not certain. The company had considered alternate sites, and only went with River City after development personnel promised an incentive package that included the city's assistance in securing a state enterprise zone grant.[5] To qualify for the grant, a local board needed to voice support for the project and certify that the firm would create at least twenty-two jobs that pay above median wage. Development personnel argued—correctly, as it turn out—that discord would kill the application because enterprise zone funds were scarce and highly sought after by other cities. Because development personnel did not want to take a divisive stance and choose between labor bodies, they invited Steve Raney, the

Labor Council's president, and Emerson Stackey, a popular United Labor leader and former councilman, onto the commission.

Trouble began when Steve noticed that Hawkeye intended to pay below-average wages. "In their applications they put that they were going to create 22 jobs that paid 14 something on average an hour, and they had one in there that was going to be a position for an engineer, it was forty bucks an hour, but there were very few if any line workers included in that average," Steve recalled, still indignant. "So what they said was, 'We are having 22 positions at 14 something an hour, the other 137 positions will be somewhat less.' So my question was, 'How much less?' Were those were going to be 7 something an hour?"

Steve stalled by requesting time to collect more information and two other commissioners sided with him: Emerson Stackey and Shirley Nolan, a union-backed county supervisor who had been in office since the 1970s. The motion was defeated 6–3. Other commission members then called an immediate vote, and the application for enterprise funds was approved 7–1, with Steve voting no, Nolan yes, and Stackey abstaining. Ultimately, therefore, the application passed with near-unanimous support and development personnel expressed public optimism. "These companies are not on a bended knee. Our communities are on a bended knee," Ben Denison told a newspaper reporter the next day. "A split vote does damage an application, [because] we are handing the state a reason not to approve it. If the application is denied, Hawkeye could decide to go somewhere else, but we are confident other steps can be taken locally." Crucially, however, the reporter also interviewed Steve, who declared, "If you think I'm just going to sit here and help Hawkeye bring 137 poverty-level jobs to River City, you're wrong!"

River City's residents had heard harsher words spoken. Before the 1980s, such a statement would hardly have been front-page news. In this case, however, Hawkeye's regional manager also read the newspaper and responded with an open letter to River City.

"The three members of the commission who did not fully support an application have done a great disservice to Hawkeye employees and the local community," he wrote. "Mr. Steve Raney, who evidently represents organized labor, is dissatisfied that many of our jobs are entry level and suggests that Hawkeye pays poverty-level wages. I consider this to be an insult to our employees and to our company. Mr. Emerson Stackey did not support our position as he withheld support by abstaining to vote. Mrs. Shirley Nolan of the County Board of Supervisors demonstrated incomplete support by voting, 'Yes,' but expressing reservations and concerns. I am hopeful that these names will be remembered by our employees and others in the community should they ever appear on a ballot." Making matters worse, the mayor of another city where Hawkeye considered relocating chimed in with his own letter to the newspaper. "We are still as interested as we were last year," he wrote. "We will be putting our best offer forward again."

Now the gloves were off. "I can personally guarantee that Hawkeye will never again be exposed to the kind of treatment it was exposed to weeks ago," Ben Denison said in another interview. "Never again will these existing 500 jobs be put into such jeopardy." The following day, an open letter from the city office of economic development accused Steve and others of overstepping their bounds, and argued that River City needed "entry-level" positions to help its citizens "move out of welfare" and into the skilled trades.

A flurry of angry letters from River Citians followed. "For the lady [from the economic development office] who thought that only skilled workers should make $13 an hour, let her stand on a line all day long, working in a meatpacking plant or foundry or shoveling sand and dirt and see if she does not think she is worth more than [minimum wage]," one working-class resident wrote. Other letters accused Hawkeye of making shoddy and overpriced products, of "whining about tax incentives," of treating workers like "computers or robots"—and many of these came from recognizable names once associated with the old labor faction. For example, Emerson Stackey took offense at Hawkeye's letter and publically criticized Hawkeye, as did Mitt O'Connell, a popular Democratic state senator who sat on the Development Corporation board. Even members of River City's old families who had largely withdrawn from public life reentered the public fray. "The comment about 'poverty-level' jobs oozes with ignorance and an order of socialist moral superiority," wrote one such figure. "Hawkeye does not dictate what its entry level or any other job pays, the market does." The letter then went on to suggest that "at least a rudimentary knowledge of market economics" be required for those serving on public the commission in future.[6] River City was sounding like its old self again.

Before 1980, such a labor–business polarization of River City's public sphere would have helped labor leaders mobilize residents and pressure local owners. But times had changed. Control now rested with Hawkeye's corporate headquarters and state agencies that controlled funds that might influence Hawkeye. Even as angry letters to the newspaper poured in, the city's partners therefore worked behind the scenes.

About a month after the initial event, representatives of the Labor Council, the Building Trades Council, and United Labor met with development personnel to formulate a common response. At one time, labor would have backed their man without hesitation, but the organizations could not agree on a common course and eventually issued a joint statement that painted the conflict as procedural: "the application was incomplete," they noted, and added that "no representative of the company was available to answer questions." The statement also underscored that River City might still get enterprise funds despite the commission's lack of unanimity. Then, United Labor leaders—minus Stackey—traveled with development personnel to Hawkeye's corporate headquarters and quietly mended fences. Most partners who had been drawn into the conflict soon repented. Two months later, for example, one errant United Labor member wrote a letter to the newspaper that described the conflict as arising from a legal "gray area." "Nobody would or could be against progress in River City," he wrote. "I can't understand why anybody would want to stop progress here . . . and nobody does."

In the end, River City did not win the enterprise zone grant, but development personnel made good on their promise and secured Hawkeye alternative sources of funding. These included $2 million worth of low-interest loans from HUD, a forgivable $700,000 loan from the Iowa Public Infrastructure Forgiveness Program, and $500,000 from a community development block grant. Next, the city council voted unanimously to provide additional local incentives, which included an unspecified tax abatement, a $1 million no-interest loan from the city's office of economic development, $2.7 million in TIF, and a number of sundry services: municipal employees would remove rail spurs from Hawkeye's preferred construction site, extend streets and utilities, and construct a landscape buffer. Apparently well satisfied, Hawkeye broke ground on the plant later that year.

Partners then settled accounts, publicly maligning those who had engaged in the conflict and removing them from public commissions. The public justification for these actions revolved around a community-politics dichotomy. Partners insisted that those who engaged in the conflict had been too partisan. Soon after, city council passed a resolution establishing its sole power to appoint leaders to state commissions and replaced Steve and Emerson with United Labor leaders who had not joined the fray. Since the Hawkeye incident, city council has appointed only United Labor leaders to public commissions, and partners justified this on the grounds that the Labor Council is labor's "political arm," while United Labor is a "community-oriented" organization.[7] And indeed, partners' categorization proved fateful, because Labor Council leaders did divert their energies into politics and ultimately achieved payback by throwing a political wrench into the wheels of Ben Denison's primary campaign.

Contradiction 2: Consensus versus Majority Opinion

Partners often experience a second tension within their public role that is the obverse of the one I discussed above: they are tempted to support a position that accords with the beliefs of a majority of their peers, but is considered divisive and off-limits by a minority of other partners. In River City, this tension arose most often in connection with social issues championed by the Democratic Party. Although River City's leaders spoke mostly in jest about the days when "Republicans could not get into city hall except to pay their taxes," the fact is that most of them identify privately as Democrats. At the time of my fieldwork, too, the city's state delegation was almost entirely Democratic. Among partners, Independent identification, or at least a public persona uncolored by public displays of partisanship, remained the gold standard. However, a few prominent partners, especially elected leaders or those who got their start in Democratic politics, flaunted this norm and openly identify as Democrats: Ben Denison, Mayor Ron Bolan, Kathy Gooding of the River Museum, the head of the Labor Management Council, and United Labor leaders like Doug Whitter and Darrell Bandy.[8]

River City's community life was officially nonpartisan, but some of the city's partners regarded it as more Democratic than Republican. And indeed, I found that Republican partners were cagier about their political views than their Democratic counterparts. Before interviews, I usually checked leaders' political registration, and whereas Democratic partners were typically open about their politics, Republican leaders declined to discuss the matter. A few Republicans even told me that they were hesitant to attend Republican Straw Poll, an event during which partners' taboo against public partisan displays is relaxed. Accordingly, the rift between River City's community leaders and the city's GOP was deeper than the one between community and Democratic leaders, and GOP activists identified explicitly as marginalized outsiders.[9] "People always say to me, 'the Republicans, that's the party of the rich,'" Andy Tuner, a GOP activist, told me. "I always say, 'Just look at my tax returns!' I probably made $20,000 last year [as an overnight security guard at a local college]!"

In this context, River City's partners found Democratic identification both a liability and a potential advantage. Elected officials especially found it useful to quietly index their Democratic sympathies while avoiding the impression of engaging in excessively partisan and un-partner-like actions. This was indeed a fine line; I will show in the next chapter that partners saw some Democratic activists' local activities—for instance, protests against visiting Republican politicians—as an outright embarrassment. However, a few public officials walked this line successfully by reframing Democratic positions as consensus positions and Republican positions as divisive and partisan. There is nothing generally remarkable about elected partners' tendency to present divisive issues as consensus positions; recall that all of partners' initiatives are backed by a socially constructed consensus and therefore supported by some partners and opposed by others who agree to "keep divisive issues off the table." In this case, however, those opposed to the proposed consensus shared a common characteristic—their Republicanism—and occasionally countermobilized along partisan lines, thereby spawning a conflict that partners on *both sides* framed as about community versus politics.

Ron Bolan, River City's mayor, was a master at this form of fuzzy self-presentation and was central to several political conflicts during my field-work. His name was particularly associated with a green city initiative and one to grant same-sex partner benefits to city employees—visionary policies as he formulated them in the early 2000s. "Council today is more open-minded, we weigh the pros and cons—not philosophical maybe, but we take a more educated point of view to make the right long-term decision," he told me. "So when the [sexual orientation] issue came up, it was not contentious for us!" he added. "You need to educate the council and the community [and when we did that] I think that the average person on the street ended up either not caring much about it or realizing that it was really not a big deal. People saw the narrow focus [of previous councils and looked at us and said], 'They are looking into the future.' [And] when outsiders look at us, they see that we are the first city in Iowa to have tried this, that we are welcoming of their employees if they want to move here, and that we are a city that is going to progress and move into the future."

River City's traditional leaders were no strangers to disagreement, but they were also not wary of it and routinely shrugged their shoulders at conflict, adding perhaps that those motivated by differing core values were bound to disagree. By contrast, partners are supposed to avoid divisiveness. Moreover, environmental sustainability and sexual-orientation equality may well become taken-for-granted features of public life, but these were not consensus issues in the 2000s. After River City's same-sex ordinance passed, for example, GOP activists picketed city hall. But note the skilled way in which Ron repositioned these initiatives as long-term consensus positions. Ron's focus on education especially erased the possibility of in-tractable disagreement and put the burden of consensus on the minority: former councils disagreed with the same-sex ordinance, but only because they refused to educate themselves, not because they were composed of different individuals with different core values than today's council. His position notwithstanding then, Ron spoke as a partner. He demonstrated partners' telltale admiration for education, placed his faith in consensus, and criticized opponents in the same terms that others might employ to critique stubborn traditional leaders: opponents are like (unteachable) children, for example.[10]

Of course, Ron's public campaigns were popular among like-minded Democratic partners, but Republican partners perceived them as especially threatening, and for good reason: these campaigns reconstitute Democratic positions as consensus positions rather than divisive ones, which made opposition to them un-partner-like. When trying to lure Microprocessor Corporation to the city, for example, development personnel created a co-alition that included Ron Bolan and other environmental and same-sex quality advocates, which they believed would convince the firm that River City was progressive—at this point, public opposition to Ron's initiatives was definitely off the table. For this reason, River City's Republican partners were especially reactive to initiatives that blurred the boundary between Democrats and partners.

Recall, for example, Jonathan Speenham's report from the introduction, which I quote in full below.[11] Jonathan was a 1990s-era council member who had kept his political beliefs private, but lost a mayoral race to Ron Bolan after he was outed as a Republican—largely because he was mar-ried to a member of a pro-life group that sometimes picketed River City's Planned Parenthood clinic. "When it comes to economic development, there are no differences [between Democrats and Republicans]. None," Jonathan said, expressing a blasé attitude toward development partner-ships that was typical of River City's GOP activists. "Ben Denison and [the city manager], they run River City and don't let anyone ever tell you differ-ent. [So the GOP doesn't] get involved with most city issues."

"Now on social issues, [there is] a core group of Democrats that gets deeply involved with those—no doubt in my mind that is true," Jonathan continued, growing heated. "You have a core group—and they just keep taking things back and back again—they are willing to keep hitting their head against the wall until it falls over. Anything related to mental health or the health clinics, you hear from the Democratic contingent on that. When they came out with their priorities this year they listed as one of their key priorities, 'Making River City a green city.' That is higher than development of the east-west [highway] corridor and drainage at city park?!? I can tell you that would have been different had I been mayor. Or the sexual-orientation ordinance—that was one we fought for years and the Democratic contingent pushed probably the hardest on it and it finally got passed."

Note that Jonathan employs many of the same discursive tricks as Ron Bolan to reposition things like the green city initiative or same-sex ordinance as divisive after all: like traditional leaders, leaders who support these issues are stubborn and rigid in their thinking, and therefore not true partners. Such fractious debates over political or cultural issues took up the majority of airtime during River City's local elections while the city's economic development practices, or any community issues for that matter, were hardly mentioned by anyone. Unlike in pre-1980s public life, however, neither side to such "political" conflicts employed a public discourse that recognized two legitimate, differing sides. Recall that traditional leaders viewed one another as friendly enemies who take opposite sides within the same political game. By contrast, the sides in political post-1980s conflicts that I observed consistently painted their opposition as publicly illegitimate, and this framing transcended the content of the conflict at hand. Both sides spoke as partners, bickered over who was supporting the *real* consensus position, and argued that the other side was too political and should be publically silenced. In this light, it is noteworthy that "political issues" appeared inherently divisive and relatively unimportant—certainly secondary to the "community" consensus that united partners.

Contradiction 3: Traditional Representation versus Consensus

Finally, partners found political conflict useful in resolving a contradiction between their accountably to other partners and to those constituencies who they purported to represent. Consider United Labor leaders' tenuous balancing act. They operated under a cloud of suspicion in the eyes of other partners, lest their traditional conflicts with business should resurface. For them, divisive positions and statements were out of the question. However, they were simultaneously accountable to their members, who were accustomed to a more contentious union tradition. The 2000s was also a period of precipitous union decline and lousy union contracts. I argued in chapter 2 that union members traditionally expected a visible conflict with the employer prior to such bad news, but United Labor leaders could not do this. Unsurprisingly, I found that United Labor leaders were acutely preoccupied with their legitimacy in the eyes of the membership. Recall Doug Whitter's report from chapter 2: "the easiest way to win a union election is to throw out some crazy statement [like], 'Enough with this in bed with business stuff, let's take them on!' Then people say, 'That man is a fighter!' and we'd be right back in the fight."

Of course, United Labor leaders and other partners always had the option of presenting themselves differently in different contexts, but public two-facedness is risky.[12] News of a fiery speech could always make its way from the union hall to other partners' ears. By contract, political conflict gave United Labor leaders the opportunity to resolve the tension with their role by double-voicing: issuing statements that were coded to appeal to both partners and their traditional constituencies.

Consider, Ron Bolan's mayoral victory over Jonathan Speenham, a campaign during which the city's Democratic partners—including and especially United Labor leaders—campaigned hard on Bolan's behalf. "You know, it's like I tell my members: politics is crucial here to what we do," Doug Whitter told me. "Just look at the last [mayoral election]. I mean, you had one candidate, a retired UAW Union member, a Democrat, and then another guy who is probably about as out there and extreme—just a real extreme Republican. You could not ask for two more stark choices. Ron has taken us forward and been very, very effective. With the other guy—well—if you are worried about the hard-core Republican agenda, that was him."

Republican activists were handy indeed, because they gave partners like Doug an opportunity to simultaneously address both the court and the gallery, so to speak. Doug's statement explicitly repudiated those who are intransigent, fanatical, and set in their ways while celebrating those who are effective (in achieving consensus). Here, Doug spoke as a partner. But he simultaneously positioned himself against the "hard-core Republican agenda," a formulation that indexed traditional business leaders to many older UAW members. However, actors like Jonathan were actually *not* members of River City's old families. Jonathan no more represented the agenda of his city's traditional business establishment than Ron Bolan represented the Labor Council's traditional labor agenda.

In other words, the type of double voicing practiced by Doug was a safe way of indexing solidarity with those who still expected traditional representation, because those targeted by such statements were mere safe stand-ins for the types of actors who dominated pre-1980s public life. In truth, figures like Jonathan lacked the ability to truly threaten River City's partnership regime. The periodic conflicts precipitated by Republican activists provided much opportunity for double voicing and occasionally served as a moment of collective effervescence for River City's democratic partners—a kind of pageant, wherein those caught between old and new were able to momentarily resolve the inherent tensions in their public roles. Unsurprisingly, I found that partners were frequently complicit in stoking such conflicts and in blowing them out of proportion, as they did in the following two cases.

Community versus Politics I: The Saturday Club

On one frigid February morning, I attended a session of the Saturday Club, a forum held monthly while the Iowa legislature was in session, when members of the city's delegation—five Democrats and two Republicans— met to address constituents' concerns. The event was held in the Grand Harbor Hotel, a crown jewel in River City's harbor redevelopment. I entered, making my way past the blinking slot machines and onto the slowly moving escalator to the upstairs convention space. The room slowly came into view: a ballroom, complete with crystal chandeliers, rows of perhaps 200 chairs, and a frosty bay of windows behind the lectern, some thirty feet high, with a view of the slowly moving ice floes in the river below.

I was early, but at least fifty people already filled the room, and no wonder. This was the only River City event attended by all of the actors in the book, including partners, disgruntled traditional leaders, and Republican and Democratic activists. All these leaders used the Saturday Club as an opportunity to socialize and keep tabs on one another. For partners, therefore, the event was tense because it was political and hence outside their control. Unlike in city council, the agenda was not set in advance, but people considered politicians' pledges binding. Therefore, real events sometimes happened. Two years before I started fieldwork, Democratic activists lambasted the city's Republican representatives over the Iraq war, and one Republican pledged never to return to the forum, thus endangering partners' efforts to secure state highway funds. On this morning, however, partners' moods were cheery as River City's delegation had just secured said highway funds and most people expected only good news, unaware than an unexpected event was about to become the gossip of the moment among River City's leadership class.

At the front of the room, Fred Billingham stood behind a lectern, gavel in hand, preparing to chair the meeting. I bypassed Labor Council leaders who were sitting in the back row for fear of appearing too chummy with them, and instead made my way to the front of the room toward an empty seat near Andy Turner. Andy was in his sixties, but seemed two decades younger with his long, unkempt gray hair and loud sweaters. A local eccentric, he had run for city council as a write-in candidate in the 1970s and had been a gadfly on various fringe issues since. More recently, Andy had become involved with the Republican Party, which is how I had met him, and with the Right to Life Coalition—a group that attracted widespread local condemnation for its pickets of Planned Parenthood.[13] Because I knew that the city's partners considered GOP activists to be relative nobodies, I thought sitting next to him a safe choice, realizing my mistake too late after noticing that Andy was sweating nervously as we exchanged hellos.

"Well, I'd like to bring this meeting to order." Fred Billingham cleared his throat, his gavel gently tapping. Each legislator gave a short synopsis of their recent activities, emphasizing especially the unity of the delegation in securing River City's development dollars. Partners were especially pleased to see Christopher Piney, a Republican legislator, who was now back in attendance after boycotting the Saturday Club. "It's great to have Chris back," one partner told me. "Because, you know, we don't see eye-to-eye on just about anything, but it is essential that we have everybody together at the table again and at least talking to each other."

Next came questions from the audience. Most focused on the possibility of securing additional state funds for River City's transportation projects. As this went on, I noticed Andy shifting in his seat. Eventually, he raised his hand, quivering nervously as he waited.

"Yes, Andy, you have a question?" Fred asked, hiding a faint smile under his mustache. Andy stood up, holding a piece of paper that he had printed from the Internet. "I have a different question for Representative O'Brien," he said in a shaky voice. "I have a question about the house bill co-sponsored by Representative O'Brien, the so-called human cloning bill, because that *is* what the bill is going to do . . . " Andy paused as the audience rumbled. "Ohhhh, Andy!" somebody declared in exasperation from a couple seats backs.

"No, no, folks, it is okay," Pete O'Brien was standing, his hand raised in a stately manner. This was a tense moment as Pete O'Brien was considered unreliable and conflict-prone by the city's partners. During the ongoing nurses' strike, for example, Pete had spoken at strikers' rallies and pickets at the businesses of the hospital's board members. "I believe the question is in reference to a bill I sponsored regarding stem cell research, and I'll tell you why I supported that bill," Pete O'Brien began. "Now I realize that there are some strong feelings about this issue, but the truth of the matter is that stem-cell research is a cutting-edge technology. Researchers are just starting to tap the potential of this technology, which could provide a cure to all kinds of things: Parkinson's, Alzheimer's," people stiffened in their chairs. In the 2000s, stem-cell research was a wedge issue; many Republicans audience members and even some Catholic Democrats opposed it. Representative O'Brien's statements threatened to divide the audience along partisan lines. "Well, and the fact of the matter is that this kind of research will be done somewhere," O'Brien continued, shifting his discourse after noting the tension. "How we feel about it is only one question, because it is also an economic development issue. I mean, if the research is going to be done, we want it to be done here. And as far as human cloning, that is a preposterous claim. Of course, nobody would support that."

The mood in the room loosened. "Thank you for your question," Fred said, looking around for the next question.

But Andy remained standing, quivering with emotion. "You're a liar!" he shouted, "I have read the research and . . . " At this point, Andy was silenced by a murmur from the audience. "You're acting like a child, sit down!" somebody shouted, eliciting a supportive murmur.

Fred remained cool, leaning against the podium and coaxing the room into silence with the gentle rapping of his gavel. "Now disagreement is one thing, reasonable people can disagree," Fred said finally, "but outbursts are something else. If you cannot respect these fine people that have come down here on a Saturday morning to answer your questions, then I'm going to have to ask . . . "; the rest of Fred's statement was drowned out by deafening applause from the audience. Andy tried to say something in response, but by this time the chief of police, who was also in attendance, had made his way to the front of the room and started speaking to Andy in a hushed tone, turning Andy's attention away from the podium as Fred maneuvered gracefully to take another question. Andy sat down and the chief of police squatted next to him, whispering for a few more moments before going back to his own seat.

In the grand scheme of things, Andy's outburst was really no big deal: a single GOP activist, nervous and acting only on his own initiative, grew a little heated in a political forum. But over the next weeks, it became the talk of the town; in some accounts, Andy had even been physically restrained by the chief of police. Although everyone blew the event out of proportion, it was interpreted differently in different circles. Partners interpreted it as a victory of partnership over politics. "I really thought [Andy] was going to become violent—thank goodness the chief of police was there," a prominent partner told me. "And Fred Billingham, he just handled it so well and respectfully. I think that really shows you how far we have come around here. It does not matter who you are. We have all learned to respect one another, set politics aside [and] try to work together for the common good." Meanwhile, GOP activists and their closeted supporters seethed with anger at being treated like unruly children; the activists busily planned their next initiative.

Democrats too found the event intensely interesting. At a party meeting soon after, one Democratic activist argued that the event demonstrated the importance of Democrats in positions of local authority and pointed out that Fred Billingham, the chief of police, and indeed the majority of the lawmakers assembled were Democrats. For her, the event was a victory of Democrats over Republicans. "It just goes to show you the kind of thing we are up against," she concluded. So it was that Fred Billingham got to be both a partner and a partisan, and in the process reproduced the division between community and politics within River City's public life.

Community versus Politics II:
The Ben Denison Campaign Revisited

The Ben Denison campaign was conceived from the get-go as being about community versus politics. This was no mere rhetoric. Ben's campaign was co-chaired by one Democrat and one Republican, although both had long ago made the transition to partnership and were no longer involved in their parties. Ben also accepted no party or PAC money and told me that this was because he did not want to be beholden to political groups if elected.[14] A true partner, Ben recognized the political gift for what it was: an effort to ensnare the receiver in ties of obligation. Ben's political speeches, too, were nothing if not an effort to colonize politics with the logic of partnership. He admitted that he had Democratic "core values," for example, but kept them "off the table" and in fact did not enumerate them until late in the campaign. He pledged to focus instead on issues that were good for River City as a whole.

Ben's campaign also drew virtually unanimous support from River City's partners, Democrats and Republicans alike. Fred Billingham told me, "So [I'm for] Ben Denison, even though it upsets a lot of my colleagues at the Labor Council. Ben did not stand up there and tell us exactly what we wanted to hear. He says, 'Hey, let's be commonsense about this whole thing.' Somebody asked him if we should [push for] Right to Work. He says, 'Well, I support that wholeheartedly, but that is not even an issue unless we have a Democratic Senate and House [in Iowa]. So why even talk about it? That is a losing no-win issue. Let's talk about the economy, not these labor issues.'"

Partners' desire to channel their community ideology through Ben's campaign and into the sphere of national politics was, I believe, genuine. What they failed to add was that the political forces arrayed against Ben were also based in community life, not political institutions that were somehow external to the city. Ben's most vocal opponents, for instance, were none other than Labor Council leaders, community leaders who had bided their time since the Hawkeye incident and now exacted political revenge.

On the night of Ben's primary loss, I stopped by a meeting of the Labor Council and found those assembled in good cheer. "I'd give twenty dollars to see Ben's face right now," somebody announced as I entered the building; "A victory for the liberal wing of the Democratic Party," someone added. "We told him—right after Hawkeye Supplies we told him—if you are ever planning to run for office, you had better watch out!" Steve Raney said to approving nods as I took my seat. Then, Michael Lombarti appeared in the doorway slouching under the weight of a case of beer. The mood turned downright festive as he walked down the aisle handing out beers.

As the men drank, they talked more about the primary, expressing a measured sympathy for Ben's loss. As veterans within their city's public game, they had all experienced the disappointment of loss. They then lamented that Ben had done as well as he had, reflected on their own diminished capacities, and finally on the significance of the campaign.[15] "We tried to tell him: 'Look, five dollar an hour jobs is not good jobs, why would we be paying companies money to bring in jobs that are going to pull wages and benefit levels down?'" Michael told me, illustrating that which I suspected: "political" differences in this case were really cover for a deeper critique of partners' stewardship of community life. "Because then when our people go in to negotiate, management says, 'Look, Joe Schmo over here is paying five dollars an hour, why should we pay you thirteen?' They give [firms] TIFs, tax moratoriums, nobody knows what is going on, but they are giving away working people's money is what they are doing. That's the problem with Denison. He's one of these pseudo-Democrats [that] don't want to be associated with labor [and] the average working Joe," he said. "Then, of course, there was Hawkeye Supplies," Michael added, sipping his beer, his face twisted in a vindictive grin.

In this particular case, partners had literally created their own political opposition. More generally, Ben's troubles reflected a structural gulf between community and politics that was also of partners' own making. Ben was overwhelmingly popular with other partners, but to win the primary he needed to operate in a political sphere anchored by institutions—the party, networks of local activists, and funders—that hardly overlap with River City's post-1980s community institutions. As my account of the Saturday Club showed, partners step into such political spaces as into a foreign land that they can neither control nor even predict, but this is only because they have voluntarily withdrawn from politics.

By contrast, Ben's main primary opponent was deeply rooted in politics. He was from Marathon, a nearby city of comparable size to River City and allegedly from a connected Democratic family. Ben's opponent also took money from numerous left-wing PACs, and used it to inundate the airwaves with ads portraying himself a true, left-wing Democrat—a presentation of self that Ben could not have effected even if he had the money to do so. What's more, partisan institutions conspired against Ben. The area's partisan blogs buzzed with discussions about whether or not Ben was too "pro-business," and such concerns were picked up by the regional media, which ran stories asking if Ben was a "true Democrat." Eventually, Ben did elaborate that he believed in helping "society's underprivileged" and spent several campaign days volunteering at River City's food bank, but this was ridiculed by journalists as a last-ditch rebranding. In effect, Ben was unable to effect a presentation of self that appealed to the partisan public he needed to win the primary, because such a presentation clashed with his existing public persona.

Many of River City's Democratic activists also backed Ben's main opponent. It did not help that Ben's campaign overlapped with a nurses' strike at an area hospital, during which the city's partners adopted a rigid stance of nonintervention. By contrast, other political candidates were actively involved in the strike. State senator Mitt O'Connell spoke at several strikers' rallies, for example, and Pete O'Brien took things even further by publically harassing the hospital's board members at their places of business. River City's Democratic Party practically sanctioned such divisive tactics by electing the president of the nurses' union party president. As head of the city's Development Corporation, Ben could not have joined such antics even if he had wanted to. Unsurprisingly therefore, many activists echoed Labor Council leaders' sentiments. "[I like candidates with] that sense of justice," one activist, a computer programmer, told me. "The big guys have their protectors. Everyone else who is not privileged has to stress out over the tiniest little thing. [Ben Denison] represents big business. [Some of my friends] tell me that I need to be inclusive, but I'm sorry, that is not the Democratic Party I know."

After the defeat, River City's partners drew a familiar lesson. "The campaign was no fun at all," Ben's Democratic campaign managers told me. "But that is how politics is: it is all about division, not bringing people together." But however much partners may paint politics as an irrational outside force, and partisans as a sort of space invader from Planet Politics, it is impossible to escape the fact that partisanship is very much locally generated, and that partisans are part and parcel of the very same public ecology reproduced by the city's partners. It is partners' hegemony over community institutions, their extreme and—dare I say—divisive intolerance of discord, that pushes dissenters toward partisan politics. So it is that partners, in trying to banish their doppelgangers from the light of public life, actually create a place for them to thrive and occasionally thwart their own carefully laid plans. In this book's final chapters, I examine the broader consequences for America's political system.

PART THREE

Neoliberalism (continued): Politics Disembedded from Community Governance

SEVEN

The Activist Party

I concluded chapters 5 and 6 with River City's and Prairieville's politics disembedded from community governance: each city's public sphere was inhabited by community-minded partners who avoided partisan politics and partisan activists who were otherwise peripheral within key community associations. In River City, Prairieville, and elsewhere, this community-politics opposition arose only recently. Before the 1980s, community leaders viewed party politics as synonymous with their exercise of community leadership, took leadership roles within parties, and disciplined incoming activists, and were thereby central to America's more-moderate postwar party system. But at the time of my fieldwork, Prairieville and River City's party politics unfolded as within a political petri dish, a breeding ground for extreme political ideologies that was occasionally seeded by disgruntled outcasts from the city's leadership class and community leaders who baited partisan activists for their own ends.

In part III of the book, I take this political petri dish—a set of grassroots partisan institutions that are distinct from key community organizations—as a starting point and consider implications for America's political system. In this chapter I zoom out and show how the transformation of grassroots parties in places like River City and Prairieville polarized American politics. In chapter 8 I turn to River Citians and Prairievillers, specify the mechanisms that communicate to them that community and politics are animated by incompatible and opposing norms, and analyze how this community-politics tension structures their political attitudes, alternatively producing partisan polarization and political apathy. Chapter 9 then discusses the 2008 and 2012 elections and shows why politics-averse voters were unable to coalesce around a single post-partisan candidate.

Central to my argument in this chapter is the transition between two

Table 7.1. Differences between community leadership and activist parties

	Community Leadership Party	Activist Party
Status hierarchy within the party	Community notable lead party. Intraparty status mirrors community status.	Flat status hierarchy. Activists see one another as community of equals.
Relationship between community leaders and activists	Community leaders within the party discipline and socialize activists.	None. Activists establish solidarity by tolerating one another's political commitments.
Activists' political focus	Focus on issues that interest community leaders, especially distribution of economic resources.	Focus on hot-button issues. Activists prefer candidates who embrace full range of extreme commitments.

ideal-typical forms of grassroots partisan organization: the pre-1980s *community leadership party* that I described in chapter 3 and the post-1980s *activist party*, which I describe here. Like the community leadership party, the activist party is an ideal type, or a conceptual model that is useful for analyzing connections between a party's organization and the intragroup dynamics that it engenders. Differences between the two types of parties are summarized in table 7.1. Recall the community leadership party's three defining features: community leaders were party leaders (and vice versa), used their positions of community prominence to maintain a party hierarchy, and thereby disciplined incoming activists, focusing their attention on the bread-and-butter economic and social issues that were central to community conflicts. The activist party is virtually opposite in all three respects: party members are activists with no connection to key community institutions or positions of community leadership, the status hierarchy between activists is flat, and this relative egalitarianism further polarizes activists and makes them appear extreme to outsiders. Activists join the party due to particular—and often peculiar—political commitments, which they often acquire through media coverage of hot-button issues. The activist party then acts as an echo chamber, amplifying fellow activists' commitments to these issues; therein, activists establish solidarity by tolerating the commitments of others, allow one another to use the party label when mobilizing in favor of whatever cause, and support candidates who appeal to the widest range of fellow activists. From the outside looking in, the activist party therefore appears more unified and extreme in program than the activists who comprise it are in reality. Because the activist party is an ideal type, River City's and Prairieville's grassroots parties deviated from the model and, in particular, Republican parties were somewhat more ideal-typically activist than Democratic parties. Nevertheless, all four parties changed fundamentally since the 1970s and came to resemble one another more than themselves in the 1970s. The activists' party best encapsulates their common trajectory.

I begin the chapter by discussing American parties in a historical perspective and showing that their grassroots reorganization—rather than, for example, voters' preferences or changes in campaign finance—best accounts for the polarization of American politics. I then explore the internal dynamics of River City's and Prairieville's parties and show how activists' effort to create solidarity in the absence of organizational structure polarizes them and produces dynamics that make the party look like a coherent, radical movement to the outside world.

National Politics and Grassroots Parties, 1970s–Present

Since the 1970s American political parties have diverged and polarized by various metrics like the discourse of legislators, their policy positions, and legislative votes.[1] Of course, Democratic and Republican legislators have always disagreed to some extent, but the nature and intractability of their disagreements has changed. Recall that Keynesian-era parties were characterized by *conflict displacement*: Republicans and Democrats debated and grew polarized on one big issue at a time—for instance, civil rights or social welfare spending—but after debate died down interparty positions on the issue converged.[2] Today, *conflict extension* is the norm: legislators hold permanent opposing positions on the full slate of partisan issues and such attitudes are reflected in their votes.[3] Analyses that map congressional votes along a partisan scale displayed a single clump with two peaks during the 1960s and '70s, a vote pattern that indicates multiple Republicans who consistently voted to the left of Democrats (and vice versa). Especially since the 1990s, such analyses have shown two distinct and distant clusters, a pattern that indicates that all Republicans are to the right of Democrats.[4] News of such polarization should hardly surprise anyone familiar with the news of the moment, which is replete with recall elections, filibusters, government shutdowns, and other do-or-die political stratagems. Mainstream accounts of such partisan polarization focus alternatively on the polarization of the American electorate and changes in campaign law, although many social scientists—myself included—now look to a reorganization of grassroots parties as the primary explanation.

Consider first the commonly held belief that American parties have grown more extreme because Americans are more extreme and intransigent in their political preferences. This explanation is intuitively appealing because mainstream political scientists conceptualize voting as an individual-level transaction—for instance, one wherein a politician "buys" voters' support by "selling them the right policies."[5] This economic conception of voting behavior has diffused to the mass media, whose pundits habitually discuss election results as unambiguous support for the winners' policies and tactics. Brazenly political mass media outlets—Fox News, MSNBC, talk radio, and partisan Internet sites—have also appeared in recent decades, and it is perhaps natural to assume that this reflects American's hunger for partisan discord. But there is little evidence that Americans have become more extreme in their political views. For example, sociologists Delia Baldassarri and Andrew Gelman show that Americans' 2000s-era political views were neither more consistently partisan nor extreme than those of their 1970s-era counterparts.[6] Rather, Americans became better at sorting themselves into the parties that shared their preferences because the parties themselves became more clearly divided and vocal about their differences—a finding that suggest that the parties' polarization is driving polarization among voters, not vice versa. Studies like these consistently find that a small group of voters on the left and the right have become more partisan and extreme in their partisan preferences, but these are voters who are virtually guaranteed to vote anyway.[7] Meanwhile, overall rates of partisan identification fell and most people today report ambivalent feelings about the two parties relative to their 1970s-era counterparts.[8] Politicians are not simply responding to changing tastes and selling the public the divisive politics it wants. In fact, just the opposite: many politicians are more ideologically extreme than the median voter in their districts, which suggests that they are positioning themselves in ways that jeopardize their chances in the general election.[9]

Explanations of partisan polarization that focus on fundraising are likewise initially appealing, not least because political donations have increased since the 1970s.[10] Recall figure 3.1, which summarized trends in political expenditures. Until the late 1970s national parties were organizationally equivalent to a few figureheads in a room with virtually no resources. In the words of one DNC chair, they had only the ability to decide where to hold a convention and to decide who could show up. Since then, parties and PACs have mobilized ever more money, largely due to advances in targeted fundraising like the RNCs successful experiments with mass mailings during the 1980s and, even more so, both parties' Internet fundraising since 2000. Accordingly, the two parties themselves and especially

PACs have expanded from a sideshow in American political life to hosts of the main event. To borrow VO Key's classic distinction, it is therefore plausible that politicians are more polarized and divided because post-1980s parties-as-organizations are institutionally robust and capable of compelling them to toe the line.[11]

Political money matters and its rise has contributed to conflict extension among politicians, but it is not the main cause of the latter trend. Consider what political donations allow parties and PACs to do: engage in what some political scientists refer to as an *air war*, or to bombard daily life with partisan messages through the mass media, but not much else. This is partially due to the peculiarities of the American legal system, which has consistently defined donations to parties or candidates as an attempt to buy influence but "independent expenditures" (money spent on media buys that are not coordinated with parties or campaigns) as constitutionally protected free speech.[12] Because of this, wealthy donors usually max out their donations to candidates and parties ($2,600 and $32,000, respectively, as of 2014), then give the rest—often substantially more—to PACs, which use it to buy attack ads.[13] The much-discussed Citizens United decision and subsequent appearance of so-called Super-PACs is merely the continuation of this legal tradition.[14] But even were this not the case, the amount of money in American politics is still grossly insufficient to allow parties an organizational presence outside of a few major cities. In 2012, for example, the operating budget of all Republican and Democratic committees was roughly $1.2 billion, which is comparable to the national advertising budget of Coca-Cola and Pepsi, but nowhere near these corporations' operating budget.[15] And in fact, the parties spent most of their money on TV advertising, leaving them incapable of building a national bureaucratic structure.[16] Effectively, party leaders are still organizationally akin to a few figureheads in a room; the only difference is that these figureheads now have a sizable advertising budget. During nearly four years researching politics in Iowa, for example, I encountered only one employee of either political party: a low-level DNC employee who slept in the attic of Prairieville's party headquarters for a few weeks, then moved on. His presence was the result of Howard Dean's allegedly revolutionary "50-State Strategy," which was intended to give the DNC an organizational presence in every state.[17] In Iowa, this strategy raised the number of paid DNC employees from one to a whopping three—hardly a political revolution after all. In effect, parties and PACs are national organizations in name only; really, they are glorified advertising agencies.

Of course, America's partisan air war has contributed to the polarization of politics by giving parties and PACs both sticks and carrots with which to coerce politicians. Such organizations can engage in supportive independent expenditures (i.e., attack ads targeting a friendly politician's opponent) to reward loyal politicians who adopt the party's hardcore positions. Conversely too, politicians may avoid moderate or conciliatory stances for fear of drawing the negative advertising dollars of PACs—a trend that has become common with the targeting of moderate Republicans in their primaries by right-wing groups, but began quite recently with the Americans for Tax Reform and Club for Growth's targeting of moderate Republicans in the early 2000s and by Democratic activists' successful defeat of Joseph Lieberman in the 2006 Connecticut Democratic primary.[18] More generally, too, political advocacy associations can flood the airwaves with fringy message ads, thus exposing voters and politicians alike to their ideas.

But however noteworthy and disquieting America's financially fueled air war may be, it cannot account for the degree of contemporary partisan polarization. If air-war expenditures were the main cause, one would expect that party polarization would have occurred first and furthest at higher levels of the federal system where political media buys are concentrated: that presidential candidates and members of Congress would have become polarized first and been followed only by state politicians in large states where candidates can reasonably expect parties and PACs to expend donations on races. By contrast, grassroots politics should have been relatively unaffected, because local parties and candidates do not receive significant donations nor expected independent expenditures from outside groups. But as I argued in chapter 3, the polarization of America's party system proceeded differently: grassroots parties polarized first around 1980, whereas Congress polarized later in the 1980s and early 1990s. For instance, the GOP was first nudged rightward by grassroots campaigns in places like Colorado, where a coalition of right-wing activists—dubbed "the crazies" by local media—first wrested control of what was then a landowner-dominated party in the late 1970s, winning control of local, *then* state, *then* federal office.[19] On the Democratic side, too, movement-like activists focused on civil rights, gender and sexual orientation equality, the environment, and other causes began a takeover of local and state parties in the late 1970s.[20] By comparison, trends like PACs' attempts to target moderate politicians are certainly more visible, but also of more recent historical vintage, dating only to the mid-2000s.[21]

For this reason, many social scientists now look to the reorganization of grassroots party organizations in places like River City and Prairieville as the proximate cause of America's partisan polarization. Key to this account is the observation that most local, state, and federal candidates' prospects are influenced more by the ground war than the air war, which makes politicians more accountable to grassroots partisan activists than their districts' median voter.[22] This is because gerrymandering and population movements have created few competitive electoral districts. In most cases, politicians who get the right party's nomination are virtually guaranteed a general election win, which makes the party primary—a contest in which a tiny proportion of eligible voters participate—the truly important electoral contest.[23] Ben Denison's primary defeat is a case in point: Denison lost by 750 votes of about 35,000 cast (roughly a 7 percent turnout). Several hundred thousand residents of the same district then voted in the 2008 general election, sending Ben's primary opponent to Congress.

In comparison to general election voters, primary voters are likely to be active and interested party members with firm political commitments, or—perhaps—whatever friend, family member, or acquaintance committed party members drag to the polls. Efforts by PACs to intervene in primary races of this type are relatively recent and, even so, political money and media buys matter relatively little to the party faithful. Another campaign ad is unlikely to sway someone who regularly engages in politics and thinks a lot about it, but influence from another friendly and trusted activist just might. Therefore, a few grassroots get-out-the-vote drives or a weekend distribution of absentee ballots to sympathetic party members might garner a few hundred votes apiece and prove absolutely decisive in a primary. For this reason, political scientists argue that rational politicians look to party activists, not the general public, as their primary audience.[24] In addition to this, I will show later in this chapter that party workers also polarize politics by interfacing disproportionately with politicians and media representatives, shaping these outsiders' understanding of local life.

What's more, grassroots parties appear a likely suspect because of the timing of their transformation: by most accounts around 1980, just prior to the most significant uptick in the polarization of congressional representatives and other politicians.[25] It was around this period that political scientists noted the exit of traditional community leaders from party politics and their replacement by activists.[26] For example, political scientist Seth Masket conducted an exhaustive study of California's grassroots parties and found most staffed by activists who were not influential in community governance, but ran operations that were "more active, better staffed, and better funded than [local parties] used to be [and able to] demand a higher level of partisanship from elected officials."[27] In some cities, Masket found a hierarchical organization dominated by a single individual or clique. The Democratic primaries in African American sections of Los Angeles were controlled by the Maxine Waters organization, for example, while Hispanic areas were contested by the Moline and Altorre-Torres-Planco organizations. In other cases, a looser confederation of activists controlled the party agenda. Orange County GOP politics, for example, was dominated by the ideologically right-wing Lincoln Club, while Fresno's GOP was controlled by a somewhat more traditional group of landowners with an interest in water politics.

Tables 7.2 and 7.3 show that Prairieville's and River City's parties experienced a similar disembedding from key community institutions. Recall that a majority of River City's and Prairieville's most central leaders took positions of public leadership within one of the two parties during the 1970s: respectively, fifteen and nineteen of thirty.[28] Not so in the 2000s. In 2000s-era River City and Praireiville, none of the city's most central leaders were formally involved with the GOP and only four in each case were involved with the Democratic Party, largely for extenuating reasons. In River City, two were Democratic politicians who were central by virtue of their guaranteed seats on key development corporations, one was a Labor Council leader not involved in community partnerships, and one was a United Labor leader who donated heavily to the Democratic Party, but was not active in it. In Prairieville, too, one was a labor leader who maintained a Democratic Party affiliation, another was a county supervisor who sat on multiple development organizations, and the remaining two were a school board member and an attorney who was deeply engaged in multiple artistic and cultural associations, but not economic development partnerships. Because of this, I often went from important community meetings to Democratic and Republican party meetings without seeing any of the same people.

In the remainder of the chapter, I examine activist-dominated parties and show how they polarize American politics. Political scientists argue that those who join activist parties feel pressured to adopt others' extreme views and I too observed this dynamic, but also other intraparty and community-wide processes that lead activists to embrace extreme political positions.[29] In particular, activists parties' flat status hierarchy sets in motion processes that render the activist party more partisan than the sum of its parts. I illustrate these dynamics in Prairieville's and River City's four parties, moving from most to least ideal-typical activist party.

Table 7.2. River City's most central leaders (2004–2006)

Leader	Local Democratic bodies	Development organizations				Partisan affiliation	Closeness centrality
		DC	DI	LMC	RA		
1. Bank executive		X	X				60.36
2. City manager		X	X	X	X		60.09
3. Bank president		X	X		X		58.77
4. Religious leader		X					58.26
5. United labor leader						Democratic donor	56.54
6. Fred Billingham (United Labor)	City Utility Board	X		X	X		56.30
7. Construction company executive		X		X	X		56.07
8. Car dealer		X			X		54.92
9. Information technology company executive	City Council, Library Board	X			X		54.69
10. Bank president		X					54.48
11. Energy company executive		X					54.03
12. United labor leader		X		X			53.82
13. School superintendent	School Board	X		X			53.39
14. State legislator		X		X	X	Democratic politician, donor	53.39
15. Hospital administrator		X					53.18
16. Community college president		X			X		52.76
17. Bank president	School Board	X	X				52.55
18. Ben Denison (Development Corporation)		X	X		X		52.55
19. Retired union leader							52.34
20. Mayor	City Commission, Planning Board	X			X		51.94

(continued)

Table 7.2. (*continued*)

Leader	Local Democratic bodies	Development organizations				Partisan affiliation	Closeness centrality
		DC	DI	LMC	RA		
21. Manufacturing company executive					X		51.94
22. Media company executive		X			X		51.74
23. Insurance company executive		X					51.74
24. Manufacturing company executive		X		X			51.54
25. Construction company owner		X			X		51.54
26. Physician							50.95
27. County supervisor	County supervisor				X	Democratic politician	50.95
28. State senator O'Connell						Democratic politician, donor	50.76
29. College president		X					50.57
30. Hospital executive							50.38

Note: DC = Development Corporation; DI = Development Initiatives; LMC = Labor Management Council; RA = Racing Association.

Table 7.3. River City's most central leaders (2004–2006)

Leader	Local Democratic bodies	Development organizations				Partisan affiliation	Closeness centrality
		DC	DI	GB	TP		
1. Processing plant owner			X				56.02
2. Teamsters union leader		X				Democratic officer	56.02
3. Retired business executive		X*					50.94
4. Construction company executive			X				50.94
5. Construction company owner			X	X			50.75
6. School board member	School Board					Democratic officer	50.19
7. Bank executive		X					50.00
8. County supervisor	County Supervisors			X		Democratic officer, politican	50.00
9. Dani Dover (Chamber)	Enterprise Zone Board		X				49.63
10. Manufacturing company executive							49.63
11. Newspaper reporter							49.45
12. Mayor	City Council	X					48.91
13. Packinghouse executive					X		48.91
14. Attorney						Democratic officer, donor	48.04
15. Community college president							48.04
16. Insurance company president							47.70
17. Hospital executive	Policy and Enterprise Zone Board						47.70
18. Plumbers' union leader							47.54
19. Bank executive	Enterprise Zone Board						47.04
20. Retired business owner							46.71

(continued)

Table 7.3. (*continued*)

Leader	Local Democratic bodies	Development organizations				Partisan affiliation	Closeness centrality
		DC	DI	GB	TP		
21. Restaurateur			X				46.39
22. Real estate executive		X					46.39
23. Manufacturing company executive							46.23
24. Retired labor council president				X			46.23
25. Manufacturing company executive			X				45.92
26. Electricians' union leader	City Electrical Board						46.76
27. University president			X				45.61
28. Retail store owner							45.61
29. Charles Browning							45.61
30. Physician							45.61

Note: During the 2004–6 period, Prairieville's most important development organization was Dani Dover's Development Taskforce, but it did publically disclose its board of directors. Some leaders on this list were certainly involved in this organization (e.g., Dani Dover) and many more probably were, which suggests that this table understates the propensity of Prairieville's key leaders to participate in development organizations at the time of my fieldwork.

* Downtown.

River City's Republicans

River City's GOP was once synonymous with the city's chamber. But during the catastrophic 1980s, the chamber broke publically with the GOP by electing Bonnie Cranston, a small-business owner and Democrat, chamber president. Although subsequent chamber presidents were all Republican, Bonnie's presidency severed any link or expectation of fellowship between business and Republicanism in River City. The 2000s-era GOP activists that I encountered were neither big-business owners nor particularly wealthy and, although they saw themselves as speaking on behalf of others, they had no particular connection to their city's other residents via positions of local leadership. Most were employed in middle- or working-class occupations: small-business owners, middle managers, teachers, office workers, government employees, service workers, or retirees of Green's and other large manufacturers. A few higher-status workers like business consultants, doctors, and attorneys were also active.

Consistent with the arguments of sociologists Doug McAdam and Katrina Kloos, River City's GOP had swelled with movement-like activists during successive waves of national partisan mobilization.[30] I argued in chapter 3 that activists had traditionally come into grassroots parties in the same manner, but community leaders subsequently socialized them, integrating them into a pre-existing party hierarchy. But with traditional business leaders gone, there was nobody to socialize and discipline activists, and each successive wave expanded the party horizontally, adding new political commitments like budding polyps.[31] "It was back in [the 1980s] when [candidates] like Pat Robertson started running that I first noticed it—a huge number of people who suddenly became active," Janice Kline, a longtime activist told me, describing an early wave of grassroots mobilization. "And I was surprised because there were so many new faces, faces I had never seen before. Most of these people had never been to a caucus before. [But] that was also when [business] people started saying, 'No, I don't believe in this, I'm not going to put my money into it anymore.'"

Because activists typically identified with their incoming cohort, River City's GOP was something of a repository of the right wing's historical fixations. Also in the 1980s, for example, Catholic pro-life activists like Andy Tuner joined the party along with Father O'Flannery, a Catholic priest who sometimes stalked the city's working-class neighborhoods, warning residents about the evils of abortion. Sergeant Fred, or simply Serge, joined the party along with a few others during the first Gulf War. He was habitually clad in marine regalia and occasionally pontificated about shooting traitors while those within earshot chuckled politely. Another wave of Christian conservatives joined the party in the late 1990s, followed by a large cohort of young Ron Paul supporters in the 2000s. Finally, a new wave of Tea Party activists joined River City's GOP shortly after I completed fieldwork, which confirmed my suspicions about the Tea Party being grassroots Republican politics as usual: the latest incoming wave of activists, which simply added new ideological flavors to the grassroots party.[32]

In sum, then, River City's GOP was a grab-bag of local characters: a few outcast traditional leaders, the occasional pre-1980s activist, but mostly local gadflies and politicos who had no particular connection to their city's leadership class and had been drawn to the party by commitments to motley causes. In chapter 5 I described how Prairieville's GOP activists were attuned to their isolation from business leaders and resented it. Although similarly isolated, most of River City's activists saw their separation from community leaders as simply natural. Outside of Democratic partners' occasional efforts to bait GOP activists, community leaders and GOP activists simply ignored one another. "The chamber tries to stay pretty much apolitical," a long-time GOP activist said. "[The director,] he just happens to be Republican, and because it is more business oriented you probably are going to find quite a few Republicans. [But] they are careful about not going where they shouldn't." Most other activists were similarly disinterested in community affairs. Many I spoke with had not even heard of Development Corporation, for example, and more still were unaware of its central importance to partners. For their part, community leaders were equally disinterested in activists' day to day. I attended nearly a dozen of the GOP's monthly meetings and no community leader or notable ever showed up.

The GOP's culture mirrored its composition and structure: activists saw themselves as nonelites and identified positively with their party's lack of status hierarchy. To them, the GOP was a sheltering space, wherein comers of all unpopular political persuasions would be welcomed without judgment—a confederation of underdogs. Activists complained bitterly about others' tendency to view the GOP as a rich man's party.[33] During meetings, few issues received as much discussion as the party's ailing finances, which activists claimed left them unable to raise the $150 in monthly rent they needed for the auditorium of a roadside motel where they held their meetings—already a far cry from the party's pre-1980s country club accommodations. During these discussions, activists held up their party's chronic poverty as a point of pride, which demonstrated that the GOP was a party of regular people and hence equals. It is likely that the limits of this inclusiveness would have been tested by, for example, the presence of visible minorities or openly gay members, but no such activists joined the party during my fieldwork. Such limits to their imagined community notwithstanding, GOP activists' events were pervaded by a palatably friendly—even family-like—atmosphere that extended to all those assembled. Despite the fact that my political views differed sharply from theirs, I felt more comfortable at River City's GOP events than at virtually any other public event.

But in fact, the GOP's egalitarian ethos polarized the grassroots party via three mechanisms: by exposing activists to others' extreme views, by investing them in conflicts involving others who used the GOP label, and by drawing their attention to candidates who appealed to all their peers.

First, activists' tolerance of one another's political commitments exposed them to these views, softening their opposition to ideas that they might otherwise discount. Some activists habitually launched into extended tirades on subjects—deporting all *legal* Hispanic immigrants, abolishing all taxes, or outlawing abortion—that other activists thought outside the realm of reasonable or practical. Monthly meetings also featured speakers making the grassroots GOP circuit, who spoke on issues that energized some activists but appeared beyond the pale of the plausible to others. For example, many older GOPers reported being uncomfortable with the in-your-face style of younger Ron Paul supporters, which several told me reminded them of "the 1960s." Nevertheless, other GOPers allowed Ron Paul supporters to invite monthly speakers who spoke about ending the Federal Reserve system and government-issued identification cards as a prelude to the police state—positions that they secretly thought crazy. Activists who championed such idiosyncratic causes did not always win over all their peers, but nobody contradicted them and other activists accepted their views as legitimate political discourse.

Second, activists' egalitarianism also provided them with neither the means nor the desire to police use of the GOP label. Because outsiders *did* assume that any initiative spearheaded by self-identified GOPers had the party's full backing, River Citians constantly criticized and poked fun at the GOP—a dynamic that reinforced activists' underdog self-identification. For instance, River Citians commonly identified GOP activists with Planned Parenthood pickets even though few of these pro-life protests were party regulars. Or recall Andy Tuner's public outbursts. During GOP meetings, many activists rolled their eyes at Andy, too, but others' criticism of Andy and Republicanism by extension led skeptical GOPers to circle the wagons. In effect, outsiders' tendency to associate the extremism of one with the extremism of all became a self-fulfilling prophecy as activists rallied around their maligned peers.

Finally, and along similar lines, activists' egalitarianism led them to collectively endorse candidates that even GOPers themselves considered fringy. The norm among activists was that anyone who ran for local office and sought GOP endorsement should get it. In cases where multiple activists wanted to run, they settled it among themselves, typically allowing the most senior activist to bear the party's mantle. Before the 1980s traditional community leaders refrained from endorsing candidates who seemed unlikely to win. By contrast, activists' willingness to endorse anyone in conjunction with a shallow pool of GOP candidates produced some bizarre campaigns that were ridiculed by other River Citians. For example, one GOP-backed Ron Paul supporter ran for county auditor on the plank of abolishing property taxes. Some GOP activists thought campaigns of this sort ridiculous, but here too they circled the wagons in the face of community ridicule.

Similar processes of intraparty polarization led activists to support state and national candidates who embraced the full menu of extreme GOP positions. Consider that in an egalitarian context characterized by a few individuals with extreme but strongly held views, the consensus position is one that embraces all the extremes. In this context, more moderate GOP candidates struggled. In 2008, for example, activists openly called John McCain a "RINO" (Republican In Name Only) during monthly meetings and snickered. A few activists with military backgrounds even charged McCain with treasonous cowardice in the face of Democratic opposition. Those activists who supported moderate Republicans reported feeling uncomfortable advocating on their behalf. One example was David Rourke, a longtime activist who supported Mitt Romney in 2008. Other activists saw Romney as a moderate in 2008, as they would again in 2012.

"I think Romney would run the country more like a business, because that's more like where his experience is from. He'd rely on his advisors, set up maybe more of like a business-type environment with a pyramid to the top, that sort of thing," David told me. "Huckabee, [the top choice of most activists at the time] is an unknown—he's a champion for all the right causes, but I don't know what his presidency would be like. He'd be a good number 2 for Mitt. That'd be a good ticket," David continued, hedging in anticipation of others' opposition. "And people have to realize that [Romney] is not like a Giuliani or a McCain maybe, who would disappoint so much of the party," he added, clarifying that Romney was *not*, after all, a RINO. "So many conservative Republicans say that if Giuliani is the choice, I won't vote for him, even if he is okay on some of the fiscal issues. [Giuliani] is now trying to backtrack and say that he'd be a strict construction-

ist and [appoint] judges who [take Christian-conservative social positions].
Well, I just don't believe it!" Note that David's conciliatory esprit de corps
makes him describe his relatively more moderate choice in partisan terms,
thus—once again—making the GOP appear more partisan than the sum of
its parts.

Prairieville's GOP

Differences between River City's and Prairieville's GOP paled in comparison to their similarities. Prairieville's old families abandoned the GOP
during the 1980s and no community leaders attended party events by the
2000s. The city's activists also identified as an egalitarian group of regular people and established solidarity by tolerating and supporting one another's political commitments. But whereas River City's GOP was familial,
the atmosphere within Prairieville's GOP was sometimes toxic as activists
tried to one-up each other in their adherence to ideologically pure Republicanism. I think that this difference was due to the larger size of Prairieville's GOP and—especially—the blurrier boundary between the party and
Prairieville's community leaders. Ultimately, however, Prairieville's GOP
usually functioned as an ideal-typical activist party and any additional intraparty dynamics—although caused by an incomplete separation between
the GOP and community governance—actually polarized activists and further distanced them from Prairieville's community leaders.

Prairieville's GOP grew much like River City's through successive waves
of national partisan mobilization. But at the time of my fieldwork, Prairieville's party was bigger, with over one hundred people regularly in attendance at monthly meetings in comparison to perhaps thirty in River City.
As in River City, Prairieville's activists identified with their entering cohort,
but Prairieville's activist cohorts were larger and thereby acquired organizational importance by dividing the party into cells: small informal networks
of like-minded activists. "[During the last election] we got a new volunteer:
Shannon," Lisa Miller, an activist in Prairieville, told me, describing the
formation of one cell. "[Shannon is] such an elegant lady and so knowledgeable about politics. She would start calling me in the morning and
say, 'I was just listening to Fox News and this such and such happened—we
have to call the White House!' I mean, this woman would call the White
House, you know? Just a fireball. The last presidential election brought out
some dedicated people, and a lot of that has to do with Shannon. She has a
group of maybe eight to twelve core volunteers, ladies who like to keep up
on things and like to talk politics. We all get together, have lunch, and talk

politics for two hours. [Then] you have a group, have names, and get email information so you can get to people between elections—track them, keep them engaged, and draw on them when you need them to get involved."

Prairieville's cells did not usually alter ideal-typical activist party dynamics. Activists sat with their cell-mates during meetings and often backed the same candidates during primaries, but they still identified primarily as members of a community of equals, listening politely to other activists' diatribes, party-sponsored lectures, and film screenings. As in River City, Prairieville's GOPers also allowed others to don the Republican mantle when championing whatever cause. For instance, a cell of Christian conservative GOPers began a campaign to force a sex shop out of Prairieville during my fieldwork. Even libertarians who opposed the campaign never condemned it, despite the fact that the anti–sex shop crusade was ridiculed in the local media and by other Prairievillers alike.

In a few situations, however, the cellular structure of Prairieville's GOP provided the building blocks for a sustained intraparty polarization, which mirrored nothing so much as the community-politics divide within Prairieville's public sphere.[34] I witnessed two such polarizations: one that I described in chapter 5 after Mark Sturley's critique of Republican "Christian Nazis" and another that began during a national wave of anti-immigrant protests when a local sheriff demanded to see proof of citizenship from area Hispanics. Recall that in the former case, Mark Sturley brazenly sided with community over politics, arguing that the GOP should expel more-extreme activists and reconcile with Prairieville's business leaders. The furor over Prairieville's sheriff also assumed the contours of a community-politics conflict. Prairieville's partners were embarrassed by the sheriff's actions and immediately denounced him. Although no activist did so, GOPers lined up along a relatively moderate to purely ideological continuum: moderates espoused tepid support for the sheriff but decried his divisive tactics, while the party's more political wing celebrated him as an American hero. Despite the apparent similarity in these positions, clashes between the party's two wings were downright nasty.

The tone of GOPers' intraparty conflicts were fueled in part by the incomplete separation between Prairieville's Republican Party and the city's leadership class. Unlike their River City counterparts, Prairieville's activists saw their separation from country club Republicans as contingent or fluid and for good reason: although Prairieville's key community leaders did not attend party meetings, a few were openly Republican. Dani Dover was openly Republican, for example, and one of Prairieville's most influential councilmen was the son of an activist with deep ties to state-level

Republican politics. A group of younger, second-tier business leaders even attended GOP meetings, sitting in a big group toward the back of the auditorium. These leaders were neither important partners nor in leadership positions within the GOP, but their presence—evidenced by a clump of blue business shirts in the auditorium—created the impression that business interests were present. Moreover, activists regularly encountered community leaders at political events other than party meetings, because—unlike in River City—Prairieville's business leaders attended the Republican primary straw poll, and even endorsed and supported the occasional moderate Republican. For example, Dani Dover was among Mitt Romney's earliest supporters.

Most activists took community leaders' occasional forays into partisan politics as evidence of public cowardice: they believed that community leaders harbored deep GOP sympathies and secretly longed for the final victory of activists' brand of Republicanism. In fact, activists were wrong to think this because business leaders had conflicted political views. Nevertheless, the discourse surrounding Prairieville's intraparty polarizations often revolved around charges of country club–ism and moral corruption. Activists who came out ahead in such conflicts did so by distinguishing themselves via a wanton disregard for the opinion of those outside the party. For example, activists who assumed party leadership after Mark Sturley's departure belonged to a cell whose members recorded similar messages on their home answering machines, which reminded all callers that human life begins at conception.

Although polarizations of Prairieville's GOP were infrequent, they had an enduring effect on the party, which—perhaps—were initial steps toward an intraparty hierarchy akin to the type of ideological machine identified by Seth Masket in a few California cities.[35] For instance, activists were generally concerned with whether or not they were "activist-y" enough and accepted that more-activist-y activists should lead the party—although some also resented this. In general, activists further identified the Christian wing of the party as more activist-y.

"[Some people are too] far right, Christian Right," Todd Rider, one of the blue-shirted professional workers who attends GOP meetings, complained. "Everything [they] do is dictated by this. [They] fought hard against one of the local judges here during the last election, because an attorney brought a divorce to him and come to find out it had been a lesbian couple. The judge signed it not knowing it was same sex. I mean, the judge had not even been a judge that long, so yes, he should have read it, but then this group jumped on a bandwagon with a [Christian Conservative

PAC] and just hammered and hammered—spent a lot of money trying to make sure this judge was not reappointed. But then in the balance you had the presidential election, your congressional elections, and your state and local offices, so [a lot of us] thought that was time not well spent." Such misgivings notwithstanding, neither Todd not anyone else publically criticized those involved with this particular initiative.

Prairieville's GOP was noteworthy in one other respect: it received PAC funding during the 2008 election cycle. "[I worked on a political campaign] and the guy [who] recruited me for that, I've maintained a friendship basis with him," Clarissa Mondale, a political activist in Prairieville, told me. "So then I was visiting with [my friend] and he says, 'I got a friend who works for [a conservative] PAC, let me get back to you.' I got an email twenty minutes later that says you [will get] a thousand-dollar check. That PAC has been good to us and last election cycle I think we got $2,500 from them." In 2008 I thought that the Prairieville GOP's PAC money was a portent of things to come. Consider that PAC donations simultaneously resolve PACs and activists' problems: PACs, which have money but no grassroots capacity, buy influence among activists, who get to keep the lights on in turn. However, none of the parties in my study received PAC money in 2012, although Sarah Palin's PAC made the maximum $5,000 donation to other local parties in Iowa.

Such details aside, the intraparty dynamics of Prairieville's GOP were similar to River City's: they polarized activists, led them to work for ideologically pure candidates, and taught other residents in Prairieville that community and politics are diametrically opposed. "Every community has got to have at least one strip club and one dirty bookstore. It is just a fact of life!" an incensed young professional told me after the GOP's anti-sex bookstore campaign. "You just have to deal with it. You can't take this bookstore that has been there maybe thirty years and make them move. Like it or not! I mean, I mean porn made the Internet! Politics [is] a bunch of me-against-the-world issues with no basis in anything. [Political people are] unable to set stuff aside and just say, 'You're this and I'm that!'"

Prairieville's Democrats

The Democratic parties I studied were less ideal-typically activist than Republican ones, but ultimately interparty differences were ones of degree rather than kind. That is, Democratic parties counted some traditional leaders and the occasional partner as members, but Democrats of all stripes agreed that activists with no particular connection to their city's leadership class were the dominant faction—a state of affairs that set in motion intra-party processes similar to those I observed among Republicans. In Prairie-ville, for example, a few Democrats who had been central within the city's community leadership party—union leaders, labor attorneys, and female campaign workers like Frannie Steele—were still engaged activists at the time of my fieldwork. However, a shift toward a fully ideal-typical activist party was well underway as these traditional leaders were older, scaling back their involvement, and had tried—but failed—to train a younger generation of traditional replacements.

Older union leaders complained bitterly that younger members never had time for politics. Before the 1980s, union leaders' peak public involvement lasted perhaps twenty years; afterwards, leaders stepped back to let younger unionists take over. But younger union members did not step forward at the time of my fieldwork, thus putting pressure on older leaders to stay engaged. "You know, I'm on the DNC for Prairie County here and everyone is always sittin' around sayin' we need to get more young people involved, but how do you do it?" a labor leader complained.

The situation was similar among Prairieville's labor attorneys, who had traditionally taken promising young activists under their wing. Hardy Schmidt, for example, had taken Abe Skipper under his wing, who later returned the favor by mentoring many young Democratic leaders, among them Stewart Warner, Prairieville's current state senator. "I remember [Skipper] came to our house when I announced that I wanted to be a page [in the Iowa House]," Stewart recalled. "And I said to myself, 'Wow, here is a representative actually coming to our house to help me.' It impressed me that a legislator would actually go out, serve people, but over the years I saw that level of commitment on a whole host of things from Abe Skipper. Some things I learned not to do, too," Stewart continued laughing. "But one of the things I took away and always try to remember is that you have to help the people who tend to get ignored—the people who are ignored because they are not rich and powerful." At the time of my fieldwork, no labor attorneys had successfully formed such mentoring relationships with younger leaders.

Frannie Steele and her coworkers also failed to train a new generation of female Democratic leaders. By the 1990s Frannie was blinded by illness, at which point Bridgette McIndoe, a close friend of Frannie's, took over day-to-day party work. But Bridgette was also in her seventies and tried to pass the mantle to Kathy Irving, the head of a large affordable housing nonprofit. "It was probably a couple years after Frannie died and then Bridgette came to me and said, 'Look Kathy, you have to learn this [electioneering] stuff, because otherwise nobody is going to know how to do it anymore,'" Kathy told me. "But women like Frannie and Bridgette, they had all day every day to put toward keep things going. Today you are trying to fit things into fewer and fewer hours. You are working another job; I work fifty-five or sixty hours a week for the job and then trying to fit politics in there, too?" Bridgette's choice of Kathy proved fateful, because she stepped down as party president without mentoring a replacement soon after our interview, thus breaking a decades-long chain of electioneering tradition and know-how.

With its traditional leadership either gone or gray, Prairieville's Democratic Party fell into the hands of nontraditional activists who, like their Republican counterparts, had no ties to Prairieville's leadership class and entered the party during successive waves of national mobilization.[36] At the time of my fieldwork, the party's central committee was entirely populated by such activists: one middle manager, one teacher and one retired teacher, two college professors, an attorney, two nonprofit workers and an administrative assistant. Some activists came into the party during national mobilizations like Meetup or anti–Iraq War marches. Others came after activist campaigns like Howard Dean's. Still others were committed to causes that they identified with the Democrats—for instance, fair housing, racial equality, or a more generous social welfare state—and a few championed idiosyncratic causes not typically associated with the Democratic Party at all. For example, the party president who followed Kathy was an enthusiastic advocate of on-line deliberative forums and their potential for revolutionizing American democracy.

Like their Republican counterparts, Democratic activists saw themselves as distinct from traditional Democratic leaders. But whereas River City's Republican activists saw themselves as naturally different from business leaders and Prairieville's activists resented them, Prairieville's Democratic activists looked down on their party's old guard. Many activists saw union leaders especially as unreflective and narrow in their political commitments. "This became a middle-class country because of two things: government spending and unions. That's why those are two things that the Republicans love to hate," one Prairieville activist told me, taking care to establish his support of union leaders' political commitments first. "[And the] union movement still has a lot of presence within the party [but they are] very economically focused. And I'm a policy wonk; I like to hear people argue through the specifics and the details, but you are not going to get that from the blue-collar folks. There's not a lot of deep reflection there. You get a lot more applause [from them] talking about universal healthcare and protecting Social Security to the death than you will talking about gay marriage or a sane foreign policy or civil liberties or not treating the Constitution like toilet paper. [With union leaders] it is a narrow focus and you won't see excitement about the social agenda [from them]."

In some respects, it is unsurprising that Democratic activists felt distant from union leaders given differences in the background of the two groups. Union leaders were working-class, whereas post-1980s activist were disproportionately professional and para-professional knowledge workers like teachers, professors, and nonprofit workers and identified as such. Much like partners, in fact, they saw themselves as educated and cosmopolitan, although—ironically—most activists were only vaguely aware of their elective affinity with Prairieville's leadership class, because for them local politics coded as parochial and hence uninteresting. But activists' critique of union leaders was also an inevitable consequence of their party's flattened hierarchy: in an egalitarian space characterized by heterogeneous but strong political preferences, those with pointy or focused political commitments looked narrow whereas partisans without constraints feel at home.

Like GOP activists, too, Democratic activists viewed themselves as an egalitarian group that accepted one another's political commitments. Party meetings consisted largely of members' speeches about various partisan issues, many of which the activists I spoke with admitted finding wrongheaded or simply "out there" in private interviews: faith in the Internet's ability to revive American democracy, fears about the emergence of a police state, and the like. Similarly, activists regularly made sanguine pro-choice statements, although ambivalent feelings about social issues were the norm among Prairieville's working class—and often Catholic—Democrats. Like Republicans, too, Democratic activists allowed one another to speak on behalf of the party in support of whatever cause. My sense was that Prairieville's residents saw Democratic activists' initiatives as less political than, for instance, GOPers' effort to drive sex shops from the city. Nevertheless, a few Prairievillers I spoke with rolled their eyes at some initiatives—for example, an activists' city council petition to impeach of George W. Bush.

Although Democratic activists established solidarity by tacitly accepting or adopting one another's political commitments just like their Republican counterparts, the two groups gave different accounts of why such political tolerance was important. Whereas Republicans identified as underdogs and accepted others' policy commitments on this basis, Democratic activists saw themselves as an educated vanguard, prided themselves on being open-minded toward others' efforts to educate them about national issues, and equated their party's flat status hierarchy with its commitment to reason and education—assuming, incorrectly, that Republicans were unthinking and therefore organized hierarchically. "Republicans have learned how to franchise. They know how to do that in business and with politics. They are a group of people that is more comfortable with command and control," one activist told me. "The Democrats are people of education, strong intellect, they are thinkers and they really want to argue everything—so with them, it has to be more of a coalition. That is great, but it is also our downfall, because it makes it hard to make decisions and move forward. But Democrats are not a group that can be dictated to, so it has to be that way." Of course, both River City's and Prairieville's Republican parties had *precisely* the kind of flat coalitional structure that this activist attributed to the Democrats, which underscores one of my main points: to outsiders, activists' inability to police use of the party brand makes them look like a monolith that supports the full range of partisan issues.

Individually, too, many Democratic activists identified as experts on a national policy, and saw their task as simultaneously one of self-education *and* as one of educating other Prairievillers. Of all of the Democratic Party's committees, none was better attended than the education committee, a forum where activists hatched media strategies and discussed overcoming the right-wing spin machine, opening the eyes of their city's residents, and the like. Similarly, activists favored educational party activities like screenings of documentaries that were then common viewing among left-leaning audiences: Michael Moore films or documentaries critical of Fox News and the Iraq War. Typically, these screenings were attended only by activists themselves. By contrast, Democratic activists shunned mundane party-building activities. "You can't get [activist volunteers] to paint anything," a traditional activist complained, "and if you ask them to phone bank for too long, they'll leave."

At the extreme, Democratic activists' self-conception as an educated, enlightened elite promoted contempt of other Prairievillers—a dynamic that I did not observe among Republican activists. Even during official party meetings, activists expressed skepticism about others' ability to grasp some issue or to care about it. They referred to other Prairievillers as "too busy watching TV" or "blinded by religion," for example. "Why people don't get more interested in politics is a mystery to me," one activist told me, illustrating this tendency. "[But] I don't see a lot of courage or thought in our population and that's why we have the politicians we've got—people will spend all their time worrying about whether Bill Clinton got a blowjob or not but lack [an understanding of] the big issues. It is that mentality of being blinded to the big picture [and] a lot of people are lazy and disinterested. I mean, how do you make $25K a year and not vote? You try to talk to them, break it down into simple steps, but then they just look at you like this," the activist concluded, making a dull-eyed face with his mouth agape.

In pointing critically to activists' occasional contempt for other Prairievillers, I do not mean to imply that party leaders need to share the cultural background of those they represent or refrain from challenging their political views. But consider activists' warrant—or lack thereof—for such critiques, particularly vis-à-vis their traditional predecessors. Some traditional Democratic leaders were not lunch-bucket Democrats either and took locally unpopular positions. For example, Abe Skipper entered the party as a flower child and decades later still used his state senator credentials to go backstage at rock concerts. Throughout his career, Skipper also opposed every American war, including Iraq One and Two, and supported gay rights before it was fashionable to do so. But unlike 2000s-era activists, Skipper could speak of these issues to Prairieville's working-class residents as one of their own, because he had been there: working on the line at the packinghouse, giving legal advice in times of crisis, staffing blue-collar charities on his days off, standing on the picket line during strikes. However colorful his personality or extreme his politics, Skipper spoke to Prairievillers as an insider. Contemporary activists speak as outsiders: as experts on a national reality that is divorced from daily life.

River City's Democratic Party

Of River City's and Prairieville's four parties, River City's Democratic Party was the most difficult to categorize because it consisted of three sets of actors: activists, traditional union leaders, and a small contingent of partners. At the time of my fieldwork, virtually everyone agreed that activists wielded more control over the party agenda than traditional leaders and that these later two groups were both more significant than the partners. "We still have a lot of old-style, lunch-bucket, blue-collar Democrats, who are mostly concerned with economic issues of organized labor," an activist once told me, presenting traditional leaders as activists' main foil. "But that is not [what] the party is about anymore. Now we have a broader coalition."

Divisions within River City's Democratic Party were evident in seating arrangements at monthly meetings, which were held in a roadhouse at the city's outskirts. Traditional union leaders all sat together at large round tables at the back or along the bar on the left-hand side of the hall. They did not normally make motions, speak, or otherwise participate. The only exception were Mitt O'Connell and Pete O'Brien, two populist politicians who everyone considered to be traditional leaders but who sat with the activists near the front of the room and participated in the proceedings. Occasionally, a group of second-tier partners attended meetings and sat together at a table near the back of to the hall and did not typically intermingle with activists. Of River City's key United Labor leaders, none regularly attended party meetings, although one gave generously to the local party. Finally, the long rows of picnic tables that dominated the center of the hall were seated with activists, who had swelled the ranks of the party in a similar manner to Prairieville's Democratic activists and espoused allegiance to a variety of causes: racial equality, gender equality, sexual-orientation equality, welfare-state expansion, pro-choice, opposition to the war on terror, and—especially—the Iraq War.

Here, too, Democratic activists lacked a clear status hierarchy. "It is more of a Party of the little people now," the party's president told me when I asked him for a list of key Democrats. "Because frankly, we don't have the big-name people anymore. Which is nice, too—it's more like a family, we work together." Another activist agreed: "I don't know if we have like two or three people who tower above the rest . . . it is pretty much a community of equals, maybe twenty-five or thirty key people at the same level." Here, too, activists identified with their party's flat status hierarchy and saw it as consistent with that of an educated background.

As in Prairieville, the party's flat status hierarchy produced dynamics that made it appear as a monolith to outsiders. Activists refrained from critiquing one another's political commitments and, like their GOP counterparts, reported feeling pressure to be right on all the issues. "I'm a liberal Democrat—in fact, I'd probably be Green Party [if they] had any chance of winning," an activist told me, establishing his radical credentials first. "[That is] unless [you compare me to] the real purists who are so busy being perfect and have to be right on all the issues." The one issue that River City's activists tiptoed around was abortion, because some long-time activists—Wally Porter, the city's former mayor, and a convent of Catholic nuns that had long supplied able Democratic campaign workers—made known their ambivalent feelings about it. Activists still spoke in favor of pro-choice, but acknowledged the complexity of the issue, then moved quickly to criticizing Republicans for their inconsistency in opposing abortion but supporting the death penalty—a line that never failed to draw loud applause.

In most cases then, River City's Democratic Party functioned as an activist party, but the presence of nonactivists within the party occasionally engendered different intraparty dynamics. This happened especially when traditional leaders tried to rally the party in favor of local initiatives. Partners, too, sometimes rallied River City's Democrats, but typically to get themselves elected to partisan office. In chapter 6 I discussed the Ben Denison campaign, which exemplified both traditional leaders' and partners' attempt at Democratic mobilization: Ben tried to mobilize activists to get himself elected, whereas labor council leaders countermobilized them to sink Ben's primary campaign. In this case some activists supported Ben on the grounds that he was a River Citian, while others opposed him due to their political commitment to society's underprivileged, questions about whether Ben was a "true Democrat," and the like. To outsiders, then, the conflicts that surrounded Ben's primary campaign appeared as a familiar one between community and politics, even though it was playing out within the party. Note the parallel to Prairieville's Republican Party: there, too, an intraparty conflict over Mark Sturley or immigration polarized activists along a continuum that looked to outsiders like a community-politics split. Virtually all efforts by traditional leaders and partners to mobilize River City's activists produced a similar community-politics polarization.

For example, traditional union leaders regularly rallied Democratic activist to support a long-running nurses' strike at an area hospital. For months, they spoke about little else at party meetings and purchased "We support our nurses!" signs, which other activists distributed, and which became omnipresent in many of River City's neighborhoods. Many activists did not have strong feelings about the dispute, but most sided with the nurses over management and—in a close and unusually contested vote— elected the head of the nurses' union party president on the grounds that the Democrats represented the underprivileged. At this point, some traditional leaders began an outright Democratic offensive against hospital management. Mitt O'Connell, one of River City's state senators, spoke at a nurse's rally and was quoted in the newspaper hurling invectives at management. Representative Pete O'Brien, a senior member of River City's delegation, called on Democratic activists to picket hospital board members at their place of business and personally attended a few such pickets.

To many other residents, the Democrats' pro-nurse mobilization appeared like a classic case of politics versus community—ironic, since it was a decidedly local affair of the sort that was the bread and butter of pre-1980s community conflicts. But partners, River City's post-1980s community leaders, took a firm nonintervention stance. Toward the beginning of the strike I interviewed Ben Denison and presented him with a number of possible scenarios that might lead the community's partners to intervene (e.g., the strike goes on for years, the hospital is bankrupt, negative national media coverage). He insisted that partners would not intervene in even the most extreme scenario and key partners stuck to this nonintervention policy for the strike's duration. Outsiders to the dispute were therefore presented with a clear public contrast: community leaders like the demure and officially neutral Ben Denison and firebrands like Pete O'Brien, who yelled at the hospital boards' suit-clad board members as they went to work.

I spoke with Christopher Weber during the strike, a partner who was on the hospital's board of directors. We had been speaking about how disappointingly divisive American politics has become. "Let me give you a prime example: Pete O'Brien. There's one politician I could do without—classic politician!" Christopher said, spontaneously switching from national to local. "His wife is a nurse and—big surprise—he comes up here and starts chewing into my [employer] on me. They had an information picket outside and everything. When you sit on a civic board like that you are going to spend a lot of hours. For somebody to exert political pressure, to try to sway how you are looking at something and weighing the options—I don't like that. Unions are a valuable element of society, but both sides need to be reasonable." I then asked Christopher if he blamed Pete's behavior on his Democratic identification. "I don't necessarily see it as a Democratic thing versus a Republican thing, it's just him [and] the way politics is: people fight for their side and don't take a moment to step back and look for what's reasonable."

The River City nurses' strike had a similar effect on partners who sometimes dabbled in Democratic politics. The activists I spoke with reported feelings of inexact fit within the party that mirrored nothing so much as those of more moderate Republicans during Mark Sturley's exit from Prairieville's party. "I feel conflicted about the strike, I do," Kathy Gooding, the director of River City's River Museum, told me. Indeed, Kathy's daily activities brought her into contact with community leaders opposed to the strike, while some Democratic meetings consisted largely of pro-union and anti-management tirades. Kathy responded by internalizing a community versus partisan split and alternated between looking at the situation as "a citizen" or "leader" versus as "a Democrat." "[As] a Democrat, I don't think they should begrudge these people who care for children and the infirm a living wage," Kathy said, looking at things politically first. "We are in a world of hurt if we destroy the middle class. And I think a lot of people—nurses, and teachers, and laborers—they will make up the middle class if you pay them a living wage." She then switched to a community viewpoint. "[But] there shouldn't be this standoff—I think there needs to be a dialogue, some kind of negotiation. It's sad," she continued. "I mean, even though [some partners and I] are on opposite sides of this, and we are Democrats and they are Republicans [there are] lots of other issues we do agree on."

Like Kathy, partners involved in River City's Democratic Party were often caught between community and politics. Most of these partners attended party meetings, because they—like Kathy—were involved with the party before they became prominent community leaders or because they seemed genuinely committed to the Democratic platform. Like Kathy, however, most partners who attended Democratic Party meetings simply stayed silent.

The two exceptions to partners' silence at Democratic meetings were politicians who identified as partners or partners running for office.[37] For example, Patty Conlon, a state representative who was considered relatively reliable by River City's partners, participated regularly in Democratic meetings. However, she mostly intervened on procedural issues and did not deliver the kinds of invectives that were the bread and butter of politicians like Pete O'Brien.[38] David Insbruck, the head of River City's Labor Management Council and a close lieutenant of Ben Denison's, also attended meetings in anticipation of a run for office. David's presence initially puzzled me, because he seemed out of place as one of the city's key partners; indeed, he never spoke prior to his run, smiling sphinx-like through party meetings instead. It was not until later, when David ran successfully for the state house with backing from many Democratic activists, that David's presence at party functions made sense. Unlike Ben Denison, who did not attend party meetings regularly or establish a relationship with activists until immediately before his run, David was laying the groundwork for a political career. Like Denison, David ran a campaign that was shrouded in the discourse of community overcoming politics: a "Campaign for the Common Good." I was not in the field to observe this campaign, but some informants I spoke with suggested that the campaign polarized activists along a familiar community-politics continuum, although apparently with more success than Denison had done.

Against all of the forces keeping community governance and politics separate, political ambitions like those of Ben Denison or David Insbruck are one potential mechanism of community-political rapprochement. As ambitious local leaders, partners often yearned for higher and better things, a yearning that traditionally drove leaders to politics. The case of

Ben Denison shows that partners' campaigns can reify community-politics divides, but if enough partners win they could nudge the Democratic Party onto a partner-like path. In all other respects, however, River City's Democratic Party—like the other activist parties that I investigated—polarized activists and pushed them further out of step with their city's public life. As I will show in the next chapter, activists represent the views of a disaffected segment of their city's residents, but not those who take positions of public leadership within community institutions.

Grassroots Parties and the Polarization of American Politics

Activists' takeover of grassroots parties in places like River City and Prairieville is important, because it has polarized American politics, producing much sound and fury in Congress but little in the way of governing ideology or political plans. Political scientists argue that this occurred because rational politicians are responsive primarily to their party's grassroots—activists only support candidates who are right on all the issues and politicians comply because they cannot win primaries without them. This position is in line with my observations, and I observed an additional mechanism of polarization: the roles that activists play as intermediaries between politicians and representatives of the media and daily life.

When a member of Congress or early stage presidential candidate comes to River City or Prairieville, party workers greet them at the airport, drive them to campaign events, share meals with them, and arrange the politician's meetings. One should not underestimate the importance of the fact that party workers were once community leaders like Frannie Steele or local business leaders—lower-status peers of the politicians but peers nonetheless—who understood local people's problems and could talk knowledgably and candidly about them. By contrast, activists today are a different. Most became politically interested via exposure to the mass media to begin with, and they are therefore likely to parrot back the partisan rhetoric that politicians already hear on television and the Internet. The shift has been from a bottom-up conduit of information to a closed partisan circuit, within which activists also generate partisan news coverage in turn. Even in small-time River City or Prairieville, grassroots partisanship—such as Mark Sturley's ousting as GOP president or a local sheriff's insistence on ID checks for Hispanics—became national news of the moment and reinforced media narratives about red states, blue states, and the partisan rancor that supposedly dwells just beneath the surface of American daily life. The Tea Party phenomenon is another case in point: although the media billed it as fundamental transformation of American politics and even an emergent third party, the movement drew perhaps 200,000 participants at its peak, virtually all of them already committed Republicans—although, in this case, wealthy donors had a hand in blowing the grassroots movement out of proportion.[39] And finally, activist parties polarize American politics through one additional mechanism besides: they are constitutive of a public sphere that is divided along community-politics lines and fails to provide local residents with a reliable heuristics for translating their local community experience to partisan preferences—a dynamic explored further in the book's final chapters.

EIGHT

What Regular People Think

Nothing during my fieldwork surprised me more than the degree to which 1980s-era changes in River City's and Prairieville's public sphere shaped the way that residents of these cities thought about politics. By this, I do not necessarily mean that residents spoke much about the 1980s, although some did. I certainly do not mean that residents knew much about their cities' grassroots leaders, read the local newspaper, or were knowledgeable about the minutia of partners' place-marketing campaigns—hardly any residents were. And yet, as if by magic, River City and Prairieville's residents had a great sense of the local game and spoke about public life as co-participants in it. Much as some older residents of River City and Prairieville still took part in a dead debate between their city's business and labor sides, many others accepted the parameters of public debate as formulated by their cities' partners. They took the opposition between community and politics as self-evident, and spoke about public life both local and national by adopting a persona from their city's public sphere: that of a partisan or partner.

My argument in this chapter complements the one I made in chapter 3, which analyzed how traditional voters used their memories of pre-1980s public life as a heuristic, or simplified model of how public deliberation and decision-making work, to make sense of politics.[1] Before the 1980s, community struggles were defined by labor-business conflicts, which led people to reason about politics through the framework of these local sides. This mode of reasoning usually led traditional voters to establish stable, reliable, and relatively moderate preferences. Pre-1980s blue- and white-collar conflicts were intertwined with the jobs that people worked, the neighborhoods they lived in, the way that they spent leisure time, and countless other aspects of daily life that people used to establish an intuitive connection with the party that corresponded with their "side." In no case, for instance, did those who identify with their city's business side within community conflicts support the Democratic Party. In simple terms, politics made sense to traditional voters and they were reliable participants in it.

In this chapter, I turn to nontraditional voters, or those who used their city's post-1980s public sphere to make sense of national politics. Like their city's leadership class, nontraditional voters perceived tension between community governance and partisan politics and responded in one of two ideal-typical ways: as partners or partisans. Partner-like voters sided with community over politics, saw it as self-evident that national politics should allow for interparty partnerships, and vacillated between support for post-partisan candidates and political disaffection. Partisans felt disaffected from their community's institutions and looked to politics as a panacea—much like the partisan activists discussed in chapter 7. In some respects, partisans were similar to traditional voters in that they were as interested in politics, and frequently more so, but they were also less predictable. With traditional voters, I could always tell how a person would vote based on how he or she talked about the community. By contrast, partisans were united by an alienation from their community's public life, but were all over the political map, expressing preferences that ranged from political resignation to support for a revolutionary left to support for a Christian theocracy. Partisans' only overarching political commonality was an affinity for candidates who pledged to change the rules of the political game, both locally and nationally. In different ways, then, neither partisans nor partner-like voters were reliable participants in America's political system.

Before proceeding to partisans and partners, I need make three caveats about my analytical approach and research design. First, this chapter continues to rehabilitate the Elmira model of voting behavior, and my focus is therefore on ways that people reason about politics, not people as such.[2] Labels like "traditional voter," "partisan," and "partner" are not meant as an absolute description of any person's political orientation; rather, these labels identify how a person reasons about politics at a single point in time. This distinction is important, because like the Elmira researchers I found that people changed the way in which they reasoned about politics over time. For instance, I spoke with many people who sounded partner-like during the primaries and searched both parties for a post-partisan candidate only to then have their partisan sympathies jolted by the partisan furor preceding the general election.[3] Because of this, my approach to analyzing how people vote is twofold. In this chapter, I analyze the connection between the models that people employ to reason about politics and their political preferences. In chapter 9 I then follow the same people through the 2008 and 2012 election cycles and analyze when and why they used different heuristics to make sense of politics.

Second, and along similar lines, I do not proceed from that assumption that people make sense of politics only via community heuristics. My claim is only that people make sense of politics often by using their intuitive sense of community life as a guide and that whereas doing so once translated into coherent political identification, doing so today produces political confusion. At the same time, I take it as given that people get meaningful political information elsewhere—for instance, via the TV and Internet. My interest is in how people reason *when* they employ community life as a heuristic. In the language of quantitative social science, my aim is to introduce the tension that many people perceive between community life and politics as a new variable into analyses of political preference formation, but I would need a differently designed study to determine the relative importance of community heuristics vis-à-vis other determinants of peoples' preferences.

Finally, I designed my study with the goal of achieving *saturation*: to maximize my chances of conducting at least a few interviews with each *type* of local voter.[4] My argument is informed by a great many of these interviews and observations of River Citians and Prairievillers: I interviewed 104 residents in 2007, reinterviewed the vast majority twice before the 2008 election, put together a team of researchers to observe a few of them during the 2008 Iowa caucuses, and tracked down and reinterviewed some of them prior to the 2012 election—over 300 high-quality, in-depth interviews. I selected interviewees by targeting neighborhoods that seemed most different from one another and by relying on snowball sampling to get at informants who might not otherwise agree to sit for in depth-qualitative interviews. I am therefore confident that another researcher studying River City and Prairieville during the same period would have uncovered the same categories of political reasoning among residents and come to similar conclusions about them, but—because my sample was not statistically random—I am unable to draw inferences about the relative proportions of different kinds of respondents.[5]

My analysis of nontraditional voters in this chapter is divided into two sections. Section 1 enumerates the many mechanisms that communicated to Prairievillers and River Citians that their city's community life had changed since the 1980s and had come to revolve around partnerships. Section 2 then discusses partisans and partner-like voters, showing the cognitive mechanisms that lead partisans to embrace extreme politics and those that lead partners to repudiate strong partisan affiliations. Section 2 also enumerates attitudes common among younger partner-like voters, which contribute to their distrust of politics: faith in educated experts, belief that everyone is the same deep down, belief that politics is abnormal, belief that voting is undemocratic, and repudiation of politics as generational solidarity. Chapter 9 then follows nine ideal-typical voters through the 2008 and 2012 election cycles and shows that whereas traditional voters and partisans were most excited and consistent before the election, partner-like voters changed their preferences or became dejected just before the vote.

Section I: How Daily Life Teaches Residents That Community Life Revolves around Partnerships

Prairievillers and River Citians were aware that the American political system had changed since the 1980s, and no wonder: they heard more partisan bickering on the radio and television and read about it on the Internet. Traditional voters usually saw this change as one of degree—politicians have always fought, now they just fought a little more—whereas partner-like voters saw political polarization as an outright catastrophe. But in either case, the mechanisms that communicated information about America's political system to them are self-evident. By contrast, it is initially less clear why Prairievillers and River Citians should have known anything about their community's public life. That they did is puzzling, because partners were relatively cut off from their city's residents. Traditional leaders traded on an ability to mobilize their city's residents and constructed vertical networks that penetrated deeply into local life. By contrast, partners inhabited a social space that I described as a flat disk of interaction: their chief concern was constructing place-marketing partnerships with one another.

This answer to this puzzle is, first, that some residents of River City and Prairieville *did not know* that their community had changed: the traditional voters I discussed in chapter 3 were effectively living in the past in that they still imagined their community's public life as a labor-business conflict—a conflict that ended roughly two decades before I began fieldwork. But others realized that times had changed, and learned this via periodic experiences that accumulated to form an accurate impression of their city's public game: the tenor of leaders' public pronouncements, their own experience of associational engagement, the character of community-wide initiatives, events and scandals, and partners' rare attempts at public relations.

Leaders' Public Pronouncements and
Engagement in Community Associations

Many Prairievillers and River Citians learned about community life via leaders' pronouncements. For example, I spoke with William, a surgeon who moved to River City in the 1970s. "[When I moved here,] River City was kind of run down. When we drove over the bridge coming into town, the only thing we saw was run-down factories, old industrial stuff. My wife just about imploded. Like, 'Why are we coming here?' [But now it] looks better," William said. I asked him why he thought the city changed.

"The [leaders] who did the waterfront renovation [partnerships], all of the sudden they started talking really positive," William replied. "It had reached a point where it all would have spiraled down had it gone any further and the mayor [Jones Berry], throughout all this, opposed everything. He was a real drag on getting things done. It must have taken concerted leadership, because things don't just happen, but it did not come from the mayor or [those who were in charge then]," William added. "There is an old River City, but there is [now] less of that old mentality; [it] is slowly dying out. You know, old River City worked at the Pack or at Green's, that kind of tied them together, [but] from where I'm sitting River City is not that way anymore. They are [becoming] more open to the world and clearly that has to be a positive."

William was not a community leader and his information about River City's public life was limited. Still, he identified figures who personified River City's traditional public style (e.g., Jones Berry) and even peppered his narrative with a few pieces of partner-lingo (e.g., the decline of an "old mentality" or "old River City"). Although hazy on the details, he used such fragments of information to construct a historical narrative that was not too different from the sort of thing that a well-connected partner might say: the city was run by a bunch of combative naysayers, a new generation of positive visionaries took over, and so on.

For many Prairievillers and River Citians, exposure to leaders' public pronouncements was further reinforced by experiences of community engagement. Most residents had no contact with key organizations like River City's Development Corporation or Prairieville's Development Taskforce, and some residents belonged to no voluntary organizations or clubs at all—although a nonnegligible number of professional residents encountered their city's leadership class via their employers' participation in a community planning forum or initiative. For instance, William worked at one of River City's hospitals, had once participated in a health planning forum, met a few of River City's partners, and recalled being impressed by them. Moreover, even associations at the periphery of Prairieville's and River City's public life were periodically pulled into community-wide initiatives, and their leaders' had adopted the language of partnership. "I think that we have become much more open to collaboration and diversity," a Maureen, a sixty-something professional in Prairieville told me, commenting favorably on her civic experiences. "Your religious or [charitable] organizations will get together and jointly sponsor a Martin Luther King fundraising event or will do big initiatives that include religious leaders, business people, minorities, high school students. There is an awareness that we can't just hold to our own little groups and our own narrow missions, but we have to be welcoming and all work together."

Of course, many others like the traditional voters I discussed in chapter 3 encountered the same pieces of fragmentary public information as William and Maureen, but saw in them evidence that community leaders "no longer care and don't listen," "just want to be in the big show," and so on. "The few and the powerful, they run everything. It's the little boys club as bad as it ever was," one of River City's working-class residents told me, reacting to the same kind of stuff that appealed to partner-like voters. "They're not involved with what the general population feels. It is what *they* want, 'I want these big new things!' They get an idea, 'We need a ballpark!' and then they do it. They think that if they do it everyone else will just follow."

Events: Scandals, Conflicts, and Development Schemes

Residents also learned about their communities' public life via scandals, conflicts, and new development schemes. I have discussed many such cases: Ben Denison's congressional race, River City nurses' strike, Sturley's ousting from Prairieville's GOP, and the wave of anti-immigrant sentiment that swept Prairieville. I conducted interviews with residents during these events, and was consistently surprised by the palatable sense that community leaders' habitual chatter morphed from a blurry object in Prairievillers and River Citians' peripheral vision to a central object of curiosity and concern.[6] Indeed, such events were teachable not only because they focused attention on what community leaders were saying, but also because most of them concerned a conflict between community leaders and partisan activists. During Prairieville's immigration scandal, for example, virtually everyone I spoke with knew that an overzealous sheriff started the conflict and had been sharply criticized by community leaders but embraced by the county GOP. Many residents with Republican sympathies were angry that community leaders had stuck their noses where they did not belong, whereas many others expressed pride in community leaders' ability to set divisive issues aside and fumed that political activists had, once again, demonstrated themselves to be beyond reason.

Along similar lines, locals were intensely interested in changes to their city's built environment. They drove by new building sites, told relatives living elsewhere about them, and speculated endlessly, reading the developments as hieroglyphics that revealed fundamental shifts in their city's leadership class. For example, I spoke with Joyce, a homemaker who lived in one of Prairieville's affluent neighborhoods. "There's a lot more entertainment," Joyce said. "It used to be you had to make your own fun, but we are trying to do more for the community now, and are a lot more family-oriented. We have the bike trails, the walking trails, the new amphitheater. We even have [a] rock climbing [wall]. Can you imagine? So people from all the little towns around here come in and use it. We have the new dance pavilion. Churches use it, people get married there. You know, *before* it would have been," Joyce paused twisting her face into a stern expression, emulating an older didactic voice, "'A dance pavilion?!?' they would have said, 'Why in the world would we need something like that?'"

"So why do you think that happened?" I asked.

"Oh I don't know! That's just how I see it," Joyce laughed, throwing her head back and crossing her arms over the snowflake embroidered on her sweater. "It is almost like we have an older half and a younger half. Things were once so conservative. Probably it was a lot of those old-timers that just, 'Oh no! uhhh uhhhhh!'," Joyce said, once again emulating an old austere voice. "They were set in their ways, against change. [Now] they are more positive and pro-active, and they are willing to spend money, because they want to draw people into the community."

Although Joyce never met Dani Dover and Prairieville's other partners, she effectively triangulated local development and quality-of-life initiatives with community leaders' periodic pronouncements, arriving at a good understanding of contrasts between traditional leaders' and partners' public style. "So let me tell you about my new project—and this is one that I'm having a lot of fun with," Dani Dover once told me, describing her role in the construction of the rock-climbing gym mentioned by Joyce. "But let me warn you, I'm an overindulgent mother," Dani added dryly, her character-istic sarcasm on display. "My son comes home from college and bemoans that there is nowhere to climb, [which is where I got the idea for a climb-ing wall. Now it is] a real asset for the community—nothing similar to it between here and Chicago! [It is like I was telling you:] ideas come from a variety of sources, literally everywhere—this one just happened to come from my son—but you need somebody to bring them together and con-stantly keep that vitality going. Because now my son says, 'Maybe I could see myself living here,'" Dani concluded. "This is something he would not have said ten years ago. And if he says that, maybe other young profession-als will feel the same."

Others encountered the same sorts of hieroglyphics as Joyce, but read therein tales of community leaders who had lapsed in their traditional obligations. One such resident was Irma, a lifelong resident of a lower-middle-class Prairieville neighborhood with strong Republican sympa-thies. "There is more entertainment, but that is more expensive now to take advantage of as far as the young families go," Irma said. "And I don't know if it is city council or what have you [but it also seems like] we never get a chance to vote on it anymore. Other towns, or used to be here, you always heard, 'Oh, they voted down this or that for the schools.' Now they just have a couple meetings, which does not do you any good anyway, and then they go ahead and do it. And Prairieville gets [nothing] in here besides your motels, your hotels, your restaurants—you know—minimum paying jobs. They've got the old opera, the events center, and the baseball team, [but] people can't go to that every night of the week. For years they been telling us how the convention center [was] putting them in the hole [and now] they are building another one right next to it! Our kids—if they even stay here—will never get it paid off till their kids are grown up. Normal young families, the ones just trying to work hard—not these crazy, get di-vorced from your husband, go down and sign up for [food stamps]—those that work hard, they can't hardly make it anymore."

Partners' Attempts at Public Relations

Finally, residents learned about community life via partners' occasional ef-forts to reach out to the public. Partners' attempts at public relations were not common, but—when they did occur—took the form of community planning forums that partners spearhead in connection with particular initiatives or developments. As in all partnership-related matters, such fo-rums were more frequent and ambitious in River City, where partners used periodic Envisioning exercises to develop city priorities as well as priorities for particular neighborhoods.[7] Prairieville's community leaders employed similar forums, albeit on a smaller scale. River City's Envisioning exercises began in the early 1990s, shortly after a partnership to improve the city's schools failed when voters rejected a general bond referendum. After that, partners decided that mercurial public sentiment was an unacceptable liability.

Envisioning exercises shifted participants' attention away from divisive issues and toward points of consensus, thus encouraging River Citians to adopt a partner-like subjectivity, however provisionally. "This is grassroots democracy at its finest," one key partner told me, voicing a common evaluation of Envisioning. A typical process began with big public meetings during which participants generated ideas for improving the city, which were recorded and passed to smaller, partner-directed committees that eliminated contradictory ideas or those they considered divisive, culling the list to 100, then 30, and finally 10 initiatives. The 10 consensus initiatives were vague (e.g., "diversify the economy to create job security"), but partners insisted the actual priorities were unimportant. "I mean, you and I could sit down together and come up with a pretty good comprehensive plan, probably as good or maybe better than what we came up with," one Envisioning organizer told me. "[But then] only you and I would have ownership of it. [The point was] having buy-in. You gotta make sure that people have been asked."

According to official estimates, over 1,000 River Citians participated in an Envisioning process. These numbers are surely inflated, but Envisioning exercises nevertheless shaped River Citians' understanding of community life by becoming events in themselves. River Citians learned about them by talking with others, reading the newspaper, watching local news, and so on. Indeed, many River Citians I spoke with held up Envisioning as ideal public engagement. Russ, a software engineer and recent transplant to River City, was one example. "Oh, I love it here, I'm really, really impressed," Russ said. "There is that feeling here that is purposeful and cohesive at the same time. From what I understand, a couple people had a vision, instead of just talking about it and arguing they made it happen. Instead of that old core of corrupt money-grubbers [running things], people who cared got all these things started. They did the Envision process, got input from the citizens, brought everyone together, and turned it around." Of course, other residents had other ideas, and dismissed Envisioning as one of partners' many place-marketing machinations. But whatever people's orientations toward their community's leaders, they—like their leaders—learned to view community as animated by norms that clashed with both traditional leaders' public style and with partisan politics.

Section II: Partisans and Partners

I now turn to nontraditional voters, Prairievillers and River Citians who perceived community life and partisan politics as animated by incompatible public norms and responded in one of two ways: as partisans or partners. Partisans were those who felt alienated from post-1980s community life and looked to politics as panacea, whereas partner-like voters identified with post-1980s community partnerships, saw nothing similar in national politics, and repudiated party politics. The terms *partisan* and *partner* refer to ideal-typical tendencies, and I will show below that some partner-like voters occasionally incorporated more traditional party preferences into their political reasoning—although, to a surprising degree, most partner-like voters explicitly criticized traditional voters' unquestioned and unwavering party preferences.

The Partisans: Politics over Community

Partisans' political reasoning was characterized by nothing so much as total unpredictability: often, respondents of this type discussed problems in similar ways, but seemed lost when the subject turned to politics and grasped at radically different—albeit frequently equally radical—political solutions. Tom, Jeff, and Steve, all middle-aged residents of River City, exemplified such divergent political tendencies. All three pointed to nearly identical community problems, but Tom identified with the far left, Jeff identified with the Christian conservative wing of the GOP, and Steve repudiated all politics.

I first came upon Tom as he raked his yard in one of River City's lower-middle-class neighborhoods. He had recently been laid off from his job as a factory worker. "I think it's crap. Just total crap!" He said as soon as I asked him about changes in the city. "In the early '90s, we got a lot of retail, more traffic, a million new restaurants. [But] all these things don't appeal to your average person," Tom said. "[We] used to have all these factory jobs, but they just demolished it and people had to settle for Wal-Mart. All of the sudden River City was trying to become a carbon copy of some of your larger cities—like your Milwaukee or Chicago," he stammered angrily. This seemed like something he had been waiting to get off his chest. "[That is why] they built the dog track and the River Museum . . . suddenly we got big businesses coming in with their money and saying, 'Your city wants it!' It makes me wonder if we are living in a democracy. That's not democracy—that's communism," Tom added. "'Oh, but it has brought so much money and jobs to River City!' [our leaders say]. But these so-called jobs are basically worthless! So *those* people," Tom continued, referring to the city's leadership, "they don't really give a shit about what happens. I think it's all just for show!"

Tom saw community as a world gone wrong: whoever was running the show had no connection to River Citians, knew nothing of their real problems, and did not care anyway. Having written off community, Tom placed his hope in politics. "We really need a working-class president—we may never get that, but the next best thing would be a Democrat," Tom told me, drawing on a more traditional Democratic ideology. "And I hate to say this about my own party, but lately they have been spineless and not shown a lot of muscle. Sometimes they act like they don't care about the public: people like me and you who have to work for a living. Any idiot can see that corporate America runs this country. But maybe if we can get a Democrat in there, somebody [thinking] about people from every walk of life, then we can make some improvements, tear things down and take them back to where they used to be."

Jeff, a resident of one of River City's middle-class neighborhoods, saw community life as equally bankrupt. "I don't like the way they are trying to expand [River City]—make it more than it is," he said. "It is almost like they are trying to make it a big city, you know what I mean? And there's no need for it. They say they are bringing in jobs now, but none of them pay what they used to. To be honest with you, I know what I see: government is basically corrupt, part of a hired class. I mean, everything is in decline—everything." Like Tom, too, Jeff placed his hopes in politics and for the same reason: he was—in Tom's words—looking for a candidate who would "tear things down" and fundamentally change the rules of the public game, both locally and nationally. "Politics is not supposed to be [the way it is now]," Jeff told me. "In order to be president nowadays you gotta be a fucking billionaire. I mean, that's probably the problem. These people have all this money and they have no idea what it's like to have to walk down in our shoes. They got no struggle in their lives, so why should they be concerned? Look at Canada, they got free health care, how come we can't [get that? Politicians] find $5 billion to put into a plane and when it comes to other things they are like, 'Ohhhh . . . I don't know.' Five billion dollars would pay for a lot of children's health visits. So I just, I follow religion. I'm a conservative Christian. I just think the world as a whole is going to hell—and from a Christian standpoint I guess it's supposed to. Conservative Republicans are more Christians. They vote on Christian values—abortion and things. Liberals, they want more gays and all that other shit."

Typically, partisans like Tom and Jeff established a firm, stable commitment to one of the two political parties, which made them superficially similar to the traditional voters I discussed in chapter 3. But note that partisans established their political preferences via a different sort of political reasoning than traditional voters. Traditional voters identified positively with one of their community's pre-1980s sides, thereby identifying with that side's political party by extension. Traditional voters' political preference therefore indexed support for the democratic status quo—both locally and nationally—and, indeed, these voters' preferences were typically moderate. By contrast, partisans began from a place of disaffection with community life and grasped at politics for an idealized alternative. Accordingly, partisans' preferences ran toward the extremes of their parties: toward those who seemed willing to tear things down. Among informants whom I was able to reinterview in 2012, for example, only those I originally classified as partisans in 2008 unambiguously embraced movements like the Tea Party or Occupy Wall Street. What's more, partisans' orientation toward community life was purely negative, and they therefore lacked a consistent positive model for making sense of actually existing national politics. It is for this reason that partisans were all over the political map. Like Tom and Jeff, some embraced the hard left or right while others vacillated between political alienation and support for outsider candidates or, indeed, a third party movement.

Steve was an exemplar of the latter tendency. His life exemplified the trajectories of many working-class younger people after the disappearance of steady, unionized jobs.[8] His father had worked at the Pack, and Steve began his working life at a small nearby assembly plant before being laid off. He moved to New Mexico to attend trade school as a gunsmith, but was unable to find steady employment and worked odd jobs. He then moved to Idaho and worked in a sporting goods store—a job he loved, which would not pay the bills. Then on one trip home to River City, he got lucky and found a job as a gunsmith. He moved back home, was doing well, and even purchased a small house, but after two years he was laid off, the house went into foreclosure, and the credit card bills mounted. To pay off the debt, Steve began working as a long-haul trucker, but wanted to quit because the job strained his relationship with his girlfriend.

"I don't know, I guess River City is changing, changing for the better, I guess—they say that," Steve told me. "[But] I just look at my parents and the system was good to them. Dad had a good job. They had a lot more than me. Back then it seemed like if you got your high school diploma there was a pretty good deal there for you. [So] they had pride in what they were doing. That's the part you never hear about [in River City]. So I don't see [that the city is improving and] I understand why people have such a negative attitude. I understand why young people today just want to listen to rap music, get a bunch of tattoos, get fucked up, fight. People think they'll never have anything: things like pride, doing a good job, satisfaction."

Like Tom and Jeff, then, Steve was downbeat about his community: there seemed to be nothing there for him, which clashed with partners' tendency to periodically announce that things were going great. Like Tom and Jeff, too, he looked for a political candidate who would shake up the whole system. He just had not found one yet. "I guess I talk politics, [although] it's more complaining and bashing on politics than talking about it really," Steve said. "These guys don't need to be wearing $11,000 suits and flying on jets that we buy. I guess I'm for reforming the whole thing. I'd like to turn this whole thing upside down, you know what I mean? The whole thing is crooked. I guess that's my attitude really: it is withdrawal. Now they got all these movie stars and rock stars telling kids to rock the vote. I just tell all my friends to ignore all that, because if nobody was buying it they'd stop putting all that stuff out. It is just like [when] you go to the store and see all these magazines about Brad [Pitt] and Jen [Aniston]. If everybody ignored that crap, it would not be around anymore." His repudiation of politics notwithstanding, Steve had strongly supported third-party candidates in the past: Independent Ross Perot and, more recently, Green Party candidate Ralph Nader. In chapter 9 I will return to Steve and his trajectory through the 2008 election cycle.

Partners: Community over Politics

In contrast to partisans like Steve, Jeff, and Tom, partner-like voters saw a political ideal within their city's public sphere: partnership. But this ideal seemed nowhere evident in national politics. My impression when conducting interviews was that partner-like attitudes were particularly common among two types of people: younger people and older people who were heavily engaged in community associations—an impression I document more systematically in the Methodological Appendix.[9] But whether partner-like voters were younger or older and civically engaged, they were unified by the perception that the public norms of their community were fundamentally mismatched with those animating America's political system. Partners responded to this mismatch in one of two ways, with the majority vacillating between tendencies over time: search for a better political system or candidate and outright repudiation of party politics.

Donald, an engineer in his fifties in River City, exemplified partners' search for an alternate political system. "Everyone who thinks about it realizes that politics is all about polarization," he said. "It's about picking out the base which is always way out on one leg or the other. That just adds to this polarizing sense you feel all around you. What about some kind of middle ground? [For politicians] to gain traction you have to stand up there and say some ridiculous thing, tweak an emotional nerve in that alligator brain down there. Crazy, crazy.

"So I can't say I feel for either side, because the middle is left unattended," Donald concluded, moving to positive solutions. "Let's all find a win-win situation to get out of this mess. If somehow people could come together, find consensus, then we could make it work. The number one thing the government could do is get good reliable information out there, so that people could see it all for themselves. [Politicians should] say, 'Here is the full cost,' show it to people, act as an honest broker. [Politicians] could then educate and bring together people, because right now it seems like all they do is divide."

Donald's ideal alternative to contemporary politics was nothing but the logic of partnership projected onto national partisan institutions—unsurprising, perhaps, because he had participated in several partner-led initiatives through his work and reported being extremely impressed. He took for granted, for example, that people would reach consensus if only they had unbiased information, and his statements were even peppered with partner-speak: "let's find a win-win," government should be an "honest broker," and the like. Therefore, Donald approached politics primarily as a search for the most partner-like candidate, although he was frequently frustrated in his search—particularly during the hyperpartisan pre-election atmosphere. "Sometimes I feel like maybe if we all stopped paying attention, [politics] would just go away," he told me before the 2008 general election.

In contrast to Donald's search for a partner-like political system, Suzanna, a thirty-something paralegal in Prairieville, exemplified partner-like voters' political avoidance. Like many in her upper-middle-class neighborhood, Suzanna was pleased with the city's new direction. "They have the pavilion downtown, the Friday Night Musicade, a group out there planting trees, the ball team, Cinco de Mayo events, just a lot of family activities that they are trying to put on," Suzanna said. "I never paid much attention to

[city] politics before, but when I got married and had kids, I started getting involved and paying attention. And, you know, the Smellyville thing had gotten around, that was a bad deal for us," she added laughing. "I think people decided that you have to get involved and you have to work. And you have to be open to input—listen to other people's point of view, and incorporate it. I don't see so much of that conservative mindset [anymore]. I remember complaining as a teenager that there is nothing to do, [but] I just think they are working on issues that are good for the city as a whole [now], trying to make Prairieville a better place to live for families."

Although Suzanna's understanding of her changing community was a little hazy, she hit the important points: leaders were once "conservative" and cliquish, but now incorporated input, focused on "consensus" issues and marketed the city. Suzanna was certain that an analogous form of engagement was absent in national politics. "I think [national politics] is getting out of control. It is ridiculous [and] both parties are equally bad in that way. They might say they are different—like one might say they are for the war and the other against—but basically they are all up there playing the same game," she said. "I don't claim to be part of any party. Too much badmouthing goes on. It is irritating. And any [politician] who starts out getting honest, by the time they get to Washington they are like, 'What is the point?' It is a losing battle probably."

Suzanna's repudiation of politics, and the reasons for it, was clear: she saw politics as inherently conflict-ridden and therefore corrupting of leaders who wanted to bring a consensus-oriented approach. In effect, her repudiation of politics was produced by the same community-politics tension that led Donald to search for ideal alternatives. Indeed, when I pushed Suzanna to formulate an ideal political alternative, she and other partner-like voters formulated one similar to Donald's. "What if we could start over, send all the politicians home and get new ones, what do you wish that would look like?" I asked. "I think they should start getting things done, that's the big thing," Suzanna said. "I mean, I'm not smart enough to figure out the immigration issue or the health-care issue, but I know that there are people out there smart enough to figure it out. They need to focus on issues that the people they are representing want solved, not the ones that people lining their pockets want them to fight about. Right now it is all about their conflicts, [not] coming together and solving the issues that are most pressing for the country." Here again, Suzanna displayed an innate belief in the possibility of finding a consensus position. Her belief in consensus was as prerational, unquestioned, and fundamental to her reasoning as traditional voters' belief that public life was characterized by zero-sum conflict between sides.

Not all voters who reasoned about public life as partners were entirely consistent in this ideology or incapable of establishing partisan preferences. In particular, some Prairievillers and River Citians mixed a preference for partner-like public institutions with either a more traditional identification or a strong preference for a hot-button political issue, thereby establishing a preference for one party by claiming that the *other party* was too divisive.[10]

Brenda, an executive in Prairieville in her forties, exemplified this tendency. She usually voted Republican. "[Partisan politics] is one area of our history where we have failed," she said, sounding partner-like. "Both sides are just battling for that power and then once they get it they struggle with other parties. It is not one party's fault over the other, just not a good working environment." She then switched tracks, focusing on places where Democrats had simply gone too far. "[Although] maybe that goes to the Democrats being ultraliberal now when they are campaigning," she said. "Once they get into office I would hope that they would become more neutral and willing to give and take, but I doubt it. I really struggle with the Dems, because they are so far left. On a lot of issues, like social issues, they seem to focus so much energy on abortion, stem cells. Well, I and a lot of other people could never go along with it."

Abby, a recent college graduate in Prairieville, felt like Brenda, only about the GOP. "Growing up I was more Republican, because I was just following my parents," Abby said. "Now I think it would take a lot of commitment for me to be one or the other. . . . The two sides have their own version of everything, [which] is so set in stone, [but nothing] can ever really be completely resolved just one way, so all that fighting seems so pointless," partner-like Abby concluded, then switched tracks. "[But] right now the Republicans are supporting Bush in Iraq, and maybe they are doing that because he is president and they have to. [But] I think he only [started the war in Iraq] to finish what his dad started. Once he comes out of the White House maybe that can change—that makes me look more to [Democratic candidates] right now; they don't seem so fixed in one point of view or the other when it comes [to the Iraq War]."

Both Brenda and Abby expressed preferences for essentially the same political system and disagreed only about which party is less partner-like. In this way, they reconciled their simultaneous preference for one political side with a preference for a politics without sides by selecting the party that was less "side-like," or—more simply—the "less political" political party.

Like traditional voters then, people like Brenda and Abby did sometimes espouse preferences for one party, but their partisan preferences differed from those of traditional voters in two ways.

First, people like Brenda and Abby typically expressed their preferences as provisional: Abby said she was more interested in Democratic candidates "right now," whereas Brenda indicated that she might warm up to Democrats who "become more neutral and willing to give and take." Unlike traditional voters then, these two and others like them did not really feel themselves to be *part* of a party, and I found that such attitudes translated into action, or rather lack thereof. Whereas numerous traditional voters I spoke with donated time or money to parties, occasionally wrote letters to their representatives about pressing issues, and were otherwise ready to participate in politics, wayward partner-like voters never did until right before the election, and then only in response to negative campaign ads.[11] Because voters like Brenda and Abby did not view themselves as "political people," their negative evaluations on politics remained private and had no impact on the political system of their day.

Ironically, voters like Brenda and Abby also overcame their innate distrust of politics only in response to hyperdivisive partisan messaging. Brenda and Abby were goaded into political positions because of strong feelings about issues like stem-cell research, abortion, or the Iraq War. These were precisely the type of hot-button issues that were the bread and butter of negative campaigning during the 2008 election cycle and the subjects of hundreds of millions of dollars' worth of PAC-funded attack ads. Brenda and Abby, who despised the tenor of partisan politics, took political positions only because of this self-same tenor. By contrast, traditional voters supported parties that they considered to be aligned with people like themselves, did not waffle, and could make up their mind without the benefit of negative campaign ads.

Other Mechanisms That Led Partners to
Feel Alienated from Partisan Politics

In addition to their basic distrust of political conflict, partner-like voters felt alienated from partisan politics for a number of related reasons, many of which are evident in the above examples: the belief that public problems are best addressed by experts, that everyone holds the same public views deep down, that politicians are abnormal, that voting is undemocratic, and that political disaffection is a mark of generational solidarity. I found most of these tendencies among all partners, including older partners, but they were particularly pronounced among partner-like voters in their twenties and thirties—those who had no personal exposure to pre-1980s public life at the time of my fieldwork.

Faith in Experts, Lack of Faith in One's Own Education

Partner-like voters often claimed to be insufficiently educated about politics, unable to formulate an opinion without doing some research, and—sometimes—stated that a matter was simply too technical and should be left up to the experts. I encountered this attitude among virtually all partner-like voters in their twenties and thirties. One example was Clark, a twenty-something repairman in River City. "As far as the [Iraq] War, [I have] friends who are over there and I really don't like it," he said. "But as far as the reasons, or what we are doing over there, I really don't know about all that. I don't know much about what is going on. All you hear about now is that Democrats, they want to stop the war; the Republicans say they need to stay. They go back and forth on it. I don't know what to think. I'm just waiting for something big to happen that will convince me. [Although now] they have a commission—full of ambassadors and generals and other kinds of experts—maybe everyone should just wait to see what they say."

"Well, what is your sense, I mean, do you have a sense that maybe one Party is approaching [the war] better?" I asked.

Clark pondered. "Well, one party is more conservative and the other is more liberal—I guess the Democrats are more conservative, right? I don't really know. I don't know about politics. I'd need to educate myself on the issues more to really make up my mind." People like Clark often pledged to educate themselves in anticipation of our next interview or before the election, but in the frenetic pace of life this never happened. But the key issue is not Clark's lack of education per se. Many traditional voters had less formal education and less political knowledge than Clark, but I *never* spoke with one who reported feeling insufficiently educated. What traditional voters had and Clark did not was an intuitive model, or heuristic, for making sense of politics. It is evident, for example, that Clark found politics counterintuitive and hence confusing: he mislabeled the Democrats as "conservative" and appeared to not know what this label meant. It is for this reason that Clark sought additional information, but in the absence of an intuitive heuristic model, anything new he learned become

so much more political noise and was quickly forgotten. He therefore concluded that the inherently confounding political issues are best left up to
the experts.

At the extreme, many younger partners I spoke with argued that a more
technocratic system would be generally preferable to our current form of
mass democracy. Kevin, a twenty-something office worker in Prairieville,
exemplified this tendency. "I don't care about Democrat and Republican,
but I know it matters a lot to other people," he told me. "It is like a mentality of I want my side to win—like the mentality of a baseball team or a
football team of something. People will cheer for their side no matter how
bad they are sucking.

"Right now, what interests people is controversy, that is what politics is.
The majority of people in Congress as well as the administration are probably reasonable people but they get pulled one way or another by extremists
who do it to get headlines. [If politicians did not appeal to the public] then
we could go back to caring about Paris Hilton and her jail time or whatever it is. And then that would make the political action seem less interesting and [politicians] could get more done," Kevin continued. "And then,
the people trying to represent us would not worry so much about getting
elected [and] they could get back to business instead of fighting one another for the camera. [We'd have] fewer pandering to the crowd type situations and they could go back to what is good for the country as a whole."

Belief That Everyone Is the Same "Deep Down"

Many younger partner-like voters were additionally confused by politics,
because they believed that everyone held the same public beliefs deep
down. Indeed, it often seemed that partners felt insufficiently educated
about politics because they considered a lack of political consensus *inherently* puzzling but could not account for it. Melanie, an unemployed
Prairieviller in her twenties, exemplified this tendency. "Politics is supposed to be everything the people want," she said. "That is the most important thing: they are supposed to be representing all of us, not what all
these little groups want or what [politicians themselves] want. Like, I feel
like they are up there saying this and this and this, but they only say those
things because that is what the people supporting them want. They should
be more realistic, definitely more realistic. They should just tell people, be
honest about it: 'We can't do [what you want] for this reason.'"

At this point, I asked Melanie how the two parties figured into this.
"Yeah, the two parties—I don't really understand the two parties, or the

differences between them," she replied. "I mean, I've taken classes [in high school] where they tell me, but I don't see the differences. I think they have different priorities, like depending on if they want more economic or—I don't know. It is hard for me to explain. I see a difference, but not a big difference, so I don't think there should be two parties. I don't understand it and it seems pointless. Because overall they must have the basic same beliefs. It is good to have different points of view, but everyone really wants the same thing deep down. Everyone is the same. Maybe one little difference or belief is what all the differences are over."

Politicians as Abnormal and Voting as Undemocratic

Because of their innate distrust of conflict, younger partners were virtually universal in their distrust of politicians. Of course, criticism of politicians is as old as politics itself and traditional voters too critiqued their elected representatives. But whereas traditional voters criticized politicians on the grounds that one or all of them had failed to live up to some ideal, younger partners saw them as fundamentally abnormal and incomprehensible. Many, for example, placed politicians in the same "otherworldly" category as reality TV stars or the sorts of celebrities who make a name for themselves by releasing sex tapes.

Greg, an unemployed twenty-something in Prairieville, exemplified this tendency. "I don't know if I can really trust any politician, like as far as how they market themselves," he said. "It seems like all you see them in is their attack ads, more than you see them really talking about themselves, what they want to accomplish, their strengths, and things like that. Like they are against other people's beliefs, but you never know what they are willing to work for. I really don't get into candidates at all. I often feel like they are both morons—maybe that's just me. Neither is worthy of being president. You'd like to see someone who will talk more human [or who has] lived like your life. Not somebody who is married into money or has had daddy's money, and is there to put on some kind of act. I don't know how those guys can know what is best for millions and millions of people. They are just from Planet Politics."

In addition to politicians, the simple act of voting appeared counterintuitive and contrary to laudatory public engagement to a few young partner-like voters. For traditional voters, voting was an intuitive extension of the public norms of their community's public sphere: just as local leaders spoke on their behalf with the expectation of future support, traditional voters gave their vote to a politician with the understanding that the politician would advocate for people like them in turn. By contrast, some younger partners viewed voting as suspect precisely because it makes politicians beholden to particular kinds of people, therefore unwilling to compromise, and therefore contributes to a fractious and unworkable political system.

Will, a young professional in Prairieville whom I quoted in the introduction, exemplified this tendency. "Our generation has grown up not trusting anything in government," he said. "Because there are all these huge issues, but if anything gets brought up it [is] immediately shot down [for not being] on the right side of the aisle. [It] is hard for me to just go out and vote. I do, but it's just like—ehh—I don't know what it is really doing. Politicians are in it for the career and they are beholden to their parties, to private industry and lobbyists, and a few crazies and they don't want to put forward new ideas. [You get] all this talk about viewpoints as either left or right. I just hate to think that way. So many things are good for the country as a whole, but politicians get pulled one way or another."

Political Avoidance as Generational Solidarity

Given that many of partner-like voters' tendencies were especially pronounced among younger people, it is perhaps unsurprising that many of them justified their repudiation of politics in terms of generational solidarity. Younger partner-like voters identified themselves in opposition to their elders, who seemed to be about politics, sides, and generally focused on division. Jessica, an office manager in Prairieville, was one such case. "To a point you want to have some [political] conflict—yes, that is the system we have," she said. "But there are some issues where you think, 'Why can't we come together on that?' Both parties could give a little bit, focus on finding compromise a lot more. I mean, there is obviously [the perception that] the Republicans are for business and conservative and the Democrats are like your working-class blue-collar people." At this point, I asked Jessica if she thought that the parties really represented these interests. "I don't know," she replied. "I feel like that's more how it used to be—that's how older people think about politics, maybe some of your politicians are still like that, those that go way back. My parents' generation, [they] vote[d] Republican no matter what the issues were, that's just what they were. They just believe in their party. I think my generation is more take-it-as-it-comes. [Before it was] a relationship to a party, [you'd say], 'That's what my Party believes and so I'm going to believe it, too!'" It should go without saying too that all of these tendencies intertwine to produce a general antipolitics orientation among partner-like voters.

The trends that I discussed in this chapter would appear to spell trouble for American democracy. Traditional voters were pitted against one another, but generally had faith in the American political system and a stable, predictable preferences for one of the two parties. But traditional voters used pre-1980s public life as a heuristic, and one would therefore expect them to disappear with time; indeed, most of the traditional voters I encountered in River City and Prairieville were older.[12] As traditional voters disappear, they are replaced by partisans and partners, who use post-1980s public life as a political heuristic. Both partisans and partners are dissatisfied with contemporary politics. For partisans, contemporary politics is not radical enough; they hope for a party or candidate who will shake things up and alter the rules of the political game. Partner-like voters see politics as hopelessly divisive, and also want to fundamentally change it to be more amenable to the sorts of partnerships that pervade community life. What is increasingly missing from electoral politics, then, are constituencies that translate their experience of daily life—however imperfectly—into support for a coherent and workable governing ideology or agenda.

From some people's point of view, a happy resolution to this impasse might look as follows: voters finally grow weary of the discord in Washington, DC, and elect partner-like politicians who focus only on consensus issues and demonstrate to everyone that Americans really all want the same things. This scenario is what River City's and Prairieville's community leaders and partner-like voters alike wanted and even expected. However, I think that the victory of partnership scenario is unlikely for two reasons.

The first reason is a point that I will develop in this book's conclusion: partnership only works in community life because neoliberal policies create conditions that allow grassroots leaders to leverage disproportionate public resources by shifting from one momentary consensus to another. There is no analogous situation at the national level, because there is no higher authority to which congressional representatives might market their national schemes. Stated differently, neoliberal policies have cloaked the harsh political reality of necessary tradeoffs via competitive, market-like systems of public finance. But at the national level, politicians cannot escape the reality of tradeoffs and are forced to make decisions that will harm some Americans and help others. In simple terms, the consensus that exists in community life is politically constructed. When push comes to shove, Americans *don't* all want the same things. It is true that skilled partners may leverage the funding for a community health center *and* attract a high-end medical services company to their city, but it is hard to see how federal politicians can avoid tradeoffs between, for instance, record healthcare industry profits and affordable healthcare for all. If people desire political conflict, the best they can hope for is the conflict displacement and begrudging respect between friendly enemies that characterized the Keynesian era.

Moreover, the victory of partnership scenario is unlikely because of the impediments to the formation of a truly bipartisan coalition in support of a partner-like candidate. These impediments are rooted in the fact that partner-like voters are less reliable than either traditional voters or partisans: they vacillate both within election cycles and across them, and are easily disheartened by negative campaign advertising. Nothing illustrates this process better than the fortunes of the Obama campaign during the 2008 and 2012 election cycles: partners initially saw Obama as a post-partisan candidate but eventually came to see his campaign as politics as usual.

I now illustrate this by analyzing several voters' trajectories through these elections.

NINE

How Obama Won the Heartland (Thrice)

It was fall of 2007 and a rainy day in River City. I was back in River Falcon auditorium, the jewel of one of the city's colleges and the home court of the much-beloved Division III basketball team of the same name. I had arrived early but ringside seating was filled, and I sat in the gallery section, my feet dangling over the metal railing. True to its reputation, the Obama campaign had drawn a crowd. My neighbor was a father of three who had taken a break from Sunday chores to see Barack Obama speak for the second time. We chatted while waiting for the event to begin. Obama was a breath of fresh air, he insisted, who could bring an end to the partisan bickering in Washington. "My wife and I both love him," he concluded. The attitudes expressed by my neighbor were exactly what had brought me to the event. I was there because I tried to catch as many political events as possible and because Obama had already begun to draw big crowds and make headlines, but—more than this—because Obama's name was coming up again and again during my interviews among those on the lookout for a post-partisan, antipolitics, even partner-like candidate.

In truth, many aspects of Obama's campaign were unremarkable relative to those of Hillary Clinton and John Edwards, his main rivals. Here we were in the same auditorium where all the other leading candidates held rallies, listening to the same patriotic rock being blasted through the speaker system: Bruce Springsteen and the like. Many of the candidates even related the same personalized anecdotes about River City, in large part because they had all heard the same stories when being driven around town earlier in the day by Democratic Party chairman Dan Mulrooney or another activist. In terms of issues, too, all the campaigns offered something for everyone and strayed little from the day's official Democratic line: end the war in Iraq, healthcare for all, more transparency in government, quality education, and—because this was Iowa—support for ethanol as an alternative to fossil fuels. When it came to issues, the campaigns mostly differed in where they placed their emphasis and in how they packaged their message.

As Bruce Springsteen finally died down, Obama's opening speaker made his way to center court: a father with two sons serving in Iraq who claimed to have been a Republican before George W. Bush lied to him about the war. I had seen this speaker at several rallies before, and he provided the sort of opening act that was red meat for Democratic activists. In part, this was because many activists saw the Iraq War as pointless, thought that George Bush's administration had lied about WMDs to get American troops there in the first place, and were still angry about it in 2007.[1] More than this, however, the Iraq War issue was near and dear to activists, because it provided sharp contrasts in a candidate pool otherwise characterized by shades of gray—a test of a candidates' true conviction. For instance, Hillary Clinton had voted in the Senate to authorize the war, which many activists saw as evidence of her lack of Democratic conviction. John Edwards had voted for the war, but admitted his mistake and apologized profusely, which satisfied activists. Obama had always spoken out against the war, and this was virtually the only thing that most activists knew about him other than his race. For many activists, this was all that they needed to know; at this point in the primary, Obama appeared to them an unspoiled outsider with the courage to pursue a hard-line Democratic agenda. In activists' minds, then, this opening speaker was putting Obama in the best possible light and—to be fair—Obama lived up to his end of the antiwar crusader image by railing against the "wrong war, in the wrong place, at the wrong time" in his typical stump speech. But that wasn't what was drawing the crowds; I glanced over at my neighbor, for example, who was nodding politely but seemed underwhelmed.

Finally, it was time for the main event. Obama made his way to the microphone and immediately began to poke fun at the petty contrivances and pageantry of it all, as if to indicate that he was keeping a safe ironic distance from this whole politics thing. "Say, what in the world is a River Falcon anyway?" he quipped upon reaching the microphone rather than lavishing praise on the hometown team as other candidates had. Later, he opened the floor to Q&A thusly: ". . . and rule number 3 is that if it's a question where my staff may be able to help, you should ask them. So if you're missing your Social Security check, I don't know where it is right now, but if you give us some time we're gonna try to find it for you." He was right: every rally I attended featured at least one crazily meandering

question from an oldster. The audience ate it up, too, laughing uproari-
ously. But aside from this, much of Obama's opening speech was fairly dry
stuff: we should respect the Constitution and avoid unnecessary war, we
should do something about healthcare—perhaps by creating different risk
pools—but my staff is still looking into the details, we should pursue alternative energy—perhaps ethanol and maybe switch-grass—but definitely
avoid relying on Middle East oil. Polite applause, polite applause, polite
applause. I found my attention drifting and thought to myself that Obama
was indeed a bit wonky. But then he came to his signature closer, which
truly engendered many in the crowd to him.

"We know these are problems that we can solve," he thundered. "So the
problem is not that we don't have solutions, the problem is that our politics is broken. The problem is that we've got a politics based on negative
ads and calling people names, talking about who is up and who is down—
it's a petty, small, politics that focuses on our differences . . ." Obama continued speaking, but it was all drowned out by a full ten seconds of thun-
dering applause and exclamations from the audience. As the screaming
finally died down, Obama's strong voice became discernible once more:
". . . that's what this election is about, changing our politics. That's why
you're here. I'm under no illusion that it is just about me—it's about you,
your hopes and dreams. I want to lead this country, but I want to lead this
country because all of you decide to take this political process and make
it your own. That you believe in democracy the way that it is supposed to
work . . ." here again, applause drowned Obama out, but he paused this
time before concluding. "And that I think is going to happen in this election: all of you are going to make decision to change the country, the country is going to change!" As the audience applauded again, my neighbor
leaned over, "He's great, isn't he?" His eyes glistened with emotion.

The rest of the campaign event went off more or less as expected, in part
because many of the questions came from activists bird-dogging on behalf
of various PACs: posing questions designed to elicit public support from
the candidate on a particular policy.[2] One elderly woman, for example,
asked if Obama would commit to scrapping the military's F-22 Raptor program. Obama maneuvered politely around the question, saying he would
look into it. The rest took the familiar form of question, expected response,
applause. Somebody asked what the United States could do about industry
leaving the United States. Answer: improve education and give companies
tax breaks to stay in America rather than relocate. Enthusiastic applause.
Somebody else asked if the union movement had a future. Answer: unions
built the American middle class. Obama then went on to say that he had

been introduced to some of River City's striking nurses and supported their plight. Rousing applause. After about twenty minutes of this the rally ended. Obama hung around for fifteen minutes, answering one-on-one questions and autographed people's napkins, T-shirts, and even shoes. Dan Mulrooney then escorted him out of the auditorium and drove him and his entourage to the campaign bus, where he would spend an hour and a half traversing the cornfields to another small Rust Belt city, be greeted by another pack of that town's activists, and do another campaign rally. Such were the humble beginnings of Barack Obama's road to the White House. And yet, for many of his core supporters, this was Obama at his finest: clean and hope-filled, a campaign and candidate as yet undefiled by politics.

In the words of Barack Obama himself, the 2008 election was not so much about him as it was about the aspirations and hopes of his supporters. Beneath this apparent truism lies the recognition that however skilled or capable a candidate may be, he or she is nevertheless separated from the public by several orders of cultural translation that are largely outside of the candidate's control. First, a candidate is typecast as a certain sort of player within a story about American politics that is told and retold across election cycles: the embattled incumbent, the outsider, the maverick, and so on.[3] Second, people then take whatever image they have of the different candidates and reconcile it with their existing understanding of what politics is and should be all about.

My interest here is primarily in this second sort of cultural translation: I take it as given that, for whatever reason, people saw Obama as the post-partisan candidate during the primary, and focus on how this category changed in people's minds during the election. Thus, I have no specific insight into the true Barack Obama, his real political intentions, or those of any other candidate, or into how campaigns maneuver to assume this or that mantle within various political discourses. Rather, I am interested in what happens to the category "post-political politician" during an election, because I think that this process illustrates a structural—and virtually insurmountable—contradiction between the kinds of politics that partner-like voters want and the way that the American electoral process actually functions.

In this vein, the interesting thing about the Obama campaign was that its core, partner-like primary supporters grew noticeably tepid in their support before the general election.[4] By contrast, traditional Democratic voters and Democratic-leaning partisans mostly supported candidates other than Obama early on, in part because they were unenergized by his calls for a post-partisan politics and—in the case of a few older voters—because they were apprehensive about his race.[5] But by election time, traditional Democratic voters supported Obama unanimously and enthusiastically along with virtually all Democratic-leaning partisans, whereas many partner-like voters were turned off by the general elections' hyperpartisan tone. Therefore, Obama won with the support of traditional Democratic constituencies, was dependent on them for re-election, and was perceived that way by traditional voters, partisans, and partners alike. A similar process occurred on the Republican side. Partner-like voters initially preferred relatively more post-partisan candidates like John McCain and Mitt Romney, but were typically demobilized by the hyperpartisan atmosphere before the general election.

To illustrate this, I now turn to a detailed analysis of nine voters that typify the trajectories of others I spoke with during the 2008 election cycle and, if I was able to track them down, the 2012 election. In chapter 8 I was interested only in the relationship between voters' way of reasoning about politics and their political preferences, and therefore divided them into three categories: traditional voters, partisans, and partner-like voters. In this chapter, I am interested in how the same people behave over the course of the election, and therefore divide voters into four categories: traditional voters (those who always reasoned traditionally), partner-like voters (who always reasoned like partners), partisans (those who always reasoned as partisans), and mixed (those who reasoned sometimes like partners and sometimes in some other way).[6] My take-home point in this chapter is simple: partner-like voters and mixed voters who lean heavily on partnership as a heuristic are not a reliable constituency, even for candidates who effectively engage in partner-speak.

Partners' unreliability in elections is succinctly summarized in table 9.1, which lists the political preferences of different types of voters at points during the 2008 election cycle.[7] Because traditional voters and partisans behaved similarly, I aggregated them. The table shows that partners and mixed voters had a clear preference for two partner-like candidates—Democrat Barack Obama and Republican Mitt Romney—but were also volatile during the election and prone to switching parties, not voting, or being unsure in their vote choice immediately before the election—an orientation that political scientists have shown is also heavily correlated with nonvoting.[8] Ultimately, therefore, traditional voters and partisans were *more* likely to strongly support Barack Obama or John McCain before the election itself than partners or mixed voters, even though traditional voters and partisans typically preferred other candidates during the primary.[9] These ideal-typical trends are summarized succinctly in table 9.2.

Table 9.1. How different types of voters behaved during election cycle

Classification after first interview	Partner	Mixed	Traditional/ partisan
Respondents with 3 interviews/initial respondents	20/22	23/30	46/53
Candidates liked during caucus			
Ever liked both parties or switched	12/20	7/23	1/46
Republicans			
Romney, McCain, Giuliani	12	14	6
Huckabee, Tancredo, Brownback	1	2	12
Democrats			
Obama, Richardson	15	8	6
H. Clinton	2	4	14
Edwards	1	4	18
General election preference			
Strong	6	17	39
Weak	11	5	3
None	3	1	4

Table 9.2. Trends among traditional/partisan, partner-like, and mixed voters

	Traditional/ partisan	Partner	Mixed
Consistently support one party during election cycle?	Yes	No	No
Confident in choice pre-general election?	Yes	No	Yes
Consistently support same party between 2008 and 2012 election cycle?	Yes	Usually	Yes

Traditional Voters

Whether they supported Democratic or Republican candidates, traditional voters were consistent in their preferences throughout the election cycle. This is because traditional voters' understanding of politics as a struggle between sides, especially as between the haves and have-nots, seemed always to fit the oppositional nature of American politics. Moreover, the charged pre-election atmosphere resonated with traditional voters' intuitive understanding of public life, making them particularly excited to exercise their preferences by voting.

Walter Bryerson

Walter Bryerson, a lifelong Republican who was in his sixties, was one such voter. He had once worked as a senior manager at one of River City's old family–owned firms, was still critical of blue-collar populist leaders like

Jones Berry, and lived in an affluent neighborhood associated with his city's old families. By the time we spoke, Walter's old-family employer had long since been acquired by an outside corporation, and Walter worked from home as a consultant for several energy companies. Our first conversation meandered pleasantly from Walter's biography, to River City, to national politics, and back again. Whenever the focus shifted to politics, Walter fretted about Democratic efforts to redistribute wealth through the tax system. "The Democrats might get into power and that frightens me," he said. "I think they are united by a struggle for power and they get that power by pandering to the have-nots. Like, 'We will give you more of this and that benefit if you just vote for us.' [But] for me the number one thing is the tax structure should not be used as a punishment/reward vehicle. People need to work for what they have, not wait for handouts."

The fact that Walter perceived politics through the framework of sides hardly requires additional commentary; his statement could almost be substituted verbatim for a traditional business leader's critique of blue-collar leaders. The two parties mapped neatly onto Walter's understanding of public life: the Republicans champion the haves, the Democrats pander to the have-nots. This is not to say that Walter was a blind follower of the GOP. In fact, he was critical of the GOP and George W. Bush administration. But Walter understood the failings of his party and its president *through* the heuristic of sides: failures, in Walter's view, were due alternatively to the machinations of Democrats and the unwillingness of Republicans to stick to their core principles. "I just wish the Republicans would be more Republican and stand up for some values of importance," Walter said. "Lately [they] have not taken any high ground, as in: 'This is our position, these are values we believe in.' It has been more reacting to the criticism. George Bush has been one of the worst. If you listen to the media, he can't do anything right and I do blame him for letting that happen. We need a more global leader, somebody more like Reagan who is a better speaker [and can] say: 'This is wrong and this is right. This is what we are going to be doing and okay, you can criticize it, I'm listening to your criticism but I'm still going to do it!'"

Walter was similar to many other traditional voters in that he selected candidates by looking for those who seemed to most embody the values of his side: he was on the lookout for a *global leader* in the style of Reagan, and was especially impressed with candidates who were unswayed by Democrats. When we first spoke in spring of 2007, for example, Walter liked Mitt Romney, who was then billing himself as a business candidate, and disliked Rudy Giuliani and John McCain, who were then perceived as more moderate. "Romney stands for a lot of [conservative] principles, especially on economic issues," Walter said. "He also has experience in an executive position, which may help him be effective. I do worry, though, because I wish he was better on TV. You really have to be great—like maybe Bill Clinton [unfortunately] was—because you have to convince people that your position is right. I don't care for Giuliani," Walter continued. "He's too liberal [and] McCain has no fire and is yesterday. Some of the bills he passed with Democrats are a farce. He is too easily swayed by involvement with them."

I interviewed Walter again just weeks before the 2008 caucuses. By then, he had switched his allegiance to Mike Huckabee, an unsurprising decision since the Iowa caucus was by then effectively a three-way contest between Huckabee, who was billing himself as an ideologically pure candidate, Romney who had taken over McCain and Giuliani's moderate mantle, and Libertarian Ron Paul. "I'm beginning to like Huckabee most of all," Walter said. "He seems honest and like a real straight-shooter. I certainly like his view that morality has to be part of government. Like, he has some interesting views on reforming taxes. We should at least rethink taxes. I feel like he is more personable and might not alienate as many people as Bush, [although he too] has the conviction to state a position and stick with it."

Walter was typical of other traditional voters in that he did not even consider Democratic candidates throughout the process, although when I asked him about it directly Walter distinguished between two sorts of Democrats: those who, like Hillary Clinton, were Machiavellian, and others, like most other Democratic hopefuls, who were merely opportunists. Interestingly, Walter initially found Obama to be among the least offensive of Democrats: "He's kind of interesting—I'd like to hear more of what he has to say," Walter said, although he then went on to describe Obama as "having a better political wind-sock than moral compass."

In the end, John McCain—Walter's least-favorite Republican—won the GOP nomination along with Barack Obama, Walter's least unpreferred Democrat. But this hardly mattered as the lead-up to the general election featured campaign advertising that resonated with Walter: McCain's advertisements accused Obama of radicalism and socialism and featured self-made paragon "Joe the Plumber," while Obama's advertisements mocked McCain's multiple houses and adopted a more traditional message focused on middle-class social welfare programs. In this atmosphere, Walter retained his existing way of thinking about politics, but grew more rigid in his partisan stance, casting the election in starker moral categories. "Obama has no right to be a president. He's a communist," Walter stated flatly, then backtracked a bit. "That may be a little strong, but he is definitely a socialist. I don't think he reflects American values and I'm afraid of him in there putting in judges whose criteria is that they are empathetic to underclass. And I think his redistribution of wealth is going to destroy the capitalist society of America. So I'm more against one candidate than I am for the other. I think McCain will stand up for America, internationally. And based on what he says it looks like he would be for creating jobs or at least not destroying them by having a punitive tax system." By election day, Walter was energized and ready to vote Republican. His unwavering political convictions, which only strengthened before the general election, were typical of traditional voters.

The Pleumer Family

Gary Pleumer was a lifelong resident of one of River City's working-class neighborhoods—one visible from the bay windows that lined one side of Walter Bryson's hilltop home. In his sixties, Gary had worked as a butcher in a unionized grocery chain. I came to his house several times during the election and interviewed him, his wife, a former nurse's aide who was also in her sixties, and—on two occasions—their daughter, Laura, a thirty-something who lived in the same neighborhood and worked part-time as a cashier and bartender. Gary and Lisa were unambiguously traditional voters. Laura was, too, although I suspect she may have been more mixed in other contexts; on several occasions, she dismissed all politicians as corrupt and said other things reminiscent of her partner-like generation. But in her parents' home at least, Laura spoke about politics as a contest between the haves and the have-nots.

It was initially difficult for me to get Gary, Lisa, and Laura to formulate a clear political preference for either party, because as soon as politics came up, the three proceeded to slander various candidates and to crack jokes about them. However, it quickly became evident that they were playing the same political game opposite of Walter Bryerson: he played for the haves, they for the have-nots. "Would you ever vote Republican?" I asked in spring of 2007. "Hell no," Gary replied. "Because I don't like them. They're out for one thing: make more money for the president and all his friends who are all Republicans. The [Democrats], they'll get out of Iraq; you don't see Republicans saying that because they want the oil. They probably got stock in the oil company and don't want to lose money. But now the Democratic campaigners have money," Gary continued, turning hopeful. "That Bama guy has 20 million, Hillary has 20 million, Edwards 14 or 15 million." Gary's family nodded as he spoke.

Needless to say then, no member of the Pleumer family ever looked to Republican candidates, and instead the three spent my first and second interview with them looking for a candidate among the champions of the have-nots. Many traditional Democrats went about this like Walter had for the Republicans: by looking for a candidate who seemed like the most effective champion for their side. A typical most-to-least, pro-have-not Democrat ran Edwards–Clinton–Obama. However, the Pleumers reasoned in another way that was also typical of other traditional voters: they discussed contenders as a pantheon of sorts, idiosyncratic in their own ways, but basically all the same. Given the nature of the Democratic field, much of these discussions revolved around issues of race and gender and—like many traditional Democrats I spoke with—the Pleumers expressed unflattering stereotypes about both.

The first time I met him, for example, Gary told me a story about a fight between a white teenager from the neighborhood and a black teenager who had recently moved to River City from Chicago.[10] "Colored people think they can get away with anything, I think it's bullshit," Gary concluded. "There's some good ones," his daughter protested. "There's a few good ones," Gary agreed, "but it is [the older black] generation [who are good. And with younger people] it is getting to where you can't [distinguish] the whites from the coloreds anymore." But when prejudice and politics mixed, the Pleumers periodically stopped their debate to let me— the interviewer—know that they were not truly prejudiced and would never vote Republican. Nevertheless, they expressed discomfort about voting for Obama on the grounds that *others* in the country were still too racist. At other times, too, Laura spoke about Hillary Clinton's gender as a disqualifying factor. The following exchange is from fall of 2007:

LISA: I think it's going to be a tossup between Hillary [Clinton] and Barack Obama, and I don't like him. A lot of people won't vote for him because he's colored.

GARY: He ain't bad, he's a smart guy. [I'd prefer] Obama or Edwards, [because] they're out front and they don't lie. Who wants a woman president? I don't want that! (*cackles*)

LISA: You are just pitiful!

GARY: She might be okay.

LAURA: Look, she had her time, I'm not racist or prejudiced, but . . .

GARY: (*to me*) I'm just kidding about Hillary, I think she could be a good president, she's smart, I'm just kidding about her being a woman.

LISA: Just like anybody else, she's for bringing the troops home and everything, that's what I want to see happen, I don't want to see any more war. I'm tired of that.

LAURA: I guess Edwards would be the one. From what I've seen of him, he looks more honest than the rest of them. He just strikes me that way. Hillary, nothing against women, but she had her claim to fame. She was there. She took care of a lot of the country when she did. A lot of women are going to vote for her cause she's a woman and she was great with people, great when she was in there, but can she run the country? No, I don't think so.

LISA: You really don't think she could? Oh my god, I'm going to move!

LAURA: Ugh! Women, she may be smart, may be strong, but dammit look: you're going to be looking face-to-face with these guys—hardcore leaders, big-time people, China.

LISA: There's been women who ran countries, look at Margaret Thatcher.

LAURA: Yeah, when?

LISA: It hasn't been that many million years ago honey!

LAURA: If you get these men pissed off, my god [Hillary Clinton] is going to piss her pants and call a maid. I'm sorry, I'm a woman and can do anything that a man can do and stuff, but running a country is a whole different story. [And] what about the money? How's she going to manage the debt? She's got a big ole heart, women got a big ole heart, you can't run the country with a big heart. They are going to eat her up!

GARY: [She] can still run the country. It don't matter. I think [any] Democrat is going to get the soldiers out of Iraq, get the price of gas down, get inflation down—these Republicans have screwed up the government big time, with social security [Democrats] will try to keep it . . .

LAURA: Edwards will.

GARY: . . . so is Obama, so is Hillary, with [Republicans] you can forget those guys, they are big jokes.

The election of 2008 was one of historic firsts, which one might reasonably expect would dislodge the loyalties of some voters, particularly ones like the Pleumers whose political discussions were peppered with casual stereotypes. But the Pleumers maintained a consistent orientation throughout the election cycle, because they viewed whatever pieces of information they gleaned from the national media through an enduring framework that divided the world into haves and have-nots, or champions thereof. By the time of the general election, all three were as energized as Walter Bryerson and lobbied their extended family to vote for Obama.

"I don't want Bush the second in, as long as McCain don't get in there, okay," Lisa told me. "I was for Hillary, but after she dropped out I'm all for Barack Obama, I think he's going to make a great president and I don't care what they say about him," she added. "I don't care if he is colored, big deal," Gary reiterated. Gary and Lisa then chatted for a bit about the news of the moment: accusations that Michelle Obama had made anti-white statements, which revived media interest in Obama's affiliation with Jeremiah Wright, a colorful African American pastor. "My cousin who lives in Florida says that Obama is going to be totally and strictly for the black people. I don't see it that way," Lisa said. "I think he's going to be fair. Truthfully, I do. They say on TV that his wife don't like white people and I'm like, 'Oh please, how do you know she don't like white people?' Now John McCain's first lady, she obviously is a tight-ass—that's a fact," Lisa snorted, turning to another piece of national news of the moment. "They are saying that she wore a hundred thousand dollar outfit to the Republican convention! That must be a nice thing to have!" Gary and Lisa then proceeded to crack jokes about the fact that John McCain could not remember how many houses he owned, a mini-scandal from some weeks earlier. The Pleumer's trajectory through the election cycle was typical of other traditional Democrats. I met many who initially reported that they would not support an African American for president, but not one who did not eventually vote for Barack Obama.

The True Partners

Like traditional voters, partner-like voters were consistent in their political reasoning throughout the election. But unlike traditional voters, partner-like voters were consistently wary of politics and hence politically unpredictable. This is to say that partners had strong preferences for an alternative political system antithetical to the existing one. During the primary season, partners generally reconciled their distaste of actually existing politics by supporting a more partner-like candidate: Democrat Barack Obama and, less so, Republicans Mitt Romney, John McCain, and Rudy Giuliani. From here, the trajectory of partners' preferences became hazy. Virtually all partners were disillusioned by the negative atmosphere that preceded the election and they responded in three ways: some supported their caucus choice as the lesser of two evils, others were unsure what to do, and others simply did not vote or voted third party. Partners' propensity to follow one of these trajectories seemed almost random, or at least based on characteristics that I was not able to observe during my interviews. I illustrate these dynamics among three Obama supporters throughout the 2008 election cycle: Greg Wishburn, an accountant in his forties who did vote for Obama, Jerome Blumstein, a business owner in his fifties who was unsure how to vote before the election, and Carla Snowden, a stay-at-home mom in her thirties who did not vote.

Greg Wishburn, Jerome Blumstein, and Carla Snowden

During my initial interviews with them, Greg, Jerome, and Carla differed in their degree of political interest and sophistication, but were of like mind when it came to political ideology: to them, it was clear that public life should be based on a search for partnership, an ideal state that they saw as incompatible with the two-party system. "Politics is all about polarization," Greg said. "People are like, I heard this or that on the news and that makes me angry!' [And] politicians are more concerned with pulling together a bunch of little constituencies than having common ground. When they gain the White House, they become the president of their parties, not the United States."

Jerome agreed with Greg's assessment of the situation. "Over time there seems to have been a taming [in River City]—especially between management and labor. I think that is a major accomplishment," Jerome said, contrasting community with politics. "And [even in our company] we have worked [at developing] a wonderful working relationship with the union leaders. We have much more to gain from working together than fighting. I don't see enough of that in politics, [but] I always say, 'Take the ball down the middle!' Bush said he was going to do that and look what happened. He wasted all that political capital to give Jerome Blumstein a tax cut! What kind of sharing the load is that? [I think] the Democrats might be starting to realize that the middle is wide open. We need a more centrist government that focuses on what unites us rather than what divides us."

Carla Snowden was not as knowledgeable about politics as Greg and Jerome, but her political intuitions were the same. "I like independent parties most of the time, because I think that they don't bow as much to what the general of their party believes [and] can have their own opinions," she said, demonstrating a partner-like distaste for factional obligations. "It is out of control and somebody needs to do something to fix it. There's too much badmouthing—you know, these are the people who are *supposed* to be running our country. I just, I feel bad for my daughter, because I'm raising her to be an honest and caring person, but [politicians act] like selfish little brats." At this point, I was still having trouble identifying the source of Carla's political disaffection, so I asked her what politicians should be doing. "[Looking] for areas where we can move forward as a country," she replied. "Like, I don't know [what to do about healthcare]. I think that everyone should be entitled to healthcare, but I don't want to foot the bill for other people. Like I said, I'm not smart enough to come up with solutions to that problem, but somebody must be," she elaborated, illustrating many tendencies common among young partners: belief that everyone wants the same deep down, faith in educated experts, and so on.

Greg, Jerome, and Carla before the Caucuses

Immediately before the caucuses, Greg, Jerome, and Carla were on the lookout for partner-like candidates and avoiding divisive ones.

"I end up voting against candidates more often than I end up voting for candidates. I really get turned off by politics," Greg told me. "If I hear someone say, 'I'm going to build a fence between here and Mexico,' I'm going to vote against that person. Often I vote against anti-ness: 'Oh, I'm anti-gay, I'm anti-this, I'm anti-that.' If you are defining yourself as being against, you're appealing to people's basest desires." At caucus time, Greg liked several non-anti candidates. "There [are two] Republican worth [their] salt: McCain and Mitt Romney. McCain, he's one of the only voices in the Senate that is ever rational and moderate [and] Mitt Romney is one of those people who is defining himself by what he's for not what he's against." Greg also liked Obama. "I don't know if I can really put my finger [on why I like him]," Greg said, pausing to reflect. "People say he is inexperienced, but I think that could be almost like a good thing. I do worry that he has been so stoked by his supporters that [he's] basically going to do whatever they ask," he continued, demonstrating a distrust of factional obligations. "I worry that he'll get a big ego, but I'd like to see him do well. So yeah, I'd like to see McCain get it [or] maybe Barack Obama." The only candidates Greg did not like were Republicans like Mike Huckabee who were then portraying themselves as Christian right candidates and Hillary Clinton. "Hillary Clinton is a very unfortunate candidate," Greg said. "She could probably make a pretty decent president, but she would polarize the race, because of what people will say about her. If she wins the primary, the

Republicans will strafe that election like nobody's business. Don't do it! They will make her look like Kim Jong Il in drag! [She won't be able] to get anything done with all that noise."

Unlike Greg, Jerome—who had voted Republican in the past—was burned out on the GOP after two terms of George W. Bush and willing to consider almost any Democrat as a more-conciliatory alternative. "[The conservative media] is always saying that Democrats are soft on this or are not always true to their core values, and I think, 'Great!'" Jerome said. "I was elated that [Democratic House Leader Nancy] Pelosi went to Syria and Iran to talk with them. Good! GW can be further isolated in his little house. Leave Cheney in the basement. [The Democrats] seem to get it. Clinton is criticized as too moderate but that is good. We need more centrists in government. Obama seems very dynamic and like he is ready to bring people together and move forward. I'm a big fan of Joe Biden—just a regular guy, terrific sense of humor, just, 'No big deal, let's just sit down together and do it.'" Like Greg, Jerome only excluded a few Democrats on the grounds that they seemed too divisive. "The only one I don't like is Edwards," he said. "He looks the role [of president], but he's running too much on the class warfare stuff. All that is just not the ticket any more—it is the past, not the future."

At the time of our second interview, Carla had not thought much about the election, but reported liking two candidates who seemed relatively apolitical: Republican Rudy Giuliani and Barack Obama, unsurprising since both had very little experience in national politics at the time. "I like Rudy Giuliani. I heard [him] speak on TV a couple years ago and I have a lot of respect for the guy [and how] he handles himself: he seemed focused on solving problems and above all the bickering. [And] I like Barack Obama," she continued, "He's like the least worst choice. He likes people working together. I don't like Hillary Clinton. She comes across as hard and I have a lack of respect for her just based on her history with her husband."

Greg, Jerome, and Carla before the General Election

The weeks before the 2008 election were a let-down for Greg, Jerome, Carla, and other true partners, who expressed disappointment at just how political things had become.

Of the three, Greg coped with his disappointment with the least handwringing and approached the election with a mixture of comical detachment and cautious optimism. "It has been entertaining to watch two candidates who are moderate getting so much vitriol from their own parties because they don't represent the extreme views," Greg said. "To me, it is off that you'd be so mad at a candidate in your own party that you'd be willing to jump ship. It's childish," he added, referring to news reports of Republican evangelicals or former Clinton supporters boycotting the election. "[But] I'm hopeful [because] I did not think our system would allow moderates to get through anymore. It is amazing and mysterious to me. I'm not sure what that says about the American public, but I'm hoping that people are tired of the extremities—this bang-bang where we swing from one side of the pendulum to the other."

Greg maintained his preference for Obama, but admitted that he had ambivalent feelings and would not be upset if the election went the other way—an orientation that political scientists argue is a strong predictor of not voting, although Greg ultimately did vote for Obama in 2008.[11] Greg's ambivalence was rooted in the fact that both Obama and McCain inhabited the same role in his mental schema—as outsiders coming to shake up the system—although Greg also had fears about their ability to live up to the role. "As individual people, I'd be happy if either one of them got it, but I have reservations about both," he said. "With McCain, I'm not sure if he'd be able to overcome the system that Bush put in place inside the government, if he'd be able to clean house. And Obama, unless he has very clear-eyed and capable advisors, I'm not sure he's capable of choosing the best people [or] if he'd just put in some angry Democrats. Both men are at tremendous risk of being overwhelmed by Washington as it exists, [but] Obama, I can see him [being] better at inspiring the populace to bring the [political] change we need."

Like Greg, Jerome also flirted with the idea of voting for Obama, but was still not completely decided just a few days before the election—a mental state that, like Greg's ambivalence, often leads people to not vote.[12] "You gotta hand it to [Obama], he's brilliant and articulate, and that is refreshing," Jerome told me. "I also don't think he will make himself out to be a king, like what we got now. He'll actually listen to people and bring them in on things, try to find some common ground. McCain just seems like he doesn't know which way to turn, so he's spitting out a bunch of slogans and hoping one of them sticks." At this point, however, Jerome paused and contemplated a scenario that excited many traditional Democratic voters: Democratic control over Congress and the presidency. To Jerome, this outcome seemed unlikely to produce political partnerships. "I am concerned that the Democrats look like they are going to win both houses of Congress," Jerome said. "It is not good for the whole government to march in lock-step. They will try to ram through things they could not have gotten past in a negotiation type situation. So that gives me pause. If I don't vote for Obama, it will be for that reason."

Whereas Greg was ambivalent and Jerome undecided, Carla was entirely turned off by the political tenor that preceded the election, even though Obama had been her favorite primary candidate. But for her, the gulf between what she thought politics should be and actually existing politics was simply too great. "The fact that they label all this stuff as Democrat or as a Republican, like the Republican is way over here and the Democrat is way over there, it bothers me because I think that people are not so extreme anymore," Carla said. "I paid attention right up until it got nasty and now I'm avoiding it. I just don't think that either one of them should be president," she added. "Neither one of them is experienced enough or cares enough. Neither one of their programs is going to work. I don't know how to fix it, I don't know what the answer is, but I don't think that either one of them knows either. It's like a high school election; it's not about running the country, it's a popularity thing and it's ridiculous!"

Greg, Jerome, and Carla's reactions are all understandable given that all three perceived a basic incompatibility between the politics of sides that seems to dominate DC and the politics of partnership that they would like to see there. Like them, other partner-like voters alternatively embraced a candidate who they imagined could transform America's political system, wrung their hands about the implications of participating in politics at all, or disengaged altogether. Because of this, partners were the least politically reliable of any voters I observed, even though they had been most fired up by the Obama campaigns' message of overcoming politics during the primary. By the general election, fully fourteen of the twenty partners had either decided not to vote or were not entirely certain about their vote choice. My study suggests that it was traditional voters and partisans who therefore put Obama over the top on election day.

Mixed Voters

Mixed voters were sometimes partner-like in their political reasoning and sometimes partisan or traditional, but these competing tendencies were pronounced at different stages of the election cycle. Recall that traditional voters were hardly impacted by the pre-election media blitz, because it merely reinforced their view of politics as conflict between the two sides. For their part, partner-like voters, who hoped for a politics without sides, were demobilized by pre-election partisan mudslinging. Mixed voters were characterized by a third temporal pattern: they were relatively more partner-like throughout the election cycle, but then totally transformed by the pre-election partisan furor, becoming virtually indistinguishable from traditional voters and partisans—ironic, because they were harshly critical of negative campaigning at other times.

Adam Meysing

Whereas Walter Bryerson held fast to traditional business principles, Adam Meysing, aged early sixties, saw himself as an evolved business leader. Adam had worked as a senior manager at Green's manufacturing and been deeply engaged in River City's public life until the late 1990s, but had since retired to enjoy the good life. When I first met him, he was packing up his middle-class home to move with his wife, a successful real estate agent, to their dream house: a bluff-top mansion just across the river from River City. We next spoke in his new living room, which had breathtaking views of lazy barges crawling along the river.

Initially, Adam seemed like an ideal-typical partner. "Every time you talk politics you get into a heated argument. [Politics is] absurdity," he said during our first interview. But sometimes, a bit of Walter Bryerson–like traditionalism crept up in Adam. During our second interview, for example, he praised a "conservative approach in terms of protecting the borders and low taxes" and criticized welfare recipients. Of Adam's traditional and partner-like tendencies, however, the partner-like persona was initially dominant. During our first interview, for instance, I asked Adam to place himself politically. "The two-party system provides too much of the same kind of stuff no matter which one you vote for," he said. "Most people are basically the same [and politics has them] hating themselves. I've been an Independent for quite some time. You might have one guy who is excellent, and I don't care if he's Democratic or Republican. And it's . . . I . . . I don't belong to [country] clubs," Adam continued, demonstrating partners' telltale distrust of faction-like commitments. "I don't like representing what someone else [thinks I should]. Politics should be the way it is in everyday life: you have to give and take a little bit, there's no absolute truth there. You are making compromises all the time, whether you realize it or not."

Immediately before the Iowa caucuses, Adam was on the lookout for a partner-like political candidate and had his eye on two: Mitt Romney and Barack Obama. "Mitt Romney looks pretty good right now," Adam said. "I think he has all that [policy] stuff and appearance and all that fluffy stuff you need to get elected. And I think he's kind of cool, too, isn't he, that Barack Obama, [he's] amazing," Adam continued, not missing a beat. "[Obama] sounds like such a nice personable guy, he's got a little bit of that JFK thing in him. Everybody likes to have a nice fresh young guy who looks like he might really do something, and it's kind of cool that he's a black guy whose made it that way with no problems—not like an Al Sharpton type making trouble—kind of like you've got Condoleezza Rice there, you got Colin Powell, excellent people who happen to be black." Adam's reaction to Obama's race was common among partner-like voters: the fact that Barack Obama was black but did not seem "only for the black community" coded to them as Obama's repudiation of traditional factional obligations. "[But] that's why Mitt Romney would be fun, too," Adam continued. "There you have the religion issue—he's of a different religion—just like JFK was Catholic. 'Mitt Romney is a Mormon, oh my god!' [the media would say]. That'd be fun, kind of interesting. I'd like to see one of them get it." Like other partners and mixed voters during this period, Adam employed a scale that ran orthogonal to left-right divides and evaluated candidates according to their capacity for partnership-building. Among voters who did so, candidates like Romney and Obama were often near the partner-like end of the scale, whereas Republicans like Mike Huckabee and Ron Paul and Democrats John Edwards and Hillary Clinton ranked as relatively unpartner-like.

But then, during our pre-election interview, partner-like Adam was gone, buried under a flood of negative adverting. Whereas partner-like voters became disillusioned when confronted with pre-election around-the-clock coverage, mixed voters like Adam had a vestigial traditional heuristic to fall back on. The transformation was near-total. Whereas Adam was laid back and reserved during our earlier conversation, before the general election he ranted angrily. In terms of content too, I found it difficult to distinguish him from the likes of a Walter Bryerson. "The Obama campaign is using class warfare," Adam declared, indignant. "'Oh, these terrible rich people who are successful,' [they say]. 'They're dirty and rotten, we hate them, let's take their money and give it to all you other people who have not been so fortunate!' And then, and then what does [Obama] do?!?" Adam demanded, "Goes back on his promise to use public finance!" he stammered, red-faced. "When I first saw Obama he seemed like a breath of fresh air and then after a while he just seemed like a regular politician, and then when it turned out that he had all these nuts in his background helping him. Like this Bill Ayers thing," Adam continued, referring to a mini-scandal involving Obama's loose ties to a 1960s-era student radical. "[The media says], 'Oh here is a guy, made a mistake a long time ago. [He] bombed the Pentagon! He's a Timothy McVeigh who got away with it! Then suddenly this guy is an all-right dude?!?"

Adam's general election reaction was typical of mixed voters, particularly the many who initially liked Obama but eventually voted Republican. Like Adam, they claimed that it was Obama, *not they*, who had changed or—at least—that new information about Obama had come to light. But Adam, like other mixed voters, had changed. He had reverted to a traditional ideology and argued that America's true political problems sprung from lack of separation between the two parties, not partisan divisiveness. "The problem that McCain is having is that there has been this ridiculous spending on both sides, so it had blurred the distinction that used to be there between the Republican Party [and the Democrats]. It is not clear cut and confusing to the public so they've got no clue," Adam said, now indistinguishable from Walter Bryerson. "Journalists themselves are just a product of the system, which is already slanted [Democratic]: a bunch of hippie radicals. Go out and get a real job! [Journalists] say [Sarah] Palin is a bad choice, but she's a great pick. She's just an average everyday person who is going to get in there and do it, and yet to see her reviled [by the media] like she is makes me disgusted with the Democratic Party and all that baloney. [Palin] seems to be more in touch with what the people out there are talking about who are conservative than [McCain] does because he's not really for the party. He's a maverick. I think that McCain will fight for what he believes in and will cross the aisle, but it is more to put something in the face of other Republicans than to get anything done!"

Mixed voters claimed to detest the negativity and divisiveness of national politics, but they were ultimately the ones most affected by it. Whereas traditional voters maintained a consistent ideology regardless of the tenor of national politics, mixed voters perceived ideal public institutions as essentially nonpartisan and needed negative ads to reorient themselves toward politics. The partisan sound and the fury revived mixed voters' partisan cognitive structure, which traditional voters simply took for granted.

Melissa McKinney-Rollins

Melissa McKinney-Rollins was Adam Meysing's Democratic-voting counterpart. She was in her forties and worked as a high school history teacher. Like Adam, she spent the majority of the 2008 election cycle in desperation over political divisiveness. At other times, though, she identified herself politically as someone who is predisposed to "look out for the underprivileged" and voiced support for social issues then championed by some Democratic politicians. "I'm an oddity [here in Prairieville]," she said. "I'm for gay marriage, I'm very pro-choice, whereas here it is a very religious, '[Everyone should] agree with my views' kind of place. I think that everybody has a choice. [You have to be tolerant] of how other people believe so that they are tolerant of how I believe." But Melissa made such statements rarely before the general election, preferring to focus on what she saw as the problems of the country as a whole.

"It's horrible; I think that things are really going down the toilet fast," Melissa said during our first interview. "We've gone too long with dishonest people making all the decisions and the regular people are the ones suffering for it. [And] I don't think that you can say, 'Oh, Republicans are a bunch of big fat white liars, old men who don't know what they are doing,' [because] I also don't trust the Democrats most of the time. The system is corrupted to a degree that is no longer acceptable. Party politics, a lot of it is based on the politics of fear," Melissa concluded. "[Party leaders] ask themselves what people are afraid of [and] that's what [they] are going to talk about." In fact, Melissa's distrust of party politics ran so deep that she had turned down several invitations from Democratic activists to get engaged with the party after speaking in support of her preferred candidate—John Kerry—at the 2004 caucuses. "That's just now where I see myself," she said. "People have a lot of fear and anger [and] extreme voices make them feel better. I mean, that is party politics, that's how it works. People are afraid of the changes they see around themselves and [that's] the group that's not willing to compromise." If more voters like Melissa had joined the Democratic Party, they might have interjected a conciliatory tone into activists' deliberations and perhaps tempered some of the dynamics of the activist party that I described in chapter 8. But Melissa, like virtually all voters with even a hint of partner-like ideology, stayed away from parties.

Like Adam Meysing, Melissa searched instead for the most partner-like candidate during our first two interviews. "I think compromise is really important," she said. "It is important to start from a value set, but then be able to talk with one another and come up with creative solutions. We need competing voices, Democrats and Republicans, to come together and say, 'Look, there are some issues where we'll never agree, but look at all this middle ground.' [We need politicians] who [are] fresh, who have big ideas, who are not so bogged down in the system that they owe everybody a favor. I don't want somebody who is repeating the exact same thing that's been said for the last thirty elections." For Melissa, two seemed to fit the bill: Barack Obama and John McCain, the two eventual nominees. "I'm a mama for Obama," she said. "It's time for an influx of honesty and to try something new. People say he does not have a lot of experience and I say good, means he does not owe anybody any favors and is not beholden to anyone. He can bring people together and move us forward as a country." Melissa then continued, not missing a beat. "[And] I like John McCain because of his past," she said. "He's not a social conservative and it takes a lot of courage to go against what everyone else in the party is saying. [That] makes me hopeful. The people with extreme voices are more represented, but there is enough positive energy at a national level for good things to happen."

By contrast, Melissa was equally distrustful of other Republican and Democratic politicians who seemed partisan. She thought Edward's "two Americas" campaign "old-fashioned" and—perhaps presciently—found him untrustworthy.[13] "Edwards is smarmy, he's always just got that smarmy grin and I'm like, 'Oh dude, he's hiding something!' he gives me the heebies," she said. Melissa was similarly down on Hillary Clinton. "Hillary Clinton, I don't trust that situation," she said. "She's polarizing. People feel one way about her or another." Similarly, Republican candidates besides John McCain seemed out of touch. "They are saying the same old things to get elected," Melissa said. "I like the hope I see in Obama and the integrity," she concluded. "Because I think that would be just about the last nail in the coffin if I were betrayed again by these stupid politicians."

But then, during the polarized atmosphere that preceded the general election, Melissa found herself transformed by politics. One might expect that Melissa was happy because her two favorite candidates—Barack Obama and John McCain—had won their parties' primaries, but just the opposite was true: "I feel dread about the future of our society as we know it," Melissa said, channeling nothing if not the politics of fear. Melissa now viewed politics as a two-way contest between intolerant Republican forces and everyone else, represented by Democrats and Obama in particular. She spoke nervously about the "hard-core GOP agenda."

Like Adam Meysing, Melissa reconciled her new model of politics with her earlier preferences by claiming that new information about John Mc-Cain had emerged. "I'm disappointed with the change that I've seen come over John McCain. He went from being a very nice man to being a snot," Melissa said during our pre-election interview. She was incensed by how rudely McCain had treated Obama during their televised debate and suspected racism as the cause. "It's like don't you have a mother? Don't you feel better than to act like that?" Melissa continued. "It disappointed me, because I thought we had two good men up there, [but it's like], you don't like somebody and you are going to give them a dirty look?" Similarly to

Adam, Melissa was also incensed by information that had "come to light" about John McCain. In fact, all the information was already public knowledge, but was merely stirred up by negative attack ads and partisan talking heads before the election: McCain's history of philandering, gambling, and ambivalent relationship with the Christian right. "[But] he's been courting conservatives now for months," she concluded. "And has a history of being a womanizer. I'm afraid of his impulsive decision making."

By contrast, Melissa argued that Obama had not changed at all. "No, I don't think he's changed. I like him for the same reasons," she said. "Maybe a more experienced person might know better how to deflect questions and attacks but—ehh—I think that he will learn those things." Note that Melissa's one critique of Obama is exactly what she once perceived to be his greatest strength: lack of political experience. Like Adam Meysing, she had been changed by the polarized pre-election atmosphere into assuming a different political subjectivity. Like Adam, too, Melissa did not appreciate this, because to her it seemed that the Republicans, not Obama or she herself, had changed between the primaries and the general election.

The Partisans

And finally, I need say a word about partisans: those who saw no place for themselves in community life, were angry about it, and looked to politics for succor. I will not discuss partisans who had already sided with either Democrats or Republicans by 2008, because they behaved largely like traditional voters: they supported one party consistently throughout the election, albeit typically with more ideological fervor.[14]

Instead, I focus here on the small subset of partisans who repudiated existing politics, but were ever on the lookout for a political candidate who might shake things up. I focus on these voters in part because they became important to media discourse about American politics in 2008 and have remained so. For instance, Barack Obama created a mini-scandal after he was recorded saying that some voters were unhappy with the state of the world, clung to their "religion and guns," and would never vote for him. Since 2008, movements like Occupy Wall Street and the Tea Party have also focused attention on twenty-first-century American populism. My sense was that Obama was right about one thing: whereas partner-like voters seemed more enamored with Democrats in 2008, uncommitted partisans gravitated toward the GOP. Ultimately, however, Obama was wrong about the causes. Whether they supported Republicans, Democrats, or neither party, I found that partisans were no more irrational than anyone else. Rather, like Obama, they hoped for a fundamental transformation of America's political system, but—unlike him—they wanted a complete do-over: total transformation of community life and politics. Linda Timmons and Steve Moreland exemplified these tendencies.

Linda Timmons

Linda Timmons, once a traditional Democrat, embraced the Tea Party during Obama's first term. But when I spoke to her in 2008, she had written off politics entirely. Linda was a forty-something office worker who lived in a middle-class neighborhood in Prairieville. She and her husband worked harder than either of their parents, earned a combined salary far above Prairieville's median, but still felt that between health insurance, activities for the kids, the mortgage, and student-loan payments, life was a struggle. Locally, too, everything about Prairieville seemed to anger Linda: high property taxes, multiple user fees, crappy city services, and pointless developments that proliferated in the downtown corridor. Politics, too, seemed contrived and hopelessly divorced from the needs of regular people.

"There should not be only two parties, because they should focus more on us," she told me. "It's like, if you are Democrat, you are supposed to vote for Democrats and stay with them or you are screwed, even if you disagree with them. My mom always said, 'Republicans are for the rich and Democrats are for the poor people." But well, you know what? Have the Democrats helped me? No, I don't think so. So I think that they should do away with [parties]."

Because of statements like these, I initially thought that Linda was expressing partner-like sentiments, as in: we should do away with the parties so that politicians focus on areas of agreement. But this is not what she meant. Parties as such were fine; Linda just wanted parties that represented regular people. "It's just gotten to be A versus B all the time, but there's no C there for people like us. We need a party that represents regular people. Personally, I think that the country may need another civil war," she said. "Some people don't appreciate what they've got and nobody listens to those who do." In past decades, Linda's populism would have been championed locally by Prairieville's blue-collar leaders and channeled into Democratic politics, but at the time of my fieldwork Linda saw no sympathetic community voices.

Given her aversion to actually existing politics, Linda entered the primary season looking for a candidate who seemed most like a regular person and, hence, most likely to shake things up. "I'm always looking for the outsider, because they won't know what to expect and will just go with their gut feelings," she said. "They'd do better. If they get someone in there who knows what they are doing they [will] know too much: a been-there, done-that sort of thing. They'll promise you things, but they will just keep doing the same thing they've been doing."

In practice, Linda's populist streak generally led her to look down on Democrats, who she saw as elitist. Much of her antipathy toward them was established through random pieces of media discourse that Linda assembled into an image of Democrats as out of touch with regular people—an impression likely reinforced by right-wing media. For example, she distrusted Hillary Clinton, because of her association with her husband, an orientation that was strengthened when, in a micro-scandal, Hillary Clinton failed to tip at lunch in an Iowa diner. "She stiffed a waitress," Linda snorted. "That really got to me." Similarly, Linda heard that Obama was in favor of granting licenses to illegal immigrants and heard that he refused to put his hand on his heart during the pledge of allegiance—another micro-scandal when Obama was photographed not doing so at an Iowa fair. On the flip side, however, Linda liked Bill Richardson, a second-tier Democratic candidate who received little press attention, because she heard that his wife was a teacher and that he supported higher pay for expert teachers. "It was interesting what he was saying," Linda said. "Teachers have a hard job." Conversely, Republicans looked more "regular" to Linda, but she was not enamored with them either. She liked Giuliani, but also heard that he had "troubles with New York City" and thought he was unfit to run the country. Some of her peers at work liked Romney, whom Linda though okay. She had not heard of Mike Huckabee or Ron Paul, two candidates popular with other partisans who leaned toward the GOP.

It was not until the general election, and specifically McCain's choice of Sarah Palin as his running mate, that Linda felt much political enthusiasm. "I like Sarah, I like her a lot," Linda said, referring to the vice-presidential candidate known for being an Alaskan, an avid hunter, a hockey mom, and for blaming media elites for her poor performances in interviews. Linda also liked one of Sarah Palin's one-liners: that the only difference between a hockey mom and a pitbull was lipstick. "She wears lipstick," Linda continued laughing. "It just shows that there are strong women out there and she's got a good head on her shoulders and stuff. I've thought about writing Sarah Palin into my ballot [instead of John McCain]. Before Sarah I was not even going to vote for president—not worth it! [But] she's young and McCain is really old and so if anything happens, she's ready to jump in."

Steve Moreland

Unlike Linda, Steve Moreland never settled on an outside-the-beltway candidate in 2008 and ultimately did not vote. Steve (discussed in chapter 8) was a thirty-something River Citian who had been forced into long-distance trucking to pay his debts and hated it. He was angry that community leaders only touted pointless building projects and place-marketing initiatives, not the needs of regular people. As an idealized alternative, Steve had developed his own populist ideology, one similar to discourses later popularized by movements like Occupy Wall Street. "I think about it when I'm out driving," he told me, "you drive through these cities and see the shiny building, but the people who [work in them] don't produce anything of value. That's not right." It was this attitude that had driven Steve to third-party candidates like Ralph Nader in the past, but in 2008 he was dissatisfied with the entire field.

The last time I spoke with Steve was by phone while his truck was stuck in the Rocky Mountains during a freak October snowstorm. The Great Recession had begun and Steve recognized the gravity of the situation, but was still undecided and concluded that he would not vote. "I don't know, it seems like everyone I know is having financial problems, but really it is just more of the same." Steve said, noting that financial problems were nothing new in his life. "[And] we can't do eight more years of Republicans, but sometimes I just look at Obama and he's just a little too charismatic, it is like he's got all the right answers [and is] too good to be true. It is hard for me to trust people in the system, I guess. And it is not a race thing—I'm not one of these southern boys on the CB [truck] radio talking about they not gonna vote for Ooobamiii," Steve added, drawing out the Obama with a southern twang.[15] "I just remember Ralph Nader from last time and always like all the stuff he says—I know that the independent guy never makes it in, but whatever, it's a statement of the whole system sucks. I'm so disgusted with all this, you know? All these people are billionaires and they all live in gated communities and none of them have a clue. There's no room for the regular Joe."

The 2012 Election

The period between 2008 and 2012 was an eventful one in American history: four years of seemingly endless recession, the rise of the Tea Party movement, the growing public awareness of inequality as the defining feature of our times, and a mounting feeling that—perhaps—America's proudest days are behind her. But for all this change, the prevailing trend among my informants was lack of change: traditional voters and partisans continued to support their parties, mixed voters still sounded like partisans on election day, and partner-like voters were—yet again—unpredictable. Indeed, the contrast between changing times and unchanging voters confirmed this chapter's overarching argument: that voters' beliefs are structured by political heuristics that are more enduring than any one election, and therefore not amenable to change in response to events or times of pressing political need.

Walter Bryerson, for example, strongly supported Mitt Romney. "I'm afraid that I'm probably the most extreme person you'll speak with today," he said. We shared a chuckle after I told him that I doubted it. He then proceeded to tell me that Obama's socialism was bringing down America's capitalist society—an almost verbatim repetition of our 2008 interview. I did not interview the Pleumers again because Lisa and Gary both died within a few months of each other in 2011. Their passing is a reminder of the fact that the stable, traditional base of the both parties is quickly disappearing. Adam Meysing and Melissa McKinney-Rollins were also, once again, transformed by the politics of fear that both claimed to detest. Adam ranted about how Obama was not who he purported to be, while Melissa talked about how much the hard-core Republican agenda frightened her.

Among partners, there was a bit more action. Greg Wishburn was supporting Obama again, although he seemed more adamant in his decision than in 2008. To him, Republicans now symbolized forces of division within American society, with Democrats their hapless, partner-like opponents. "I'm really stunned at the kind of crazed anti-Obama-ness that seems to have gotten built into everything," he said. "It's a brilliant strategy: you tie the guy's hands behind his back and then say, 'Look, he can't punch!' But it's scary. That's how the Nazis came to power: [they] repeated untruth over and over until they made their own version of truth. I'm not a conspiracy theorist, but there must be something larger than the Republican Party going on, something that is manipulating them in ways that they don't realize. [So] I think Obama was naïve," Greg concluded. "He did not surround himself with people who understand how to make things happen." But conversely, Jerome Blumstein thought that Obama had acted divisively and was switching back to the GOP. "I've always considered myself a moderate, but enough is enough with all these new regulations, they make me want to choke!" he stammered. "And I'm in the 1 percent that they keep talking about, and I just met with my accountant and it turns out I now have to work until July before I'm not working any more just to pay my taxes. I'm so mad at Obama. I have no problem with paying my fair share, but—come on—talk about dividing the country." Were I to classify Jerome in 2012, I would have labeled him a mixed voter. His transformation shows the difficulties that partner-like candidates have maintaining their post-partisan image when forced to govern in a hyperpartisan system.[16] Finally, Carla was, once again, politically dejected and did not vote.

For Linda Timmons, too, things continued to take their natural course. She still distrusted the traditional GOP, but now counted herself a Tea Party supporter. "[With] the [traditional] political parties it is just like if you had a king and queen," she told me. "The king don't care what happens to the people. Yeah, he's there and yeah, he takes their money, but they don't see it, they don't know. Do they want to know? I don't know. Your guess is as good as mine," she said, then continued. "I think we need fresh blood. The Tea Party is a young party, so they are bound to make mistakes [but] they are looking out for the regular people."

And finally, there was Steve Moreland. I thought about Steve often in the intervening years between 2008 and 2012 and, naively, hoped to get some resolution after interviewing him again. This is partially because I liked him and found myself generally in agreement with his views of community and, perhaps a little less so, politics. Moreover, his biography embodied the new post-2008 normal for many young people: incomplete, frustrating career trajectories, mounting personal debt, and a lack of faith in public institutions, both local and national. I hoped that Steve had found something political to be hopeful about. But in the end, I could not find him. Between 2008 and 2012, he had moved with his girlfriend to the Pacific Northwest, but he was no longer there either. It was as if the continent had swallowed him up. And perhaps it is just as well, because whatever Steve himself was thinking, my research had already told me that there was no reason to be hopeful about the participation of other voters like Steve Moreland in America's political system. The federal reforms of the 1970s and 1980s had robbed them of grassroots leaders who once provided a model and avenue toward moderate, constructive political participation. The post-Keynesian society offered them only a naïve, unworkable faith in consensus on the one hand, and political resignation or extremism on the other.

The Politics of the Post-Keynesian Society

At the heart of this book are three key arguments. First, I argued that 1970s and '80s-era federal reforms changed the types of coalitions that allow community leaders to leverage outside resources, thereby creating a structural opportunity for River City's and Prairieville's politics-averse partners to push their cities' traditional leaders from public prominence. Second, I argued that newly ascendant partners broke their predecessors' traditional ties with political parties, left them in the hands of partisan activists, and generally reorganized their cities' public spheres from a conflict between Democratic labor leaders and Republican business owners to one between community-minded partners and their partisan opponents. Finally, I argued that River Citians and Prairievillers—who draw on their community's common sphere of public talk, memory, and affect when thinking through complex public problems—increasingly view community and partisan politics as antithetical, an orientation that alternatively produces political apathy and extremism. In simplified form, then, my argument is that 1970s and '80s-era neoliberal reforms reconstructed the political reasoning of grassroots leaders and regular citizens.

In this final chapter, I recap the book's arguments, discuss caveats and the degree to which my account applies to trends outside of River City and Prairieville, and address normative implications for American democracy. Scholars typically evaluate the public sphere's moral significance by relying on dramaturgical metaphors that focus on how people act in public—for instance, on whether or not they formulate rational arguments—but this approach yields ambiguous conclusions about River City and Prairieville's public transformation. Therefore, I build upon my analysis throughout the book to develop a relational framework, which equates the public sphere's normative value with its ability to communicate information between people and policymakers. In this respect, River City's and Prairieville's public transformation is problematic because it introduces a phenomenon that I characterize as *structural deceit* into America's system of intergovernmental relations. The overall effect is that the organization of River City and Prairieville's public institutions communicates misleading information about citizens' daily lives to policymakers and, in turn, misleading information about politics to locals.

A Summary of the Book

In the book's first half, I analyzed the organization of River City and Prairieville's public sphere before the 1980s, which I summarized as *politics embedded in community governance*. Central to these arrangements was the community leadership party, a mode of grassroots partisan organization that also appears in other historical accounts of the postwar period. The community leadership party's defining feature was the involvement of public figures who were simultaneously leaders of their city's key economic, civic, and municipal associations. In River City and Prairieville, public life was contested by business owners and union leaders, who simply turned their individual and collective energies toward, respectively, Republican and Democratic politics at election time. In Prairieville, for example, the chamber became de facto Republican headquarters while confederates of Frannie Steele—who held a weekly meeting of labor union leaders, attorneys with working-class clientele, and other community activists in her home—became Democratic electioneers, disciplining incoming activists and focusing their attention on the bread and butter economic and social issues that preoccupied community leaders. Institutions like these were central to pre-1980s party politics. They served as the organizational base of the two parties, exercised influence over candidate selection, and communicated community priorities to candidates. Community leadership parties were partisan, but moderate. Community leaders took the contours of political contestation for granted, both at the community and national scale, avoiding the hot-button issues that occupy today's activists.

Community leadership parties also blurred the boundary between community governance and partisan politics in the minds of River Citians and Prairievillers. Pre-1980s community institutions were defined by labor-business conflicts and, because those central to these conflicts were also central to party politics, residents saw Democratic and Republican politics as an extension of community cleavages. Drawing on interviews with older River Citians and Prairievillers, I showed how this community-politics blurring accounts for the relative orderliness of Keynesian-era politics: an electorate that identified with parties at high rates but was ideologically moderate. Because older residents saw their community's conflicts simultaneously as partisan political conflicts, the latter seemed intuitively familiar and legitimate, and community life provided a heuristic for making sense of politics. Older residents used virtually any aspect of daily life—their job, education, neighborhood, or ways of spending leisure time—to establish a stable partisan preference. Recall one voter from chapter 3: "Being a teacher, I'm definitely a Democrat, so that's my stand on that . . . the Democrats try to represent the middle class, keep an eye out for them . . . the Republicans represent money, they represent the upper class. [Both] are very important, because we have to make sure we don't have like a monarchy—just a government that is run solely by one group of people."

In the book's first half, my aim was to explain why River City's and Prairieville's traditional community leaders were engaged in party politics—a tendency that I analyzed by examining their competition for public prominence. I argued that three aspects of Keynesian-era federal policies—financial sector regulations, social service funding, and urban development funding—structured community leaders' game, making its inner logic compatible with partisan engagement. Financial sector regulations sheltered locally owned businesses from corporate acquisitions, thereby protecting an indigenous class of business owners and labor union leaders, who were additionally protected by the period's relatively labor-friendly policies. Politicians also created programs with broad social service and urban development priorities, but—due to an inability to expand the size of the federal bureaucracy—administered them via discretionary and frequently noncompetitive transfers to local bodies and nonprofits. In the words of John Mollenkopf, federal bureaucrats operated a "banker government" that encouraged community conflict by allowing grassroots leaders to exert unilateral control over federal funding and, therefore, giving them an incentive to fight over policy implementation.[1] The sum total of these policies was a public sphere that was rooted in community institutions and understood that way by community leaders. Keynesian-era policies embedded resources in community institutions, and wherever community leaders looked, they were confronted by what appeared to be a local economy, a local civil society, and a local politics.

Keynesian-era policies went hand-in-hand with a grassroots public sphere defined by conflict between local business owners and union leaders, who opposed one another in economic, civic, and political life, but were united by a common public culture.[2] However different figures like

Jones Berry, River City's motorcycle-riding, union-backed mayor, and the patricians who dwelt on the city's bluffs seemed, they played the same public game. Both sides attained public prominence by winning control over local institutions and using their resources, whether local or federal, to shape the city's collective future in accordance with the visions of their supporters. Both sides traded on an ability to construct vertical networks of gift and reciprocal obligation that penetrated deeply into local life and allowed them to mobilize community support. For this reason, traditional leaders understood their relationship with the public as reciprocal. To them, their position of public prominence was a gift from their side of the public, which they reciprocated by advocating for their constituents at work, helping labor or business charities, or running for local office and championing initiatives intended to help their side. In this light, community leaders saw party politics as just another way to champion their people and strengthen ties with them and saw no distinction between community and partisan cleavages.

In the book's second part, I turned my attention to 1970s- and '80s-era reforms and examined their transformative public impact, which I summarized as culminating in *politics disembedded from community governance.* The most dramatic of these reforms were financial deregulations, which fueled the twentieth century's largest merger movement during the 1980s, led to the acquisition of most of River City's and Prairieville's locally owned firms, and thereby thinned the ranks of business and labor leaders, robbing both cities of their traditional leadership class. Subsequent reforms of federal social service and urban development funding transformed the large, discretionary transfers of the Keynesian era into a complex system of small, targeted, hypercompetitive grants controlled by a shifting mix of federal agencies, state agencies, and middle-men nonprofits. Grassroots leaders were effectively questing after the same federal dollars as before, but needed to market their plans to this, that, and the other outside institution to get them. Remaining leaders reported feeling like the "world had grown larger than the city limits," because the resources they needed to their problems were controlled by outsiders.

A central argument of the book is that neoliberal reforms reshuffled River City's and Prairieville's public sphere by creating a structural opportunity for a new type of leader: the partner. In the hypercompetitive context of the post-1980s period, those willing to enter into broad-based, shifting, and flexible partnerships could make the city appear as all things to all people, leverage the necessary outside resources to impact public life, and rise to prominence in their city's public game. A bevy of previously marginal or nonexistent figures—leaders of cultural and artistic institutions, municipal employees, and economic development planners—proved adept partnership-builders and thrust into the center of public life. Some traditional leaders made the transition to partnership, but not without abandoning the oppositional identities of their predecessors, while others clung to their traditional mode of engagement but could not leverage the resources they needed to impact public life and receded from the public limelight. Other traditional leaders—the old families, for instance—simply retired and left town. Finally, some like River City's Labor Council leaders contested the rise of partners within their own ranks, but were deemed an unacceptable liability by their peers and ostracized. When the dust settled, partnership was the official public ideology of both cities.

Unlike their traditional predecessors, partners assiduously avoid politics, viewing it as incompatible with their public personae. This is because partners see themselves as flexible, collaborative, and capable of enacting multiple presentations of self to work with anyone or anything, and look down on those deemed *narrow* or *divisive*, terms of derision that index the traditional style of their predecessors. Within this new public game, partners trade on an ability to participate usefully in the maximum number of different partnerships, which requires them to avoid engagements that code to others as divisive, inhibit their flexibility, or otherwise tie them to a rigid identity. Recall, for example, that River City's mayor attained public prominence by representing himself as a labor leader in one context, an environmental advocate in another, and so on. Because of the value that partners place on public flexibility, the factional obligations of traditional leaders are anathema to them and it is for this reason that they avoid party politics. To them, to be political means to be rigid, divisive, traditional, and hence less partner-like. A few partners occasionally flaunted their own political taboo, but cautionary tales like River City's Fred Pommel—a chamber leader who paved the way for the city's partnerships but was then pressured to withdrawal from them because union leaders found his past GOP involvement too divisive—ward off most.

Paradoxically, partners' avoidance of politics polarized America's political system by giving rise to a form of grassroots partisan organization that political scientists identify as activist parties.[3] As community leaders left grassroots parties, activists who were unconstrained by concern for local problems took over. These activists were frequently drawn into politics by waves of partisan furor, and their parties acted as echo chambers of sorts, amplifying collective commitment to hot-button issues. Because activists established solidarity by tolerating one another's political commitments, they were exposed to extreme viewpoints, favored candidates who espouse the full menu of hot-button partisan issues, allowed anyone to use the party label, and circled the wagons in the face of inevitable community criticism and ridicule. Their takeover of grassroots parties polarizes politics in multiple ways: they get politicians elected, serve as intermediaries between these politicians and daily life, and play a disproportionate role in media stories about American politics at the grassroots.

This institutional disembedding of politics from community institutions altered River Citians' and Prairievillers' commonsense understanding of public life. Partners oversee a grassroots public sphere defined by opposition between community-directed partners and divisive political activists and regularly stoke this community-politics divide—by labeling their community opponents as political, publicly maligning political activists, and occasionally running for office as post-partisan candidates. Via interviews with River City and Prairieville's residents, I showed that many viewed community and politics similarly: as irreconcilable opposites. I identified two ideal-typical responses to this perceived tension. Some residents, the partners, viewed their community's public life as ideal and distrusted politics on the grounds that it is factional and divisive. They saw politics as an unfamiliar public world animated by "the mentality of a football team, you cheer for your side no matter how bad they are sucking" and vacillated between withdrawal and uncertain support for post-partisan candidates. Others, the partisans, saw no place for themselves in community life and looked to politics as a cure-all. This search produced unpredictable but generally extreme political orientations, which varied from radical left to Christian conservative right. Partisans were united only by a desire to shake up public life, both locally and nationally. In the words of one partisan, "I'd like to turn this whole thing upside down." But whether voters identified as partisans or partners, they lacked one thing that united traditional Democrats and Republicans alike: a model of public life that allowed them to translate their intuitive daily experience into support for a governing agenda within America's actually existing political system. Partisans and partners are both utopians in their way. They have in common a politically constructed common sense that leads them to yearn for political systems that do not exist. The puzzling, contradictory nature of post-Keynesian politics is the consequence of their quests for unattainable ideals.

The major takeaway point is this: political policies create the arena in which public life unfolds, define the relationship between community institutions and America's political system, and ultimately structure the way that we think about public life. As shorthand, my argument is that the public sphere that we take for granted as natural is politically constructed—specifically, by neoliberal federal policies. I will discuss this argument's normative implications shortly. But first, three quick caveats about causality, my arguments' external validity and scope conditions, and Keynesianism and neoliberalism are necessary.

Caveats and Scope Conditions for the Argument

First, I need underscore a caveat about causality: I argued that neoliberal reforms transformed River City and Prairieville's public spheres, but I do not mean to imply by this that only these reforms can explain all of the ways in which these cities' public life has changed over several decades. Important things besides neoliberal federal reforms occurred during the last several decades, some of which I treated as exogenous to my argument: the declining profitability of manufacturing or advances in political fundraising techniques, for example. One could add many other factors to these like feminist, racial, and sexual orientation equality movements or the Internet and other technologies that circumvent traditional media. My argument is not that, absent a 1970s and '80s era reorganization of the American state, River City's and Prairieville's public spheres would look exactly as they did in the 1970s.

Rather, my argument is that, absent neoliberal reforms, River City's and Prairieville's public institutions would look different from how they appear today and probably more reminiscent of pre-1980s public institutions in a few important ways. I have shown in exhaustive detail how changes in American federalism allowed politics-averse partners to rise, pushed leaders who did not change with the times to the margins of public life, and promoted polarization among those left holding the reins of political institutions. It is therefore reasonable to conclude that, absent changes in American federalism, River City's and Prairieville's community leaders would feel less pressure to adopt partnerships and therefore be more willing to argue about the just distribution of their community's resources, speak on behalf of particular constituencies, and engage more freely in partisan political debates.

My second caveat is related to the first and revolves around external validity: the degree to which the processes that I observed in River City and Prairieville occurred elsewhere. In considering this issue, one must first distinguish between the big milestones in River City's and Prairieville's histories and my account of why these developments occurred. The milestones themselves are certainly part of national or international trends, because I

focused my analysis on trends that other scholars identify as such: 1970s-
and '80s-era changes in American federalism, the corporate merger movement, the disappearance of traditional community leaders, the emergence
of entrepreneurial partnerships in urban politics, activists' takeover of the
two parties, and the tendency of people—especially young people—to
abandon them. My aim in looking to River City and Prairieville was to develop ideas about the causal processes that connect these widely observed
trends in order to explain why they occurred in tandem. Here, too, I have
partially leaned on standard social scientific accounts; for instance, other
scholars have documented that 1980s-era merger movements thinned the
ranks of traditional business elites in other American cities.[4] I also identified a new causal process by showing that post-1980s federal policies
transformed River City's and Prairieville's public institutions in similar
ways, which promoted the emergence of activist-dominated partisan institutions in turn. Throughout the book, I triangulated this account with records of federal spending and other scholars' accounts of American federalism, post-1980s urban governance and civil society, and grassroots parties,
showing it to be more consistent with the timing and form of historical
change than alternative accounts—for instance, changes in party nomination procedures or campaign finance.[5] This suggests that neoliberal reforms
induced a broadly similar transformation in the public life of other American cities. However, my study focused only on the relationship between
neoliberal reforms and the public sphere in River City and Prairieville, and
further research is needed to determine the myriad ways in which these
phenomena could be related in different contexts.

    With regard to my argument's implications for other cities, it is impor-
tant to underscore that I see River City and Prairieville as paradigmatic
cases—or ones that are good to think with—not wholesale stand-ins for
other cities. That is, my interest is less in River City and Prairieville per se
than a set of scope conditions that exist within them: first, the decline of
Keynesian-era protectionism and emergence of competitive, market-like
systems of resource allocation and, second, leaders' style of problem-
solving and means of jockeying with one another for public prominence.[6]
River City and Prairieville are noteworthy in illustrating the degree to
which neoliberal federal reforms transformed public life absent mitigat-
ing circumstances and—stated this way—one readily sees a number of hypotheses about why other cities' historical trajectories should have been
different. If community leaders do not feel compelled to compete for outside employers and funding, for example, one would expect pressures toward partnership to be lower. Indeed, this hypothesis seems supported by

Prairieville's experience during 1990s-era corporate mergers, when the city found itself the momentary headquarters of three Fortune 500 companies and local business leaders abandoned their drive toward partnership.[7] Similarly, there is much variation in state revenue sharing arrangements; a few East Coast states particularly make relatively discretionary—or Keynesian-like—transfers to their cities, and here one would expect community leaders to have more incentives to engage in factional conflict and perhaps party politics.

Or consider cities outside the American context, where scholars have also noted the emergence of a neoliberal policy logic, entrepreneurial partnerships, and the decline of traditional party organizations. I have tailored my argument to the unique nature of American federalism, wherein city-federal relations are broadly similar to those of other former British colonies but radically different from elsewhere. Relative to the United States, urban actors in France and southern Europe exercise little community-level autonomy but play a larger role in national policymaking, those in Germany and Scandinavian nations are less autonomous vis-à-vis federal policymakers across the board, and those in the global south differ in myriad ways that I hesitate to categorize.[8] The causal connections between federal policy, partnership, and partisan politics would play out differently in a French or Brazilian "River City." Nevertheless, American River City provides a possible starting point for such analysis by pointing to an object of inquiry: those elites—whether they self-identify as urban or not—who are tasked with marketing plans to faraway funders, their public culture, and their relationship with political parties.

Conversely, one would expect the scope conditions of my argument to also apply to scales and contexts besides cities. For example, sociologist Mark Mizruchi argues that 1980s-era mergers thinned the ranks of long-serving Fortune 500 CEOs and diminished their positions of influence within the Republican Party—a trend that allowed politically motivated activists to dominate the national GOP, during the same period and for exactly the same reason that activists took over the GOP at the grassroots. Similarly, my understanding from talking with those who work in social service nonprofits is that whereas marginal nonprofits often fight on behalf of this or that constituency, large and well-endowed nonprofits that rely on competitive grants eschew conflict and embrace broad-based partnerships with other nonprofits—essentially, a partisans-versus-partners mode of organization within a different sector and at a different scale. One could further imagine partner versus partisan–like dynamics developing among public school officials competing for federal race-to-the-top grants, public hospital administrators forced to quest after competitive grants, donations, and better rankings to remain solvent, and any other context in which leaders rely on market-like, competitive mechanisms for critical resources.[9] In short, I think it likely that neoliberal reforms have introduced a conflict between partners and partisans into many facets of American public life and feel confident that future studies will bear this out.

Finally, and along these lines, a word about Keynesianism and neoliberalism. In using these terms and generally focusing on broad periods of American political history, I do not mean to imply that 1970s and '80s-era reforms were simple, orchestrated by a single group, or neatly periodized. Instead, neoliberal reforms were alternatively supported and opposed by Democrats and Republicans, unfolded during different periods, and took different forms in different policy domains: financial deregulation during the 1970s, deep cuts to urban funding programs in the early 1980s, the downscaling of social services to lower levels of government later in the 1980s, and across-the-board reliance on targeted, competitive grants and market-like mechanisms for funding delivery. Some policies such as these predated the 1970s, while some Keynesian-era programs persist today. For instance, some community development block grants are still apportioned on a fixed-formula basis and therefore fit my definition of a Keynesian program. Because Keynesianism and neoliberalism are shorthand for complex arrays of interrelated policy transformations, some social scientists may frown on their usage, insisting that they merely serve as placeholders for a more precise explanation of state-society relationships.

But in my view, social science advances partially through the articulation of what sociologist Max Weber identified as ideal types, or conceptual models that facilitate analysis of reoccurring patterns of action (or deviations from them) by stripping away real-world complexity and focusing on critical causal or constitutive relationships.[10] For instance, scholars identify the turn of the twentieth century as America's Progressive Era. This term does not perfectly describe a messy and multifaceted underlying reality, but rather identifies key components of an underlying turning point in American politics—an attack on urban ethnic party machines, emergence of social movements organized as lobbies, new styles of political discourse— and invites analysis of interrelationships between such trends.[11] Similarly, even critics of terms like *Keynesianism* and *neoliberalism* generally identify the 1970s and 1980s as a turning point in American political economy, and we understand the period better in part because social scientists have described ideal-typical shifts in aspects of social reality during the period: from "managerialism to entrepreneurialism" in urban governance, corporate managers' tendency to view firms as "bundles of assets," the emergence of activist grassroots parties, and the like. However, social science lacks conceptual frameworks for understanding connections between 1980s-era changes in different political domains. In this light, I see River City and Prairieville as useful paradigmatic cases for thinking through the relationships between different aspects of post-Keynesian politics. Community leaders' public activities occur in an interesting institutional bottleneck, because they are simultaneously impacted by a myriad of federal, state, nonprofit, and corporate initiatives and produce a myriad of diffuse consequences, and—by looking at them—it is therefore possible to reconstruct the broader consequences of ideal-typical neoliberal reforms. Any argument about ideal types leaves one open to charges of oversimplification. I am surely guilty of this in small ways, but I have anchored my analysis in concrete processes and am therefore able to plead innocent to, at minimum, felonious charges of telling stories about the forest that do undue violence to the trees. Although the reforms of the 1970s and '80s are complex, I nevertheless showed exactly how they mattered by pinpointing turning points in local life: for instance, the moment when traditional leaders could no longer exercise public influence and sat on their hands as partners formed their first coalition to capitalize on new politically constructed opportunities.

Ultimately, then, my analysis maps the contours of ideal-typical Keynesian and neoliberal political systems by examining the diffuse consequences of policymakers' prevailing paradigms of statecraft, or their general understanding of society, social problems, and the proper role of government. Indeed, recent historical scholarship suggests that there is more commonality in the ideological outlook of Keynesian- and neoliberal-era policymakers than their reforms may suggest. Prior to the 1970s, Democratic and Republican politicians and policy experts alike were characterized by an outlook that historians describe as "institutional realism": they saw society as messy and imperfect and viewed social and economic pathologies as amenable to improvement via state involvement and tinkering. Throughout the Keynesian era, this prevailing viewpoint was challenged by conservative intellectual movements, think-tanks, journals, policy-entrepreneurs, and experts—actors who were unified by the belief that human moral and economic progress was best achieved through market-competition, which the state should facilitate.[12] In the tumultuous economic climate of the 1970s, such ideas suddenly gained currency on the left and right, and politicians began to seek advice from this new class of neoliberal policy experts—a shift that reshuffled the careers of politicians and policy experts

alike, much as neoliberal policies subsequently reshuffled the status hierarchies of River City and Prairieville's traditional leaders.[13] Those who
favored bureaucratic political solutions lost ground to those who favored
public austerity, private sector–like accountability, and initiatives that created competitive, market-like public sector institutions. Summarizing this
shift, sociologist Stephanie Mudge argues that Keynesian-era politicians
approached problems by asking, "How much government?" Today's politicians ask, "How much market?"[14]

This book tracks the consequences of this paradigm shift across America's system of intergovernmental relations and, indeed, deeper into public
life. In the words of sociologist Andrew Abbott, the actors who make political claims in River City and Prairieville are unknowing avatars of faraway
policy initiatives, or projections of policy logics embedded in particular
local contexts.[15] So it is that Keynesian-era community leaders looked to
community problems and asked, "How can I get control over (political)
resources?" while the partners who contend with neoliberal realities ask,
"How can I market my initiative to people from the outside?" The threads
of these policy logics manifest themselves differently still in the words of
River City's and Prairieville's other residents. When dwellers of River City's
blue-collar flats or Prairieville's patricians talked as if it were self-evident
that people like themselves voted Democratic or Republican, they were un-
knowingly mirroring the logic of the Keynesian system. When we say that
reasonable people avoid politics and that things would be better if only
politicians put divisive issues aside, we are merely parroting the implicit
logic of the neoliberal policies that structure our public life. We do not realize that we are doing it, and yet we do it.

Our public common sense, including our political common sense, is
politically constructed; that is my argument's implication in a nutshell.[16]
Our society's collective public imagination follows, albeit indirectly, from
the types of regulatory and intergovernmental policies pursued by politicians, and could be changed by these policies. It therefore seems appropriate to conclude with reflection on River City and Prairieville's Keynesian and neoliberal public spheres, and to ask which is more conducive to
meaningful democratic participation.

Because the answer to this question involves no small value judgment,
my goal is not to answer the question definitively for the reader. Rather, I
begin by laying out standard ways in which scholars make value judgments
about public culture—the dramaturgical approaches—and show that they
provide ambiguous guidance for thinking through the normative implications of River City's and Prairieville's public transformation. Here, the

reader will have to make up his or her own mind. To de-muddy the water a bit, I develop a relational framework for evaluating the public sphere's democratic potential that builds on my analysis throughout the book. The relational framework evaluates the democratic potential of the grassroots public sphere in terms of its capacity to act as a conduit of communication between daily life and national politics. In this light, the neoliberal public sphere is normatively problematic because it systematically distorts communication between citizens and national policymakers.

Keynesianism, Neoliberalism, and Democracy

Political theorists have traditionally addressed normative questions about the public sphere using dramaturgical metaphors, which focus on how people act in public: public life is moral if people participate for the right reasons, discuss the right issues in the right way, and come away appropriately transformed. Popular commentators typically evaluate the public sphere similarly, and—whether they realize it or not—most commonly apply normative standards similar to those articulated by Alexis de Tocqueville and Jurgen Habermas.[17]

The Tocquevillian approach holds that the ideal public sphere is organic, grassroots, self-organizing or unspoiled: a pure outgrowth of people's popular will rather than an instrumental response to economic and political constraints or incentives. Scholars in this tradition argue that public activities are moral when deliberation and engagement occur independently of the state or other organizing authority, a position Tocqueville took when idealizing public life in colonial America. "It may almost be said that the [American] people are self-governing in so far as the share left to the administrator is so weak," Tocqueville wrote. "The American people reign in the American political world like God over the universe. [They are] the cause and aim of all things, everything comes from them and everything is absorbed in them."[18] The Tocquevillian position resurfaces often in academic arguments—most recently, for example, in the writings of Robert Putnam—and is ingrained in popular political discourse.[19] Consider, for example, that the labeling a phenomenon as "astro-turf," or not really motivated by a spontaneous outpouring of grassroots popular will, is sufficient grounds for discrediting it in everyday political talk.[20]

Another approach accepts that public activities are structured by economic and political institutions, but argues that participants can subsume such interests to the power of human rationality by adopting the right sort of talk. Jürgen Habermas takes the most well-known exemplar of this position by arguing that public talk should consist of rational-critical discussion, or "a kind of social intercourse that disregards status altogether, [one animated] by a tact befitting equals. The parity on whose basis alone the authority of the better argument could assert itself [and] carry the day [necessitates] the parity of a 'common humanity.'"[21] In other words, Habermas argues that democratic deliberation should consist of people who check their interests at the door and evaluate others' positions according to abstract principles like justice, fairness, and rational consistency and—in Habermas's words—surrender to the forceless force of rational arguments. This position parallels many people's moral judgments about deliberative democracy. In everyday talk, people often say that if others just stepped outside their own point of view, educated themselves on the issues, and engaged in rational discussion, they would eventually arrive at a consensus—a political consensus that usually approximates the position of the person making this claim.[22]

My arguments about the political construction of the public sphere is a critique and alternative to the Tocquevillian position. In my view, Tocquevillianism is impossible to reconcile with our complex society because virtually all public activities are directly or indirectly intertwined with the state. The self-supporting colonial hamlet is now fiction, as is the idea that grassroots leaders come together, pool their meager resources, and solve their collective problems alone.[23] As River City's and Prairieville's leaders know all too well, "grassroots" problems are linked to social, economic, political forces far outside the scope of local control and cannot be solved without intergovernmental monies, coordination, and regulation. Were one to apply the Tocquevillian standard consistently, one would conclude that River City's and Prairieville's traditional leaders and partners' were equally influenced by the incentive structure of the American state, and therefore equally far from the democratic ideal. Real democracy in these cities, one would argue, exists only in the margins of public life: in self-organized bowling leagues, spontaneous block parties, and the like.

Moreover, the Tocquevillian ideal is premised on a false tradeoff between instrumental action and authentic public culture: the implicit assumption is that people who are constrained by public institutions or stand to gain public resources will abandon the true public good to attain material benefits. River City and Prairieville show that the relation between structural incentives and public culture is one of co-evolution and involves no straightforward tradeoff. I hope to have intuitively clarified this issue by analyzing these cities' public cultures through the anthropological metaphor of game-play; like a game, public culture is structured by external realities, but players experience these as constitutive of the game's organic flow rather than as externally imposed constraints.[24] Keynesian-era leaders gained material benefits and social esteem by stoking conflicts, but they were also genuinely motivated by a desire to fight for their people; indeed, some continued to play their traditional game even after it ceased to bring them material benefits in the 1980s. Similarly, contemporary leaders find partnerships useful for leveraging outside resources, but my genuine impression was that they also believed in partnership as an end in itself. To them, it was self-evident that cooperation and avoidance of conflict were morally superior to public discord. There is nothing surprising about this, indeed just the opposite: psychologists tell us that contradictions between one's behavior and ideological justifications create deep source of psychic tension that usually lead to a change in either behavior or public persona.[25] To paraphrase sociologist Nina Eliasoph, people either wear public masks that suit their private actions or change their private faces to fit their public masks.[26] The Keynesian and neoliberal public sphere are both equally authentic *and* structured by the state, depending on how one chooses to look at it. Tocquevillianism offers no clear guidelines for adjudicating one as normatively preferable to the other.

The Habermasian narrative is also problematic because it is utopian— both in its emphasis on rationality and the power of talk to bridge intergroup divides—and places undue normative emphasis on the public talk's form rather than its effect on speaker and audience.

First, it seems evident that a political society characterized by citizens who rationally deliberate en masse will never exist on this earth. Most people do not talk about politics in this way. There is nothing wrong in principle with ideals that are rosier than reality, but the Habermasian ideal is problematic because it leads to prescriptions that undermine people's capacity for actual political communication. Social scientists have long argued that politics is simply too complex for human comprehension and that people require some form of heuristic, or mental shortcut, for making sense of it.[27] In his 1922 classic *Public Opinion*, for example, Walter Lippmann wrote that "the real [political] environment is altogether too big, too complex, and too fleeting for direct acquaintance. . . . People construct a pseudo-environment that is a subjective, biased, and necessarily abridged mental image of the world. [We] live in the same world, but think and feel in different ones." In simple terms, we do not contemplate the political world as it is, but rather continually update our simplified models of it.

The Habermasian ideal ignores this pre-conscious basis of communication and therefore introduces the false expectation that people can overcome their differences just by talking about them. In contrast to the Habermasian view, linguistic anthropologists argue that deliberation is a second-order communication strategy, one that elaborates speakers' implicit assumptions rather than challenging them.[28] Social psychologists, too, have shown that collective deliberations about contentious issues tend to sharpen intragroup differences, not reduce them.[29] For examples, one need hardly look further than River City and Prairieville, where traditional leaders take it as self-evident that public life consists of a zero-sum conflict over public resources, whereas partners see public life as an arena of collaborative partnership-building. This key difference is leaders' implicit model of how public life should work, not how they talk about it. Indeed, both sets of speakers occasionally constructed sound rational arguments about what community life and national politics should look like and arrived at entirely different conclusions.

Finally, the Habermasian narrative places too much normative emphasis on a rational-critical mode of communication rather than its effects on speakers and audience. Sociologist Jeffrey Alexander refers to this Habermasian tendency as the *fallacy of misplaced abstractness*: the assumption that abstract, inclusive claims can only be made in abstract, inclusive language.[30] Real political talk is full of innuendos, ad hominem attacks, rumors, appeals to emotions, untrue stories about a mythical political past, equally fanciful tales about unattainable political utopias, and so on. What's more, many of Habermas's critics emphasize that challengers to the status quo ordinarily make claims that sound less rational than powerful stakeholders who are accustomed to playing a game whose rules are stacked in their favor.[31] It is a mistake to assume that people cannot construct an inclusive political community using linguistic building blocks that are more uncouth than the rational-critical ideal, and insisting on rational-critical discussion as the democratic gold standard therefore seems misguided as it is seldom the language of the weak. For example, traditional labor leaders constructed their public imagination largely by slandering their city's well-to-do employers, but also argued that, at least potentially, everyone is a worker. They also actualized their battle with business leaders by, among other things, volunteering for working-class charities night after night, week after week, and year after year. Conversely, a public culture that celebrates universalism and inclusivity does not guarantee inclusive public action. It was in the name of preserving consensus, for example, that River City's partners publically humiliated Labor Council leaders and excluded them from public life—even though the latter were simply trying to prevent the use of public monies for a corporate give-away. The key point is that people's collective understanding of public life is not akin to a whole-sale script or absolute guide to action.[32] Rather, people selectively and creatively use pieces of their collective understandings and commitments to make various claims and, as such, there is no basis for judging one public ideology as inherently preferable to another.

Tocquevillian and Habermasian narratives are merely the most common dramaturgical narratives that people tell to evaluate the morality of public life and do not exhaust the range of these types of normative arguments.[33] But other approaches that focus solely on River City and Prairieville's public sphere also lead to ambiguous conclusions. For example, one could employ a participatory democratic framework, which evaluates public interaction as moral when it transforms participants from passive observers into informed, capable decision makers.[34] The trouble here is that traditional leaders and partners tell different stories about public engagement's transformative impact: traditional leaders see is as helping participants identify with their people and ultimately advocate on their behalf, whereas partners view it as giving people the wisdom to recognize that some differences are irreconcilable and must be set aside.

One might even be tempted to eschew theory altogether and evaluate River City's or Prairieville's pre- and post-1980s public spheres according to their policy consequences. For instance, partners appear key to the well-being of their cities because they are skilled at negotiating political contradictions and harmonizing the activities of different levels of government, but such interorganizational virtuosity matters only in the context of a federal system that makes it difficult to otherwise accomplish leaders' public goals. Traditional leaders were equally adapted to their times. Similarly, one might look to traditional leaders and partners' worst excesses. It is true that traditional leaders often pursued questionable policies: for instance, Prairieville's old families used urban renewal to reengineer their city's built environment against the wishes of some residents, which may attest to the moral bankruptcy of their public style.[35] But partners too engage in troubling machinations. At the time of my fieldwork, both cities' economic development personnel oversaw elaborate fiscal schemes that quietly accumulated debt and diverted school funding toward flashy, speculative high-end building projects—a common development strategy in many contemporary cities.[36] Here again, the normative implications are ambiguous. In one key respect, however, the normative implications of the neoliberal public sphere are unambiguous: its ability to enhance meaningful political communication between citizens and policymakers.

To clarify this point, I develop a relational public sphere framework as an alternative to Tocquevillianism, Habermasianism, and other dramaturgical models. This narrative is motivated by the simple truism that social phenomena are never inherently significant, but acquire significance only in relation to other phenomena. That is, I proceed from the assumption that the democratic value of the grassroots public sphere lies not in itself, but in its ability to communicate information between two pieces of the political system: citizens and policymakers in centers of political power. Students of the public sphere do sometimes evaluate it in this relational manner, but seldom develop their normative intuitions.[37] For example, Habermas compared grassroots democracy to a "warning system with sensors that, through unspecialized, are sensitive throughout society," and historical institutionalists often discuss it as a sort of "nagging system" that focuses politicians' attentions on pressing issues in daily life.[38] Relational metaphors come in many forms, but I find optical images especially useful: the grassroots public sphere is democratically valuable when it functions as a window that gives people and faraway policymakers insight into one another's activities.

Neoliberalism as Structural Deceit, from Top to Bottom

Consider first what River City's and Prairieville's public sphere communicates about citizens to policymakers and other consequential outsiders: its capacity to provide a window into these cities' daily life.[39] During the Keynesian era, the communicative capacity of River City's and Prairieville's public life was enhanced by robust connections between citizens, their grassroots community leaders, and faraway policymakers and other consequential outsiders. This appears to also have been true elsewhere. Sociologist Theda Skocpol argues that postwar civic life was structured by federated associations with grassroots local branches, regional or state-level coordinating bodies, and national mouthpiece organizations. This federated structure created a two-lane highway of information. Peoples' hopes, ideas, and grievances flowed toward centers of political power along with their representatives, who brought back information about conditions elsewhere, the limits of federal power, and so on. In River City and Prairieville, I identified a similar mode of organization particularly within each city's informal party system, which acted as base of the two-party system. Recall that Frannie Steele's house—a political power base to be sure, but one in a small, unremarkable city—hosted America's most powerful congressional representatives, governors, two future vice presidents, and one future president.

For me, the key question has been *why* traditional community leaders maintained communicative ties to local residents and policymakers. I have argued that they did so because they viewed their public game as consistent with the logic of national politics and—more precisely—equated public leadership with an ability to represent their constituents. Recall that Keynesian-era politicians operated a *banker government* that effectively made community leaders co-participants in the politics of the Keynesian state. Community leaders, like federal policymakers, fought over how best to allocate society's scarce resources and, like federal policymakers again, traded on an ability to mobilize local coalitions on their behalf. Therefore, community leaders understood their relationships with their city's residents as reciprocal: they expected to be able to call upon particular constituencies when needed, but also felt obliged to advocate on their behalf.

In contrast to partners, then, traditional leaders saw contact with policymakers as an opportunity to advocate for their people and altered their advocacy based on their constituents' needs. Here, I do not mean to idealize the public role that traditional leaders once played. They saw themselves as working-class or business-class leaders, conceptualized the public in the same way, and were therefore not a neutral conduit of communication as either the two-lane highway or window metaphors suggests. It is unclear whether residents could have communicated grievances not based in class identity—ones motivated by gender, racial, or sexual inequality, for example—through traditional leaders, and that is normatively troubling. But relative to partners, traditional leaders are noteworthy in that, at minimum, their interactions with consequential outsiders communicated *something* about local constituencies: information about the actual economic, civic, and political cleavages in their communities and, however imperfectly, information about the grievances and hopes of those on whose behalf they spoke. The conduit of grassroots to national communication they created was problematic in many ways, but it existed.

In the abstract, nothing prevents River City's and Prairieville's partners from creating a similar conduit of communication between daily life and faraway policymakers, but they do not do so in practice. Instead, partners inhabit a social space that I described throughout the book as a flat disk of interaction, one relatively insulated from their city's residents and outside policymakers alike. By this, I mean first that partners are less interested in cultivating the kinds of reciprocal ties with local residents and policymakers that traditional leaders saw as synonymous with public leadership. Before the 1980s, River City's and Prairieville's key leaders built vast personal networks that penetrated deeply into daily life and were simultaneously on a first-name basis with, at minimum, their city's Iowa House, Iowa Senate, and congressional representatives as well as the governor, provided of course that they were of the right party. Partners are uninterested in such personal relationships. Recall partners' blasé attitudes about traditional forms of democratic representation, which they view as a hassle: "[Democratic bodies] are important because [sometimes] you have to give people a chance to get up there and bitch, but [they] make it difficult to do things creatively."[40] To be sure, partners care about the well-being of their city's residents and the opinions of consequential outsiders, but the conduit of communication that they create revolves around marketing, not representation.

River City's Envisioning process (described in chapter 8) provides a fitting illustration.[41] The ostensible goal of the process was to produce common community priorities, which were typically vague: "strengthen and diversify the economy to create job security," "support livable neighborhoods," and the like. But for partners, establishing common priorities was not the point. "[Envisioning], that's the heart of the democratic process, it gives you goosebumps," the partner who headed the process told me, a sincere twinkle in his eye. "[You and I] could probably sit down together and come up with a pretty good comprehensive plan, probably as good or maybe better than what [the process] came up with. The difference would be that only [we] would have ownership of it. If [people] don't participate, so be it. And even if their idea does not make it to the plan, they have been part of the process and you can say, 'This is ours!' [and] justify whatever plan you can link to it." Such statements are consistent with sociologist Caroline Lee's study of Envisioning processes, which advocates tout as a way of "plucking more feathers with less squawking."[42] But in the context of my discussion, the fact that partners use Envisioning instrumentally is the sizzle and not the steak; traditional leaders, too, used public forums instrumentally to mobilize support for their agendas. Rather, partners' mode of public engagement is different in kind from that of traditional leaders' because of its uni-directionality, which alters the communicative potential of forums like Envisioning.

Because traditional leaders saw themselves as beholden to a particular group, their advocacy created a representation of a political constituency with social, economic, and political needs and grievances. But partners speak for no particular constituency and selectively keep some of what residents communicate in forums like Envisioning and take the rest off the table. If something does not fit with their plan, they simply ignore it and say, "At least [people] have been part of the process." Partners see nothing wrong with this, because it is consistent with how they form relationships with other partners: they engage publically by keeping divisive issues off the table and focusing on win-win initiatives. But the fact that partners speak on behalf of no constituency makes their forums devoid of communicative potential. No matter what River Citians say in Envisioning forums, partners strategically omit inconvenient information and include only those views that concur with their agenda. The neoliberal public sphere does not provide consequential outsiders with a window into daily life, because it communicates something about partners' own plans, not their community's residents.

But in fact, River City's and Prairieville's public life does not even communicate much that is meaningful about partners, because partners are primarily focused on marketing to outsiders. As marketers, partners collaborate to create a representation of grassroots life that matches whatever consequential outsiders like corporations, and competitive federal, state, and nonprofit grant-making bodies demand. If they are attracting a packing plant, they create coalitions that make their cities look like blue-collar meccas, if applying for a National Endowment for the Arts grant, a hotbed of youthful creativity, and so on.[43] In short, the way that partners communicate with outsiders is actually more harmful for meaningful democracy than if they did not communicate at all, because they systematically reinforce—rather than inform—powerful outsiders' understanding of grassroots life. Their primary communicative function is to reflect corporations' and grant-makers' priorities. For this reason, I have described the neoliberal public sphere as mirror-like. If Congress passes a program of competitive grants for the restoration of historic downtowns, for example, then partners across the country will definitely create coalitions that make it look like their communities care desperately about downtown restoration, even if lack of affordable healthcare, housing, or early childhood education are more pressing.

For all their differences with partners, activists activities are similarly mirror-like: they reinforce, rather than inform, outsiders' understanding of citizens' daily lives. I have argued that activists are often pulled into politics by waves of media attention to particular partisan issues and collectively create an echo chamber of sorts wherein activists feel compelled to be right on all the issues. Arguably, this is not all bad because—as sociologists Doug McAdam and Katrina Kloos have pointed out—grassroots activists thereby create conditions amenable to the success of certain types of social movements.[44] But of crucial importance to my argument is the origin of most contemporary movements for social and political change: not the grassroots, but with associations that sociologist Theda Skocpol identifies as "bodiless heads"—lobby groups and other mouthpiece organizations, largely based in Washington, DC, which rely on targeted partisan messaging to raise funds and have no particular connection to, or take input from, grassroots leaders.[45] Because activists often just channel the messages of such organizations, they are arguably more integrated into a closed-circuit of manufactured partisan communiqués than they are in community life.[46] They largely amplify the partisan messages of Washington, DC, rather than presenting policymakers and other consequential outsiders with a meaningful alternative to the status quo.

One can summarize this state of affairs thus: the neoliberal public sphere introduces a structural deceit into America's political system by systematically communicating misleading information about River City's and Prairieville's daily life to centers of political power. By this, I do not mean to imply that partners and partisans are deliberately deceitful. Rather, the deceit originates in the very organization of public life, and even more fundamentally in a mismatch between federal politics and the type of politics that neoliberal federal reforms induce at the grassroots. To better appreciate this deceit, it is helpful to imagine things from the perspective of a politician or other dignitary on an official state visit. She lands in her chartered plane in River City or Prairieville's tiny airport, looking down at the mysterious city below. Who will greet her at the airport and tell her about the place, its people, and their troubles?

If the politician were landing in the Keynesian era, she would be greeted by key community leaders, who were simultaneously leaders within their political parties, and—therefore—people who were known to her and who she was eager to cultivate relationships with. As representatives of local constituencies, these community leaders would talk impassionedly and at length about *their people*, advocating for this or that on their behalf. Community leaders would provide the politician with partial and incomplete information about daily life to be sure, but nevertheless communicate something meaningful about daily life—all in all, an informative visit.

By contrast, consider what the politician will learn after her plane sets down today. It is likely that key community leaders will not show up at the airport at all. If she does meet with the city's partners, she will be disappointed to learn that they are not involved in party politics and therefore of little immediate use to her. And if she were to meet them, partners would likely remain in marketing-mode, present a rosy picture of the city, its successful utilization of past federal programs, and their eagerness to have an opportunity to do so in future. Of course, the politician will certainly meet with party activists, but in talking with them she is likely to hear about abortion, the border fence, or any number of hot-button partisan issues upon which she is already regularly lobbied (but which community leaders assiduously avoid). Between these two groups, nobody will try to say much that is meaningful about the community's daily life. The politician therefore departs with mistaken impressions: competitive, market-like federal programs are popular and regular people care deeply about the hot-button political issues of the day.

Neoliberalism as Structural Deceit, from Bottom to Top

The neoliberal public sphere introduces a different kind of structural deceit into America's political system if one contemplates the system from the bottom up: it communicates the false impression to citizens that community-level politics, particularly an emphasis on setting aside divisive issues and engaging in broad-based partnerships, will work at a national scale. Here again, the contrast with Keynesianism is useful. River City's and Prairieville's traditional public spheres by no means provided local residents a perfect window into the internal workings of national policymaking, but did not systematically communicate misleading information about the nature of politics. Here again, too, the Keynesian-era public sphere's window-like characteristics were inseparable from the fact that community leaders were co-participants in federal politics.

At base, politics is about the allocation of limited resources and necessarily involves tradeoffs: one group gets and another does not, or one group gets and another must give. Agreement over the impossibility of total political consensus is virtually the only true consensus between political theorists on the left and right—from leftist radicals like Karl Marx to Friedrich von Hayek, the godfather of America's neoconservative movement, who compared political consensus to a group of friends who have agreed to go on a trip but not yet selected a destination.[47] By this, I do not mean that politicians need be in constant combat or that they are incapable of bargaining and arriving at a reasonable compromise.[48] Nevertheless, politicians must necessarily make decisions that benefit some people more than others at some point and, in such cases, make subjective judgments about the right course of action. That's politics.

The distinctive communicative feature of the Keynesian-era public sphere was its ability to communicate the reality of political tradeoffs to River City's and Prairieville's residents. Federal policymakers passed large, discretionary chunks of money onto community leaders, and unsurprisingly they and their city's residents saw it as self-evident that politics is a zero-sum game.

Neoliberal policies construct a different kind of public sphere. Because 1970s and '80s-era reformers distrusted political leaders' ability to out-think the market, simply transferring scarce resources to local leaders and letting them make due was out of the question. Their solution to the scarcity problem was to apportion resources through competitive, market-like mechanisms to those grassroots leaders who could show that they have or would make good use of these resources. Note the critical communicative problem with this system: market-like scenarios hide the reality of scarcity from grassroots leaders. Instead of scarcity, grassroots leaders are faced with the prospect of a high ceiling if they market their city successfully and a low floor if they fail to do so; they might go the way of Flint, Michigan, or Charlotte, North Carolina. It is for this reason that River City's and Prairie-ville's partners believe that they have everything to gain from collaboration and everything to lose from conflict—they actually *do*.

But partnerships only work in River City and Prairieville because partners operate within a politically constructed neoliberal context. Nationally, federal politicians are still engaged in a zero-sum game.[49] For them, partnerships will not unleash a flood outside resources, because there is no higher authority to whom they might market their initiatives. At the top of America's political system, difficult tradeoffs are still the name of the game.

Herein lies the neoliberal structural deceit from the point of view of River City's and Prairieville's residents: their intuitive understanding of how public problems get solved is a misleading guide for understanding national politics. Many of those who identify with their community's public culture repudiate politics altogether and see it as self-evident that conflict over difficult tradeoffs will bring ruin, whereas simply setting these tradeoffs aside will—somehow—produce the best of all possible worlds. This utopian celebration of the antipolitical is problematic firstly because it is self-reinforcing—or, in the words of philosopher Slavoj Žižek, a constitutive misrecognition of underlying realities. People see the latest crackpot to be elected governor and exclaim that reasonable people should stay out of politics. But their governor, who was championed by otherwise publically marginal activists, was elected precisely because community leaders desired to be reasonable and avoided partisan politics. Moreover, it is difficult to imagine a meaningful political system without significant tradeoffs. If America is to have a single-payer healthcare system, one that other nations' experience suggests would lower costs for most Americans, then some insurance company executives might lose their jobs. If we are to have more social services, some people will need to pay more taxes. That many of River City's and Prairieville's residents see such political tradeoffs as un-pragmatic is ironic, because it is precisely politically motivated neoliberal reforms that have produced this view.

This basic tension between the political construction of an antipolitical subjectivity is at the heart of the story that River City and Prairieville have to tell about the nature of contemporary politics. Theirs is the story of poli-cymakers' utopian effort to erase partisan politics and the resulting mis-match, both paradoxical and troubling, between yearning for post-political consensus in some quarters, gaggles of sign-waving activists in others. This two-facedness of our political culture is fundamental to its structure and, when viewed in this way, there is nothing especially surprising about it: if one constructs a political system that leads grassroots leaders to devalue politics, those with a real axe to grind will eventually take over political institutions.

My aim in this book has been to show how 1970s and '80s-era reforms introduced this conflict between partisans and partners into America's po-litical system. I have no particular insights into when or how this state of affairs is likely to change. My analysis does suggest that if policymakers' continue their efforts to depoliticize American federalism via competitive, accountable, and market-like systems of resource allocation, they will sim-ply double-down on the status quo and further fuel conflicts between par-tisans and partners, raising the tenor of partisan politics to fever pitch. This status quo is interesting as it appears to please no one, yet persists. The reasons are deeply structural. At the grassroots, the discontented find two public role models: the partners for whom solutions appear as technical fixes to immediate problems and partisans who are unschooled in public leadership and look to politics as a panacea, not the frequently mundane art of the possible.[50] Both lack Keynesian-era leaders' deep ties to local people, understanding of local problems, and willingness to build bridges with partisan politicians, engaging in actually existing politics on their con-stituents' behalf. In the absence of the latter, policymakers look to society and see widespread disaffection with partisan politics among some, an-ger about everything and nothing in particular among others—hardly the makings of a coalition for systemic change. There are only two visible roads away from our current historical moment. Both lead back to the present.

ACKNOWLEDGMENTS

As in any ethnographic study, my greatest debt is to my informants: River City's and Prairieville's leaders and other public characters. To extend this book's central metaphor, all those I encountered appeared to engage in public life for the love of the game—its potential for transformative acts of city-building and operatic struggles over the public good. I have yet to encounter a group of people who believe in their work more or whose importance to the lives of others is so large in proportion to their extrinsic rewards. It was only through dumb luck that I stumbled into their world, and I was fortunate to be able to participate in it, however marginally, for several happy years in Iowa. River City's and Prairieville's other residents, too, deserve special mention for their willingness to repeatedly interrupt their lives for interviews. As someone who lives and dies by my schedule now, I cannot imagine extending the same generosity to a stranger.

I am also grateful to numerous researchers for practical assistance. The Labor Center at Iowa State University and Iowa's Secretary of State, Board of Elections, and Legislative Services helped with archival records and initial contacts. Numerous academic researchers also helped me go door-to-door in search of interviews, drove with me across Iowa, and participated as members of two ethnographic research teams that conducted simultaneous observations of the 2008 caucuses and straw polls: Len Albright, Geoff Bakken, Stefan Bargheer, Jean Chen, Maria Czyzewska, Cassie Fennell, Jackie Hartley, Julie Keller, Monica Lee, Dan Menchik, Troy Peters, Jean Rattle, Paki Reid-Brossard, Abigail Rosenthal, Carly E. Schall, Anjie Chan Tack, and John Zinda,

Naturally, I benefited too from the practical assistance of River Citians and Prairievillans, who I can thank only collectively.

My greatest intellectual debt is to the University of Chicago, where I conducted most of the research for this book. I arrived to find Chicago steeped in the old model of graduate education: people placed little emphasis on early publication and generally making oneself look good on paper, and most faculty instructed new arrivals to go out and do big projects instead. I found this imperative initially terrifying and—because I had trouble securing outside funding for my research—financially devastating, but the university also created meaningful opportunities for intellectual development that were enhanced by an interdisciplinary workshop system. I soon found my home in the Political Communication and Society Workshop, which was organized by Michael Silverstein, Susan Gal, Andreas Gleaser, and Lisa Wedeen, and benefited from participation in an intellectual community that was excited to engage with my work precisely because it seemed outside the mainstream of academic sociology and was likely to evolve in unexpected directions. My sense is that few departments today would encourage young researchers to undertake a multiyear study of two unfamiliar cities without clear expectations about likely findings, which I think sensible but sad. I was lucky to be part of a university that encouraged a leap into the unknown.

Those who advised me at Chicago went above and beyond: Andreas Gleaser, Susan Gal, Elisabeth Clemens, and Andrew Abbott. Andreas took it upon himself to acquaint me with social theory—all of it—and discussed a book with me weekly over many months. He also pushed me to focus on political-economic arguments earlier in my research, advice I should have followed. Sue Gal's enthusiasm for my project was contagious and her incisive understanding of language inspired me to try to learn more about it myself. Lis influence on this book, from my engagement with historical-comparative works to my interest in American federalism, is everywhere apparent. She saw more clearly than I did that the project's ultimate payoff lay in engaging with institutional theories of the state and provided invaluable feedback on countless issues as she gently steered me in this direction. The research for this book would not have been completed without Andy's constant support and tireless advocacy for the project. It will surprise no one that his feedback proved invaluable, but perhaps even more critical was an advising style that I can describe only as leading by example. I am consistently impressed by Andy's ability to write clearly, ask big questions, produce insights into social processes that I do not understand at first (but prove indispensable after reflection), and generally work in world far nobler than actually existing social science. To the extent that my ability to produce ideas has improved, it has done so largely due to my desire to co-participate in the production of Andy's brand of social science.

At Chicago, I also benefited greatly from other scholars who provided critical feedback at multiple stages. Those not mentioned elsewhere include Mary Akchurin, Kim Austin, Mike Bare, Jason Beckfield, Andrew Bauer, John Brehm, Jessica Cattelino, Terry Clark, Ben Cornwell, Erica Coslor, Bobby Das, James Evans, Gary Alan Fine, Lis Gaumer, Eric Hedberg, Gary Herrigel, Ryon Lancaster, Edward Laumann, Greg Liegel, Sida Liu, Masha Medvedeva, Etienne Ollion, Michal Pagis, Andrew Papachristos, Steve Raudenbush, Steven Rosenfeld, Raphael Santana, Dave Schalliol, Kristen Schilt, Dan Slater, Mario Small, Craig Tutterow, Danielle Wallace, Liza Weinstein, and Dingxin Zhao,

The book also benefited greatly from multiple presentations at Stanford University, where I spent two years as an ASA/NSF Postdoctoral Fellow (fun fact: this postdoc was funded by the American Recovery and Reinvestment Act, which makes me the proud beneficially of a Keynesian-stimulus job). Upon catching my first whiff of eucalyptus wafting on the wind, I knew that Stanford would be different, and it was. I am especially grateful to participants of the Economic Sociology Workshop, which was headed by Mark Granovetter, Xueguang Zhou, and Steve Barley. This workshop proceeded according to an interrupt-frequently-with-questions model, which helped me to simplify my ideas and introduced me to many arguments about contemporary capitalism that informed this book. For critical engagement, feedback, and much needed good times, I am also grateful to Diana Dakhalla, Corey Fields, Warner Henson, Tomas Jimenez, Monica McDermott, Lindsay Owens, Paolo Parigi, Bogdan State, Mitchell Stevens, and Patricia and Cristobal Young.

This is as good a place as any to also thank the many fine people who co-inhabit the strange world of sociology and have shaped my thinking during frequently too brief conversations in hotel lobbies, walks through random cities, on academic panels, over after-conference drinks, during campus visit, over Skype, or other encounters: Woody Abbott, Jacob Avery, Christopher Bail, Delia Baldassarri, Tim Bartley, Claudio Benzecry, Bart Bonikowski, Rogers Brubaker, Bruce Carruthers, Austin Choi-Fitzpatrick, Claire Decoteau, Andrew Deener, Matt Desmond, Wendy Espeland, Kurtulus Gemici, Blackhawk Hancock, Chris Hausmann, Jerome Himmelstein, Dan Hirshman, Rob Jansen, Colin Jerolmack, Monica Krause, Greta Krippner, Daniel Laurison, Jooyoung Lee, Omar Lizardo, Richard Lloyd, Matt Mahler, Jeff Manza, Nicole Marwell, Damon Mayrl, Doug McAdam, Michael McQuarrie, Rory McVeigh, Tom Medvedz, Ajay Mehrotra, Ben Merriman, Anne Mische, Alex Murphy, John O'Brien, Becky Pettit, Elizabeth Popp Berman, Monica Prasad, Susanna Ramirez, Fiona Rose-Greenland,

Jake Rosenfeld, Marc Schneiberg, Jeremy Schultz, Jennifer Silva, Lyn Spill-man, Erica Summers-Effler, Iddo Tavory, Sarah Thebaud, Todd van Gunten, Steve Viscelli, Edward Walker, Rachel Weber, Damian Williams, Andreas Wimmer, and Michael Young.

In am additionally grateful to Brown University, where I have written most of the book *and* managed to remain gainfully employed, appearing to outsiders like a functional member of society—a new one for me. One could hardly ask for a friendlier and more professionally supportive department, and my work has benefited from an environment that is virtually free of the kind of fear-and-loathing that I hear about from other junior faculty. I am especially grateful to Rebecca Carter, Nitsan Chorev, Scott Frickel, Margot Jackson, John Logan, Hilary Silver, Tyson Smith, and Sandy Zipp for intellectual engagement and friendship. I have also benefited greatly from a network of interlocutors who provided feedback on various chapters: Andrew Abbott, Cedric De Leon, Barry Eidlin, Nina Eliasoph, Dan Hirschman, Patrick Heller, Michael Kennedy, Caroline Lee, Isaac Martin, Dan Menchik, Isaac A. Reed, Adam Slez, Mark Suchman, and Nicholas Hoover Wilson. Of these interlocutors, Stephanie Lee Mudge deserves special mention. Shortly after arriving at Brown, I approached Stephanie about forming a book-writing group that ended up being just the two of us. Stephanie subsequently kept me accountable, read every chapter multiple times, and made the otherwise solitary task of book writing enjoyable. Many of the better ideas in the book both small (e.g., the opening of chapter 4) and large (e.g., engaging with the political parties literature) were hers.

Some material within the book has also been published in the *American Journal of Sociology*, *Social Problems*, and *Socio-Economic Review* (the latter two published by Oxford University Press) and benefited from anonymous reviewers at these journals. My fieldwork during the 2012 election cycle was generously supported by an American Sociological Association Fund for the Advancement of the Discipline Grant. The manuscript was further improved and ushered along by three anonymous reviewers at the University of Chicago Press, developmental editor Brad Erickson, editorial associate Kyle Adam Wagner, and my fearless editor, the ineluctably pleasant Doug Mitchell.

Finally, my family deserves special mention. I have often spoken about the project with Maria Czyzewska, my mother, who even made a trip out to Iowa with us to observe the caucuses. She has also helped us financially over the years, as has Piotr Pacewicz, my ever-supportive father, and my wife's parents, Dianne and Samuel Rattle. Nobody deserves my thanks more than Jean Rattle, practically the only thing that has been with me longer than this project. This project put a strain on our life by sending our finances—which, at the time, were more *her* finances—into free fall. I am forever indebted to her for those years, but not half so much as for the friendship and love she's shown me since. It is impossible to articulate gratitude to someone whose adult life is entirely intertwined with one's own, except perhaps by saying that it would be fun to do it over again, especially with the knowledge that many of the personal, financial, and professional trials that we've jointly faced along the way would work themselves out. Finally, I would be remiss if I did not thank my daughter Josephine, a pleasant-natured, funny person of three, and her infant brother, Emmett, who already vacillates between the easy-going and the dramatic disposition that seems to be our family's defining characteristic. Much of this book was written in the early morning hours before Josie wakes up, so last my gratitude goes out to her for being such a solid sleeper and—by extension—to Dr. Pamela High, a sleep specialist who helped us restore order after several trying months. After waking up, Josie sometimes comes in to help me work by tapping away randomly on my keyboard and moving the mouse around. I hope to always be amused by such devastating critique of my life's work.

September 2015
Providence, Rhode Island

This appendix addresses my ability to draw inferences about politics outside of River City and Prairieville, case selection, ethnographic approach, the practical and ethical considerations of studying public figures (including anonymity), my procedure for selecting nonleaders for interviews, and details about my social network analysis.

Analytical Approach

River City and Prairieville are not typical or average American cities; they are idiosyncratic and even statistically unusual—older than the average American city, until recently whiter, and so on. Some readers may worry that this undermines my ability to make claims about politics elsewhere. But statistically speaking, all cases are equally unique and a study of an average American city—according to one website, Indianapolis, Indiana— would yield insights into American politics that are no more generalizable than a study of anywhere else. Representativity is a property of samples, not cases. By analogy, consider that interviewing an average American gives one no special insights into Americans' political opinions. Instead of relying on induction, I first isolated commonalities in River City's and Prairieville's historical trajectories, then employed historical-comparative techniques and engagement with other scholars to generalize about trends outside River City and Prairieville.

First, I looked to River City and Prairieville to generate ideas about the relationship between historical trends, notably the emergence of partnerships in urban politics and activists' takeover of grassroots parties. In the language of quantitative social science, I was generating hypotheses, although I hesitate to use that word because quantitative analysts view one hypothesis as equal to another until tested and hence associate the term with trivial insights. By contrast, sociologist Mario Small argues that one should distinguish between trivial and logically compelling hypotheses.[1] Whereas trivial hypotheses are based purely on induction, logically compelling ones proceed from observations of causal or constitutive relationships and provide a logical reason why phenomena should co-occur similarly elsewhere.

My ability to compare River City and Prairieville facilitated my ability to formulate logically compelling hypotheses by allowing me to separate important commonalities in their historical trajectories from each place's idiosyncrasies. Had I studied only River City, for instance, I might have focused on the particular characteristics of the traditional union leaders who were traditionally dominant. But having Prairieville and its history of business leaders' public dominance as a comparison allowed me to see that labor leaders and business leaders in each city, whether publically dominant or subordinate, (a) created similar interpersonal coalitions, monopolized resources in similar ways, and approached the public similarly, (b) understood partisan politics as part of this public game and engaged in to elevate their local esteem, and (c) abandoned this traditional mode of community engagement and withdrew from politics in the 1980s. After isolating such commonalities, I made three logically compelling hypotheses about American politics: that 1980s-era federal reforms promoted the rise of partners, that partners left grassroots parties to activists, thereby polarizing American politics, and that these trends impacted the political reasoning of voters.

Throughout the book, I evaluate these arguments using historical-comparative techniques, which rely primarily on the logic of triangulation: assessing claims according to their consistency with the sequencing of historical change, their logical coherence, and a wide array of different accounts, sources, and records.[2] At this stage, too, I used my ethnographic investigation as one vantage point, which was particularly helpful in identifying where other scholars' interpretations of historical trends were simply implausible. For example, political scientists argued that community leaders once engaged in party politics because they relied on graft from national party leaders to maintain local patronage networks, but I spoke with leaders from this era and found them wholly disinterested in national party conventions except maybe as a fun perk—something akin to a partially funded trip to political Disneyland.[3] I therefore sought out urban histories, which suggest that the decline of urban machines happened earlier in the twentieth century—a fact that contradicted political scientists' prevailing accounts of grassroots party change. Where my other arguments about connections between federal policy, community governance, and grassroots politics are concerned, too, *Partisans and Partners* effectively works on two levels: I use ethnographic portions to show how things did happen in River City and Prairieville, and historical-comparative arguments to establish that these cities' trajectory is the most plausible account of what happened elsewhere. For instance, anyone reading critical urban geographers' accounts of urban partnerships side by side with political scientists' treatment of grassroots parties would likely realize that the two trends are related and could confirm this intuition by looking at different kinds of archival data. But crucially, I only knew to bring these literatures together because my informants showed me that the public persona of partners was incompatible with overt partisan displays.

Overall, then, I think it likely that the relationship between community governance and grassroots politics was similar enough in other American cities to create dynamics similar to those that I observed. The one notable exception is my analysis of nonleaders' political reasoning, which is more speculative due to the dearth of open-ended qualitative studies of voting behavior. Here, my study was purely ethnographic, and claims that I make about the probable connections between a community's public sphere and citizens' political reasoning should be read as plausible hypotheses.

Studying Community Leaders

In discussing River City and Prairieville as cases, I report how I came to think about them after my ethnographic research was complete, which is decidedly more systematic than my initial ideas about the project. When I started this study in 2005, George W. Bush had just been re-elected and people in my social circle, I myself, and popular books like *What's the Matter with Kansas?* were interested in why people vote Republican.[4] Around this time, I became acquainted with classic community studies. I was particularly taken with the Elmira study and was also part of a workshop at the University of Chicago with linguistic and cultural anthropologists who impressed upon me that one should study people's ideological commitments by examining how they piggyback on interpersonal loyalties and tensions. My idea was to marry these insights and conduct an Elmira-like study informed by up-to-date cultural scholarship and ethnographic methods. Some of my intuitions about the advantages of this approach were consistent with my eventual findings—namely, I hoped that examining how people use daily life as a model for making sense of politics would allow me to say something new and interesting about their political preferences. But in most other respects, I imagined doing a different project than the one I did. I was mostly interested in why people vote Republican and expected to spend most of my time studying voters; issues like community leaders' public game, grassroots party organizations, and federal policies were off my radar.

I selected River City and Prairieville with the intention of explaining why one was more Republican than the other, not to study their political convergence as I eventually did. Because Chicagoland seemed too vast, unmanageable, and unique in its machine politics, I was on the lookout for smaller places within a day's drive and considered municipalities in Michigan and Indiana, but settled on Iowa as the right state. Iowa's clearest advantage lay with the Iowa caucuses, which I thought would make the project interesting to a broad audience. Municipalities at the state's eastern edge are also heavily Democratic but become Republican as one moves west, which seemed to invite comparison. I focused on larger municipalities of 25,000 to 100,000 residents, of which Iowa contains over a dozen. After examining these cities' demographics, voting patterns, and what information I could glean from the Internet, I identified several candidate pairs for comparison and—after a road trip to see them for myself—settled on River City and Prairieville, which appear similar on paper, save that voters in River City are typically more Democratic than Prairieville's voters. Prior to my road trip, I had never set foot in either city nor had I spent much time in any similar place.

In sum then, I arrived in River City and Prairieville as an outsider with virtually no knowledge about these places and a different project in mind than the one I ended up conducting. Unsurprisingly, my initial research was driven by happenstance. I began the project by interviewing members of local historical societies to learn background information about each city and—during one interview in River City—a local historian suggested that I interview the city manager for his perspective. Because I had never spoken with anyone involved in local politics before and felt out of my element, I was frightfully nervous before interviewing the city manager, but the interview nevertheless proved conceptually and practically helpful. The city manager spoke about a transformation of River City's public life, which local historians had also discussed. He also suggested additional people I could speak with. I followed up with these contacts, who ended up being key local partners in turn, and from then on I employed a top-down recruiting strategy that worked well in accessing community leaders: I contacted those I thought the highest status members of any group first and, after the interview, asked them for contacts.[5] Before I knew it, I was studying River City and—later—Prairieville's public life, and the study seemed virtually to drive itself. Each informant supplied additional contacts, and I kept interviewing them because each filled in more pieces of a story about their cities' public transformation, which I found intuitively compelling but did not initially know how to situate relative to my interest in political preferences.

At the time of my fieldwork, most ethnographers seemed to identify with one of two modes of ethnographic investigation: grounded theory and the extended case method. Grounded theory is an inductive method, and ethnographers in this tradition proceed by abandoning their preconceived interests and assumptions and instead reconstruct their informants' worldview via a recursive process of observation, taking detailed field notes, searching their field notes for patterns, and repeat observation. The extended case method is more deductive in that practitioners begin with a theory and then select field sites where the theory's applicability may be challenged in order to extend the theory's scope or explanatory potential. I began my fieldwork with an interest in politics and even vague ideas about the kind of arguments I wanted to make and therefore proceeded more opportunistically than grounded theorists. But unlike practitioners of the extended case method, I had no commitment to a particular theory. I was therefore unable to identify with either tradition. My initial fieldwork was also driven largely by intuitions about what seemed important, which made me worry about whether my research was systematic enough. As my fieldwork advanced, however, I developed a recursive process of hypothesis-making and testing that was similar to an approach since identified by sociologists Iddo Tavory and Stefan Timmermans as the abductive method.[6]

The goal of the abductive method is to capitalize on one's theoretical intuitions to arrive at novel insights about social life. Because such insights frequently begin with chance observations or lucky accidents, the abductive method codifies a procedure for capitalizing on happenstance. One begins by focusing on phenomena that appear novel, anomalous, or otherwise surprising relative to existing scholarship, not necessarily those that interest informants (as in grounded theory) nor phenomena identified as significant by prior scholars (as in the extended case method). One then formulates hypotheses about these surprising phenomena and tests them through additional fieldwork. This is largely what I did. My initial fieldwork uncovered two surprising phenomena. Key community leaders identified as partners, expressed distaste for politics, and associated partnership with a 1980s-era public transformation. I had also encountered traditional leaders, many of them politically engaged, who had fallen in public esteem since the 1980s. These findings surprised me, because I expected community leaders to simply share the partisan preferences of their community's residents. Based on my initial observations, I abduced—or hypothesized— that a 1980s-era political-economic shift displaced politically engaged traditional leaders and elevated politics-averse partners to central positions in public life. Because partners' aversion to partisan bickering coincided with hyper-polarized partisan politics both nationally and at the grassroots, I further hypothesized that partners' avoidance of politics and conflicts with partisan activists polarized the latter.

Much of my fieldwork focused on evaluating my hypotheses by learning more about differences between partners', traditional leaders' and activists' style of public engagement. I focused heavily on juxtaposing pairs of organizations that were otherwise similar, but identified by community leaders as animated by opposing public styles (e.g., the Labor Council and United Labor Council). I also employed several tracking strategies identified by anthropologist George Marcus: I "followed the people" by examining leaders in different public contexts and "followed the conflict" by identifying the root causes of tensions between partners, traditional leaders, and partisan activists.[7] I focused especially on deviant cases—notably partners who dabbled in politics—in order to uncover how the internal logic of partnership clashed with partisan engagement. I did not take terribly systematic field notes, but tape recorded everything and followed versions of procedures recommended by grounded theorists for sifting through data and identifying the native meanings of informants: I listened to interviews and transcribed key snippets, analyzed terms of distinction used by my informants, and wrote memos about the meanings of these *codes* or distinctions throughout the project, often under the auspices of writing updates to my advisors or early papers, which were little more than annotated field notes.

I viewed my research as ethnographic throughout and still do, but gleaned most of my key insights through in-depth qualitative interviews. This approach was appropriate for my field site, because my central object of analysis was the public sphere, a phenomenon that consists of "interactional orders" and "micro-situations" that do not occur in any one privileged site and are separated from one another by time and space.[8] That is, I observed interaction in any accessible setting where public talk occurred: the city council, the chamber, the Labor Council, the Labor-Management Council (in River City), the two parties, and community planning forums. Generally, however, face-to-face interaction was less revealing than what people said about it later, largely because leaders orchestrated public meetings to appear uncontroversial to a general public. As I argued in the book, community leaders interact in their city's public sphere largely by observing one another's behavior from afar and reading the tea leaves, looking to snippets of available information for clues of one another's intentions. When leaders did act, they schemed alone or in small groups long before spearheading initiatives they hoped would make a big splash, but—mostly—they waited, watched, and gossiped incessantly with trusted confidants. It is not for nothing that my informants revered their peers for an ability to "smell shit coming from miles away." My ethnographic investigation simply tracked these processes: I happily gossiped with community leaders about their city's past, present, and future and relied especially on long-term relationships with trusted informants, whom I contacted periodically to assess reactions to various events. I also used various archival sources to triangulate leaders' memories of public initiatives with written reports.

Rapport and Professional Ethics in Public Conflict Zones

Because my fieldwork consisted partially of gossiping about acrimonious conflicts, establishing rapport and proceeding ethically proved problematic. It is noteworthy that ongoing conflicts did *not* complicate my project in the way that I expected: throughout the project, I worried that my contact with both sides in ongoing conflicts would anger someone and doom the project, but this never happened. Instead, securing access to informants proved unproblematic in virtually all cases, which—in retrospect—I think primarily due to a lucky fit between my own biography and qualities valued by community leaders. This was especially true of partners, who identify with youthful thinking, education, cosmopolitanism, education, and celebrate personal quirks and idiosyncrasies. I was in my mid-twenties, had come from Chicago, was born outside the United States and subsequently lived abroad, and was writing a PhD dissertation about partners' small Rust Belt city—something most people took to be quirky and odd. I was therefore able to take for granted that my rapport with partners would be instantaneous, and my interview transcripts are full of ethnographically invaluable statements that suggest an unquestioned commonality of outlook.

Relations with traditional labor leaders were also unproblematic, because I originally approached them through the Iowa Labor Center and was therefore perceived as a "labor historian," a label I initially contested but eventually accepted. My status as a friendly outsider was likely bolstered by the fact that I sympathized with traditional labor leaders' plight and made no great effort to hide it. Partisan activists too were happy to speak with me, because they were marginal in their city's public life and pleased that I contacted them at all. Although my contact with Prairieville's GOP became problematic after the Mark Sturley's ouster as party president (described in chapter 5), this event ultimately taught me more about Prairieville's activists than seamless access probably would have.

The only informants who proved difficult to access were members of the old families who were initially contemptuous and un-swayed by contacts I had established with others. For example, I called one long-time business owner in River City who—not five seconds into my introduction—said, "I know who you are, young man, but I have no time for your questions," and hung up. So it was that I learned first-hand why many older informants still deplored the old families who once ran their town from on high. But even here I got lucky in Prairieville where two long-time old business owners had read classic community studies in college, enjoyed them, and associated the University of Chicago with this tradition. To them, I was not a "young man," but rather a "University of Chicago researcher" or even "University of Chicago Josh," and they were giving with their time and instructed me to use their name to get further contacts.

My easy access to informants notwithstanding, River City and Prairieville's public conflicts proved problematic because I found it difficult to maintain sympathy with all sides. Sympathy with informants is important for ethnographers, because the goal of the method is to understand the world from informant's point of view. Moreover, conversation is fundamentally interactive and frequently guided as much by the speaker as the listener, who gives the speaker permission to state opinions via a series of verbal and nonverbal cues. In effect, the ethnographer gets data by giving informants implicit approval and encouragement for articulations of views and presentations of self, even when he disagrees with these views or find presentations of self off-putting. In this respect, all ethnographers are—in the words of sociologist Erving Goffman—"finks," but one's ability to establish rapport is particularly difficult when studying actors who dislike one other.[9] In my case, I found myself sympathizing with Democrats over Republicans and with traditional leaders over partners.

My tendency to take sides was more pronounced in community conflicts than partisan conflicts. I am a Democrat, had been involved in various kinds of left-wing activism in college, and was secretly rooting for a Democrat to win the 2008 Election. Nevertheless, contacts with GOP activists proved less problematic than I expected. This was perhaps because I had spoken with my fair share of Republicans while an undergraduate at the University of Texas, where it was normal for students with an interest in politics to congregate and debate at social events. Because I had many happy memories of arguments with Republicans that had run long into the hot Texas night, it was easy to view GOP activists as those with a passion for politics that was similar to my own, and I felt comfortable at party functions and even participated in Republican's political talk during the Iowa primary by rooting for my favored GOP candidate (Mitt Romney). My sympathy for traditional leaders over partners ran stronger, probably also due to various aspects of my biography. I spent my teens and college years in the sprawling, affluent suburbs of Austin, and River City and Prairieville's histories of industrial production and blue-collar, union-tinged politics struck me immediately as excitingly exotic. Partners' tendency to bad-mouth this past rubbed me the wrong way and I was un-swayed by their visions of a cosmopolitan city dotted with craft breweries, music venues, and other cultural amenities that—having recently come from Austin—I took for granted. I was also sinking into personal debt throughout my project and economic inequality was at the forefront of my thinking about politics, which made me unsympathetic to partners' efforts to take "divisive issues" like inequality off the table. Whatever the reasons, I found myself rooting for traditional leaders, despite the fact—or perhaps because—they seemed destined to lose to partners.

My main response was to hide that I had taken sides from informants and to try to minimize my own tendency to do so. If asked directly about my opinion, I replied that I needed to remain neutral for the sake of the project; sometimes implying that I could not state personal opinions as a condition of doing academic research (something that I thought practically true, but not administratively or legally true). Luckily, partners took my lack of explicit opinions as tacit approval, but everyone respected my desire to remain "neutral," including GOP activists who—I later found out—un-surprisingly suspected me of being a Democrat. I also made a conscious effort to identify with informants based on traits that I found sympathetic or redeeming, such as my aforementioned sympathy for Republicans' passion for politics or—in the case of partners—their often humble roots, their individual and collective ambition, their legal and technical mastery, and their willingness to work toward remote goals. It became easier to sympathize with partners after I presented early findings at professional conferences and discovered that some audience members were prepared to demonize partners outright. One person, for example, asked if partners were "on the take" from corporations. Because I did not think my informants nefarious, I felt thereafter compelled to specify how their behavior was structured by broader opportunities and incentives, which likely led me to my eventual interest in federal policy.

Nevertheless, *Partisans and Partners* is not always a feel-good story, and in writing it I encountered ethical considerations related to the reporting of potentially unflattering information. In deciding how to treat such information, my aim was to protect individual informants from public criticism, legal trouble, and regulatory scrutiny while relating the maximum amount of factual details about River City and Prairieville's public life. To this end, I made two distinctions. First, I distinguished between information that concerned an individual's behavior versus that which concerned collective behavior or which I could attribute to a group member (e.g., things said or done by "an influential partner" or a "well-known Democratic activist"). Next, I distinguished between information that was public knowledge or in the public record, sensitive (known to most community leaders but not publically discussed by them), and secret (known to some community leaders but not others).[10]

I erred on the side of caution when reporting information about particular individuals. If information seemed potentially unflattering, I reported it only if informants related it to me themselves or if their activities were public knowledge. Where individual community leaders' behavior appeared illegal or scandal-worthy, I did not report it unless it was in the public record. Many community leaders were less discrete with me than they should have been and reported on scandal-worthy behaviors ranging from conflicts of interest to solicitation of prostitution. I have kept such information in confidence. Where I thought that an individual's role in a collective endeavor portrayed them in an unusually unfavorable light, I additionally masked informants' identities by changing details about them, moving them between cities, or—in one or two cases—splitting a single informant into two characters.[11] Protecting informants from harm was also the reason I anonymized my field sites, a decision I discuss shortly.

By contrast, I freely reported community leaders' collective activities unless I happened upon information that was truly secret, or known only to a subset of community leaders (e.g., one group's effort to spread rumors, an unsuccessful attempt to lure a company). There are therefore many things in the book that community leaders do not discuss publicly and might not like to see in print (e.g., the lengths to which partners go in wooing outside corporations) and other things that community leaders see as unproblematic, but which I have presented in a potentially negative light (e.g., partners' tendency to view democratic participation as a tool for generating "buy-in."). My decision to report such information runs counter to the advice of some ethnographers, who recommend obtaining informants' consent prior to publishing potentially unflattering information. Nevertheless, I think that my approach is appropriate, because my informants—unlike most subjects of ethnographic research—were in positions of public authority. Community leaders participated knowingly in this study and were accustomed to dealing with the media and therefore in a position to appreciate how I might use their reports. They also have much influence over their own public image and are unlikely to be permanently impacted by the publication of this book. If community leaders take any notice of an anonymized academic press book, its publication will be—at most—one small episode in their stewardship over public life, not a rare and defining moment.

Perhaps most important, community leaders exercise public influence. The presumption within democratic society is that those who play the public game should be subject to special scrutiny, which I see as applicable here. My ultimate goal is to report accurately on the exercise of community power in order to generate frameworks for thinking about contemporary democracy. Where the imperative to report accurately conflicted with a desire to avoid divulging collectively unflattering information, I divulged this information anyway. If the actions of community leaders sometimes appear unflattering, it is because they—like all of us—operate in a world that is only minimally under their control and forces them to do half a dozen things that they might rather not do in order to achieve one or two goals that they find worthwhile. My hope is that in reporting accurately on community leaders' machinations, I do them the service of presenting them as they were: three-dimensional and well-meaning people making do in complex and difficult circumstances

Anonymity

Although my main priority is reporting accurately on River City's and Prairieville's public life, I see protecting my informants from duress as a competing and nontrivial imperative. To this end, I have refrained from reporting information that was not in the public record and seemed likely to harm particular informants, but the significance of information changes over time in ways that make it hard for anyone to know what may prove harmful. For example, I conducted my research during a period when many Iowa cities were expanding their reliance on nontraditional financing mechanisms like tax increment financing (TIF), and River City and

Prairieville's leaders boasted proudly about devising new ways to use the practice. Since the 2007–8 financial crisis, TIF has come under regulatory scrutiny from the Iowa legislature, and many of the ways in which River City and Prairieville's leaders used TIF have produced scandals in other Iowa cities. In discussing my study with community leaders, I presented its primary audience as academics or those with a general interest in American politics, not journalists, regulators, legislators, or others capable of sanctioning community leaders for their behavior. I have therefore employed pseudonyms for both informants and their cities to minimize the probability that my research will be employed by the latter.

These days, a determined reader could use the Internet to reasonably guess at River City and Prairieville's true identities, but suspicion is different from confirmation in print and anonymity grants my informants two types of protection. First, anonymity makes it difficult for journalists to produce media accounts based on particular events in my book, because they could only do so responsibly by conducting independent research and re-interviewing River City and Prairieville's leaders to verify that events in this book are actually about them. Moreover, academic research and community leaders' public initiatives are retrievable via the same Internet search terms, and anonymizing my cities lowers the probability that others will happen upon my research when seeking out information about River City and Prairieville for their own purposes—for instance, when conducting an Internet search for "economic development," "mayor," and River City's or Prairieville's real name. To date, my anonymization of River City and Prairieville has had the desired effect. During debates over TIF reform in Iowa, virtually all Iowa-specific academic research appeared in journalistic and regulatory reports, but a paper I wrote about TIF in River City and Prairieville has not, even though I have received inquiries about it from journalists, politicians, and developers in other parts of the country.

Ethnographers most often object to anonymization on two related grounds: that it complicates efforts to verify research findings and makes it difficult to conduct follow-up research and otherwise engage in ethnographic research as a collective enterprise.[12] To me, neither of these objections suggests that sociologists need to abandon anonymization outright, particularly because there are cases wherein ethnographers could not realistically or ethically do their research without promising anonymity to their informants—just as, for instance, other scholars could not reasonably compile datasets without promising anonymity to respondents. It seems preferable to develop realistic standards that are distinct from those often enforced by institutional review boards and which allow fellow researchers to both fact-check ethnographic research and conduct follow-up studies.

That such a thing is possible is nicely illustrated by cases on anonymization that preceded institutional review boards. Consider the classic community study *Middletown* (Lynd and Lynd 1929). The book garnered the Lynds media attention, which prompted some "Middletown" notables and other residents to argue to the media that the Lynds misrepresented them and their city—criticism the Lynds addressed in subsequent publications. Middletown was also subject to several follow-up studies, some conducted by the Lynds and others by unrelated researchers who agreed to employ the Middletown pseudonym.[13] Some critics of anonymization draw parallels to journalism and argue that anonymous reporting creates perverse incentives to make up facts, but the Middletown case suggests that—in ethnography as in journalism—such incentives can be counteracted by others rooted in institutionalized standards for reporting information to one's professional peers. Stated differently, it seems reasonable to adopt looser standards of anonymization that treat anonymity as one imperfect layer of protection that hides informants' identity from the public, not other academic researchers who want to verify research findings and conduct follow ups. I effectively employed this standard in my study, because The University of Chicago's IRB made clear distinctions between social scientific research and research in fields requiring stricter standards of anonymity (e.g., medical research). For instance, the IRB allowed me to enlist several fellow graduate students' help in interviewing nonleaders and even allowed me to assemble a team of a dozen researchers from three universities to simultaneously observe the 2008 Iowa primaries. This was both practically helpful and can help verify the general contours of my arguments about River Citians' and Prairievillers' political attitudes. The problem is not anonymization per se, but rather an all-or-nothing conception of anonymity that is unnecessary in social scientific research, often ignored in practice, and frequently impedes legitimate social science if adhered to strictly.

Interviews with Regular People

I conducted a baseline interview with 104 residents of River City and Prairieville in spring/summer of 2007, reinterviewed 87 in the months that preceded the Iowa caucuses, 90 before the 2008 general election, and finally reinterviewed a small number (35) before the 2012 election. My goal in selecting informants was to achieve saturation: to conduct interviews with each type of local voter, not a representative sample of either city.[14] To this end, I targeted residents of five neighborhoods with each city, which I identified by sitting over a map with various community leaders and partisan activists and asking them to tell me about political types and where they lived. The neighborhoods included an old family hilltop neighborhood, a suburb associated with young professionals, a middle-class Republican-leaning suburb, a working-class Democratic neighborhood, and a politically mixed suburb. I interview roughly ten informants per neighborhood, employing strategies like asking neighbors for contacts and going door-to-door with a fieldworker of the opposite gender to maximize response rates, which were over fifty percent among those who answer the door—extremely high for in-depth qualitative interviews.

Because I did not obtain a representative sample of either city, I was unable to rely on statistical inference, but am able to formulate plausible hypotheses about the connection between people's orientation toward community life and their partisan preferences—namely, that younger residents (who were exposed only to post-1980s community life) and older civically engaged residents (who were differentially exposed to post-1980s community life) would be more likely to reason as partners and identify more loosely with partisan politics vis-à-vis older civically unengaged voters. The patterns that I observed among my informants were consistent with this hypothesis, thus lending my hypothesis additional plausibility. I show this by employing a simple ethnographic coding scheme. I first classified interviewees as relatively more or less civically engaged, using engagement in a central community institution (e.g., the chamber of commerce, Rotary Club) or three or more secondary community institutions (e.g., a service club, charity, PTA, church) as the cutoff. I did not count people as highly engaged if their associations were in frequent conflict with their city's partners—as was the case with several unions headed by Labor Council leaders and an activist evangelical in River City. Next, I categorized interviewees as more or less partner-like based on their response to a question that I posed halfway through my first interview, which asked the person to imagine an ideal alternative to America's political system. I classified those who said existing politics was fine or expressed preferences for more partisan conflict as un-partner-like, those who espoused support for much less or no partisan conflict as partner-like—although, of course, many in the latter category changed their tune later in the election cycle (i.e., "mixed voters" whom I discuss in chapter 9). Finally, I classified respondents as "young" (under forty) or "older" (over forty), sometimes based on direct questioning and sometimes my best guess based on interview details (upon

Table A.1. Political reasoning and community engagement among interviewees

	Civic Engagement	
	Lower	Higher
Partner-like voters	Over 40 = 8 Under 40 = 14	Over 40 = 20 Under 40 = 2
Traditional voters and partisans	Over 40 = 48 Under 40 = 6	Over 40 = 5 Under 40 = 1

relistening to interviews, I realized that my initial impressions of people's ages were terrible; I classified many people in their thirties as "older," especially if they had children!).

Table A.1 supports the assertion that partner-like voters tended to be younger or older and civically engaged. Consider the table in quadrants, clockwise from the lower left-hand side. Quadrant 1 consists of traditional voters and partisans and includes mostly older informants along with a few younger partisans. Quadrant 2 includes civically unengaged partner-like voters, who are almost exclusively "younger." Quadrant 3 includes civically engaged partner-like voters and includes both older and a few younger informants. Finally, quadrant 4 is relatively empty, which supports the assertion that to engage in community life is to engage as a partner. Although the analysis does not provide statistical proof of my claim, it lends additional plausibility to the hypothesis that orientation toward community mediated River Citians' and Prairievillers' perceptions of partisan politics.

Social Network Analyses

My social network analyses throughout the text are based on a datasets that I compiled of six types of associations: the board of directors or senior management of local and non–locally owned businesses, labor unions with at least one locally based representative, voluntary associations, city and county elected bodies, appointed city commissions, and the local Democratic and Republican party institutions. Below, I detail data sources and their biases, and my technique for analyzing the data.

Major locally based businesses. I collected information on the board of directors and senior management of large, locally based businesses largely from *Dun's Million Dollar Directory*, a directory that lists information about firms based on several criteria, including geography. I included data on all firms that employed at least 100 workers. *Dun's* publishers claim not to collect data on retail and professional service firms, but they did collect information on several such firms in both my cities, and—where information was available—I included it. A major drawback of *Dun's* is its inconsistent inclusion, and frequent omission, of locally based subsidiaries of companies headquartered elsewhere—a source of bias since corporate subsidiaries were virtually absent from River City's and Prairieville's economies during the 1970s, but dominated it by the 2000s. Therefore, I crosschecked *Dun's Million Dollar Directory* against the company's *Billion Dollar Directory*, which contains more accurate subsidiary data, and documents stored by both cities' chamber and public libraries, which frequently contained list of important companies, their officers, and boards of directors. Luckily, corporate subsidiaries during the 1970s were few, whereas it was comparatively easier to find information about employers during the 2000s. In several cases I had to make a choice between omitting information about a company or sampling company information from slightly outside the time period of interest, and opted for the latter.

Labor Unions. River City's labor newspaper periodically published complete lists of all official union representatives and leaders of union coordinating bodies like the Labor Council. Prairieville's labor newspaper did not contain such lists, and I was unable to find more than a handful of historical copies, as it was never archived. My analysis of Prairieville's unions is therefore based on what fragmentary data I was able to assemble. My information about the 2004–6 period was based simply on observation of Prairieville's Labor Council, because—unlike River City's—all key labor leaders attended. For the 1974–76 period, I relied on surviving copies of the labor newspaper, oral histories, lists of interviewees compiled by the Iowa Labor Center's oral history project, and informal records kept by informants (particularly Daniel Steele's treasure trove of 1970s-era photographs, which I describe in chapter 4). I also cross-identified labor leaders from nonprofit reports, which often included leaders' union affiliation or—sometimes—listed their labor union office as their home address. I could not reliably date some leaders to the 1974–76 period and surely missed some, which suggests that better historical data on Prairieville's unions would have shown them to be more central in public life.

Voluntary Associations. My data on voluntary associations is based largely on nonprofit reports filed with the secretary of state for the 1970s and on self-collected board membership data for the 2004–6 period. Nonprofit reports filed with the secretary of state contain three sources of bias: the volume of nonprofit fillings increases with time, union leaders report their activities less frequently as nonprofits than business leaders, and the

detail of information that the Iowa secretary of state collects on nonprofits decreased in the late 1990s. The volume of nonprofit reports for the
1974–76 period was manageable, and I proceeded inductively, collecting
information on any nonprofit that listed its mission as publically oriented,
rather than merely recreational or religious. Most of these nonprofits were
outliers to the network, and I dropped them. While compiling the data,
it became apparent that business leaders overreported their civic activities
and labor union leaders underreport them (e.g., they formed nonprofits
to spearhead their company's philanthropic activities, whereas unions did
charitable works without forming separate nonprofits). I partially dealt
with this bias by eliminating some business associations that had no analogous union counterparts (e.g., company foundations). I also collected additional information on key participants in major union initiatives from
the city's labor newspaper or other archival sources and included them
as the directors of *associations* (e.g., the editorial board of each city's labor
newspaper, a perennial labor-directed Christmas drive to collect toys for
needy children in River City). Despite this, some reporting bias remained,
and I think that the centrality of 1970s-era labor union leaders in River
City's—and even more so Prairieville's—public life is understated in my
analyses. By the 2000s, the volume of nonprofits rose to many hundreds,
rendering an inductive approach prohibitive. I therefore included information on voluntary associations that I knew to be important players based
on my ethnographic study or that had been important during the 1974–
76 period. Additionally, I scanned the complete list of nonprofit reports
stored by the secretary of state for anything I might have missed during
fieldwork. Beginning in the late 1990s, the secretary of state converted nonprofit reports to an electronic format, scanning the first page of the report
and throwing the rest—including the complete list of directors—away. I
therefore relied on printouts of key organizations' boards of directors that
I made during my fieldwork and the Wayback Machine, a digital Internet
archive.

City and County Elected Bodies. I collected complete data on elected
city officials, members of the school board, and county officers from primary records stored by these organizations.

Appointed City Commissions. I collected complete data on key city
commissions for the 2004–6 from records kept by each city's auditor. To
facilitate presentation, I amalgamated boards into types (e.g., the Cable TV,
Electrical, Transport, and Airport Commission into "Infrastructure Commissions"). Unfortunately, both cities had cleared out 1970s-era records. In
River City the county auditor helped me to compile a list of commission

members by conducting a computer scan of city council records for the word "commission" between 1970 and 1976—a word that came up when council representatives were appointed or reappointed to a commission. This procedure was far from perfect and certainly missed important names, which I made no further effort to compile. Therefore, the high importance of commissions during the 1970s is likely understated vis-à-vis their importance in the 2000s. I found a complete list of Prairieville's 1970s-era commissions in the historical correspondence of a city council representative who received a facsimile of all local board members in 1975.

Democratic and Republican Party Institutions. I collected data on elected state representatives, party officers and workers, and major party donors. I compiled data on elected representatives from an annual yearbook of Iowa's legislators. I employed a loose definition of party *officer*: anyone serving in an official leadership capacity (e.g., party president, recording secretary, head of the membership committee) or representing the party as a precinct or caucus captain. Data on party officers for the 2004–6 period are based on a complete record of both parties' official representatives, a list of all precinct captains during the 2004 caucuses and 2006 precinct convention (for Democrats), and 2004 straw poll workers and 2006 county convention delegates (for Republicans). I found complete records of party leaders during the 1970s from paperwork filed with Iowa's Ethics and Campaign Disclosure Board, but no records of election-day workers and convention delegates. I therefore compiled partial lists from any archival party materials that I could find and from local newspaper coverage of the caucuses and general election, listing anyone mentioned as a precinct delegate or as formally involved in election day organizing as a party officer. In River City this procedure resulted in a list of comparable size in the 1970s and 2000s period, but the actual number of party workers was probably higher in the 1970s. For example, many precincts in 2004–6 sent no representatives to the county convention, which my informants told me rarely happened during the 1970s. Prairieville's hometown newspaper did not cover the primaries as thoroughly as River City's, and—on the Democratic side—I included more names from other archival materials and from pictures of Democratic events taken by Daniel Steele. Nevertheless, my analysis likely underestimates the centrality of 1970s-era party officers vis-à-vis their 2000s-era counterparts, particularly the centrality of Prairieville's 1970s-era GOP officers.

My definition of major party donor includes those who engaged in a donation pattern that signaled partisan affiliation to their peers. During the 1970s, Iowa's Ethics and Campaign Disclosure Board required parties to report donations of over $250—a large sum that signaled a major commitment to the local party. I counted these individuals as major donors along with others mentioned in historical records as having made especially generous donations to parties. By contrast, 2000s-era campaign law required parties to list any donor who contributed $25 or more. In actuality, party leaders sometimes reported smaller donations to the ECDB for both periods, but nevertheless the two lists were incomparable. For example, River City's Democratic Party reported two dozen party donors during the 1974–76 period and over 350 people who donated between $5 and $500 during the 2004–6 period, even though fewer than 100 unique individuals regularly attended either party's events. Many 2000s-era donations did not signal partisan allegiance. In Iowa, it is common for individuals to donate to parties to gain preferential access to high-profile political candidates: a base annual donation of $100 dollars gets one an invite to a backstage reception with an important visitor, and attendees of such receptions—who often tag along with friends—are expected to donate by purchasing a $50–$125 ticket. Community leaders did not view attendance of such events as a signal of partisan allegiance; many did so out of curiosity, for entertainment, to lobby politicians directly, or find a postpartisan candidate. Indeed, cross attendance at partisan events was common; for instance, five River Citians made an annual $100 donation to both parties, presumably to get themselves onto both invite lists. My aim was to isolate donation patterns that were bigger or more frequent than necessary to gain access to candidates—a standard that mirrored party leaders' tendency to publicly praise those who they identified as *big money* and *reliable* donors, and I employed the same strategy to do so in both cities: I counted all those who gave more than $225 during the 2004 presidential election year (i.e., a sum indicating more than the standard $100 annual donation and attendance of one high-profile event) or more than $100 dollars in 2005 or 2006 as major donors. I also counted those who made more than two donations in any amount in 2004 or more than one donation in 2005 or 2006. Even by this restricted criteria, my lists of River City's 2004–6 party donors vis-à-vis their 1970s counterparts was triple the size for the Democrats and 1.5 times as large for the GOP, which suggests that the 2000s-era centrality of River City's donors is overstated.

I lost the 1970s-era list of donors that I originally compiled for Prairieville, and employed a different procedure. For the Democrats, I simply included three individuals who older activists widely believed to have been extremely generous to the party (needless to say, the centrality of Democratic donors during the 1970s is therefore understated). For the GOP, I relied on an archived collection of papers belonging to Prairieville's congressional representative (a Republican), which included a letter from local party officials that essentially said: "if you want to hold a fundraiser, these are the people you should definitely invite." This list was incomparable to my procedure for identifying donors in the 2004–6 period, and probably overstated the centrality of 1970s-era GOP donors: the former list included 56 individuals in comparison to 22 during the 2004–6 period, although this disparity may also just reflect a real decline in the Prairieville GOP's *big money donors* (see chapters 5 and 7). Nevertheless, I justified using this 1970s-era donors list because my list of GOP officers during this period was woefully incomplete. Between GOP *officers* and *donors*, I captured most of the known Republicans who came up frequently in my informants' oral histories, which my 2004–6 procedure also appeared to do.

Analysis of Network Data. I used Freeman's *closeness* to assess centrality in all analyses, which was appropriate given both cities' changing community structure and native understandings of structural power.[15] Perceptions of structural power and the metrics that ideally capture them depend on a network's macro structure, and River City's community structure changed from a cluster of labor Democrats and business Republicans who opposed one another on the city's democratic bodies to a single cluster of partner-dominated associations and periphery of traditional and political groups.[16] During the 1970s leaders saw intercluster brokers, politicians especially, as publically central. This attitude is consistent with a brokerage metric like *interclique betweenness*, but—in this case—is not consistent with commonly used eigenvector centrality measures like Bonacich's centrality, because business leaders were more likely to form formal organizations to pursue their initiatives vis-à-vis labor leaders, and measures that weight ties according to adjacent nodes' number of ties exaggerated this reporting bias.[17] By contrast, 2000s-era leaders perceive those engaged in multiple partner-dominated associations as central, viewing those who engaged, or *brokered*, with traditional or political organizations as suspect—an attitude well captured by measures like Bonacich's centrality but abysmally by betweenness measures. Closeness did not perfectly capture leaders' structural intuitions during either period, but also yielded no misleading findings. It can be interpreted simply as an actor's visibility, or the propensity of information about them to diffuse to others in the network, all other things equal.

In both associational and individual centrality analyses, I disregarded overall associational size by, respectively, not controlling for it and dropping all leaders who belonged to just one association. This decision reflected key community leaders' lack of consistent preference for small organizations populated only by other key leaders and is consistent with qualitative studies of structural power, which show that leaders within an *inner circle*—those with more than one board membership—possess a different collective identity and understanding of network structure from those who belong to just one board.[18] I intend the more-than-one associational membership cutoff as a rough proxy for those who community leaders would likely regard as peers, as opposed to regular people who just happen to sit on one board. Because community leaders saw associations as desirable if they were populated by their peers (i.e., they seemed to regard a small board dominated by a couple key leaders and a large board with a few key leaders on it as equally desirable, all other things equal), I simply counted them as central insofar as they were close to other key leaders and dropped those with only one board membership from my analysis when assessing leaders' centrality.

NOTES

PREFACE

1. On divergence of political parties, see Poole and Rosenthal 2007; Cohen et al. 2008; Layman et al. 2010; Heaney and Rojas 2015. The two parties' policy positions have also converged in some domains as Democrats have adopted pro-market positions previously associated with the right (Hacker and Pierson 2011; Mudge 2011), but my overarching argument is that the latter shift toward neoliberal policies promotes partisan polarization on other issues, albeit indirectly via policies' impact on community governance and grassroots politics.

2. Dimoch et al. 2014.

3. About 20% according to Dimoch et al. 2014. On lack of issue polarization among most Americans, see DiMaggio, Evans, and Bryson 1996; Evans 2003; Fiorina, Abrams, and Pope 2005; Fiorina and Levendusky 2006; Fiorina and Abrams 2008; Abramowitz and Saunders 2005; Abramowitz 2013. For evidence of party-driven polarization of electorate, see Baldassarri and Gelman 2008.

4. The American National Election Study (ANES) reports that 39.1% of respondents identified as Independent or unaffiliated in 2008 (50.5% of 18–34-year-olds did so), whereas 25.7% of respondents did in 1952 (and 30.1% of 18–34-year-olds did so). Shifts in aggregate rates of Independent identification can be misleading, because of period effects (Fiorina and Levendusky 2006, 92; Galston and Nivola 2008, 7): temporary shifts among all voters, which disproportionately impact younger cohorts (Mayer 1992). For instance, rates of Independent identification increased sharply in the late 1960s and early 1970s possibly because both parties supported the Vietnam War, rising especially among the large baby boom generation (50.3% of 18–34-year-olds did not identify with a political party in 1972). During this period, scholars began discussing partisan dealignment (see, e.g., Broder 1972), and contemporary commentators who claim that rates of Independent identification have *not* increased among younger Americans typically use this anomalous period as baseline. But examining intergenerational trends shows a persistent rise in Independents (Stonecash 2006, 114–15): 30.1% of 18–34-year-olds identified as Independents in 1952, 30.4% in 1960, 42.7% in 1968, 47.9% in 1976, 43.2% in 1984, 48.4% in 1992, 55.9% in 2000, and 50.5% in 2008. Some argue that young Americans became more partisan after 2001 (Green and Coffey 2007; Kimball and Gross 2007), but this is true but only vis-à-vis 2000, which was a high-water mark

of partisan disaffiliation among 18–34-year-olds. In this note, I classify Independents as those who did not state an initial party preference to ANES interviewers, including "leaners" who reported preferences for a party when pressed. Some scholars argue that leaners develop nearly identical vote preferences to party identifiers (Keith et al. 1992; Dimoch et al. 2014)—which is consistent with my findings in chapters 8 and 9. But leaners reason differently from identifiers and with important consequences: they are less likely to vote, donate, and work for a campaign, and otherwise engage in the political process (for similar national trends, see Dimoch et al. 2014).

5. I have cut words from quotes by eliminating false starts, hedges, tangents, and repetition to make ethnographic data maximally accessible (for a similar approach and justification, see Bourgeois and Schonberg 2009, 13). Ellipses indicate that an informant paused, trailed off, or was interrupted, not omitted words. I have not inserted clarifying terms, connecting clauses, or any other words into quotes except where indicated with brackets.

6. Eliasoph 1998.

7. Downs 1957.

8. On pre-World War II period, see Ansolabehere, Snyder, and Stewart 2001. On post-1980s period, see Aldrich 1995; Poole and Rosenthal 2007; Fiorina 1999; Layman et al. 2010; Masket 2009.

9. Wright and Berkman 1986; Canes-Wrone, Brady, and Cogan 2002; McAdam and Kloos 2014.

10. For a similar focus on grassroots parties in political science see Aldrich 1995; Layman et al. 2010; Masket 2009; Bawn et al. 2012. My explanation complements many accounts of individual-level predictors of partisanship. For instance, Carmines, McIver, and Stimson (1987, 380) argue that New Deal–era patterns of partisan identification declined because "all political alignments tend toward entropy": commitments to conflicts and issue configurations lose emotional salience with time, particularly when transmitted intergenerationally. But I will show that Keynesian-era community institutions reified the emotional salience of political divisions by embedding them in local conflicts, a community-level dynamic that ceased after the 1980s. My discussion of grassroots parties also accounts for the rise of inter-issue correlations among party identifiers (Baldassarri and Gelman 2008).

11. River City and Prairieville were most notably different from other American cities in their relative absence of racial politics until the 1990s and 2000s. But my overarching argument is about community leaders' mode of exercising power, which could apply also to cities in which community cleavages are racial (see chap. 3).

12. See Methodological Appendix.

13. Katznelson (1981) argues that American workplace and community politics have always been separate, including during the Keynesian era, but I found that many community allegiances—for instance, to white ethnicity or neighborhood—were interwoven with labor-business conflicts and partisan divides. For a similar take on Keynesian-era community conflicts, see Mollenkopf 1983.

INTRODUCTION

1. Social scientists commonly identify the 1970s and '80s as a turning point in American political economy, but characterize it differently. Some political scientists identify the post-1970s period with Republican electoral successes (Bartels 2008) or Democrats' adoption of GOP policy positions (Hacker and Pierson 2011). For oth-

ers, the 1970s was a period of changing policy paradigms: the rise of economistic reasoning (Smith 2007; Berman 2014) and affinity for market-like models of society among policymakers in both parties (Fourcade-Gournichas and Babb 2002; Prasad 2006; Mudge 2008; Peck 2010; Krippner 2011; Rodgers 2011; Mirowski 2013). I adopt the latter view. See chap. 4 for further discussion.

2. See Aldrich 1995; Poole and Rosenthal 2007, 2007; Jacobson 2001; Layman et al. 2010; Masket 2009.

3. McAdam and Kloos (2014) argue that polarization among congressional representatives grew most pronounced in the early 1990s.

4. Political scientists identify this earlier strategy as "conflict displacement" (Key 1952; Sundquist 1983; Carmines and Stimson 1989; Aldrich 1995; Gelman 2010, 116). For discussion of partisan polarization among Americans, see n. 3 in the preface. Conflict extension may appear incompatible with both parties' growing proclivity for pro-market policies, but the two phenomena are separable. Consider the Affordable Care Act debate: Democrats and Republicans staked policy positions that were more market-like than—for instance—government-administered health care, then fought vociferously.

5. See n. 4 in the preface.

6. See, respectively Krippner 2011; Rodgers 2011; Rothenberg 1984; Fourcade 2009; Medvetz 2012; Berman and Milanes-Reyes 2013; Mudge 2015; Hirshman and Berman 2014.

7. See Aldrich 1995; Lyman et al. 2010; Masket 2009; Bawn et al. 2012.

8. Specifically, urban development and social services funding, both of which received steep cuts as a result of Reagan's New Federalism policy (see chap. 4).

9. On merger wave, see Espeland and Hirsh 1990; Fligstein 2001; Davis 2009.

10. Which exercised de facto authority over federal funds (see Mollenkopf 1983).

11. This was due to Reagan's New Federalism but the Carter administration also tried unsuccessfully to transform city-federal relations (see chap. 4). Reagan's New Federalism hobbled the Department of Housing and Urban Development in the 1980s, reducing its expenditures from 8% to 2% of the federal budget (Biles 2011).

12. This was a shift in grant funding across federal bureaucracies (Smith and Lipsky 1993; Mudge 2008; Biles 2011).

13. On proliferation of partnerships, see Brenner 2004; Peck, Theodore, and Brenner 2009. On political parties, see Aldrich 1995; Layman et al. 2010; Bawn et al. 2012; De Leon 2014; Mudge and Chen 2014.

14. See Mollenkopf 1983.

15. On traditional importance of United Way and locally sourced philanthropy, see Galaskiewicz 1985; Smith and Lipsky 1993; Barman 2006.

16. See Lippmann 1922.

17. Converse 1964, 215–18. See also Stokes 1963.

18. See Schuman and Presser 1980; Zaller 1992; Alvarez and Brehm 2002; Bartels 2008; Hacker and Pierson 2011, 109–11.

19. Berelson, Lazarsfeld, and McPhee 1954. The Elmira study followed an earlier study by Lazarsfeld, Berelson, and Gaudet (1944), which showed that voters are political disinterested, uninformed, but consistent over time. Some political scientists view the Michigan model (Campbell et al.1960; Miller and Shanks 1996), which assumes that citizens vote based on enduring partisanship affiliation, as the solution to this apparent puzzle. But the Michigan model assumes a process of preference formation that is inconsistent with that observed by Elmira researchers and which I

rediscovered in River City and Prairieville: people change their preferences over the election cycle, then re-establish habitual preferences before the election.

20. The Elmira study is associated with the "sociological approach" to the study of political preferences, but I avoid the term as its meaning changed over time. Scholars who followed the Elmira researchers were interested in predictive voting models and equated the "sociological approach" with variables that measure social categories, as have subsequent scholars who identify with this tradition and efforts to map the field (Knoke 1976; Manza and Brooks 1999; De Leon 2014, 11; Mudge and Chen 2014). The Elmira researchers defined the sociological approach as focused on process and context, not variables and outcome: "one should take into account respondent's broader institutional position. . . . We should not be concerned with individual vote decisions. . . . One should relate individual level data to changes in . . . institutions" (Berelson, Lazarsfeld, and McPhee 1964, 297). For a similar characterization of the Columbia school, see Christensen 2015.

21. See Pierce 1932; Silverstein 2003; Garfinkel 1984; Ochs 1990.

22. Layman et al. 2010.

23. Fiorina, Abrams, and Pope 2005; Fiorina 2006; Baldassari and Gelman 2008.

24. See Aldrich 1995; Poole and Rosenthal 2007; Jacobson 2001; Layman et al. 2010. For a review and analysis, see Masket 2009.

25. Hacker and Pierson 2011, 150.

26. DiMaggio, Evans, and Bryson 1996; Fiorina, Abrams, and Pope 2005; Fiorina 2006; Baldassari and Gelman 2008.

27. See n. 4 in the preface.

28. See n. 4 in the preface for a discussion of this trend.

29. Subsequent political scientists discounted the Elmira approach on the latter basis (see De Leon 2014, 35–36, 42–44).

30. Following Martin (2011), I understand sound explanation as an account that focuses on an actor's situated reasoning without attributing causal power to nonpersons (e.g., demographic categories). See also Reed 2011. I employ this approach throughout, but as part of a multi-sited or linked ecology framework (Abbott 2005) wherein some people's actions (i.e., policymakers) have far-reaching consequences for others' decision-making context.

31. Clark and Lipset (1991), who argue that materially confident actors value lifestyle issues over class-based ones.

32. Theirs was an analysis of the social construction of political interests before the term was fashionable. For similar contemporary research, see Clemens 1997; Skocpol 2003; McLean 2007; De Leon, Desai, and Tuğal 2009; Slez and Martin 2007.

33. I do not begin from the premise that River City and Prairieville are "typical" or "representative," but rather triangulate commonalities in their historical trajectory, analysis of nonlocal trends, and various academic literatures to establish that these cities' historical trajectory is probably similar to that of other American cities. See end of introduction or Methodological Appendix for further discussion of my comparative logic or conclusion for discussion of my arguments' scope conditions.

34. On politicians' rhetoric, see Smith 2007; Rodgers 2011. On expansion of public expenditure that accompany neoliberal reforms, see Levy 2006.

35. For a review, see Mudge 2008 and Mirowski 2013.

36. See Lefebvre 1979; Harvey 1989; Brenner 2004; Peck, Theodore, and Brenner 2009.

37. Mollenkopf 1983. I draw on urban theory for theoretical models of community leaders' collective activities—especially Stone's (1989) regime theory.

38. Scholars of urban governance have long argued that public culture reflects community leaders' economic and political interests (e.g., Hunter 1953; Molotch 1976; Logan and Molotch 1987). Scholars of grassroots democracy argue that public life has *become* more like this (see esp. McQuarrie 2013; Lee, McNulty, and Shaffer 2013).

39. For a recent exception, see Eliasoph 2011. Development scholars have focused more on relationships between material constraint and civil society (see, e.g., Auyero 2001; Baiocchi 2005). Historical comparativists have analyzed the connection between the voluntary sector and the state (e.g., Clemens 1997; Schudson 1998; Skocpol 2003; Neem 2010), but not the grassroots production of public consciousness.

40. Like Alexander (2006, 31), I assume that the public sphere is irreducible to a single site of face-to-face communication. Following Mead (1934), the public consists of a sphere of mutual intelligibility and a capacity for reflexivity: when engaging publicly, actors are able to anticipate others' attitudes and responses and adjust their activities accordingly.

41. It may appear self-evident that democratic talk should consist of policy arguments crafted to appeal to others' reason, but real people seldom speak this way, and this form of talk often stifles debate. Some people use particularistic appeals—to workers' solidarity, for example—to make universalistic claims: everyone who works deserves life's necessities (Alexander 2006; Haydu 2008; Spillman 2012). Self-interested speakers have traditionally insisted on rational detachment to exclude the uneducated or excessively partisan from public debate (Fraser 1990; Young 1996; Mansbridge 2003).

42. That is, public talk is anchored in an informal pecking order similar to Stone's (1989) urban regimes.

43. See Hunter 1953 on institutional standing and the exercise of urban leadership.

44. On opportunity structures and political incorporation, see Amizade 1993 and Clemens 1997.

45. Social scientists frequently employ game metaphors to analyze symbolic competition (Goffman 1959; Geertz 1973; Bourdieu 1984), including Long's (1958) previous characterization of urban politics as an "ecology of games." Most sociologists associate this style of argument with Bourdieu, who informs my argument. For instance, I discuss leaders' public personae similarly to Bourdieu's analysis of habitus (see opening of chap. 4), and community leaders' public game is effectively a field-like phenomenon (Bourdieu 1984; Levi-Martin 2003; Fligstein and McAdam 2012). Such parallels are unsurprising, because Bourdieu (1985, 13–14) presented concepts like "field" and "habitus" as useful in delineating a scholar's *disinterest* in certain types of explanation: to "revoke the opposition . . . between objectivism and subjectivism [and] revoke the commonsense duality between the individual and the social" (Wacquant 2004, 316)—in other words, to avoid both a "strong program" style form of cultural structuralism (e.g., Alexander 2006; Sewell 2005) and rational choice-style objectivism. Like Bourdieu, I also aim to avoid both extremes, but also avoid the terms "habitus" and "field" in the text because they are jargon-y and occasionally counterintuitive. By public persona, I mean something akin to publicly visible habitus, or the tacit dispositions, tastes, perceptions, and mundane judgments that impact a leader's style of public behavior. I discuss the arena in which leaders play their public game rather than their "field," because the latter conjures images of impersonal forces (e.g., magnetic fields), and therefore promotes the kind of agent-less cultural account that Bourdieu tried to avoid (see Lizardo 2011). Terms

like "arena" and "game" more naturally underscore that any cultural forces "act" only through people.

46. Aldrich 1995; Jacobson 2001; Saunders and Abramawitz 2004; Fiorina, Abrams, and Pope 2005; Baldassari and Gelman 2008; Masket 2009.

47. See, especially, Masket 2009.

48. For an exception, see Chong 2000.

49. Rodgers (2011, 62) actually uses the term "institutionalist realism." The term is not central to his analysis, which focuses on society metaphors in multiple domains, but I find it useful as my focus is on policymakers' prevailing understanding of society—something akin to policy "paradigms" (Kuhn 1962): implicit models of how society works, which make certain problems appear salient and methods for addressing them appear appropriate. My discussion of Keynesianism and neoliberalism is also similar to organizational scholars' discussions of "institutional logics." These scholars also note the spread of market-like logics to many noneconomic domains in recent decades (for a review, see Thornton, Ocasio, and Lounsbury 2012). Some scholars equate Keynesianism with countercyclical economic policies, but this policy preference was rooted in the general understanding that microeconomic principles operate only if governments stabilize macroeconomic conditions (see chap. 1 for discussion).

50. Rodgers (2011, 44) argues that Keynesian-era policymakers thought about markets as concrete, physical places in cities or as markets for particular kinds of goods or services (e.g., labor markets, agricultural markets).

51. See especially Mudge 2008, and also Fourcade-Gournichas and Babb 2002; Prasad 2006; Krippner 2011.

52. In effect, I contrast Keynesianism and Neoliberalism as two ideal-typical political systems. Weber (1978 [1922], 30) pointed to such an account: "A so-called 'social system'—a 'state,' a 'church,' a 'guild' . . . consists purely and exclusively in the possibility that someone has acted, is acting, or will act in such a way that one agent's meaning varies in relation to another . . . a 'state' ceases to 'exist' sociologically as soon as there is no longer the possibility that certain types of meaningful social actions will be performed."

53. By this definition, some ideal-typically Keynesian policies remain in American politics while ideal-typically Neoliberal ones were in place before the 1970s. Such historical overlaps do not preclude analytical periodization. To paraphrase Sahlins (1985), the social world is a world in becoming, not in being.

54. Although Lamont and Swidler (2014) argue that ethnographic studies should also employ triangulation to substantiate arguments.

55. River City and Prairieville were as different as I reasonably could manage, which helped me separate the general from the particular. Naturally, these two cities do not exhaust the full range of possible relationships between political context and the public sphere but—given my aims—two cases were better than one.

56. My arguments about regular people's political reasoning rely on induction due to a dearth of qualitative voting studies. See Methodological Appendix for further discussion.

57. As shorthand, activists do not play community leaders' public games. The term "politics disembedded from community governance" parallels a spontaneous distinction that partners make between community and politics, thereby incorporating a constitutive ambiguity in partners' exercise of public power: it is by defining partisans as "not community" that partners exclude them from governance. Actually, I

show in chapter 6 that activists are part community governance, because partners occasionally bait them and otherwise use them to attain their community goals. Partisans' "disembeddedness" is therefore shorthand for a complex set of dynamics that I unpack fully later. In economic sociology, references to economic action as "embedded" in society (Polanyi 1944; Granovetter 1985) creates a similar ambiguity, because economic action cannot be distinct from social relationships (Krippner 2002; Gemici 2008) or even political relationships if one takes a broad enough view of politics (Gemici 2015), even if it sometimes unfolds according to its own logic. I use the term "disembedded" largely to signal that activists do not orient their activities toward community governance, but also hope to invite critical reflection about the degree to which partisans are truly "disembedded" from contemporary public life rather than constitutive of it.

CHAPTER ONE

1. Berelson, Lazarsfeld, and McPhee 1954.
2. Mauss 2000 [1922].
3. Although there are parallels between my description and those of "machine politics" (e.g., Banfield and Wilson 1966, 115–16), my claim is not that the old families or their clients were materially motivated. Like Auyero (2001), I argue that pre-1980s leaders valued material exchanges because they created social relationships, not vice versa.
4. Rodgers 2011, 3, 62.
5. Ibid., 41–42.
6. Hence Keynesian-era politicians' obsession with attaining full employment via countercyclical spending, but also labor policy, regulation, and much else besides (Rodgers 2011, 47, 49). On Keynesian-era economic textbooks, see also Mirowski 2013, 20. Following Polanyi (1944), Keynesian-era policymakers believed in markets, but not necessarily a self-regulating market society.
7. Mudge 2015.
8. Notably members of the Mont Pelerin Society (Mirowski 2013) and their business backers (Phillips-Fein 2010). This applies also to interest groups that represented the business community (Mizruchi 2013).
9. Quoted in Hacker and Pierson 2011, 189.
10. Davis 2009. See also Espeland and Hirsh 1990; Fligstein 2001; Zorn et al. 2009.
11. See Johnson and Kwak 2011. Restrictions on interstate banking were established as part of the 1927 McFadden Act. Until the 1970s, Iowa law was especially restrictive, preventing banks from operating multiple intrastate branches and effectively ensuring multiple locally owned banks per city.
12. Krippner 2011.
13. Chandler 1990.
14. Fligstein 2001.
15. This is consistent with contemporaneous studies of other urban economies (Galaskiewicz 1985; Safford 2009).
16. The insight that "localism" is constructed by broader political economies originates with urban geographers (e.g., Lefebvre 1979; Harvey 1989; Brenner 2004).
17. See Hunter 1953.
18. I was unable to fact-check this incident, but ones like it occurred, drawing the National Guard.
19. I used a Freeman's closeness to assess centrality.

20. Scott 2013, 82.
21. The Central City Commission was large (39 members), and its centrality therefore somewhat overstates its public importance. The Methodological Appendix discusses why I did not normalize by size.
22. I employ a relational framework throughout: different features of social life enter into mutually reinforcing relationships that allow them to persist coherently over time (Abbott 2001).
23. Local historians told me that Madam Scarlet never existed, but the legend persists, probably because it captures residents' feelings about local inequalities.
24. This is not a reference to the city's actual population, which flat-lined in the 1950s.
25. In chapter 5, I argue that Prairieville emerged as a brief winner during the 1990s-era corporate merger wave; many old families were willing "globalizers" until their businesses were bought out by larger corporations.
26. On "embedded economies" see Granovetter 1985 and Uzzi 1997 for case study employing the concept. The term "embedded" is misleading because all economic relationships are necessarily social and hence "embedded" in society (Krippner 2002; Gemici 2008). It is nevertheless significant that, unlike the "new guys," the old families self-consciously balanced interests that they viewed as economic against those they viewed as noneconomic.
27. Uzzi 1997.
28. Pacewicz 2013b. For historical studies, see Lynd and Lynd 1929; Warner 1963; Hunter 1953; Galaskiewicz 1985.
29. Rather, they were economic and noneconomic.
30. See Mauss's discussion of professions that incorporate the logic of gift and counter-obligation (2000 [1922], 69).
31. For this reason, "embedded exchange" is not "altruistic" (Uzzi 1997): social obligations are not inherently less pressing than economic ones. In either case, there is no free gift (Mauss 2000 [1922]).
32. See Mizruchi's (2013) account of Fortune 500 CEOs.
33. See Chandler 1990; Fligstein 2001.
34. Uzzi (1997) attributed these economic benefits to embedded economies, but also notes possible economic drawbacks: such systems may stifle innovation and lead profitable firms to become "welfare agencies" for others. For more on each city's local economy, see Pacewicz 2013b.
35. Malinowski 2002 [1896]; Caplow 1984.
36. Conversely, refusing to give creates social exclusion (see below discussion of Valley Beef).
37. Some members of River City's patricians described Rhomber Sr. as "too generous" and "want[ing] to be liked by everyone and [giving] away too much."
38. On calling out, see Althusser 1971 and De Leon 2014, 143–45. People identify in multiple ways, but engaging publicly locks in and reifies a particular identity—here, an elite, business-class identity. For similar analyses of public self-presentation, see Mische 2008; Tavory 2016.
39. Other community studies of the postwar period note a similar phenomenon (e.g., Hunter 1953; Warner 1963).
40. On institutional realism, see footnote #49 in Introduction. On Keynesian-era policymakers' inability to expand federal bureaucracies, see Hacker 2002; Clemens 2007; Morgan and Campbell 2011.

41. Hacker 2002; Morgan and Campbell 2011.

42. Smith and Lipsky 1993, 10.

43. Barman 2006. See also Clemens and Guthrie 2010. Policymakers saw nonprofits as more accountable and subject to public pressure (Morgan and Campbell 2011).

44. Prairieville's union leaders were civically active but sometimes identified *all* civic associations with business leaders. "We don't go in for community clubs or organizations," one leader said. "A bunch of old ladies from Sheppfield might play cards once a week and call that a community club. We get together [to] really help people."

45. She might mean the Central City Commission (i.e., no. 1 in table 1.2).

46. On post-1980s chamber endorsements, see chap. 4.

47. Another union-backed councilman briefly served alongside Hal Swift in the 1970s.

48. They also engaged in horse-trading. One union-backed member of the commission reported that "we used [business] people on the board to help our side—and those people used us too. [Like they'd say] 'I got a problem with a furnace.' [We'd say] 'I know a plumber, maybe I'll talk to him, have him go down and fix it for you. Now do me a favor.' That kind of shit." Traditional leaders viewed horse-trading as distinct from faction-building exchanges, because it was one-off and instrumental. It is not unusual for multiple types of gift exchange to co-exist—for instance, the Gimwali, an aggressive bartering that co-occurred with the honorific Kula (Malinowski 2002 [1896]).

49. Data is from the Lincoln Land Institutes' Fiscal Standardized Cities (FiSC) Database and therefore only includes the 100 largest American cities. The Census of American Governments suggests that smaller cities suffered a larger cutback in federal aid in the 1980s.

50. According to Tabb (1982), until New York City's mid-1970s fiscal crisis.

51. Mollenkopf 1983, 137; Biles 2011.

52. Biles 2011; Monkkonen 1995. I discuss patterns in state transfers to municipalities in chapter 4.

53. During his 1974 State of the Union address. Martin (2008, 82) argues, Nixon tried to goad localities into abolishing property taxes by presenting revenue sharing as an alternative revenue source.

54. Fox 1972.

55. Urban scholars' demonization of urban renewal notwithstanding (Jacobs 1961; Gans 1962), I argue in the conclusion that one cannot place sole blame on the fiscal mechanism abused by urban leaders—as opposed to, for instance, institutional racism or 1960s-era urban planners' professional ethos.

56. Like many American municipalities, Prairieville and River City abandoned their strong mayor government in the 1950s in favor of the manager-council form.

57. That is, traditional leaders understood their relations as agonistic rather than antagonistic (Mouffe 2000).

CHAPTER TWO

1. See Moody 1988. The fact that they did so is a significant counterpoint to trends among leaders of national labor organizations like the AFL-CIO, which historians argue adopted a "business unionism" orientation by the 1950s: a narrow focus on workplace and wage issues accompanied by a strategy of cementing gains via legal procedures and alliance with the Democratic Party, not mass mobilization or

working-class appeals (Moody 1988; Eidlin 2015). Scholars argue that business unionism led unions to avoid broader alliances with 1960s-era social movements and hence vulnerable to employer onslaught during the 1970s and '80s, particularly after many Democratic politicians began courting big-business campaign contributions (Moody 1988; see also Hacker and Pierson 2011, 180–82; Eidlin 2015). This chapter illustrates how Keynesian-era policies promoted social-movement unionism at the grassroots, even as other factors promoted union conservatism at the national scale, and may therefore point to a reason for tension between the grassroots rank-and-file and national union leadership in the 1970s (see, e.g., Moody 1988).

2. For more on unions' importance in advocating on behalf of the working-class perspective, see Bartels 2008; Hacker and Pierson 2011; Rosenfeld 2014.

3. Older River Citians sometimes joked about "living in the state of River City," to emphasize the distinction between their Catholicism vis-à-vis mostly protestant Iowa. Younger residents said this, too, but in reference to River City's Democratic heritage relative to historically Republican Iowa.

4. Lynd and Lynd (1929) report similar activities among Middletown's nineteenth-century unions.

5. Fligstein 2001.

6. Denial of Greenfield's rezoning request is in the City Council record, but not the details of the debate. This event contradicts growth machine theory, which emphasizes that local elites are united by a pro-growth ideology (Molotch 1976; Logan and Molotch 1987). However, academic critics of pre-1980s urban governance described local elites as primarily controlling, not growth-obsessed (e.g., Hunter 1953). My suspicion is that growth actually *became* an overarching local interest during the urban crises of the 1970s, hence the appearance of academic treatments emphasizing it (e.g., Molotch 1976; Mollenkopf 1983). For a similar argument, see Harvey 1989.

7. Unionized workers at these three plants constituted over 20% of the city's private sector workforce, according to my rough estimate based on local documents and conversations with older union leaders.

8. The disparity may have been greater. One informant told me that he left a woodworking job that paid 15 cents an hour with no benefits for a job at Green's that paid $1.20 an hour plus benefits and pension in the 1940s.

9. River Citians may also have understood business-union conflicts in generational terms. In the 1960s many union leaders were in their twenties or thirties while many business owners were in their fifties or sixties. For instance, Wally Porter became mayor in his early thirties. It was hard to confirm this hypothesis, because everyone who was active then was over sixty by the time of my fieldwork.

10. See Pacewicz 2015 for exact figures.

11. I count leaders listed as business owners, managers, board of directors, or associated with the Republican Party as business leaders and union leaders, and those associated with the Democratic Party as labor leaders. One Democratic officer, a small business owner, sat on the board of River City Bank. This individual was not involved in any other business clubs or charities. Davis (2009) argues that social relationships with bankers were once necessary to capital from community banks—perhaps that is what happened here.

12. My informants suggest that the latter were sites of conflict during this period. Lynd and Lynd (1929) find similar conflict over symbolically important organizations like those focused on youth activities.

13. United Labor began as an umbrella group for AFL-CIO and non–AFL-CIO unions.

At the time of my fieldwork, the breakdown of leaders who participate in each group did not break down along these lines.

14. For a similar argument, see Clawson and Clawson 1999.

15. Consider, Kimeldorf's (1988) discussion of early twentieth-century unions, which successfully organized service workers like waiters.

16. Clawson and Clawson (1999, 96). The authors make this claim based on review of prior studies.

17. McCammon 1990. See also Rhomberg 2012.

18. Bronfenbrenner and Juravich 1998, 102. For more recent data, see also Brofenbrenner 2009. Since the 2000s, employers have intensified their anti-union tactics and become more reliant on sticks (e.g., threat of firing) over carrots (e.g., unscheduled raises).

19. See Cornfield 1991; Clawson and Clawson 1999.

20. Mizruchi (2013) argues that the leaders of many of America's largest corporations also accepted unions as a political reality during the Keynesian era.

21. Data on contestation of union drives suggests that this was true nationally: employers contested 53.9% of unionization drives in 1962 and 91.4% by 1997 (see, respectively, Prosten 1979; Clawson and Clawson 1999).

22. According to Lin and Tomaskovic-Devey (2013) reliance on financial capital is a strong predictor of intrafirm inequality, likely due in part to corporations' resistance to unionization.

23. In a few cases, leaders followed relatives into positions of union leadership and others identified them as belonging to "union families." But even those with family connections began as line workers, moving up to positions of leadership in the normal way.

24. For more on the difficulty or pressuring a nonlocal employer, see Hawkeye conflict in chap. 6.

25. This is not to say that bargaining units' economic characteristics determined their leaders' public orientation. Some Labor Council leaders represented amalgamated locals *because* they were active in organizers.

26. The local rootedness of locally owned and public sector employers is self-evident. Amalgamated locals consisted of tiny units based in different employers—a dispersion of members that, I think, minimized risk of capital flight by a single firm and encouraged pan-unionism. My interpretation of amalgamated unions differs from Moody (1988), who characterizes organizing unrelated units as a substitute for sustained intra-industry mobilization.

27. Transportation and construction locals have traditionally been business-friendly because many contract directly with employers.

28. This estimate is based on self-reports.

29. I recorded in field notes that this confrontation was over a "certification" issue, but must have misunderstood as a school board cannot decertify a union. According to public records, Denise was involved in closed-door contract negotiations between the school board and several public sector unions in the early 2000s. Labor Council probably leaders objected to something that happened during these negotiations.

CHAPTER THREE

1. On ideal types, see Weber 1978 [1922].

2. Key 1961. See also Aldrich 1995.

3. See n. 1 in the preface.

4. See Aldrich 1995; Neem 2010; De Leon 2014.

5. Except indirectly through correspondence committees and the partisan press (Aldrich 1995). On transition to mass parties, see De Leon 2010; Klinghard 2010.

6. Aldrich 1995; Masket 2009.

7. Clemens 1997. America's first mass parties also arose when self-identified party representatives made new kinds of alliances with social movements and lobbies (Klinghard 2010; De Leon 2010). Activists' 1970s era takeover of grassroots parties was therefore perhaps an American political realignment par excellence.

8. My analysis is based on FEC documents (after 1972) as reported in the Financing the Election series (e.g., Alexander 1971). The "Democratic Party" includes the Democratic National Committee (DNC), the Democratic Senatorial Selection Committee (DSSC), the Democratic Congressional Selection Committee (DCSC), the Democratic Governors Association, and the Democratic National Convention Committee. The "Republican Party" includes the Republican National Committee (RNC), the Republican Senatorial Selection Committee (RSSC), the Republican Congressional Selection Committee (RSSC), and the Republican Convention Committee.

9. I do not include 1968 in the chart, because I was unable to find estimates of non-party spending.

10. See Aldrich 1995.

11. Alexander 1971.

12. This changed with Republicans' discovery of direct mail fundraising in the late 1970s, which brought a windfall of donations (Hacker and Pierson 2011, 173).

13. Ehrenhalt 1992, xix, 45, 69, 105, 88.

14. Ibid., 164. Cases like Alabama suggest that, consistent with my argument, Keynesian-era policies promoted the emergence of factions, which included representatives of racial minorities in places with higher minority populations than River City and Prairieville. Stone (1989) also describes opposition between a white coalition to downtown business owners and black leaders based predominantly in neighborhoods in 1960s Atlanta (he also found more interfactional bargaining than I found in my cases). Alternatively, Mollenkopf (1983) argues that tensions between the Democratic Party's white-ethnic and minority supporters ultimately splintered the new Deal Coalition in the 1970s, but—due to the absence of the latter group—such intra-Democratic conflicts never occurred in my cities. Perhaps their 1970s-era politics was more akin to the 1950s- and '60s-era politics of other American cities.

15. See Key 1952; Sundquist 1983; Carmines and Stimson 1989; Aldrich 1995; Fiorina 1999; Aldrich and Rohde 2000; Fiorina, Abrams, and Pope 2005; Layman et al. 2010.

16. See Aldrich 1995; Skocpol and Fiorina 1999; Jacobson 2001; Fiorina, Abrams, and Pope 2005; Masket 2009.

17. See Baldassari and Gelman 2008; Layman et al. 2010; Masket 2009 on the polarization of party identifiers.

18. Skocpol (2003) argues that community leaders lost interest in politics after the decline of federated civil associations. I have addressed this argument extensively elsewhere (Pacewicz 2015).

19. See McAdam and Kloos 2014 for an account of why party leaders allowed changes in delegate selection.

20. For other social movement–based accounts of parties, see Mudge and Chen 2014; De Leon 2014. Elsewhere, McAdam and Kloos (2014, 19–20) argue that postwar

social movements "spared" parties from pressure or that those who did not—like the "suburban warriors" who succeeded in getting Ronald Reagan governor of California (McGirr 2002; Martin 2008)—were not significant enough to permanently impact parties.

21. McAdam and Kloos 2014, 216. The authors focus only on congressional politics.

22. In chapter 8.

23. On California, see McGirr 2002; Martin 2008; on Colorado see Ehrenhalt 1992, 194. On dearth of histories of grassroots parties, see Masket 2009, 44.

24. See Masket 2009.

25. Layman et al. 2010, 4. See also Polsby and Wildavsky 1991.

26. Congressional races were characterized by competitive primaries long before and state and local elections by a patchwork of idiosyncratic practices (see Boatright 2013). Traditional leaders also maintained an ability to dominate the county nominating conventions that actually select delegates. Two of Prairieville's 1984 DNC delegates were none other than Daniel and Frannie Steele.

27. This is a good a place as any to note parallels between my account and histories of Progressive-era urban reforms. Progressive reformers and partners' aims were similar (e.g., create an unbridgeable gap between urban and partisan politics), but ultimate goal was different: progressive reformers wanted to insulate partisan politics from the influence of ethnic urban machines (see, e.g., Clemens 1997; Klinghard 2010), whereas partners wanted to more successfully market their city to outsiders (see chap. 4).

28. Fuchs 1992. Ware (1985, 45), for example, conducted a survey of American cities and found that in supposed machine strongholds like 1960s-era Detroit, only 17% of precinct captains showed up on election day and performed all of the tasks assigned to them by the party boss.

29. For instance, Banfield and Wilson (1966, 115) compare political machines to "a business organization in a particular field of business—getting votes and winning elections." My critique is similar to Auyero's (2001), who argues that the material exchanges are constitutive of an ideology of reciprocation, a point he documents by showing that only a minority of residents in a Peronist Argentinean slum actually received benefits from "bosses."

30. Following Mauss (2000 [1922]), most gifts bind collectivities, not individuals.

31. Traditional community leaders also did not reap big economic rewards—indeed, they certainly forwent economic gain if one considers their unpaid labor on public initiatives. For instance, Frannie Steele enjoyed some perks like a partially financed trips to political conventions, but it is unclear why one would view a hectic political convention as a "material benefit" unless one were passionate about politics. Similarly, Dahl (1961) observed that political notables "took care" of their supporters' parking tickets—by secretly paying them themselves.

32. See Mizruchi 2013.

33. Kabaservice 2011; McAdam and Kloos 2014.

34. DNC and RNC convention delegates' views on most issue polarized most sharply later in the 1980s, a decade after changes to party nomination procedures (see Layman et al. 2010, 331).

35. Skocpol (2003) argues that civic life is increasingly dominated by "body-less heads" like the Sierra Club or NRA that rely on mass campaigns over federated chapters for funding. But politics is an exception, because politicians need votes, which require

grassroots mobilization, especially in early primary states like Iowa. Indeed, community leaders' avoidance of politics is especially surprising in Iowa, because they are key to the prospects of powerful politicians and have unparalleled access to them.

36. Those who are most central in my historical narrative did not always register as most central in social network analyses. As Hunter (1953) notes, powerful people often wield authority through surrogates. I found social network analysis useful for locating populations of important individuals, but not establishing an ordinal status ranking.

37. See Methodological Appendix.

38. Prairieville leaders' high engagement in democratic bodies is partially due to the centrality of the Central City Commission. This organization included many prominent figures, but my analysis also counted some leaders as central by virtue of involvement in this association and at the expense of others who were not so engaged and more prominent. Charles Browning Sr. served on ten business and Republican associations, but wielded influence on public commissions indirectly via his contacts and did not register as one of Prairieville's thirty most central leaders.

39. See Mische 2008, 21.

40. Members of Iowa's Educational Associations typically do not identify as blue-collar or union leaders.

41. Labels like "mother" and "party home" indicate a tendency to define women's work as emotional and private, men's work as instrumental and public (see, e.g., de Beauvoir 2014; Hochschild and Machung 1989). Nevertheless, the fact that people understood Frannie's Table as feminine (and hence caring, nurturing, and so on) underscores that there is nothing inherently "machine-like" about a politics of gift and counterobligation.

42. I heard the term "labor lawyer" only in Prairieville, not River City.

43. Democratic activists no longer seemed to do this at the time of my fieldwork.

44. To clarify: the reported aim of this practice was to allow activists to quickly hide that they had mixed union and voter lists if confronted (i.e., by shaking out one deck of cards).

45. River City's Rotary Club conducted a similar poll, with similar results. I was unable to find historical lists of Rotary club membership and do not include the organization in network analyses.

46. Prairieville's chamber still endorses candidates, but occasional supports Democrats (see chap. 4).

47. De Leon, Desai, and Tuğal 2009.

48. Berelson, Lazarsfeld, and McPhee (1954) argued that people often use memories of past political realities to make sense of current ones. I did not select interviewees randomly from within either city and am therefore technically unable to conclude that traditional voters were older. I describe traditional voters as "older residents" throughout, because this association was theoretically consistent with my model of preference change (see Methodological Appendix).

49. Like the Elmira researchers, I found that models of thinking about politics and the people who employ them are loosely coupled: people reason about politics differently depending on who they talk with, the period of the election cycle, and idiosyncratic factors.

50. The alternative to this two-stage causal model is to assume that voters are charac-

terized by fixed, context-independent political preferences—an assumption that is demonstrably false (Alvarez and Brehm 2002).

51. See Sniderman, Brody, and Tetlock 1993; Zaller 1992; Alvarez and Brehm 2002; Baldassari 2013. Many scholars in this tradition argue that group identification—what I label the logic of sides—is most voters' primary heuristic (see, e.g., Brady and Sniderman 1985).

52. These is therefore nothing surprising about people's political preferences being inconsistent with their factual knowledge, a finding that social scientists sometimes trumpet as significant (e.g., Prasad et al. 2009). I never contradicted my informants, but sometimes interviewed jointly with others who did, and was always struck by how unconcerned people were upon having their grasp of the facts challenged. They simply moved to a different set of facts.

53. Note that any attempt to formally classify Shirley's ideology would place her in the lowest category of political sophistication—Converse's category E (1964). But her justification makes perfect sense in her social context.

54. Political scientists typically argue that high educational levels and political knowledge are positively correlated with strong and stable political preferences (Berelson, Lazarsfeld, and McPhee 1954; Miller and Shanks 1996). But while educational levels and access to political information increased in recent decades, rates of partisan identification have declined, especially among young people, which suggests that the variable may have no context-independent effects.

55. See n. 17 in the introduction.

56. People also reason under conditions of bounded rationality (March and Simon 1958): they have access to selective information, are unable to obtain better information without making unacceptable sacrifices, and satisfice by using the best information available. In pre-1980s River City and Prairieville, voters were unable to verify if candidates were sincere in their promises without great effort; it was arguably rational for them to trust community leaders to vet candidates—provided that community leaders were accountable to residents.

57. Mollenkopf 1983.

CHAPTER FOUR

1. Partnership is also based on implicit gift-giving norms, but the gift is not a reciprocal one between actors; rather, it is a joint gift to the community. The gift of partnership is analogous to Mauss's discussion of joint sacrifices to a deity—acts that create a sense of spiritual kinship, not direct interparticipant ties (2000 [1922], 15–16).

2. See Sellers 2002.

3. Like Bourdieu (1985, 13–14), I invoke habitus (and, more frequently, public persona) to signal *rejection* of both a rational choice framework that portrays actors as responding instrumentally to structural incentives and a cultural paradigm that portrays actors as merely the agents of a coherent cultural system (e.g., Alexander 2006; Sewell 2005). "Culture" and "structure" are analytical constructs and cannot operate on the same ontological plane as human action (see, e.g., Lizardo 2011). I employ terms like "public persona" and "public game" to avoid an untenable antipathy between culturally and structurally induced action by focusing on people's situated reasoning (see also Reed 2011).

4. See, respectively, Evans-Pritchard 1956; Malinowski 2002 [1896].

5. Like Bourdieu, I assume that changes in historical conditions—namely, 1970s-era

federal reforms—matter not because they bear continuously on the rational calculations of individuals, but because people internalize an affinity for forms of action that allow them to attain immanent necessities. Community leaders' public personae are a repository of past efforts to leverage resources, rise in esteem, and establish solidarity with one another.

6. Harvey 1989. Urban geographers commonly equate partnerships with neoliberalism, but seldom specify why urban actors find them useful (see, e.g., Jessop 2002; Brenner 2004; Brenner and Theodore 2002).

7. Similarly, McQuarrie (2013) argues that new models of public engagement allow leaders to discipline the public. That is true of partnerships, but I think tangential to why community leaders embraced them.

8. On urban leaders' adherence to a neoliberal script, see Sellers 2002. My critique of scholars' treatment of urban culture is directed at growth machine theory (Molotch 1976; Logan and Molotch 1987), which presents cities' public life as subsumed to elites' overriding desire for growth. Molotch (1993, 5–6) sought to incorporate culture by arguing that elites use their cultural capital to hoodwink politicians and regulators, but this formulation presents culture as an ideological script rather than an embodied sensibility. Missing is the fact that urban leaders, like all actors, operate within a social system, attain their ends only by working with others, and adjust their behavior to their own and one another's understanding of proper and useful action—an insight that is more evident in approaches like urban regime theory (Stone 1989; see also Pacewicz 2015).

9. Following Stone (1989), community leaders rely on informal institutions to coordinate their activities and internalize these institutions' norms, viewing them as synonymous with their own interests. That is, culture is an intersubjective agreement that constrains via "in order to" propositions. To be a sociologist, I need to be hired by a university; to be a mid-life success, I need to buy a home and cannot spend my money on beer.

10. In this way, "structures" constrain and enable actors (Sewell 1992) by providing the resources they need for certain types of performances. For a similar formulation, see Bourdieu and Johnson 1993.

11. On rising inequality, see Pikkety and Saez 2003, which Bartels (2008, 296) notes is due to American public policy, not globalization or a postindustrial transitions (i.e., because other advanced democracies have not seen an increase in inequality akin to the American one). Bartels attributes this trend to the GOP's electoral successes after 1972, but Republicans have also been more anti-Keynesian (52). Recall that Eisenhower denunciation of Republican opponents of the New Deal (Hacker and Pierson 2011, 189). Contrast to Reagan's economic positions (Smith 2007, 137–38), who was tame in turn relative to the post-1994 GOP (Hacker and Pierson 2011, 163). After Republicans abandoned their commitment to fiscal conservatism, Democrats like Clinton stepped in to fill the void, essentially abandoning their commitment to countercyclical and social spending (Hacker and Pierson 2011, 177–82). For more on the right-ward shift of left parties, see Mudge 2011.

12. On institutional realism, see n. 48 in the introduction.

13. This is a reference to the Samuelson textbook, the gold standard within economics and public policy programs (Rodgers 2011, 44–47; Mirowski 2013, 21).

14. Rodgers 2011, 4, 66.

15. See Mudge 2008; Wacquant 2012.

16. On Mont Pelerin society, see Mirowski 2013, Harvey 2005, 22. Eisenhower quote from Hacker and Pierson 2011, 189.

17. On proliferation of organizations associated with the Mont Pelerin society, see Smith 2007, 82–87; Mirowski 2011. Business associations before the 1970s were sometimes favorable to aspects of the New Deal (Mizruchi 2013) and did not advocate for across-the-board deregulation (Smith 2007, 105–7; Hacker and Pierson 2011, 119–23), although some businesses supported the Mont Pelerin society from its inception (Phillips-Fein 2010).

18. Rodgers 2011, 50. Krippner (2011) describes a similar crisis of confidence among policymakers, but attributes it to an inability to meet constituents' conflicting demands (see also Mollenkopf 1983).

19. Rodgers (2011) argues that "slippage" across partisan divides occurred with other "thin society" metaphors. This trend was reinforced by economist who had long been central to parties on the left and experienced their own shift away from Keynesianism in the 1970s (Mudge 2015).

20. On Ralph Nader's role in deregulation, see Smith 2007, 105; Prasad 2006, Krippner 2011.

21. Hayek 1944, 42. On Hayek's role within the Mont Pelerin society, see Mirowski 2013. Proponents of neoliberalism initially emphasized Hayek's moral arguments over the superior efficiency of markets, as did extreme candidates like Barry Goldwater (Smith 2007).

22. Hayek 1944, 45. Members of the Mont Pelerin Society like Milton Friedman initially referred to themselves as "neoliberal" and equated their program with state intervention, but later espoused laissez-faire and libertarian positions in public pronouncements—possibly as a public relations tactic (see Mirowski 2013, 29, 38).

23. Mirowski 2013, 57. Some scholars equate neoliberalism with expanding of incarceration (Wacquant 2001). The argument is that the poor have nothing (economic) to lose and require extramarket incentives (Mirowski 2013, 65).

24. Levy 2006.

25. Wacquant 2006; Mudge 2008; Peck 2010; Mirowski 2013. This formulation sidesteps many critiques of the idea of neoliberalism, which hinge on the fact that neoliberalism is not a coherent program supported by academic economists (e.g., Venugopal 2015). Others critique the concept because neoliberalism sometimes refers to apparently disconnected historical trends. I think this second critique accurate, but public policies' multifaceted nature should not dissuade scholars from discussing the ideal-typical features of post-1980s political systems—provided that one views the 1970s and '80s as a political-economic turning point, something which even critics of the concept of neoliberalism typically accept. See the conclusion for further discussion.

26. Mudge 2008; Wacquant 2012.

27. Chandler 1990; Davis 2009; Krippner 2011.

28. Galaskiewicz 1985; Fligstein 2001; Safford 2009.

29. Krippner (2011) attributes this to a little-know policy: regulation Q.

30. Private sector initiatives like new investment vehicles and securitization also allowed individuals to circumvent financial subdivisions by tapping into markets (Davis 2009). Financial regulations were also loosened by federal bureaucrats, rather than congressional action, and generally via "drift," or policymakers' failure to create new programs and regulations to keep up with a changing world (Hacker

and Pierson 2011)—for instance, by failing to regulate new financial derivatives (Funk and Hirschman 2014).

31. Fligstein 2001; Davis 2009; Krippner 2011.

32. Fligstein 2001. This was also due to changes in antitrust enforcement; legal scholars previously defined monopoly in terms of market share, but later came to regard monopolies as undesirable only where they undermined efficiency—a view legitimated by perspectives like Williamson's (1981) transaction cost perspective (Rodgers 2011).

33. Zorn et al. 2009; Fligstein 2001. For intrafirm consequences, see Lin and Tomaskovic-Devey 2013.

34. Espeland and Hirsch 1990.

35. On merger wave, see Fligstein 2001. On rates of mergers, see Zorn et al. 2009.

36. Krippner (2011) argues that prices, unlike governmental controls, are poor economic restraints.

37. Davis 2009.

38. Galaskiewicz 1985; Smith and Lipsky 1993.

39. Biles 2011, 252. Reagan's New Federalism is not to be confused with a Nixon-era policy doctrine of the same name. Nixon and Reagan's new federalism were both touted as increasing local autonomy, but Nixon's primary policy lever was revenue sharing while Reagan's was cuts in federal funding—clearly, a different kind of autonomy.

40. This was due to Title XX of the Social Security act, which replaced Title VI (Smith and Lipsky 1993).

41. The policy initially increased accountability in fields like mental health when states replaced large mental hospitals with community health centers, achieving both savings and better mental health outcomes.

42. This was especially true for nonprofits that received disproportionate federal cuts (e.g., job training, child welfare services, women's shelters). Chernick and Reschovsky (1999) call this "leakage."

43. Morgan and Campbell 2011.

44. Clemens and Guthrie 2010; Morgan and Campbell 2011.

45. Barman 2006.

46. Biles 2011, 236, 243–50.

47. Following Mudge 2008, Carter era politicians still looked at urban policy and asked "how much state?" while Carter's solution offered the answer to "how much market?"

48. Cited in Biles 2011, 237. According to Rothenberg (1984), a new generation of 1980s-era Democrats (e.g., Gary Hart, Al Gore, Bill Bradley, Robert Reich) equated attention to such wonky policy details with good governance.

49. Biles 2011, 237. UDAG grants were enacted two years later, but in limited form.

50. Ibid.

51. Via the administration's flagship "Choice Neighborhoods" program (see Dodds 2013).

52. Biles 2011.

53. Several New England states are currently experimenting with social service bonds, which are backed by projected savings achieved via outsourcing of public sector programs.

54. For more on TIF, see Weber 2010; Pacewicz 2013a.

55. Hackworth 2007.

56. Sbragia (1996) argues that they also favor municipalities that engage in public-sector rollback, aggressive place-marketing, and are inhabited by middle- and upper-class residents.

57. The latter is important, because partnerships are predicated on the ideology of win-win, but public consensus is notoriously difficult when tight budgets necessitate tradeoffs. A reoccurring theme in partnerships is the critical importance of revenue streams that are more Keynesian-like—that is, un-earmarked for particular functions—which allow leaders to preserve consensus when unexpected shortfalls in competitive funding (see, for instance, the Hawkeye incident in chap. 7). Those who have access to such discretionary funding are particularly advantaged in their city's post-1980s public game (Pacewicz 2013a).

58. There is no reason to expect that any city dominated by partners would contain a single key broker; for instance, larger places might have a key partnership-builder within each policy domain. But for reasons that I discuss below, the logic of partnership favors one key partnership-builder per partnership.

59. Prairieville's Development Corporation later became less important, but Dover's Taskforce adopted its ethos.

60. Prairieville experienced a massive 1990s influx of Hispanic immigrants who worked in area packing plants, hence the latter partnership. Prairieville's leaders struggled to identify Hispanic leaders to include in this partnership.

61. Prairieville development taskforce did not make its board public and is not in this analysis.

62. In River City and Prairieville, Democratic Donors and Officers appear relatively central because these groups include otherwise disconnected individuals: traditional labor leaders, partisan politicians who are some development organization seats, and a few leaders of artistic and cultural nonprofits. I discuss these anomalies in chapter 8.

63. Data quality makes it difficult to definitively compare 1970s- and 2000s-era social network analyses, but density appears to have declined during this period—fewer leaders were involved in multiple associations and those who were so-engaged were involved in fewer associations than their 1970s-era counterparts (recall too Charles Browning's report in the introduction: there are fewer people to "call on"). With leaders relatively disconnected, the ability of big tents to provide formal brokering was especially useful.

64. An incentive worth an estimated $3 million. Developers I spoke with believed that city land is overvalued, but it is almost always sold at half-price (see Pacewicz 2013b)—so Sunflower still got a good deal.

65. De Certeau (1984) makes this argument about a city's spatial makeup. When one takes a different path between two points, one performs a locutionary or speech act-like act, enacting a particular version of the city (see Austin 1962; Searle 1969). In using this metaphor, I de-emphasize De Certeau's focus on the built environment, but import the assumption that there is no single authoritative representation of the city

66. See Pacewicz 2013a, 2013b.

67. This historical account of the politics of emergency food aid is based on Bouek 2014.

68. Lipsky and Thibodeau 1990. The United States has historically supported domestic agriculture by subsidizing commodity prices and purchasing surpluses (Pollan 2006).

69. See Kantor et al. 1997; Morenoff 2002.
70. Feeding America also maintains a monopoly over corporations' food donations, but only nationally. Regional foodbanks are free to contract with regional distributors.

CHAPTER FIVE

1. When I began fieldwork, my informants frequently used the term "Country Club Republican," then abandoned the term in favor of "Republican in Name Only" or "RINO." I think that RINO was popularized on right-wing radio stations, but gained popularity only by piggy-backing on the existing "Country Club Republican"—Activist split.
2. Skocpol and Williamson (2012) observed a similar more-moderate libertarians and purist Christian conservative split among tea party activists.
3. Layman et al. 2010.
4. Masket 2009.
5. Eliasoph 1998.
6. For similar critiques, see Lee 2011; McQuarrie 2013; Lee, McQuarrie, and Walker 2014.
7. See Skocpol 2003; Skocpol and Fiorina 1999.
8. Goffman 1959.
9. Only one of River City's homegrown industries successfully deployed this strategy: River City's newspaper, which acquired nearby cities' newspapers.
10. Prairieville's business leaders also mentioned restarting the Labor-Management Council.
11. The number increased to two after Dani Dover lobbied the US Census to expand Prairieville's MSA to include a far-flung, but affluent satellite city. Because consumer-oriented businesses make location decisions based on MSA demographics, higher-end stores also subsequently appeared in Prairieville.
12. See Florida 2002. Amenity-driven development usually does not pay off for reasons identified by critics (Harvey 1989): place-entrepreneurs value creativity, spontaneity, and uniqueness, but pursue similar amenities. There is hardly a rust-belt city without a farmer's market, art walk, and flashy debt-financed redevelopment effort.
13. Traditional leaders were not exactly intolerant of difference, but they expected their peers to foreground common identities (i.e., blue- or white-collar credentials). See chap. 3 for further discussion.
14. For similar dramaturgical models of action, see Mead 1934; Goffman 1959; and Bourdieu 1984, 1990.
15. This energetic versus passive distinction later appeared as a polarizing principle within the Tea Party (Skocpol and Williamson 2012), which I argue in chapter 7 was a mere formalization of pre-existing Republican splits.

CHAPTER SIX

1. The concept of constitutive exception parallels Žižek's (1989) discussion of constitutive misrecognition: a mistaken assumption about social order, which recreates that social order. Žižek (2006) illustrates this concept with the caricatured subjectivity of financial traders. One says, "there's nothing special about finance, I'd fix cars if I thought I could make as much money," and believes himself to be critiquing the ideology of his profession, but has actually just articulated the mindset that makes for a successful trader.
2. See table 4.1.

3. I tried in vain to find this t-shirt, and several amateur historians eventually confirmed that it was an urban legend. A "copy" of the original *was* sold en masse during the 25th anniversary of River City's hard times.

4. These accounts are plausible given that early partners came from those in unique economic niches. Local bankers like Pete were also uniquely positioned to recognize the extent of local economic troubles. Greenfield's union leaders represented workers in a single plant, which corporate headquarters was considering moving to Mexico.

5. This was a state program, not the federal Enterprise Zone program.

6. This was a misguided statement to be sure as the conflict revolved around a public-sector subsidy, which classical liberals and neoliberals alike decry as antithetical to free markets (Smith 2003 [1776]; Hayek 1944).

7. The Labor Council is the official political representative of labor in River City, but was also labor's pre-1980s community mouthpiece.

8. None of these individuals took actual leadership positions in the party and only Kathy Gooding and Doug Whitter made party donations sufficient to count as "donors" (see chap. 7).

9. See also figure 4.2.

10. Ron portrayed his green city initiative similarly. "I started educating: in the future communities will be judged by how green and sustainable they are," he explained. "The kind of people we need to attract and keep here, [also] really see that as a priority. When I explained [this to city council, they] became excited about the initiative."

11. See n. 5 in the preface for information about shortening quotes.

12. Social psychologists argue that two-facedness is an inherently source of cognitive stress, or dissonance, one that most people avoid by changing their behavior or beliefs (Festinger 1962).

13. Gadflies like Andy once frequented city council, but gravitated toward partisan politics by the 2000s.

14. This is how River City's partners explained the loss. The account is plausible, because Ben turned down PAC funding and was unable to compete effectively in outlying towns without TV advertising.

15. Labor Council leaders recognized that Ben carried a majority of River City's Democrats, but also mobilized their regional network of union contacts against his campaign. This in connection with Ben's low advertising budget may accounts for Ben's loss.

CHAPTER SEVEN

1. See n. 1 in the preface.

2. On issue displacement, see Schattschneider 1942; Sundquist 1983; Carmines and Stimson 1989; Miller and Schofield 2003.

3. On conflict extension see Jacobson 2001; Aldrich and Rohde 2000; Fiorina, Abrams, and Pope 2005.

4. See Cohen et al. 2008; Masket 2009, 5; McAdam and Kloos 2014.

5. The median voter theorem (Downs 1957).

6. Baldassari and Gelman 2008.

7. Chapter 4 for a discussion of these trends. On vote propensities see Berelson, Lazarsfeld, and McPhee 1954.

8. See nn. 3 and 4 in the preface.

9. See Canes-Wrone, Brady, and Cogan 2002; Fiorina 1999; Masket 2009; McAdam and Kloos 2014.

10. Skocpol 2003.

11. Following VO Key's distinction, it is equally plausible that political donations have strengthened parties-in-legislature: congressional leaders' ability to coerce legislators. But political scientists identify strong legislative parties with the early twentieth century, when "party czars" controlled committees with access to graft (Aldrich 1995, 232). Today, one is more accustomed to hearing about legislative leaders "losing control" of their parties to extreme elements (e.g., to the Tea Party caucus).

12. See especially *Buckley v. Valeo* 1976, which struck down the Federal Election Campaign Act's independent expenditures cap. This decision established the "magic word" clause: independent expenditures can contain any information if they do not mention candidates by name (Thurber and Nelson 2014, 82).

13. PACs typically engage in attack ads, because it is easier to present these as uncoordinated with a campaign.

14. The Citizens United established that unions and corporations can fund independent expenditures without forming a PAC. A later decision, Speechnow.org v. the F.E.C. 2010, established that PACs can make unlimited independent expenditures provided that they do not donate to candidates, parties or other PACs. Thus the "Super-PAC" was born: an organization that can take in unlimited contributions and use them only on (largely negative TV) advertising. Figure 3.1 indicates that nonparty organizations' political expenditures did increase substantially in 2012.

15. See Financing the Election Series (e.g., Alexander 1971), which habitually makes this comparison.

16. Thurber and Nelson (2014, 83) estimate that 75% of all political money during the 2012 election was spent on advertising, two-thirds of which went to television commercials.

17. On Howard Dean's 50-State Strategy, see Bai 2007, 154.

18. On Republican efforts, see Hacker and Pierson 2011, 208. On Democratic efforts, see Bai 2007, 260–74.

19. On California, see McGirr 2002; Martin 2008; on Colorado see Ehrenhalt 1992, 194.

20. Ehrenhalt 1992; McAdam and Kloos 2014.

21. See Bai 2007.

22. Aldrich 1995; Masket 2009.

23. In chapter 3, I argued that party rules concerning nomination procedures were not primarily responsible for activists' grassroots takeover, which may appear inconsistent with this discussion. But primaries actually *diminished* party leaders' influence over nominations; the key change is who runs the party, not whether they wield their influence in back rooms as traditional leaders once did or low-turnout primaries like contemporary activists.

24. See Masket 2009 or Layman et al. 2010 for a review.

25. See Layman et al. 2010, 331.

26. Political scientists were slow to note activists' takeover of parties, because they ceased studying grassroots parties after interpreting traditional leaders' exit as party breakdown and shift to candidate-centered politics (e.g., Polsby 1983; Rosenstone and Hansen 1993). See Aldrich 1995, Masket 2009; Mudge and Chen 2014; De Leon 2014.

27. Masket 2009, 3. Masket argues that these ideological parties serve the same func-

tions as traditional machines, but notes that some resemble a network more than a hierarchy (19).

28. See tables 3.1 and 3.2

29. See Layman et al. 2010, 9, on interpersonal influence within activist parties.

30. McAdam and Kloos 2014.

31. An organization akin to Durkheim's "segmental form" (1997 [1893]).

32. Elsewhere, Tea Party members were also mostly active Republicans (Skocpol and Williamson 2012; Heaney and Rojas 2015).

33. This shift among GOP grassroots *leaders* may explain the common and mistaken belief that low-income voters became more Republican in recent decades (Bartels 2008; Gelman 2010).

34. This phenomenon is described by Abbott (2001) as the fractal-like organization of social life: subdivisions of institutions tend to be organized similarly to larger institutions.

35. Masket 2009, 3.

36. Activists who were sympathetic to Prairieville's partners cycled in and out of the party, but rarely stayed for long. Kathy Irving was probably the one who stayed engaged longest. One regular Democratic activist, an attorney, was active in many artistic groups but not economic development partnerships.

37. One exception was Wally Porter, River City's first union-backed mayor who served as a Democratic officer *since* the 1960s and was vocally anti-Republican. I struggled to categorize Wally because he was friendly with everyone: development planners and partners, Democratic activists, and even traditional union leaders. I finally concluded that he played the role of elder, indeed eldest, statesman who was simply beyond the public norms that bound others.

38. But a few divisive statements would not have endangered Patty's community status because partners applied different standards to politicians, viewing them as an unreliable—if necessary—class (see chap. 6).

39. See Skocpol and Williamson 2012; Heaney and Rojas 2015.

CHAPTER EIGHT

1. On heuristics, see Sniderman, Brody, and Tetlock 1993; Zaller 1992; Alvarez and Brehm 2002.

2. Berelson, Lazarsfeld, and McPhee 1954.

3. This presents a problem for contemporary voting studies that establish correlations between types of voters and voting preferences. Berelson, Lazarsfeld, and McPhee (1954, 14) write: "an election is partially a race against time as well as against the opposition. What matters is who is ahead on election day." They argue that holding an election two weeks early could change the outcome, although this may overstate an election's unpredictably, because they also showed that a predictable process of repolarization occurs immediately before the vote—an issue I discuss in chapter 9.

4. Glaser and Strauss 1967.

5. Many methodologists (Lamont and White 2008; Small 2009) argue that aiming for representative samples wastes qualitative researchers' time as numbers of respondents and response rates will never allow for statistical inference.

6. Following Schutz (1970), they become "topical."

7. On Envisioning, see Lee 2011, 2015.

8. For a similar characterization of working-class life trajectories, see Silva 2013.

9. As I note in the appendix, there is no way to know if this pattern holds for River City

and Prairieville as a whole absent a representative sample. The pattern is consistent with my theoretical model: younger and civically engaged people were especially exposed to partner-dominated institutions.

10. Not unlike Democratic partners who denounced GOP sympathizers (see chap. 7).

11. This is consistent with national trends: Independents who "lean" toward a political party vote, donate money, and volunteer for campaigns at rates nearly identical to true Independents (Dimoch et al. 2014).

12. See Methodological Appendix.

CHAPTER NINE

1. As a Democrat myself, I felt similarly.

2. Many activists bird-dogged on behalf of a PAC.

3. On narratives, see Somers 1994; Polletta 1998; Abbott 2007. Although the media frequently defined candidates, Iowa was unusual in that candidates could self-construct narratives in rallies like this one.

4. This makes partner-like voters opposite of voters described by Elmira researchers, who were typically politically disinterested, then energized pre-election.

5. Conversely, a few older working-class whites identified African Americans as a traditional Democratic constituency and supported Obama because they expected him to deliver New Deal–style policies.

6. Some informants mixed traditional and partisan orientations (i.e., they identified with pre-1980s leaders, but sometimes said that all leaders had been co-opted). But these orientations were difficult to distinguish and, since traditional and partisans were similarly impacted by electoral dynamics, I did not do so.

7. I did not interview a random sample of residents and cannot conclude that these patterns are representative of other River Citians and Prairievillers. My aim here is to demonstrate the analytical utility of my ideal-types—a goal distinct from statistical inference (see Methodological Appendix).

8. Berelson, Lazarsfeld, and McPhee 1954.

9. In 2007–8, John McCain did not actively campaign during the Iowa caucuses and did not come up often in interviews, but partner-like voters seemed to like him when he did.

10. Most Iowa cities differ from the United States in that they contain few racial minorities until recently—a fact that may make their politics somewhat unusual (see n. 17 in chapter 3). A lack of information about minority respondents is a limitation of my study. However, River City and Prairieville experienced large influxes of African Americans and Hispanic immigrants during the 2000s, which created racial tensions and discussions among whites that were probably similar to those elsewhere.

11. According to a post-election email survey.

12. Berelson, Lazarsfeld, and McPhee 1954.

13. John Edwards' political career was ended by an affair he had while his wife battled breast cancer. But a lot of smart people did not see that coming! In 2008, I was an Edwards supporter.

14. Only partisans advocated extreme measures like political violence if their candidate lost and gravitated toward movements like the Tea Party.

15. I take no position of informants' racism or lack thereof. Overt racism is relatively rare in twenty-first-century public life and I find it more productive to describe the ways that people communicate political information in potentially racially coded ways (Hartigan 2010): for instance, via references to (probably white) "average Joes"

or (possibly minority) "people waiting for handouts." Because race was not my research focus, I did not probe into such statements' undertones, except to note that people deployed racially coded statements flexibly depending on their orientation toward Obama. For instance, some working-class whites perceived Obama's race as a sign that he was committed to the downtrodden, whereas partners evaluated him positively as a political outsider due to his race.

16. The only other informant who abandoned Obama between 2008 and 2012 was also an affluent partner-like voter.

CONCLUSION

1. Mollenkopf 1983.
2. I use culture as shorthand for intersubjective agreements, not a wholesale script (see chap. 4).
3. See chap. 7.
4. Galaskiewicz 1985; Mizruchi 2013.
5. See especially chaps. 3 and 7.
6. This is not to say that there is nothing particular about the urban scale of analysis. People experience social processes viscerally when they are interwoven with spatial organization (Jacobs 1961; De Certeau 1984).
7. Relative to other American cities, River City and Prairieville were probably most different in their lack of racial diversity, particularly during the pre-1970s period, which may have prevented the type of intra-Democratic faction fracturing observed in other American cities (see n. 17 in chapter 3).
8. Sellers 2002, 17–19. American politics is unique in other ways (e.g., parties exercise little top-down control, federal policymakers are unconstrained by super-national bodies like the EU).
9. Although public school funding might be an interesting exception as educational leaders both compete for competitive grants and engage in a zero-sum conflict over students (i.e., with charter and private schools) since federal funding is apportioned largely on a per-student basis (and is therefore relatively Keynesian).
10. Weber (1978 [1922]) argues that ideal-types are simplified model of a phenomenon's analytically useful features, not common or "average" exemplars of a category.
11. See Clemens 1997. The analogy to the progressive era is apt, because it anticipates two critiques of neoliberalism: that policymakers may not self-identify as "neoliberal" (neither did all "progressives") and that aspects of neoliberalism predate the "neoliberal era." One can hardly discuss the present in historical context without recourse to periodization; if terms like neoliberal did not exist, we would invent them.
12. See chap. 4.
13. Mudge 2015.
14. Mudge 2008.
15. Abbott 2005.
16. This formulation bears superficial parallels to Gramsci's hegemony (Gramsci and Buttigeig 1992): the idea that most people adopt ruling classes' interests as their own. My account differs in that (a) I show how political common sense is produced partially by conflicts (e.g., between partisans and partners), and (b) my account has no ruling class in the Marxist sense. People adopted partners' outlook, but partners did not control great fortunes and were at the mercy of nonlocal corporations, outside funders, and the like. That is, people adopt the outlook of those who respond to public policies, not to those who formulate or lobby for those policies.

17. See Tocqueville 2003 [1835] and Habermas 1989. I discuss both thinkers as "–isms" to focus on common interpretations, not nuances of their original arguments.

18. Tocqueville 2003 [1835], 71. This is a caricature of Tocqueville, who distinguished between governmental centralization (an interest "shared by all national groups") and administrative power ("a special interest of certain national groups"), which is harmful to democracy (103).

19. Putnam (2001) argues that even purely recreational voluntary associations have positive democratic externalities, thereby striking a more Tocquevillian tone than Tocqueville, who discussed only publically oriented associations.

20. See Walker 2014.

21. Habermas 1989, 238.

22. Perhaps the best evidence for the pervasiveness of this view is the repeated attention that arguments about Americans' political ignorance attract even though social scientists have consistently produced such findings for nearly a century (see, e.g., Lippmann 1922; Converse 1964; Frank 2007).

23. It was already a fiction in Tocqueville's day. Neem (2010) argues that eighteenth-century American civil society was constructed by infrastructure and communication projects, political parties, and the partisan press.

24. Unless somebody breaks the rules and a penalty is called.

25. Festinger 1962.

26. Eliasoph 2011, 56.

27. See Sniderman, Brody, and Tetlock 1993; Zaller 1992; Alvarez and Brehm 2002.

28. Because genres of speech necessarily index a community of speakers (Silverstein 2003; Ochs 1990). Habermas (1979) identified his theory as a "universal pragmatics," literally a genre of speech that calls out all of humanity as a speech community. But insofar as speech presupposes a community of speakers, it cannot be universal unless a universal community of speakers is possible. Otherwise, one would expect "universal" pragmatics to function like any other genre of speech: to sound universal to its own speakers, and particular to outsiders.

29. Tajfel 2010; Turner 1975

30. Alexander 2006, 49; see also Young 1996, 122.

31. See, e.g., Fraser 1990; Mansbridge 2003; Young 1996.

32. See chap. 4.

33. I am most sympathetic to an ideal identified by Purcell (2008) as Radical Pluralism: the moral capacity of public deliberation lies in subalterns' ability to articulate opposition to the status quo (see also Fraser 1990; Mouffe 2000). From this perspective, Keynesian-era public life appears morally preferable to the neoliberal alternative. My relational analysis articulates an alternate justification for radical pluralism.

34. See Baiocchi 2005.

35. Elsewhere, community leaders used urban renewal to displace African American neighborhoods (Jacobs 1961; Gans 1962). But I wonder if one should blame this outcome on federal policy tools rather than the racism of American society and 1960s-era urban planners' high-modernist ideals. The end of urban renewal has hardly prevented the displacement of minority residents from desirable urban areas.

36. For further discussion of local consequences see Pacewicz 2013a, 2013b. One might also consider the consequences for grassroots and thereby national politics. It is easy to see traditional community leaders' tendency to displace conflict as unambiguously positive in the contemporary hyperpartisan climate, but one might argue that they also kept important issues (e.g., civil rights) off the table. Put another way,

traditional leaders were "pointy" whereas contemporary activists are "rounded." One's reaction to this likely depends greatly on the importance that one places on the sorts of issues that traditional leaders displaced in favor of economic issues.

37. For a noteworthy exception, see Mead: "The ideal of human society is one which does bring people so closely together in their interrelationships, so fully develops the necessary system of communication, that the individuals who exercise their own peculiar functions can take the attitude of those whom they affect . . . the problem is one of organizing a community which makes this possible" (1934, 327). Like Mead's framework, my relational perspective identifies the public sphere's moral value with its capacity for allowing people to internalize other's reactions to their actions: voters should understand communicative potential of their votes (i.e., what it does and how politicians react to it) while policymakers should understand the consequences of their policies for voters.

38. Skocpol 1999, 359. Many political theorists also compare grassroots civic life to a "school for democracy" that teaches people about public problems and inculcates public skills (e.g., Putnam 2001).

39. This capacity is important, because policymakers otherwise rely on oversimplified models of society, which sometimes gain currency simply because bureaucrats find them useful during jurisdictional struggles (see Steinmetz 2008; Wilson 2011). Scott (1998) argues that many of the twentieth century's greatest tragedies—for instance, famines produced by collectivization of agriculture—resulted from elites' efforts to organize societies into more legible forms, which occurred only where a hobbled or nonexistent civil society was unable to exert a countervailing force.

40. Daniel Feegan in chapter 5.

41. Partners themselves identify Envisioning with an ideal democratic process.

42. For a similar argument, see McQuarrie 2013.

43. See chap. 4.

44. McAdam and Kloos 2014. For instance, it is difficult to imagine the gay rights movement gaining widespread acceptance from traditional party leaders like Frannie Steele, because their aim was to minimize party members' points of disagreement in favor of overarching commonalities (i.e., their commitment to the have-nots in community and partisan conflicts).

45. Skocpol 2003. Such arrangements create opportunities for well-funded but dispersed advocates of various causes, but do not create a continuous flow of information between the grassroots and centers of policymaking.

46. Following Mead (1934), policymakers think that they are learning to take on the attitudes of regular people toward themselves when interacting with activists. They are actually taking on the amplified attitudes of institutionalized political movements and lobbies.

47. On Hayek's influence on contemporary politics, see Mirowski 2013.

48. See Mouffe 2000, 104.

49. Although policymakers do not always see themselves as making tradeoffs. Krippner (2011) argues that politicians turned to financial deregulation because it appeared as an alternative to picking winners and losers via allocation of scarce credit. But the consequences of financialization show that the policy did ultimately benefit some people more than others. At the scale of the city, some entrepreneurial strategies can arguably provide widespread benefits by leveraging disproportionate outside resources.

50. Some political theorists look to urban grassroots movements as a possible vector

of political change, but many of these formulations double down on the insiders-versus-outsiders binary similar to River City and Prairieville's actually existing public sphere. Laclau and Mouffe (2001) write enthusiastically about a "chain of equivalence": alliance between groups with only their exclusion from grassroots statecraft in common—an orientation Purcell (2008) sees as realizable via a positive "right to inhabit the city." But to me, an alliance of equivalence between—for instance—River City's Labor Temple Unionists and GOP activists seems unlikely.

METHODOLOGICAL APPENDIX

1. Small 2009.
2. See Lamont and Swidler 2014; Wilson and Mayrl 2013.
3. See chap. 4.
4. Frank 2007.
5. Later, I learned that this top-down recruiting procedure worked partially because it replicated how newcomers made themselves known to their city's leadership class: they made appointments with a few key leaders, who told these newcomers to "use their names" for additional contacts.
6. Tavory and Timmermans 2014.
7. Marcus 1995.
8. See, respectively Goffman 1959 and Fine and Fields 2008.
9. Goffman 1989.
10. In a few cases, I used my own experience rather than community leaders' evaluation to determine what was public knowledge, because community leaders were sometimes poor judges of what other people knew. For example, several informants told me "in confidence" that the old families once kept outside corporations from moving into their city but asked me to guard their secret, even though this stylized fact was likely told to me by citizens of both cities more frequently than any other. In such cases, I respected informants desired not to be linked to a publically known fact, but naturally reported on it anyway.
11. That is, I did this even if the individual told me about the behavior him- or herself.
12. Some also critique pseudonyms for allowing ethnographers to make backhanded arguments for the statistical generalizability of their findings (Small 2009)—essentially, by allowing a reader's imagination to do the work of statistical inference by substituting "Middletown" or "Groveland" for whatever preconceived notions the reader previously held about similar places. But this argument conflates knowledge production in the social sciences with the particular epistemic standpoint of quantitative social science. Consider that quantitative social science did not become widespread until the mid-twentieth century; social scientists did not read the classic community studies as making a case for statistical generalizability, because they did not yet think in those terms. Stated differently, the problem identified by Small is rather that readers read qualitative case studies as making representative claims (and, perhaps, that ethnographers themselves sometimes make such claims), not an inherent problem with the theory-building role that ethnographic studies have traditionally played in knowledge production. Case studies can also serve as paradigmatic cases, which illustrate how to tell a particular kind of analytical story about a particular class of phenomena and—in this respect—ethnographies are useful *precisely* because they encourage the reader to think about cases as akin to those described by the ethnographer (e.g., as experiencing a similar process of urban

transition to one described in Zorbaugh 1929, not as demographically identical to Chicago).

13. See, e.g., Caplow 1984.
14. See Glaser and Strauss 1967; Small 2009.
15. Freeman 1979.
16. On centrality measures' structural assumptions, see Gould 1989.
17. Bonacich 1972. On interclique betweenness, see Gould 1989.
18. See, for instance, Useem 1984.

BIBLIOGRAPHY

Abbott, Andrew. 2001. *Time Matters: On Theory and Method*. Chicago: University of Chicago Press.

———. 2005. "Linked Ecologies: States and Universities as Environments for Professions." *Sociological Theory* 23 (3): 245–74.

———. 2007. "Against Narrative: A Preface to Lyrical Sociology." *Sociological Theory* 25 (1): 67–99.

Abramowitz, Alan. 2013. *The Polarized Public? Why American Government Is So Dysfunctional*. Boston: Pearson.

Abramowitz, Alan, and Kyle Saunders. 2005. "Why Can't We All Just Get Along? The Reality of a Polarized America." *Forum: A Journal of Applied Research in Contemporary Politics* 3 (2): article 1.

Aldrich, John. 1995. *Why Parties? The Origin and Transformation of Political Parties in America*. Chicago: University of Chicago Press.

Aldrich, John H., and David W. Rohde. 2000. "The Consequences of Party Organization in the House: The Role of the Majority and Minority Parties in Conditional Party Government." In *Polarized Politics: Congress and the President in a Partisan Era*, ed. John Bond and Richard Fliesher, 31–72. Washington, DC: CQ Roll-Call Group Books.

Alexander, Herbert. 1971. *Financing the 1968 Election*. Lexington, MA: Heath Lexington Books.

Alexander, Jeffrey C. 2006. *The Civil Sphere*. Oxford: Oxford University Press.

Althusser, Louis. 1971. "Ideology and Ideological State Apparatuses." In *Lenin and Philosophy and Other Essays*, ed. L. Althusser, 253–67. New York: Monthly Review Press.

Alvarez, R. Michael, and John Brehm. 2002. *Hard Choices, Easy Answers: Values, Information, and American Public Opinion*. Princeton, NJ: Princeton University Press.

Amizade, Ron. 1993. *Ballots and Barricades: Class Formation and Republican Politics in France, 1830–1871*. Princeton, NJ: Princeton University Press.

Ansolabehere, Stephen, James Snyder, and Charles Stewart. 2001. "Candidate Positioning in US House Elections." *American Journal of Political Science* 45:136–59.

Austin, John. 1962. *How to Do Things with Words*. Oxford: Oxford University Press.

Auyero, Javier. 2001. *Poor People's Politics: Peronist Survival Networks and the Legacy of Evita*. Durham, NC: Duke University Press.

Bai, Matt. 2007. *The Argument: Billionaires, Bloggers, and the Battle to Remake Democratic Politics*. New York: Penguin Press.

Baiocchi, Gianpaolo. 2005. *Militants and Citizens: The Politics of Participatory Democracy in Porto Alegre*. Stanford, CA: Stanford University Press.

Baldassarri, Delia. 2013. *The Simple Art of Voting: The Cognitive Shortcuts of Italian Voters*. Oxford: Oxford University Press.

Baldassarri, Delia, and Andrew Gelman. 2008. "Partisans without Constraint: Political Polarization and Trends in American Public Opinion." *American Journal of Sociology* 114 (2): 408–46.

Banfield, Edward C., and James Quinn Wilson. 1966. *City Politics*. New York: Vintage Books.

Barman, Emily. 2006. *Contesting Communities: The Transformation of Workplace Charity*. Stanford, CA: Stanford University Press.

Bartels, Larry. 2008. *Unequal Democracy: The Political Economy of the New Gilded Age*. New York: Russell Sage Foundation.

Bawn, Kathleen, Martin Cohen, David Karol, Seth Masket, Hans Noel, and John Zaller. 2012. "A Theory of Political Parties: Groups, Policy Demands, and Nominations in American Politics" *Perspectives on Politics* 10:571–97.

Berelson, Bernard, Paul Lazarsfeld, and William N. McPhee. 1954. *Voting: A Study of Opinion Formation in a Presidential Campaign*. Chicago: University of Chicago Press.

Berman, Elizabeth Popp, and Laura M. Milanes-Reyes. 2013. "The Politicization of Knowledge Claims: The 'Laffer Curve' in the U.S. Congress." *Qualitative Sociology* 36:53–79.

Berman, Elizabeth Popp. 2014. "Not Just Neoliberalism: Economization in U.S. Science and Technology Policy." *Science, Technology and Human Values* 39:397–431.

Biles, Roger. 2011. *The Fate of Cities: Urban America and the Federal Government, 1945–2000*. Lawrence: University of Kansas Press.

Boatright, Robert G. 2013. *Getting Primaried: The Changing Politics of Congressional Primary Challenges*. Ann Arbor: University of Michigan Press.

Bonacich, Philip. 1972. "Factoring and Weighing Approaches to Status Scores and Clique Identification." *Journal of Mathematical Sociology* 2 (1): 113–20.

Bouek, Jennifer. 2014. "Big Cheese: The Rise and Falter of the Emergency Food Assistance Program." MA thesis, Brown University.

Bourdieu, Pierre. 1984. *Distinction: A Social Critique of the Judgment of Taste*. Cambridge, MA: Harvard University Press.

———. 1985. "The Social Space and the Genesis of Groups." *Theory and Society* 14 (6): 723–44.

———. 1990. *The Logic of Practice*. Stanford, CA: Stanford University Press.

Bourdieu, Pierre, and Randal Johnson. 1993. *The Field of Cultural Production: Essays on Art and Literature*. New York: Columbia University Press.

Bourgois, Philippe I., and Jeffrey Schonberg. 2009. *Righteous Dopefiend*. Berkeley: University of California Press.

Brady, Henry, and Paul Sniderman. 1985. "Attitude Attribution: A Group Basis for Political Reasoning." *American Political Science Review* 79 (4): 1061–78.

Brenner, Neil. 2004. *New State Spaces: Urban Governance and the Rescaling of Statehood*. Oxford: Oxford University Press.

Brenner, Neil, and Nik Theodore. 2002. "Cities and the Geographies of 'Actually Existing Neoliberalism.'" *Antipode* 34 (3): 349–79.

Broder, David. 1972. *The Party's Over: The Failure of Politics in America*. New York: Harper and Row.

Bronfenbrenner, Kate. 2009. *No Holds Barred: The Intensification of Employer Opposition* to Organizing (Briefing Paper no. 235). Washington, DC: Economic Policy Institute. Available at: http://digitalcommons.ilr.cornell.edu/reports/38/.

Bronfenbrenner, Kate, and Tom Juravich. 1998. "It Takes More Than House Calls: Organizing to Win with a Comprehensive Union-building Strategy." In *Industrial Relations: Labour Markets, Labour Processes, and Trade Unionism*, ed, John Kelly, 19–36. New York: Routledge.

Campbell, Angus, Phillip Converse, Warren Miller, and Donald Stokes. 1960. *The American Voter*. New York: Wiley Press.

Canes-Wrone, Brandice, David W. Brady, and John F. Cogan. 2002. "Out of Step, Out of Office: Electoral Accountability and House Members' Voting." *American Political Science Review* 96 (1): 127–40.

Caplow, Theodore. 1984. "Rule Enforcement without Visible Means: Christmas Gift Giving in Middletown." *American Journal of Sociology* 89 (6): 1306–23.

Carmines, Edward, John McIver, and James Stimson. 1987. "Unrealized Partisanship: A Theory of Dealignment." *Journal of Politics* 49 (2): 376–400.

Carmines, Edward, and James Stimson. 1989. *Issue Evolution: Race and the Transformation of American Politics*. Princeton, NJ: Princeton University Press.

Chandler, Alfred. 1990 *Strategy and Structure: Chapters in the History of the Industrial Enterprise*. Cambridge, MA: MIT Press.

Chernick, Howard, and Andrew Reschovsky. 1999. "State Fiscal Responses to Block Grants: Will the Social Safety Net Survive?" In *The End of the Welfare? Consequences of Devolution for the Nation*, ed. Max Sawicky, 157–93. New York: ME Sharpe.

Chong, Dennis. 2000. *Rational Lives: Norms and Values in Politics and Society*. Chicago: University of Chicago Press.

Christensen, Michael. 2015. "Reestablishing 'the Social' in Research on Democratic Processes: Mid-Century Voter Studies and Paul F. Lazarsfeld's Alternative Vision." *Journal of the History of the Behavioral Sciences* 51 (3): 308–22.

Clark, Terry, and Seymour Lipset. 1991. "Are Social Classes Dying?" *International Sociology* 6 (4): 397–410.

Clawson, Dan, and Mary Ann Clawson. 1999. "What Has Happened to the US Labor Movement? Union Decline and Renewal." *Annual Review of Sociology*, 95–119.

Clemens, Elisabeth S. 1997. *The People's Lobby: Organizational Innovation and the Rise of Interest Group Politics in the United States, 1890–1925*. Chicago: University of Chicago Press.

———. 2007. "Lineages of the Rube Goldberg State: Building and Blurring Public Programs, 1900–1940." In *The Art of the State: Rethinking Political Institutions*, ed. Ian Shapiro, Stephen Skowronek, and Daniel Galvin. New York: New York University Press.

Clemens, Elisabeth S., and Doug Guthrie. 2010. *Politics and Partnerships: The Role of Voluntary Associations in America's Political Past and Present*. Chicago: University of Chicago Press.

Cohen, Marty, David Karol, Hans Noel, and John Zaller. 2008. *The Party Decides: Presidential Nominations before and after Reform*. Chicago: University of Chicago Press.

Converse, Philip. 1964. "Ideology and Discontent." In *Ideology and Its Discontents*, ed. David E. Apter, 206–61. New York: Free Press of Glencoe.

Cornfield, Daniel B. 1991. "The US Labor Movement: Its Development and Impact on Social Inequality and Politics." *Annual Review of Sociology*, 27–49.

Dahl, Robert Alan. 1961. *Who Governs? Democracy and Power in an American City*. New Haven, CT: Yale University Press.

Davis, Gerald. 2009. *Managed by the Markets: How Finance Reshaped America*. Oxford: Oxford University Press.

De Beauvoir, Simone. 2014. *The Second Sex*. New York: Random House.

De Certeau, Michelle. 1984. *The Practice of Everyday Life*. Berkeley: University of California Press.

De Leon, Cedric. 2010. "Vicarious Revolutionaries: Martial Discourse and the Origins of Mass Party Competition in the United States, 1789–1848." *Studies in American Political Development* 24 (1): 121–41.

———. 2014. *Party and Society*. Cambridge: John Wiley and Sons.

De Leon, Cedric, Manali Desai, and Cihan Tuğal. 2009. "Political Articulation: Parties and the Constitution of Cleavages in the United States, India, and Turkey." *Sociological Theory* 27 (3): 193–219.

De Tocqueville, Alexis. 2003 [1835]. *Democracy in America and Two Essays on America*. New York: Penguin Classics.

DiMaggio, Paul, John Evans, and Bethany Bryson. 1996. "Have Americans' Social Attitudes Become More Polarized?" *American Journal of Sociology* 102:690–755.

Dimoch, Michael, Jocelyn Kiley, Scott Keeter, and Carroll Doherty. 2014. "Political Polarization in American Public Life: How Increasing Ideological Uniformity and Partisan Antipathy Affect Politics, Compromise, and Everyday Life." Pew Research Center, Washington, DC (June 14, 2014): http://www.people-press.org/2014/06/12/political -polarization-in-the-american-public/.

Dodds, Alex. 2013. "What President Obama's Budget Proposal Means for Community Development Programs." Washington, DC: Smart Growth America (April 10, 2013): http://www.smartgrowthamerica.org/2013/04/10/what-president-obamas-budget -proposal-means-for-community-development-programs/

Downs, Anthony. 1957. *An Economic Theory of Democracy*. New York: Harper and Row.

Durkheim, Emile. 1997 [1893]. *The Division of Labor in Society*. New York: Free Press.

Ehrenhalt, Alan. 1992. *The United States of Ambition: Politicians, Power, and the Pursuit of Office*. New York: Three Rivers Press.

Eidlin, Barry. 2015. "Class vs. Special Interest Labor, Power, and Politics in the United States and Canada in the Twentieth Century." *Politics and Society* 43 (2): 181–211.

Eliasoph, Nina. 1998. *Avoiding Politics: How Americans Produce Apathy in Everyday Life*. Cambridge: Cambridge University Press.

———. 2011. *Making Volunteers: Civic Life after Welfare's End*. Princeton, NJ: Princeton University Press.

Espeland, Wendy, and Paul Hirsch. 1990. "Ownership, Changes, Accounting Practice, and the Redefinition of the Corporation." *Accounting, Organizations, and Society* 15:77–96.

Evans, John. 2003. "Have Americans' Attitudes Become More Polarized? An Update." *Social Science Quarterly* 84:71–90.

Evans-Pritchard, Edward. 1956. *Nuer Religion*. Oxford: Clarendon Press.

Festinger, Leon. 1962. *A Theory of Cognitive Dissonance*. Stanford, CA: Stanford University Press.

Fine, Gary Alan, and Corey D. Fields. 2008. "Culture and Microsociology: The Anthill and the Veldt." *Annals of the American Academy of Political and Social Science* 619 (1): 130–48.

Fiorina, Morris. 1999. "Further Evidence of the Partisan Consequences of Legislative Professionalism." *American Journal of Political Science* 43 (3): 974–77.

Fiorina, Morris, and Samuel Abrams. 2008. "Political Polarization in the American Public." *Annual Review of Political Science* 11:563–88.

Fiorina, Morris, Samuel Abrams, and Jeremy Pope. 2005. *Culture War? The Myth of a Polarized America*. New York: Pearson Longman.

Fiorina, Morris, and M. Levendusky. 2006. "Disconnected: The Political Class versus the People." In *Red and Blue Nation?* vol. 1, *Characteristics and Causes of America's Polarized Politics*, ed. Pietro S. Nivola and David W. Brady, 49–71. Stanford, CA: Stanford University Press.

Fligstein, Neil. 2001. *The Architecture of Markets: An Economic Sociology of Twenty-First Century Capitalist Societies*. Princeton, NJ: Princeton University Press.

Fligstein, Neil, and Douglas McAdam. 2012. *A Theory of Fields*. Oxford: Oxford University Press.

Florida, Richard. 2002. *The Rise of the Creative Class: And How It's Transforming Work, Leisure, Community and Everyday Life*. New York: Perseus Book Group

Fourcade, Marion. 2009. *Economists and Societies: Discipline and Profession in the United States, Britain, and France, 1890s to 1990s*. Princeton, NJ: Princeton University Press.

Fourcade-Gournichas, Marion, and Sarah Babb. 2002. "The Rebirth of the Liberal Creed: Pathways to Neoliberalism in Four Countries." *American Journal of Sociology* 108 (3): 533–79.

Fox, Douglas. 1972. *The New Urban Politics: Cities and the Federal Government*. Palisades, CA: Goodyear Publishing Company.

Frank, Thomas. 2007. *What's the Matter with Kansas? How Conservatives Won the Heart of America*. New York: Macmillan.

Fraser, Nancy. 1990. "Rethinking the Public Sphere: A Contribution to the Critique of Actually Existing Democracy." *Social Text*, 56–80.

Freeman, Linton. 1979. "Centrality in Social Networks: Conceptual Clarification." *Social Networks* 1 (3): 215–39.

Fuchs, Ester 1992. *Mayors and Money: Fiscal Policy in New York and Chicago*. Chicago: University of Chicago Press.

Funk, Russell J., and Daniel Hirschman. 2014. "Derivatives and Deregulation: Financial Innovation and the Demise of Glass–Steagall." *Administrative Science Quarterly* 59 (4): 669–704.

Galaskiewicz, Joseph. 1985. *Social Organization of an Urban Grants Economy: A Study of Business Philanthropy and Nonprofit Organizations*. Orlando, FL: Academic Press.

Galston, William A., and Pietro S. Nivola. 2008. "Delineating the Problem." In *Red and Blue Nation?* vol. 2, *Consequences and Correction of America's Polarized Politics*, ed. Pietro S. Nivola and David W. Brady, 1–48. Washington, DC: Brookings Institution Press.

Gans, Herbert. 1962. *The Urban Villagers: Group and Class in the Life of Italian-Americans*. New York: Free Press.

Garfinkel, Alan. 1984. *Forms of Explanation: Rethinking the Questions in Social Theory*. New Haven, CT: Yale University Press.

Geertz, Clifford. 1973. *The Interpretation of Cultures*. New York: Basic Books.

Gelman, Andrew. 2010. *Red State, Blue State, Rich State, Poor State: Why Americans Vote the Way They Do*. Princeton, NJ: Princeton University Press.

Gemici, Kurtuluş. 2008. "Karl Polanyi and the Antinomies of Embeddedness." *Socio-Economic Review* 6 (1): 5–33.

———. 2015. "The Neoclassical Origins of Polanyi's Self-Regulating Market." *Sociological Theory* 33 (2): 125–47.

Glaser, Strauss, and Anselm Strauss. 1967. *The Discovery of Grounded Theory: Strategies for Qualitative Research*. Herndon, VA: Aldine Transaction Press.

Goffman, Erving. 1959. *The Presentation of Self in Everyday Life*. Chicago: University of Chicago Press.

———. 1989. "On Fieldwork." *Journal of Contemporary Ethnography* 18 (2): 123–28.

Gould, Roger. 1989. "Power and Social Structure in Community Elites." *Social Forces* 68 (2): 531–52.

Granovetter, Mark. 1985. "Economic Action and Social Structure: The Problem of Embeddedness." *American Journal of Sociology* 91 (3): 481–510.

Gramsci, Antonio, and Joseph Buttigieg. 1992. *Prison Notebooks*. Vol. 2. New York: Columbia University Press.

Green, John, and Daniel J. Coffey. 2007. *The State of the Parties: The Changing Role of Contemporary American Politics*. Lanham, MD: Rowman and Littlefield.

Habermas, Jürgen. 1979. "What Is Universal Pragmatics." *Communication and the Evolution of Society* 1:2–4.

———. 1989. *The Structural Transformation of the Public Sphere*. Cambridge, MA: MIT Press.

Hacker, Jacob. 2002. *The Divided Welfare State: The Battle over Public and Private Social Benefits in the United States*. Cambridge: Cambridge University Press.

Hacker, Jacob S., and Paul Pierson. 2011. *Winner-Take-All Politics: How Washington Made the Rich Richer—and Turned Its Back on the Middle Class*. New York: Simon and Schuster.

Hackworth, Jason. 2007. *The Neoliberal City: Governance, Ideology, and Development in American Urbanism*. Ithaca, NY: Cornell University Press.

Hartigan, John. 2010. *Race in the 21st Century: Ethnographic Approaches*. Oxford: Oxford University Press.

Harvey, David. 1989. "From Managerialism to Entrepreneurialism: The Transformation in Urban Governance in Late Capitalism." *Geografiska Annaler B* 71:3–17.

———. 2005. *A Brief History of Neoliberalism*. Oxford: Oxford University Press.

Haydu, Jeffrey. 2008. *Citizen Employers: Business Communities and Labor in Cincinnati and San Francisco, 1870–1916*. Ithaca, NY: Cornell University Press.

Hayek, Friedrich A. von. 1944. *The Road to Serfdom*. London: Routledge.

Heaney, Michael, and Fabio Rojas. 2015. *Party in the Street: The Antiwar Movement and the Democratic Party after 9/11*. New York: Cambridge University Press.

Hirschman, Daniel, and Elizabeth Popp Berman. 2014. "Do Economists Make Policies?" *Socio-Economic Review* 12:779–811.

Hochschild, Arlie, and Anne Machung. 1989. *The Second Shift: Working Families and the Revolution at Home*. New York: Viking.

Hunter, Floyd. 1953. *Community Power Structure: A Study of Decision Makers*. Chicago: University of Chicago Press.

Jacobs, Jane. 1961. *The Death and Life of Great American Cities*. New York: Vintage Press.

Jacobson, Gary. 2001. *The Politics of Congressional Elections*. New York: Longman.

Jessop, Robert. 2002. *The Future of the Capitalist State*. Cambridge: Polity Press.

Johnson, Simon, and James Kwak. 2011. *13 Bankers: The Wall Street Takeover and the Next Financial Meltdown*. New York: Vintage Books.

Kabaservice, Geoffrey. 2011. *Rule and Ruin: The Downfall of Moderation and the Destruction of the Republican Party, from Eisenhower to the Tea Party*. New York: Oxford University Press.

Kantor, Linda Scott, Kathryn Lipton, Alden Manchester, and Victor Oliveira. 1997. "Estimating and Addressing America's Food Losses." *Food Review* 20 (1): 2–12.

Katznelson, Ira. 1981. *City Trenches: Urban Politics and the Patterning of Class in the United States*. Chicago: University of Chicago Press.

Keith, Bruce, David Magleby, Candice Nelson, Elizabeth Orr, and Mark Westlye. 1992. *The Myth of the Independent Voter*. Berkeley: University of California Press.

Key, V. O. 1952. *Politics, Parties, and Pressure Groups*. New York: Thomas Y. Crowell.

———. 1961. *Public Opinion and American Democracy*. New York: Knopf Press.

Kimball, David C., and Cassie A. Gross. 2007. "The Growing Polarization of American Voters." In *The State of Parties*, ed. John Green, 265–78. Boulder, CO: Rowman and Littlefield.

Kimeldorf, Howard.1988. *Reds or Rackets? The Making of Radical and Conservative Unions on the Waterfront*. Berkeley: University of California Press.

Klinghard, Daniel. 2010. *The Nationalization of American Political Parties, 1880–1896*. Cambridge University Press.

Knoke, David. 1976. *Change and Continuity in American Politics: The Social Bases of Political Parties*. Baltimore, MD: Johns Hopkins University Press.

Krippner, Greta. 2002. "The Elusive Market: Embeddedness and the Paradigm of Economic Sociology." *Theory and Society* 30 (6): 775–810.

———. 2011. *Capitalizing on Crisis: The Political Origins of the Rise of Finance*. Cambridge, MA: Harvard University Press.

Kuhn, Thomas. 1962. *The Structure of Scientific Revolutions*. Chicago: University of Chicago Press.

Laclau, Ernesto, and Chantal Mouffe. 2001. *Hegemony and Socialist Strategy: Towards a Radical Democratic Politics*. New York: Verso.

Lamont, Michèle, and Ann Swidler. 2014. "Methodological Pluralism and the Possibilities and Limits of Interviewing." *Qualitative Sociology* 37 (2): 153–71.

Lamont, Michèle, and Patricia White. 2008. "Workshop on Interdisciplinary Standards for Systematic Qualitative Research." Washington, DC: National Science Foundation.

Layman, Geoffrey Thomas Carsey, John Green, Richard Herrera, and Rosalyn Cooperman. 2010. "Activists and Conflict Extension in American Politics." *American Political Science Review* 104 (2): 324–46.

Lazarsfeld, Paul, Bernard Berelson, and Hazel Gaudet. 1944. *The People's Choice: How the Voter Makes Up His Mind in a Presidential Campaign*. New York: Duell Sloan and Pearce.

Lee, Caroline. 2011. "Five Assumptions Academics Make about Deliberation and Why They Deserve Rethinking" *Journal of Public Deliberation* 7 (1): 1–48.

———. 2015. *Do-It-Yourself Democracy: The Rise of the Public Engagement Industry*. Oxford: Oxford University Press.

Lee, Caroline, Kelly McNulty, and Sarah Shaffer. 2013. "'Hard Times, Hard Choices: Marketing Retrenchment as Civil Empowerment in an Era of Neoliberal Crisis." *Socio-Economic Review* 11:81–106.

Lee, Caroline, Michael McQuarrie, and Edward Walker. 2014. *Democratizing Inequalities: Dilemmas of the New Public Participation*. New York University Press.

Lefebvre, Henri. 1979. "Space: Social Product and Use Value." *Critical Sociology: European Perspectives* 285:295.

Levi-Martin, John. 2003. "What Is Field Theory?" *American Journal of Sociology* 109 (1): 1–49.

Levy, Jonah D. 2006. *The State after Statism: New State Activities in the Age of Liberalization*. Cambridge, MA: Harvard University Press.

Lin, Ken-Hou, and Donald Tomaskovic-Devey. 2013. "Financialization and US Income Inequality, 1970–2008." *American Journal of Sociology* 118 (5): 1284–1329.

Lippmann, Walter. 1922. *Public Opinion*. New York: Macmillan.

Lipsky, Michael, and Marc A. Thibodeau. 1990. "Domestic Food Policy in the United States." *Journal of Health Politics, Policy and Law* 15 (2): 319–39.

Lizardo, Omar. 2011. "Pierre Bourdieu as a Post-Cultural Theorist." *Cultural Sociology* 5 (1): 25–44.

Logan, John, and Harvey Molotch. 1987. *Urban Fortunes: The Political Economy of Place.* Berkeley: University of California Press.

Long, Norton 1958. "The Local Community as an Ecology of Games." *American Journal of Sociology* 64 (3): 251–61.

Lynd, Robert S., and Helen M. Lynd. 1929. *Middletown: A Study in Contemporary American Culture.* New York: Harcourt, Brace.

Malinowski, Bronislaw. 2002 [1896]. *Argonauts of the Western Pacific: An Account of Native Enterprise and Adventure in the Archipelagoes of Melanesian New Guinea.* New York: Routledge.

Mansbridge, Jane. 2003. "Rethinking Representation." *American Political Science Review* 97 (4): 515–28.

Manza, Jeff, and Clem Brooks. 1999. *Social Cleavages and Political Change: Voter Alignments and US Party Coalitions.* Oxford: Oxford University Press.

March, James, and Herbert Simon. 1958. *Organizations.* New York: Wiley.

Marcus, George. 1995. "Ethnography in/of the World System: The Emergence of Multi-sited Ethnography." *Annual Review of Anthropology* 24:95–117.

Martin, Isaac William. 2008. *The Permanent Tax Revolt: How the Property Tax Transformed American Politics.* Stanford, CA: Stanford University Press.

Martin, John Levi. 2011. *The Explanation of Social Action.* Oxford: Oxford University Press.

Marx, Karl. 1972 [1844]. "Economic and Philosophical Manuscripts." In *The Marx and Engels Reader,* ed. Robert Tucker, 66–125. New York: W. W. Norton.

Masket, Seth. 2009. *No Middle Ground: How Informal Party Organizations Control Nominations and Polarize Legislatures.* Ann Arbor: University of Michigan Press.

Mauss, Marcel. 2000 [1922]. *The Gift: Forms and Functions of Exchange in Archaic Societies.* New York: W. W. Norton.

Mayer, William. 1992. *The Changing American Mind: How and Why American Public Opinion Changed between 1960 and 1988.* Ann Arbor: University of Michigan Press.

McAdam, Doug, and Karina Kloos. 2014. *Deeply Divided: Racial Politics and Social Movements in Postwar America.* New York: Oxford University Press.

McCammon, Holly. 1990. "Legal Limits on Labor Militancy: U.S. Labor Law and the Right to Strike since the New Deal." *Social Problems* 37 (2): 206–29.

McGirr, Lisa. 2002. "A History of the Conservative Movement from the Bottom Up." *Journal of Policy History* 14 (3): 331–39.

McLean, Paul 2007. *The Art of the Network: Strategic Interaction and Patronage in Renaissance Florence.* Durham, NC: Duke University Press.

McQuarrie, Michael. 2013. "No Contest: Participatory Technologies and the Transformation of Urban Authority" *Public Culture* 25 (1): 143–75.

Mead, George Herbert. 1934. *Mind, Self and Society.* Chicago: University of Chicago Press.

Medvetz, Thomas. 2012. *Think Tanks in America.* Chicago: University of Chicago Press.

Miller, Gary, and Norman Schofield. 2003. "Activists and Partisan Realignment in the United States." *American Political Science Review* 97 (2): 245–60.

Miller, Warren Edward, and J. Merrill Shanks. 1996. *The New American Voter.* Cambridge, MA: Harvard University Press.

Mirowski, Phillip. 2013. *Never Let a Serious Crisis Go to Waste: How Neoliberalism Survived the Financial Meltdown.* New York: Verso.

Mische, Ann. 2008. *Partisan Publics: Communication and Contention across Brazilian Youth Activist Networks*. Princeton, NJ: Princeton University Press.

Mizruchi, Mark. 2013. *The Fracturing of the American Corporate Elite*. Cambridge, MA: Harvard University Press.

Mollenkopf, John. 1983. *The Contested City*. Princeton, NJ: Princeton University Press.

Molotch, Harvey. 1976. "The City as a Growth Machine: Toward a Political Economy of Place." *American Journal of Sociology* 82 (2): 309–32.

———. 1993. "The Political Economy of Growth Machines." *Journal of Urban Affairs* 15 (1): 29–53.

Monkkonen, Eric 1995. *The Local State: Public Money and American Cities*. Stanford, CA: Stanford University Press.

Moody, Kim. 1988. *An Injury to All: The Decline of American Unionism*. NY: Verso.

Morenoff, David. 2002. "Lost Food and Liability: The Good Samaritan Food Donation Law Story." *Food and Drug* 57:107.

Morgan, Kimberly, and Andrea Campbell. 2011. *The Delegated Welfare State: Medicare, Markets, and the Governance of Social Policy*. Oxford: Oxford University Press.

Mouffe, Chantal. 2000. *The Democratic Paradox*. New York: Verso.

Mudge, Stephanie Lee. 2008. "What Is Neo-liberalism?" *Socio-Economic Review* 4:703–31.

———. 2011. "What's Left of Leftism?" *Social Science History* 35 (3): 337–80.

———. 2015. "Explaining Political Tunnel Vision: Politics and Economics in Crisis-ridden Europe, Then and Now." *European Journal of Sociology* 56 (1): 63–91.

Mudge, Stephanie, and Tony Chen. 2014. "Political Parties and the Sociological Imagination: Past, Present and Future Directions" *Annual Review of Sociology* 40:305–30.

Neem, Johann. 2010. "Civil Society and American Nationalism, 1776–1865." In *Politics and Partnerships: The Role of Voluntary Associations in America's Political Past and Present*, ed. Elisabeth Clemens and Doug Guthrie, 29–53. Chicago: University of Chicago Press

Ochs, Elinor. 1990. "Indexicality and Socialization." In *Cultural Psychology: Essays on Comparative Human Development*, ed. James Stigler, Richard Shweder, and Gilbert Herdt, 287–308 Cambridge: Cambridge University Press.

Pacewicz, Josh. 2013a. "Tax Increment Financing, Economic Development Professionals and the Financialization of Urban Politics." *Socio-Economic Review* 11 (3): 413–40.

———. 2013b. "Regulatory Rescaling in Neoliberal Markets." *Social Problems* 60 (4): 433–56.

———. 2015. "Playing the Neoliberal Game: Why Community Leaders Left Parties to Ideological Activists." *American Journal of Sociology* 121 (3): 826–81.

Peck, Jamie. 2010. *Constructions of Neoliberal Reason*. Oxford: Oxford University Press.

Peck, Jamie, Nik Theodore, and Neil Brenner. 2009. "Postneoliberalism and Its Malcontents" *Antipode* 41:94–116.

Phillips-Fein, Kim. 2010. *Invisible Hands: The Businessmen's Crusade against the New Deal*. New York: W. W. Norton.

Pierce, Charles. 1932. *Collected Papers*. Vol. 2. Cambridge, MA: Harvard University Press.

Piketty, Thomas, and Edward Saez. 2003. "Income Inequality in the United States, 1913–1998." *Quarterly Journal of Economics* 118 (1): 1–39.

Polanyi, Karl. 1944. *The Great Transformation: The Political and Economic Origins of Our Times*. Boston: Beacon Press.

Pollan, Michael. 2006. *The Omnivore's Dilemma: A Natural History of Four Meals*. New York: Penguin.

Polletta, Francesca. 1998. "Contending Stories: Narrative in Social Movements." *Qualitative Sociology* 21 (4): 419–46.

Polsby, Nelson. 1983. *Consequences of Party Reform*. Oxford: Oxford University Press.

Polsby, Nelson, and Aaron Wildavsky. 1991. *Presidential Elections: Contemporary Strategies of American Electoral Politics*. New York: Free Press.

Poole, Keith T., and Howard Rosenthal. 2007. *Ideology and Congress*. New Brunswick, NJ: Transaction.

Prasad, Monica. 2006. *The Politics of Free Markets: The Rise of Neoliberal Economic Policies in Britain, France, Germany, and the United States*. Chicago: University of Chicago Press.

Prasad, Monica, Andrew J. Perrin, Kieran Bezila, Steve G. Hoffman, Kate Kindleberger, Kim Manturuk, and Ashleigh Smith Powers. 2009. "'There must be a reason': Osama, Saddam, and Inferred Justification." *Sociological Inquiry* 79 (2): 142–62.

Prosten, Richard. 1979. "The Rise in NLRB Election Delays: Measuring Business' New Resistance." *Monthly Labor Review* 120 (2): 38–40.

Purcell, Mark. 2008. *Recapturing Democracy: Neoliberalization and the Struggle for Alternative Urban Futures*. London: Routledge.

Putnam, Robert. 2001. *Bowling Alone: The Collapse and Revival of American Community*. New York: Simon and Schuster.

Reed, Isaac Arial. 2011. *Interpretation and Social Knowledge: On the Use of Theory in the Human Sciences*. Chicago: University of Chicago Press.

Rhomberg, Chris. 2012. *The Broken Table: The Detroit Newspaper Strike and the State of American Labor*. New York: Russell Sage Foundation.

Rodgers, Daniel. 2011. *The Age of Fracture*. Cambridge, MA: Harvard University Press.

Rosenfeld, Jake. 2014. *What Unions No Longer Do*. Cambridge, MA: Harvard University Press.

Rosenstone, Steven, and John M. Hansen. 1993. *Mobilization, Participation and Democracy in America*. New York: Pearson Press.

Rothenberg, Randall. 1984. *The Neoliberals: Creating the New American Politics*. New York: Simon and Schuster.

Safford, Sean. 2009. *Why the Garden Club Couldn't Save Youngstown: The Transformation of the Rust Belt*. Cambridge, MA: Harvard University Press.

Sahlins. Marshall. 1985. *Islands of History*. Chicago: University of Chicago Press.

Saunders, Kyle, and Alan Abramowitz. 2004. "Ideological Realignment and Active Partisans in the American Electorate." *American Politics Research* 32 (3): 285–309.

Sbragia, Alberta. 1996. *Debt Wish: Entrepreneurial Cities, US Federalism, and Economic Development*. Pittsburgh: University of Pittsburgh Press.

Schattschneider, E. E. 1942. *Party Government*. Westport, CT: Greenwood.

Schudson, Michael. 1998. *The Good Citizen: A History of American Civic Life*. New York: Free Press.

Schuman, Howard, and Stanley Presser. 1980. "Public Opinion and Public Ignorance: The Fine Line between Attitudes and Nonattitudes." *American Journal of Sociology* 85 (5): 1214–25.

Schutz, Alfred. 1970. *Alfred Schutz on Phenomenology and Social Relations*. Vol. 360. Chicago: University of Chicago Press.

Scott, James. 1998. *Seeing Like a State: How Certain Schemes to Improve the Human Condition Have Failed*. New Haven, CT: Yale University Press.

Scott, John. 2013. *Social Network Analysis*. 3rd ed. Thousand Oaks, CA: Sage.

Searle, John. 1969. *Speech Acts: An Essay in the Philosophy of Language*. Cambridge: Cambridge University Press.

Sellers, Jefferey. 2002. *Governing from Below: Urban Regions and the Global Economy*. Cambridge: Cambridge University Press.

Sewell, William, Jr. 1992. "A Theory of Structure: Duality, Agency, and Transformation." *American Journal of Sociology* 98 (1): 1–29.

———. 2005. *Logics of History: Social Theory and Social Transformation*. Chicago: University of Chicago Press.

Silva, Jennifer M. 2013. *Coming Up Short: Working-Class Adulthood in an Age of Uncertainty*. Oxford: Oxford University Press.

Silverstein, Michael. 2003. "Indexical Order and the Dialectics of Sociolinguistic Life." *Language and Communication* 23 (3): 193–229.

Skocpol, Theda. 1999. "Advocates without Members: The Recent Transformation of American Civic Life." In *Civic Engagement in American Democracy*, ed. Theda Skocpol and Morris Fiorina, 27–65. Washington DC: Brookings Institution.

———. 2003. *Diminished Democracy: From Membership to Management in American Civic Life*. Norman: University of Oklahoma Press.

Skocpol, Theda, and Morris Fiorina. 1999. "Making Sense of the Civic Engagement Debate." *Civic Engagement in American Democracy*, ed. Theda Skocpol and Morris Fiorina, 1–23. Washington DC: Brookings Institution.

Skocpol, Theda, and Vanessa Williamson. 2012. *The Tea Party and the Remaking of Republican Conservatism*. Oxford: Oxford University Press.

Slez, Adam, and John Levi Martin. 2007. "Political Action and Party Formation in the United States Constitutional Convention." *American Sociological Review* 72 (1): 42–67.

Small, Mario. 2009. "'How Many Cases Do I Need?' On Science and the Logic of Case Selection in Field-Based Research." *Ethnography* 10 (5): 1–54

Smith, Adam. 2003 [1776]. *An Inquiry into the Nature and Causes of the Wealth of Nations*. Oxford: Oxford University Press

Smith, Mark. 2007. *The Right Talk: How Conservatives Transformed the Great Society into the Economic Society*. Princeton, NJ: Princeton University Press.

Smith, Steven, and Michael Lipsky. 1993. *Nonprofits for Hire: The Welfare State in the Age of Contracting*. Cambridge, MA: Harvard University Press.

Sniderman, Paul, Richard Brody, and Phillip Tetlock. 1993. *Reasoning and Choice: Explorations in Political Psychology*. Cambridge: Cambridge University Press.

Somers, Margaret. 1994. "The Narrative Constitution of Identity: A Relational and Network Approach." *Theory and Society* 23 (5): 605–49.

Spillman, Lyn. 2012. *Solidarity in Strategy: Making Business Meaningful in American Trade Associations*. Chicago: University of Chicago Press.

Steinmetz, George. 2008. "The Colonial State as a Social Field: Ethnographic Capital and Native Policy in the German Overseas Empire before 1914." *American Sociological Review* 73 (4): 589–612.

Stokes, Donald. 1963. "Spatial Models of Party Competition." *American Political Science Review* 57 (2): 368–77.

Stone, Clarence. 1989. *Regime Politics: Governing Atlanta, 1946–1988*. Lawrence: University Press of Kansas.

Stonecash, Jeffrey. 2006. *Political Parties Matter: Realignment and the Return of Partisan Voting*. Boulder, CO: Lynne Rienner Publishers.

Sundquist, James. 1983. *Dynamics of the Party System: Alignment and Realignment of Political Parties in the United States*. Washington DC: Brookings Institution.

Tabb, William. 1982. *The Long Default: New York City and the Urban Fiscal Crisis*. New York: NYU Press.

Tajfel, Henri. 2010. *Social Identity and Intergroup Relations*. Cambridge: Cambridge University Press.

Tavory, Iddo. 2016. *Summoned: Identification and Religious Life in a Jewish Neighborhood*. Chicago: University of Chicago Press.

Tavory, Iddo, and Stefan Timmermans. 2014. *Abductive Analysis: Theorizing Qualitative Research*. Chicago: University of Chicago Press.

Thornton, Patricia, William Ocasio, and Michael Lounsbury. 2012. *The Institutional Logics Perspective*. New York: John Wiley and Sons.

Thurber, James, and Candice Nelson. 2014. *Campaigns and Elections, American Style: Transforming American Politics*. Boulder, CO: Westview Press.

Turner, Victor. 1975. *Dramas, Fields, and Metaphors: Symbolic Action in Human Society*. Ithaca, NY: Cornell University Press.

Useem, Michael. 1984. *The Inner Circle: Large Corporations and the Rise of Business Political Activity in the U.S. and U.K.* New York: Oxford University Press.

Uzzi, Brian. 1997. "Social Structure and Competition in Interfirm Networks: The Paradox of Embeddedness." *Administrative Science Quarterly* 42:35–67.

Venugopal, Rajesh. 2015. "Neoliberalism as Concept." *Economy and Society*, 1–23.

Wacquant, Loïc. 2001. "Deadly Symbiosis When Ghetto and Prison Meet and Mesh." *Punishment and Society* 3 (1): 95–133.

———. 2004. "Following Pierre Bourdieu into the Field." *Ethnography* 5 (4): 387–414.

———. 2006. *Parias urbains: Ghetto-Banlieues-État*. Paris: La Découverte.

———. 2012. "Three Steps to a Historical Anthropology of Actually Existing Neoliberalism." *Social Anthropology* 20 (1): 66–79.

Walker, Edward T. 2014. *Grassroots for Hire: Public Affairs Consultants in American Democracy*. Cambridge: Cambridge University Press.

Ware, Alan. 1985. *The Breakdown of the Democratic Party Organization, 1940–1980*. Oxford: Clarendon Press.

Warner, Lloyd. 1963. *Yankee City*. New Haven, CT: Yale University Press

Weber, Max. 1978 [1922]. *Economy and Society: An Outline of Interpretive Sociology*. Berkeley: University of California Press.

Weber, Rachel. 2010. "Selling City Futures: The Financialization of Urban Redevelopment Policy." *Economic Geography* 86 (3): 251–74.

Williamson, Oliver. 1981. "The Economics of Organization: The Transaction Cost Approach." *American Journal of Sociology* 87 (3): 548–77.

Wilson, Nicholas Hoover. 2011. "From Reflection to Refraction: State Administration in British India, circa 1770–1855." *American Journal of Sociology* 116 (5): 1437–77.

Wilson, Nicholas, and Damon Mayrl. 2013. "What Do Historical Sociologists Do All Day? Measuring the Field of Methods in Historical Social Science." Paper presented at The Social Science History Association meeting, Chicago. Available at: https://sites.google.com/site/damonmayrl/research.

Wright, Gerald, and Michael Berkman. 1986. "Candidates and Policy in United States Senate Elections." *American Political Science Review* 80 (2): 567–88.

Young, Iris. 1996. "Communication and the Other: Beyond Deliberative Democracy." In *Democracy and Difference: Contesting the Boundaries of the Political*, ed. Seyla Benhabib, 383–406. Princeton, NJ: Princeton University Press.

Zaller, John. 1992. *The Nature and Origins of Mass Opinion*. Cambridge: Cambridge University Press.

Žižek, Slavoj. 1989. *The Sublime Object of Ideology*. New York: Verso.

———. 2006. *The Parallax View*. Cambridge, MA: MIT Press.

Zorbaugh, Harvey. 1929. *The Gold Coast and the Slum*. Vol. 227. Chicago: University of Chicago Press.

Zorn, Dirk, Frank Dobin, Julian Dierkes, and Man-shan Kwon. 2009. "Managing Investors: How Financial Markets Reshaped the American Firm." In *The Sociology of Financial Markets*, ed. Karin Knorr-Cetina and Alex Preda, 269–89. Oxford: Oxford University Press.